Other Putnam Berkley titles by Carl Hiaasen

Kick Ass: Selected Columns of Carl Hiaasen,
edited by Diane Stevenson

Paradise
SCREWED

Selected Columns of

CARL HIAASEN

edited by

DIANE STEVENSON

G. P. PUTNAM'S SONS
NEW YORK

G. P. Putnam's Sons
Publishers Since 1838
a member of
Penguin Putnam Inc.
375 Hudson Street
New York, NY 10014

Library of Congress Cataloging-in-Publication Data

Hiaasen, Carl.
Paradise screwed : selected columns of Carl Hiaasen / edited by Diane Stevenson.
p.   cm.
Columns originally published in the Miami Herald.
ISBN 0-399-14791-8
1. Dade County (Fla.)—Social life and customs—20th century—Anecdotes.
2. Dade County (Fla.)—Social conditions—20th century—Anecdotes.   3. Dade
County (Fla.)—Politics and government—20th century—Anecdotes.   4. Miami
(Fla.)—Social life and customs—20th century—Anecdotes.   5. Miami (Fla.)—
Social conditions—20th century—Anecdotes.   6. Miami (Fla.)—Politics
and government—20th century—Anecdotes.
I. Stevenson, Diane, date.   II. Title.
F317.D2 H53   2001   2001031850
975.9'38063—dc21

Printed in the United States of America

1   3   5   7   9   10   8   6   4   2

This book is printed on acid-free paper. ∞

Book design by Victoria Kuskowski

Acknowledgments

I am especially grateful to Bob Radziewicz, my longtime editor at the *Miami Herald*. His steady hand guided many of these rants into print, sometimes at peril to his own career (not to mention his sanity). I am also privileged to have worked for years with Jim Savage, one of the finest investigative minds in the business. If every newspaper had editors like these, you'd see more ball-busting journalism and less useless crap being published on the front pages.

To Sam Terilli, legal ace, I must say thanks for your razor-sharp advice and stalwart defense of the First Amendment. Thanks, also, for keeping me out of court.

Last but not least, I am again indebted to my friend, the indefatigable Diane Stevenson, for slogging through another swamp of columns to prepare this second collection. I'm no expert on the clinical symptoms of masochism, but be assured that I've advised Diane to seek professional help.

CARL HIAASEN, JANUARY 2001

Contents

Part

1

WELCOME TO FLORIDA

July 2, 1985

TANNING ACTION PROVES BEAUTY CAN BE BEASTLY

A true tale from the Miss Universe extravaganza:

On Sunday, something called a "Squirtmobile" was supposed to "dispense" suntan lotion all over 10 of the most beautiful women in the world—this according to the official Miss Universe press apparatus.

I drove out to Key Biscayne envisioning the spectacle of a mass squirting and musing over how far we have come as a civilized species. It seemed only right that the incident would be televised and shown to the entire world on July 15.

A word about official press kits: Don't believe them.

The Squirtmobile arrived at the Sonesta Beach without a drop of Coppertone. An irate TV director to a chastened Squirtmobile functionary: "The whole idea is this thing squirts out the product!"

An emergency call went out over the walkie-talkie and six bottles of suntan oil were collected, hardly enough for the promised geyser. A major squirt was clearly out of the question; a creative huddle ensued.

Finally, 10 of the Miss Universe contestants arrived, wearing patient smiles and lustrous swimsuits. I'm not sure who was who because they were commanded by bullhorn to remove their sashes.

As the Squirtmobile was driven into position for the cameras, it nearly squashed two tourists lying under an umbrella. They were James and Marjorie Najarian from New Jersey, and they wanted to know what was going on. I told them.

"This is low class," James said, evenly. "Low-class commercialism."

"It sounds like something out of the 1950s," Marjorie added. "I'm waiting for Annette Funicello."

The Najarians are annual visitors to Miami, and they seemed like nice, intelligent folks. They couldn't believe the state legislature had kicked in $500,000 for a beauty pageant.

"They think it brings in tourists," I said.

"The thing that brings tourists is peace and quiet," James remarked, turning back to his magazine.

Soon the Squirtmobile was in place and the reigning Miss Universe, the Miss Universe, was told to get inside. This was the new plan: As the Squirtmobile sped down the crowded shore, Miss Universe would dangle her legs out back and pass bottles of Coppertone to contestants prancing after the little truck.

Something you see every day at the beach, right? And safe, too.

After about the sixth take, the TV producers were getting hacked off. The contestants were running too fast, then too slow, then waving when they weren't supposed to. And the swimmers! They kept staring at the camera, screwing up the shots. "If you keep looking this way, we'll have to do it all over again, and these girls are getting very, very hot," warned a big shot TV guy named Ray on a megaphone.

Then something terrible happened.

Somebody yelled, "Action!" and the Squirtmobile roared away with two stunning beauty queens in pursuit—all according to script. But suddenly the contraption hit some soft sand and threw about half a ton of beach straight into one of the contestant's face and hair.

I don't think I've ever felt as sorry for anyone.

The woman (Miss Austria, according to a chaperone) was trying to smile and be a good sport, but behind her smoky eyes you could tell what she was thinking—that it would be nice to use a claw hammer on the jerk who dreamed up this stunt.

The poor girl had been so thoroughly slathered with Coppertone that all the gritty sand now stuck to her legs and arms like spackle. The TV crew took a break while she cleaned off.

Meanwhile, someone got a shovel to dig out the Squirtmobile.

As other beachgoers were herded into place for the next take, I noticed that the teeming Miss Universe entourage—photographers, escorts, TV grips and groupies—had now completely obstructed the Najarians' modest view of the ocean.

James looked up from under his umbrella and mouthed the words: "Low class."

Marjorie just smiled and said, "Do you think they'll let us swim?"

October 13, 1986

EXTORTIONISTS FIND SICK FUN IN LOST PETS

New frontiers of human depravity (continued):

Not long ago Sue Sinclair placed a classified advertisement in this newspaper. She was trying to find her lost cat, Tristy.

"An exceedingly pretty cat," Sue says. "Looks like an Angora." One day Tristy was lounging in the front yard, the next day she was gone. The Sinclairs figured she went exploring and befriended some neighbors.

One Sunday a young man phoned to say he had found the fluffy white cat. He asked Mrs. Sinclair to meet him on a street corner in North Miami Beach. She and her husband drove 15 miles to the location, but couldn't find anyone waiting.

In the meantime, the man phoned Sue Sinclair's house again and talked to her mother-in-law, Helene. This time he wanted money. "If they call the police, I'm going to kill the cat!" he said.

He said he'd spotted the Sinclairs driving near the designated intersection, and he described their car perfectly. He instructed Helene Sinclair to tell her daughter-in-law to go to Greynolds Park and place $30 under a rock at a specific spot.

The cat, he said, could be found in a box hidden in the restroom.

Sue Sinclair couldn't believe that somebody would extort money for a family pet. She and her husband decided not to go to Greynolds Park, and instead they called the police. A Metro officer sympathized, but said there wasn't much he could do.

"The man told us no laws had been broken," she said.

The cat-extortionist called back several times with the same threat. By now Sue Sinclair didn't believe he was holding Tristy hostage. She demanded to see a photograph of her pet. Finally she told the creep: "Go ahead, kill the cat!"

A few minutes later Tristy wandered home. "Fat and happy," Sue reports.

The next day the cat-extortionist telephoned again.

"Meow, meow, meow," he said.

Helene Sinclair told him to forget it, the cat had already come home. "Then how about $5?" the man asked, before hanging up.

Says Sue Sinclair, "Obviously my own problem is solved, but anyone who loses a pet is fair game to these sick people."

In fact, several persons who took out lost-pet advertisements the same week as Mrs. Sinclair received similar phone calls. The Greynolds Park con man tried the same flimflam on a Miami Shores woman who'd lost her miniature poodle, Snoopy.

"Well, I have your dog," the man said. "He's all right, but he's crying big tears."

He told the woman to take $30 to the park and bury it. "No police," he warned.

Snoopy's owner said no. She said she knew the man didn't really have her dog. He called back numerous times, finally cutting his ransom demand to $10.

Anyone who has lost a pet knows that this isn't funny; it's the act of a subterranean thug. "A new low," agreed Sgt. Ralph Nelson of the Metro-Dade Economic Crimes Unit.

The detective had not heard of the new scam. "Never in my life," he said incredulously. He said that the I've-got-Fido hoax is certainly illegal, though it's probably just a misdemeanor because the money demands are so small.

"It's a fraud, at least," Nelson said. "Anytime you try to extort money it's a crime."

Money isn't the only thing these lowlifes have tried to extort.

After Janis Hooker's pet Samoyed disappeared, she took out a newspaper advertisement offering a reward for its return. A man called and announced that he found her pet. "Instead of money," she said, "he wanted sex in exchange for the dog."

A week later a legitimate caller answered the advertisement and returned the Hookers' missing puppy. It was a happy ending, but Janis couldn't help but thinking: "There's a real looney tune out there spending his time reading the ads."

Mused Sgt. Nelson: "We've got everything in Miami."

November 3, 1986

CASINOS OR NOT, GANGSTERS LOVE BEING IN MIAMI

Tomorrow is the day we vote on whether we want ruthless gangsters scurrying all over Florida—at least, that's what the anti-casino people have warned us.

So great is this fear that some of our civic stalwarts would sooner do business with the Yahwehs than Resorts International.

I suppose the idea of a Mafia invasion should strike terror into our hearts, but this is Miami, Florida, not Madison, Wisconsin. While Mafia criminals are a rotten lot—predatory thieves, money launderers and knee-breakers—

they look like the Brady Bunch compared to some of the violent lunatics already loose down here.

At least Mafia triggermen don't randomly spray bullets into shopping plazas and residential neighborhoods, like some of our local cocaine gangs. They don't go in for home-invasion robberies. They don't dress up like cops and rob people. They don't shoot it out with the FBI. When they do terminate somebody, it's usually one of their own.

Another reason it's hard to get worked up about the Mob is that they're already here, in droves. Just last Friday, 24 alleged Mafia figures were arrested in Broward County. These characters weren't just sitting around waiting for gambling to be legalized; they allegedly were quite busy loansharking, extorting, defrauding and doing all the nasty things that mobsters do. They were prospering nicely without casinos.

Face it—these guys are just wild about Florida.

They adore the climate, the racetracks, the beaches, the par-3 golf. Ever since the days of Al Capone, Mafia travel agents have given Florida a four-star rating. Santo Trafficante settled in Tampa. Meyer Lansky fell in love with Miami Beach and moved there with his dog. Johnny Roselli was a regular, too, until he accidentally stuffed himself into an oil drum and rolled into Biscayne Bay.

Recently, you might have read about a big-time mafioso who purchased a $400,000 home in Fort Lauderdale. He is Little Nicky Scarfo (one of the all-time great names for a gangster. Mario Puzo couldn't dream up a name like that).

At any rate, the anti-casino sentinels warn that Nicky Scarfo's arrival is proof that the Mob is interested in South Florida casinos. To which any halfwit might reply: OF COURSE THEY'RE INTERESTED IN CASINOS! THEY'RE THE MOB, DUMMY! It doesn't mean they wouldn't be here anyway, soaking up the sun.

For the sake of argument, let's say that the polls are wrong and the casino-choice referendum passes tomorrow. What do we do about this predicted stampede of wise guys—Cadillac after Cadillac racing down the turnpike from Jersey.

This is how we handle it. You know those Welcome Stations at the Florida-Georgia border? The ones that give away thimble-size cups of orange juice? We set up a special one just for the Mafia, only the sign doesn't say WELCOME. It says: AS LONG AS YOU'RE HERE . . .

Inside, we give away free linguine with clam sauce. We throw in discount coupons to Epcot Center and Metrozoo. Then we ask the mobsters very politely, before they get back into their cars, would they please mind filling out this brief questionnaire from the Florida Department of Law Enforcement.

We ask for their real names, plus their three favorite aliases.

We ask which Family they're associated with—Gambino, Bonanno, Bruno, etc.—and we ask the name of their designated car-starter.

We ask for their new address in Florida (what's the harm? I mean, are the neighborhood kids really going to toilet-paper Nicky Scarfo's house? Not likely).

We ask which Teamsters' pension fund is paying their salary.

We ask for their official Mafia nicknames—Jimmy the Meathook, Joey the Icepick, Sal the Salami, whatever—so we'll know who's who on the wiretaps.

Most important, we ask where they intend to eat lunch, so we can steer clear of the place.

Then, because oil drums don't always sink, we ask for next of kin.

April 22, 1987

SNAKE'S ALIVE? YOU BETTER CALL REPTILE RESCUE

Spring is the time when Jeff Grigg's fancy turns to pythons.

When the weather warms, snakes stir. So does Grigg's phone. When you dial 361-6222, a recorded voice says: "Reptile Rescue!"

Grigg himself wears a beeper. This is, after all, South Florida.

He says ruefully: "The snake is the only animal that people will kill first, and ask questions later."

His job is saving snakes from the ignorant hoe, shovel, hatchet and handgun. Last year Reptile Rescue got more than 5,000 phone calls and collected more than 300 critters from Florida City to Carol City. Most were police referrals, since many cops would rather take on a hit man with a MAC-10 than a two-foot green snake in a mango tree.

When the going gets scaly, they call Jeff Grigg.

"The superstitions are unbelievable," he says with a sigh. "I get women calling me up, crazy, hysterical, afraid the snake is going to climb into bed and impregnate them. Afraid that they'll suck the breath out of a baby—that's another one. That if you cut the snake in two parts, it'll crawl off in different directions and join up later.

"Just about anything that can be attributed to a snake can and will be, almost all of it nasty."

Grigg, 33, was raised in Dade County. He lives on Key Biscayne, where his normal job is fixing outboard motors. He charges nothing for Reptile Rescue missions but gladly accepts small donations for gas and snake-related expenses. One time a Bay Point patron sent him a $25 contribution and box of unhatched lizard eggs, via UPS.

He keeps a log of all captures: the king snake residing in the U.S. Army recruitment center; the Savannah monitor lizard patrolling Barry University; the four pygmy rattlesnakes set loose in a bizarre North Dade domestic dispute.

"Now here's a boa," Grigg says, opening another cage. "He was in an apartment in North Miami. Lady went to the bathroom about 2 in the morning and she found it. . . ." No need for details.

Rating his quarry, Grigg says iguanas are the fastest (he got five out of an attic on Old Cutler Road), crocodiles the most dangerous (he corralled a zoo escapee on Key Biscayne), and snakes the most harmless and misunderstood (his biggest was a 16-foot Burmese python).

Recent captures include a large boa constrictor sunning itself at Biscayne Boulevard and NE 135th Street; another boa coiled serenely on a car at a Metrorail station ("Nine Metro police officers on the scene," Grigg noted); and 58 baby loggerhead turtles "saved" from drowning by a concerned Sunny Isles tourist, who put them in a dresser drawer.

Not long ago, Miami police summoned Reptile Rescue to the scene of a neighborhood crack sting, where one of the suspects was found to have a scarlet king snake and a live ferret in his car. Grigg took care of the animals until the fellow made bail.

Native species such as racers and rat snakes are immediately freed into the wild. However, the law forbids the release of exotics such as boas and pythons, and these Grigg must keep himself or give to licensed animal dealers.

On most phone calls Grigg simply tries to identify the snake and calm the agitated human. Given time, reptiles usually will depart of their own volition. Manpower shortage prohibits on-site visits to all sightings; Reptile Rescue consists of Grigg, his wife, Barbara, and only one other volunteer. ("It's hard getting people to go pick up snakes," he explains.)

One tricky rescue took place in the infamous housing project known as The Graveyard. "I didn't know it was called The Graveyard," Grigg says. He drove out there at 1 A.M. on a routine rat-snake call.

Before he even got out of the car, he was accosted by several drug dealers. "No thanks," he told them, "I'm here to pick up a snake." The pushers backed off with noticeable haste.

The sleepy reptile was captured and Grigg departed without further incident. "Nobody ever messes with the guy with the snakes," he says.

November 18, 1988

ZUCCHINI COULD LOSE SUPERMARKET CITIZENSHIP

(A story that wouldn't surprise us . . .)

Waspo Supermarkets announced today that it is changing the labels on all foreign grocery items to English.

The unprecedented move comes only a day after another language dispute caused an embarrassing uproar in a Waspo store.

In the latest incident, a cashier was suspended without pay and locked in a meat freezer for asking a customer, "How much is that zucchini?" (Or, in English: "How much is that zucchini?")

"Enough is enough!" snorted corporate spokesman Merle (Bucky) Fuqua. "This is a grocery store, not the danged United Nations."

He said the cashier violated company policy by speaking a foreign language on the front line. Instead of using the word *zucchini,* the cashier should have asked the customer: "How much is that long green Italian summer squash?"

Beginning today, stock boys in each of the 329 Waspo stores will painstakingly comb the shelves aisle by aisle, pasting English subtitles on any brand product with a foreign name.

For example, the popular salad topping known as croutons will henceforth be marked as OVERPRICED FRENCH BREADCRUMBS.

Customers shopping for sauerkraut will find it newly packaged as SUSPICIOUS-SMELLING GERMAN COLESLAW.

And shoppers in the mood for gazpacho should keep an eye out for COLD ANDALUSIAN TOMATO PORRIDGE.

The goal, store officials said, is to create an environment where no one will ever be subjected to a foreign language—be it a word, a phrase or a sentence.

The English-only rule applies to customers and employees alike. At one store, an elderly shopper was detained by security officers after the terms *matzoh balls, tortillas* and *suey choy* were found scrawled on her grocery list.

Explained spokesman Fuqua: "This is America, dammit. When you're talking perishables, there's no margin of error."

The language controversy began last week when the manager of a Publix supermarket in Coral Gables suspended a cashier for speaking Spanish to another employee. The incident ignited a furor in the competitive retail grocery industry.

"Until headquarters looked into it, we had no idea how much foreign mumbo-gumbo was being spoken around our stores," Fuqua said.

Fearing an outbreak of language-related altercations, the Waspo chain decided it would be safer to sell all items in one language.

"We seriously considered French," Fuqua said, "because there's so much French food. I mean, there's French bread, French toast, French dressing. But then they went ahead and passed this Official English deal, so there you have it. We were stuck."

The task of manually changing the labels on the foreign food products is expected to cost the giant supermarket chain hundreds of thousands of dollars. In many cases, the English labels are larger and more complicated than the originals.

"Pasta is going to be an absolute nightmare," confided one store manager. "You've got your lasagne, your linguine, your manicotti, your rigatoni. We're talking serious overtime here."

Officials seemed particularly concerned about the new English label for vermicelli, which translates to "little worms."

Cashiers and bag boys who violate the new English-only rule will be subject to strict discipline, including reprimands, suspensions or—in the case of repeat offenders—a permanent transfer to the cheese-and-dairy department.

"One word about Brie and they're history!" Fuqua vowed.

Some store employees privately assert that many customers don't mind buying food with foreign names, or hearing those words spoken aloud at the cash register.

"The only time we had any trouble is when Frusen Gladje first came out," one cashier confided. "That Norwegian pronunciation is very tricky—mess up one lousy vowel and all of a sudden you're asking for walrus glands instead of ice cream."

May 1, 1989

DADE DAY: POWER TOOLS ON PARADE

This is an exciting week in Tallahassee. Everyone is awaiting the arrival of "Dade County Day."

The purpose of Dade County Day is to remind legislators from Okaloosa and Santa Rosa that there is a Dade County. To accomplish this, the capitol grounds will be transformed into a festive and colorful showcase featuring many of our best-known attractions.

The Seaquarium, Monkey Jungle, Vizcaya, Fairchild Garden and the Coral Castle are among many popular tourist spots worthy of mention, but that's not all. To counter the publicity surrounding the opening of rival Disney World's new movie studio, the folks who organized Dade County Day pulled out all the stops.

For example, tentative plans call for a boat to be displayed at the capitol—a real 36-foot cabin cruiser! Apparently many of the legislators have never seen a boat before, so this will be a huge thrill.

The agriculture industry is set to provide displays of real Dade County avocados and limes, in addition to "mechanical fruit." I'm not sure what the mechanical fruit exhibit does, but it's probably a lot like Space Mountain, only with a citrus theme.

To celebrate other made-in-Dade products, Burger King is scheduled to deliver a three-foot-wide hamburger and a mess of three-foot-long French fries. Mmmmmm, you can almost smell it from here.

Higher education will be showcased by giant textbooks listing the names of every local college and university. To underscore its growing reputation for academic achievement, the University of Miami will be represented by a five-foot replica of an ibis, which is a bird that eats fish and snails.

Sports also gets a share of the spotlight, from a Miami Heat basketball hoop to a Dolphins football helmet to a Doral Ryder putting green. You're wondering: What, no gun range? No cockfights? Hard to explain, but my guess is that they're saving those for next year's gala.

No tribute to Dade would be complete without a flashy tourism promotion, and this one will be no exception. Among the items scheduled for display: a three-foot tennis ball, a three-foot baseball, a surfboard, palm trees and "beach umbrellas with sand bases." Boy, those Tallahassee travel agents better brace for a stampede.

To show off how modern Dade County is, transportation officials will present a model of Metrorail. Perhaps the model train will even be pulling tiny half-empty cars. This would be an excellent way to compare the breezy, uncrowded Metrorail experience with the noisy, tourist-clogged Disney monorail.

Our unique cultural mix will be in the spotlight, too. At lunchtime on Dade County Day, the lobby of the capitol will fill with the aroma of several metric tons of paella. Meanwhile, the Miccosukee Indians will bring a live Florida alligator and allow anyone to wrestle it! This could be great fun, especially if some Miccosukee prankster were to substitute a wild foul-tempered alligator for the tame lazy one.

The best part of the Dade County Day festivities is the decorations. The theme of the exhibit is: "Dade County, Partners in Building Florida's Future." Here's a sneak preview, right off the drawing board:

"Legislators will be greeted by a moving robot with construction sounds &

holding a sign with the Dade Day logo. . . . The entire area will be surrounded with construction material . . . 55-gallon drums, ladders, wood, construction signs, power tools, rotating displays of three-foot tools . . . pliers, saw, hammers, tape measure, T-square, compass, wood plane."

I know what you're thinking: How do you top an exhibit of pliers and power tools for sheer excitement?

Try giving away free hard hats! That's right, free hard hats. Then surround the entire panorama with actual Bob's Barricades, flown in especially for the celebration (this is the absolute truth).

Few could disagree that what you'll see in the capitol rotunda this week is an authentic re-creation of life in South Florida—one big, chaotic construction site. All that's missing is a toy bulldozer and some mangroves.

July 26, 1989

LIKE LEMMINGS, BATHERS PLUNGE

Grim events of the weekend have underscored the indomitable nature of the tourist mentality—to have fun, by God, even if it kills you.

A picture in Monday's newspaper told the whole story: The body of a dead swimmer lay on the beach, while other bathers frolicked merrily in the surf, unconcerned about dangerous run-out currents that could have swept them away in seconds.

The death toll for Sunday was three, all drowning victims lost in the powerful tug of the sea. Part of the blame certainly can be placed on the county, which has left a long stretch of beach unguarded in the Sunny Isles area. Of all the millions of dollars frittered away each year by the Metro Commission, you'd think it could spring a couple hundred thousand to put up a few lifeguard stands. One guard station is being proposed at 163rd Street, but that's hardly enough.

The other side of the tragedy is human stubbornness. On the morning of the three drowning deaths, lifeguards at Haulover Beach tried vainly to clear the water. Hundreds of beachgoers jumped in anyway.

Lifeguard Capt. Marcus Breece: "We had 15 flags up that said: DANGER — NO SWIMMING. We had 30 lifeguards using whistles, warning people to get out. And we still had 21 rescues. Does that tell you anything?"

Who knows what provokes such mindless behavior. A sunny beach seems to bring out the lemming in people.

Imagine the scene at Sunny Isles—two bodies in the water, sirens, police,

Coast Guard helicopters, rescue vehicles. This is known as a clue. But still people plunged in, some even taking their kids.

I don't care what country or state or planet you happen to come from, the sight of floating corpses means it's time to get your butt out of the ocean.

Some of the tourists interviewed near one of the drownings exhibited mind-boggling nonchalance and high spirits. "People were walking around the body as though it were a dead fish that had washed up. They didn't seem concerned at all," said Don Stewart, who lives in Golden Shores.

Stewart is a former New Jersey lifeguard who has been pushing for increased protection along Dade's unprotected beaches. Not only should there be lifeguards, he says, but they ought to be vested with police authority.

The problem wasn't always so bad because there wasn't always so much beach. The stretch between 163rd Street and 192nd Street has been "renourished" with sand pumped off the sea bottom. Tourists who once dog-paddled in small hotel swimming pools now head for the beach. Ironically, the high-pressure pumping that spit up all that nice new sand also created underwater gullies and shoals that act as a natural funnel for strong rip currents.

Says Stewart: "We've got to educate these bathers—they're like a wild bunch down there. They've never had a beach before. We are inviting people literally to come down here and drown."

Even on a guarded beach such as Haulover, lifeguards have grown accustomed to being ignored. On Sunday, Marcus Breece and his men were warning visitors that the runout was so fierce that three people had already succumbed to it. This grisly news failed to impress a large number of swimmers, including one man who ventured offshore with several children.

Breece whistled, waved, finally sent a rescue boat. The lifeguards told the man to keep his family in knee-deep water near the lifeguard station. He got very angry. "The man was very adamant about his right to swim," Breece said. "He wanted to know the exact statute that allowed me to get him out of the water. I had to go get a police officer."

Incidents like this are so common that, in moments of black humor, lifeguards have proposed radical methods of getting bathers' attention—such as hanging human mannequins upside down from warning flags.

After what happened Sunday, Breece isn't sure anybody would get the message. "If a body lying on the beach isn't going to do it . . ."

July 30, 1990

IN FLORIDA, YOU GET BANG FOR THE BUCK

Shame on those who say there's no industry in the Sunshine State: We are now among the leading producers of semiautomatic assault pistols!

After years of rapid growth, the Tec-9 semiautomatic—a handy 9mm manufactured right here in Dade County—has overtaken the traditional Uzi and MAC-10 as the national weapon of choice among street gangs and crack dealers.

Last year the Bureau of Alcohol, Tobacco and Firearms received 694 police requests for traces on Tec-9s—more than any other gun. By contrast, the agency got only 448 total requests for traces on Uzi rifles and pistols, and 485 for MAC-10s and MAC-11s.

The success story of the Tec-9 is one of economy pricing (as low as $300 retail) and canny marketing (which advertises the pistol to a blue-collar clientele as a "high-spirited" companion).

They're not kidding, either. The lightweight Tec-9 can fire more than 30 rounds without reloading. Last February, one of these guns was used against Broward Sheriff's deputy Jack Greeney, who was murdered when he tried to stop a robbery. When captured, one of the suspects still carried the sales receipt for the Tec-9.

The gun is one of several models made by a South Dade company called Navegar, also known as Intratec USA. In May 1989, Intratec filed under Chapter 7 in U.S. bankruptcy court, listing assets of only $100 and debts of $3,112.

That same month, however, Intratec owner Carlos M. Garcia was telling the *Palm Beach Post* that business was going great guns. Production had doubled from the previous year, he said, due largely to the growing popularity of the Tec-9—a boom that seems confirmed by U.S. firearms statistics.

Garcia explained the Tec-9's appeal this way: "The survivalist groups, people of that nature, they like to keep a weapon so that if anything ever happens, a war ever breaks out, they'd like to have it in their house."

Other satisfied consumers include drug assassins and armed robbers, who have been acquiring the gun in record numbers. Garcia candidly acknowledged the problem to the *Post:* "I know some of the guns going out of here end up killing people. But I'm not responsible for that. The ultimate user is you—the public."

And the public is buying. From 1985 through 1988, Intratec manufactured almost 53,000 Tec-9s, most of which haven't killed anyone yet. Nonetheless, police have seen enough of the paramilitary-style pistols to be worried.

A crime bill recently passed by the U.S. Senate includes a ban on several assault weapons, including the Tec-9. The legislation faces a tough battle, but Tec-9's manufacturer isn't taking any chances.

Recently Sen. Jack Gordon of Miami Beach got a hefty stack of letters urging him to vote to keep assault weapons legal. Every letter was exactly the same, word for word: "Banning semiautomatic firearms and magazines is unconstitutional and not the answer to our nation's crime problems."

Each envelope bore a different return address, but one of Gordon's staff noticed something interesting: All the address labels had been glued to cover up a company letterhead—"INTRATEC." It wouldn't have taken Dick Tracy to figure out what was going on.

The mail-in campaign to Gordon was a misdirected volley. He is a state senator, not a U.S. senator—an important detail that eluded the folks at Intratec. "I was puzzled when I received your letter," Gordon wrote back. "I do not, nor does any other Florida state legislator, have any jurisdiction in federal legislation pending before Congress."

Oh well. Who needs a state senator when you've got the NRA on your side. In coming weeks, the gun lobby will unleash all its political ammo trying to kill the proposed ban on assault weapons. If it succeeds, Tec-9s will keep rolling off the assembly line.

And Florida finally will be famous for exporting something besides oranges.

December 6, 1992

IDEA IS TACKY BUT MAYBE NOT ALL THAT WACKY

From the Truth is Sicker than Fiction Department: Plans to build a Hurricane Museum as a tourist trap in South Dade!

A member of We Will Rebuild's Innovation Committee (yes, that's what it calls itself) recently suggested with a perfectly straight face that a museum dedicated to the wreckage of Hurricane Andrew would help "rebuild our tourism base."

Among the exhibits contemplated are a wind tunnel and an actual house destroyed by the storm, but "preserved so that people could walk through it."

It's such a morbidly tacky idea that I'm surprised I didn't think of it myself. Why not cash in on the surplus of devastation and human suffering? Why not turn one of the darkest chapters in Florida history into a money-grubbing enterprise?

I see billboards, TV spots, maybe a circling blimp. I hear catchy radio jingles: "If you missed the storm, don't miss the aftermath!" Disney, eat your heart out.

Tourists are tourists, and they go for disasters in a big way. If we build a hurricane museum, they will come. Like flies to a roadkill, they will come.

We wouldn't be the first community to profit from the public's appetite for destruction. An attraction on San Francisco's Fisherman's Wharf features a simulated earthquake, and out-of-town visitors eagerly line up to experience it. The place was packed the last time a real earthquake hit.

If Florida tries a hurricane exhibit, let's not do a half-ass job of it. If good taste isn't an issue (and apparently it's not), why stop with a dull old museum? Make it a theme park!

"Arvida's House of Flying Gables." Tourists huddle in a realistic suburban bathtub while a wind tunnel re-creates the force of Andrew, ripping off the roof in three seconds flat.

"The Dancing Building Inspectors' Jamboree." A comic musical romp through Dade's building and zoning department, featuring the hit show tunes "Which End of This Ladder Goes Up?" and "Don't Cry for Me, Joaquin Avino."

"Wild West Dade Showdown." Rival unlicensed roofers meet at high noon, firing staple guns.

"Tetanus Alley." An exciting walk through a field of authentic hurricane rubble—shattered glass, fiberglass, rusty nails and twisted metal.

"Mr. Andy's Wild Ride." Just like Disney's twirling teacups, only with mobile homes.

"You Loot, We Shoot." Tourists portray frustrated homeowners, taking aim at ruthless post-hurricane bandits.

"Tent City Revival." To recapture the Andrew experience, the adventurous visitor shares an open tent, fine Army food and a Port-o-Potty with hundreds of other hurricane sightseers.

Crude, you say? Coldhearted? Plenty of sensible folks would agree. The sick thing is, a hurricane theme park would probably work. The market looks strong.

Ever since Andrew blew through, carloads of geeks with video cameras have descended on the worst-hit neighborhoods in search of flattened homes, demolished playgrounds and mangled automobiles. Their only disappointment is the absence of human dead and wounded.

In fact, Florida tourism officials say one of the most frequent queries from incoming visitors is: "Which way to the damage?"

Gawkers and carnage freaks must be dealt with, but the question is how.

My personal choice would be to drag these vultures from their rental cars and gently disassemble their Sonys. Then put them to work with a hammer or a saw. Unfortunately, that solution presents legal snags.

The other strategy is to separate them from their money, which is what the hurricane theme park would accomplish.

But let's build one with staples and particleboard, just for the thrill of it.

April 13, 1995

AT COURTHOUSE, EVEN CHICKENS NEED BODYGUARDS

The rules are different here (Chapter 137):

Janitors at Dade's criminal courthouse have a special "Voodoo Squad" to clean up messy animal sacrifices dumped by friends and families of defendants.

The purpose of scattering critter remains is to influence the justice system by pleasing ancient saints and gods.

Let us stipulate, for the record, that no other courthouse in America has a chronic problem with nocturnal appearances by dead roosters and goats.

We shall also proffer that most people view Miami's blood customs as primitive, cruel and unquaint. While many locals are equally disturbed by the occult killing of animals, no less an authority than the U.S. Supreme Court has sanctioned these ceremonies as religious.

I also submit that even the most indignant nonbelievers might contemplate a mass sacrifice of chickens, if there was the tiniest chance it would bring an end to the O. J. Simpson trial.

Since there's no shortage of advocates for the doomed barnyard contingent, I'd like to speak out on behalf of the Metro courthouse janitors, upon whose daily work sheet the following duty is actually listed:

"Report any voodoo objects which need to be removed."

Whatever they're paying these folks, it's not enough. Scooping up slaughtered livestock is beyond the call of duty.

I say that, having worked as a janitor at a veterinary clinic—no romp in a spring meadow, to be sure. However, never once was I ordered to search the premises for dead goats.

Today, animal corpses are being tossed willy-nilly around the courthouse grounds. It's unsanitary, inconsiderate and often ineffective, deity-wise.

We need altars, and we need 'em fast. Three would do fine:

- A "Misdemeanor Altar" for deposit of your downsized offerings such as hens, pigeons, mice and gerbils.

  Theoretically, the smaller the crime, the less fresh flesh is required to influence the court. So the Misdemeanor Altar needn't be large—probably no bigger than a picnic table.
- A "Felony Altar" for your bulkier sacrifices, such as full-grown roosters, goats and sheep.

  Hexing a major felony case is a chore, especially if the size of the sacrifice depends on the size of the indictment. Dade's courts being the nation's most overcrowded, the Felony Altar should as spacious as a basketball court.
- An "Appellate Altar" to be used only after a defendant is convicted.

  It would serve as a clearinghouse for families wishing to unleash vengeful spirits on prosecutors, judges and inept defense attorneys. To avoid backlogs, curses could be submitted no later than 60 days after the trial.

Sure, voodoo altars cost money. But Dade County has a big heart for accommodating not-so-mainstream lifestyles. Remember, it spent $18,500 for a wheelchair ramp at a nudist beach.

Everyone using or visiting the courthouse would benefit from tidier animal rites. The best location for the three altars is the corner of Northwest 13th Court known as "Chicken Central," because of its popularity among sacrificialists. To avoid traffic jams, I recommend drive-through lanes. That way the altars could be as accessible as recycle bins, or drop boxes for the Salvation Army.

You pull in, dump your dead roosters, say your little chant and leave. No more creepy scavenger hunts for the janitors; they'll know exactly where to find the night's furry and/or feathered deposits.

The only other capital investments would be a fire hose, half a dozen jumbo Dumpsters and a tanker full of Lysol. Maybe Lady Justice can't see, but nobody ever said she can't gag.

June 29, 1995

MICKEY AND MINNIE NEED SOME FIRE ANTS

Well, Disney kicked us in the coconuts again. Maximum Mousketeer Michael Eisner has unveiled plans for a $750 million expansion of Walt Disney World in Orlando.

Swell. Clearly the goal is to contain all tourists on Disney property until their vacation money runs out. Only the occasional straggler will escape to other Florida resort areas.

By adding a fourth major theme park—Wild Animal Kingdom—Disney delivers another cruel blow to Miami's woeful family tourism trade. Even folks brave enough to come here won't be able to afford it after Mickey and Minnie finish rifling their pockets.

Disney's new attraction will be twice the size of Epcot. The centerpiece will be a re-created African jungle/savanna, with real live lions and ele-phants—hardly an original concept, but a risky one for Disney.

Previously its attractions have featured robotic critters instead of real ones. That's because robotic lions don't rut in public, spray sightseeing buses or oth-erwise jeopardize the company's wholesome image.

That's why the Wild Animal Kingdom is something of a gamble—the first exhibit in Disney's history that cannot be completely controlled by com-puters and engineers. The prospects for spontaneity are startling.

For once the animation will be performed by real animals. Consequently, the bears will not play banjos, the rodents will not whistle, and the lions will not break into song. Instead they'll do what real critters do, not all of which deserves videotaping.

Some animal-rights groups are already mobilizing against the project. They cite the unfortunate incident a few years ago when overzealous Disney staffers, faced with an infestation of turkey buzzards, addressed the problem with blunt instruments.

To prevent such episodes at the new theme park, Disney has enlisted re-spected zoologists and naturalists. Still, it doesn't seem right to employ African animals when Florida has so many interesting species of its own.

True, there are only about 50 panthers and a couple hundred manatees left, but we've got jillions of opossums and armadillos. And gators! What would you pay to see Donald Duck up to his feathery butt in alligators?

By ignoring local fauna, Disney is making a big mistake. Florida is acrawl with exotic beasts, some native and others that have escaped from collectors.

Just the other day, police in Palm Beach Gardens captured a 5½-foot mon-itor lizard ambling along a busy highway. The monitor, which comes from Borneo, is ill-tempered and snacks on small mammals. (Are you thinking what I'm thinking?)

The way I see it, Miami tourist leaders have two options for combating the new Disney project. One is to open a competing animal kingdom of our own. That would be costly and controversial, particularly with the possibility of a Santeria pavilion.

The other option is . . . well, *sabotage* is such an ugly word. But what would be so wrong about surreptitiously "enhancing," if you will, Orlando's imported menagerie?

Whenever you and the family visit Disney World, take a little friend to be released on the phony African savanna, when the security guards aren't looking. Perhaps a Bufo toad or two. Some walking catfish. Buzzard chicks. A small box of fire ants.

And don't forget snakes. I've got a feeling Disney won't be ordering nearly enough snakes for its new park.

Before long, all sorts of fun will spontaneously break out at the Animal Kingdom. We'll teach that snob Eisner.

How dare he open a wildlife park in Florida and expect to keep Florida's wildlife out.

November 28, 1996

JUST THE TICKET: A MONEY MAG ALL OUR OWN

Five months ago, *Money* magazine named Fort Lauderdale as the fourth-best place to live in all America. This week it ranked Fort Lauderdale as one of the country's most dangerous pits, ranking 175th out of 202 cities.

Confusing? Not at all.

Obviously, rampant crime and domestic tranquillity go hand-in-holster. Just because you live in an urban war zone doesn't mean you can't enjoy some serious golf.

Money magazine is keen on best-of lists and, as we know, South Florida (Miami in particular) often rates poorly. For this we must blame those nit-pickers who do the FBI statistics, and also the media for making such a fuss.

One way to invert our dismal rankings is to put out our own magazine called *Dirty Money*. Demographically it would aim at career con artists and white-collar crooks seeking to relocate in a sunnier, more tolerant clime.

We've got no shortage of thugs, but there's a huge untapped market for upscale scammers with dough. Dirty money is good here, always has been. You can buy cars, houses, speedboats, even a whole bank with no questions asked. Why, with the right connections a felon can even get a street named in his honor.

Maybe it's time to let everybody know what the Mafia has known for years: Few places offer the breadth of opportunities available year-round here on the Gold Coast.

Where else would a goober who never attended medical school feel relaxed enough to hang out his shingle as a plastic surgeon? Where else would the feds allow a known criminal to finish a housing subdivision with laundered drug profits?

Where else would the world's biggest cocaine smuggler feel perfectly at ease buying a $10 million apartment building—in his own name?

Each month *Dirty Money* magazine would feature such inspiring success stories, as well as useful how-to articles:

January: "How to Bribe a City Commissioner."

February: "How to Avoid Being Set Up by a City Commissioner."

March: "How to get Elected City Commissioner."

South Florida is teeming with colorful characters for magazine profiles. Consider the heartwarming story of Sweetwater's Gabriel Hernandez.

After serving a five-year prison hitch for drug smuggling, Hernandez turned over a new leaf. He apparently went into the medical-supply trade.

Prosecutors say he started 25 dummy companies that ultimately billed the state about $4 million for equipment that never existed, for Medicaid patients who were never seen.

Business was so brisk that, according to authorities, Hernandez was able to provide employment for his sister, wife, mother-in-law, father-in-law and assorted other relatives. They raked in more than $2 million until Hernandez's arrest Tuesday.

He says he's innocent—actually, that's what his attorney says. Which brings up another of South Florida's attractions for the itinerant felon: We've got the best defense lawyers anywhere.

No matter what you get nailed for, from grand theft to immigration fraud, there's an attorney down here who specializes in it. In fact, there's probably some attorney who's done time for it.

Dirty Money would fill a niche on the magazine rack, appealing to those thousands of readers tired of sweeping their homes for electronic bugs; fed up with pesky probation officers, nosy grand juries and rude pre-dawn visits from process servers.

These folks yearn for a new start in a new place—and *Dirty Money* could be their guide. And when the time comes to rank the 10 most hospitable places in the country, maybe we'll finally be No 1.

Or there'll be hell to pay.

July 10, 1997

WHERE MONKEYS CAN FLY: DESTRUCTIVE CRITTERS HAVE WORN OUT WELCOME

Citizens of Oz aren't the only ones to worry about flying monkeys.

Folks in the Lower Keys are worried, too. Nearly a thousand rhesus monkeys have infested two offshore islands, and the critters could go airborne if a hurricane strikes.

Should that happen, the Environmental Protection Agency predicts "devastating" consequences for the Keys. The monkeys are aggressive, destructive and habitually lax in hygiene.

Lower Keys residents have been trying for years to get rid of them. The state has often talked about eviction, but taken no action. This week, a long-overdue hearing to determine the future of the marauding monkeys is being held in Key West.

The animals are not native, but captive-bred and raised for commercial research by Charles River Laboratories, a subsidiary of Bausch & Lomb.

In 1973, the monkeys were unleashed on Key Lois and Raccoon Key, both of which are partly owned and leased by Charles River. Key Lois, also known as Loggerhead, is a few miles out on the ocean side. Raccoon Key sits on the flats bordering the Gulf.

Unfortunately, neither offers much in the way of primate recreation—monkeys don't fish or snorkel. So, out of utter boredom, they began eating the mangrove islands, leaf by leaf.

Before long, Raccoon Key was withering and Key Lois was nearly dead, virtually stripped. A napalm attack couldn't have smoked the place so thoroughly.

As a consequence, bounteous quantities of monkey poop washed off the bare shores into the surrounding water, creating a murky brown ring. Ill winds would carry the fetid slick to populated islands such as Sugarloaf, Cudjoe and Summerland Keys.

On occasion, the winds also carried the offending poopers. Though not Olympian swimmers, monkeys are capable of rafting long distances on floating tree limbs and other debris.

Their arrival on neighboring islands was unwelcome, and once resulted in a dramatic police-involved shooting. (The death of the AWOL monkey went largely unmourned.)

Amid howls of human protest, Charles River Labs had promised to "contain" the animals and plant new trees to replace the ones that were being gobbled.

Not surprisingly, the resourceful rhesuses chose not to remain fenced, caged or otherwise detained, and continued to supplement their drab Purina diet with delectable red mangroves.

After appraising the devastation wreaked on both islands, Gov. Lawton Chiles finally agreed that enough was enough. A few months ago, he and the Cabinet ordered the state to court. Its mandate: Boot the monkeys off Lois and Raccoon.

At this week's hearing, officials for Charles River once again are pleading for a reprieve. They claim the monkeys are the victims of bad press and politics.

The company says it has reduced the free-galloping rhesus population by hundreds in recent years, and has replanted 20,000 baby mangroves.

They also tried an unusual strategy to prevent further defoliation: caging the trees instead of the monkeys.

It proved unduly optimistic to suppose the animals wouldn't figure a way to break into the new enclosures, just as they'd figured a way to break out of the old ones. Needless to say, the trees are still being devoured.

Even more urgent is the threat of hurricanes. The EPA has warned that a storm could scatter Bausch & Lomb's wild bunch throughout the Keys, imperiling not only mangroves but wild birds, domestic pets and people.

The average rhesus weighs only a few pounds, not enough ballast to withstand even a mild hurricane. Imagine a thousand ticked-off monkeys flying all over creation, with no great and powerful wizard to stop them.

September 2, 1999

MIA IS GOING TO THE DOGS

The answer to Miami International Airport's embarrassing security woes is simple: dogs.

Acres and acres of dogs. Large, fleet-footed, white-fanged dogs. Dogs all over the place—at every X-ray machine, every ticket counter, every duty-free shop, every concourse.

Drug-sniffing dogs, explosive-sniffing dogs, firearm-sniffing dogs . . . dogs that can sniff out anything. At MIA, no human crevice should go unsniffed.

Pilots, passengers, skycaps, mechanics, ramp workers, religious pamphleteers (them especially)—everybody who sets foot in the airport gets a thorough once-over from a nosy Lab or an inquisitive German shepherd.

If that happened, smuggling would no longer be a problem, because smugglers get absolutely freaked out by search dogs. The fear is deeply primal and sort of fun to watch. The eyes twitch. The palms drip. The voice quavers.

A veteran cocaine mule might save his coolest nod for the Customs man, but he'll tremble like a cornered gerbil at the sight of Muffy the golden retriever, pawing curiously at his Samsonite.

Another swell thing about dogs: Not only would they make Miami International a safer place, they'd make it an infinitely more pleasant place, too.

You're thinking: So would an infestation of deer ticks.

True, travel guides rank MIA as one of the least hospitable major airports in the United States. Passengers complain that workers are often unhelpful, and that service is slow, hostile or nonexistent.

The mere idea of pricing a candy bar at $1.50 is so uproarious that you'd think MIA's concessionaires would always be in high humor. Yet the only time they seem to break into a genuine smile is when they close down their registers, just as it's your turn in line to pay.

Dogs could fix all that, because they tend to brighten people's moods. Even the surliest vendor might be forced to crack a smile if a frisky Weimaraner started licking the neon magenta polish off her toenails.

Another advantage of keeping a couple thousand large dogs around the airport would be the drastic improvement in the behavior of passengers.

South Florida is known for having some of the most obnoxious air travelers in the world, and fisticuffs are not unheard of at MIA. Dogs would put an end to such nonsense, if not with their deterring presence then with their gleaming canines.

Think of all those times you've waited 45 minutes while some jerk in front of you ranted and cursed at a ticket clerk, and all you kept thinking was: Wouldn't it be great if a 150-pound Rottweiler came along and dragged this bozo off by the earlobes?

Well, why not? And what a nice treat for the dog, after a long day of sniffing out hand-grenade smugglers and baggage thieves.

Which brings us to the bleak plight of American Airlines, recently the target of a humiliatingly productive drug sting. Heroin in the beverage carts gave new meaning to the slogan "something special in the air."

Solution? A search dog on every plane. Give 'em the run of the joint, from cockpit to cargo hold.

Imagine. No dope, no incendiary devices, no drunks hassling the flight attendants, no creep in row 27 bitching about his Salisbury steak.

Put a hungry-looking Doberman in the aisle, and every flight would become orderly and civilized. If some fool dared to act up, it would be better entertainment than any in-flight movie.

Soon, American would be the most asked-for carrier in the hemisphere. Fang Air.

And Miami International? Suddenly the nation's most popular airport, a secure and tail-waggingly friendly destination where passengers are more inclined to carry Liv-a-Snaps than Thai stick.

2

BUILT UP, WASHED AWAY

December 7, 1987

U.S. POINTS OUT THE BRIGHT SIDE OF OIL SPILLS

Silly us. All that fretting about what offshore oil drilling might do to Florida's coastline—what a bunch of worrywarts!

The U.S. government just released a hefty environmental impact study containing this reassuring, computer-generated conclusion: If oil exploration commences up and down the Gulf of Mexico, there's merely a 48 percent chance that a major spill will smear the beaches within 35 years.

Gee, what a relief. With the odds of an ecological disaster being only about 50-50, we needn't be concerned that the Interior Department has extended its oil-leasing program to include most of the Florida Keys.

The phone-book-size study on the Gulf of Mexico asserts that offshore oil exploration is abundantly safe, and that "state-of-the-art" technology should minimize damage to reefs, tidal banks, water quality and marine life.

For instance, the Interior Department has brilliantly determined that the use of high-powered explosives to dismantle abandoned oil rigs "could cause injury or death" to certain sea life. To prevent this, the government and the oil companies will arrange for special observers to watch for sea turtles and marine mammals around drill platforms that are about to be blown up.

The report doesn't specify what the observers will do if they actually spot any turtles, or in what way the turtles will be warned of the impending dynamite. Merely shouting at the animals is probably not sufficient.

In assessing the risks of oil drilling off Florida, the government is equally mindful of potential harm to tourism: "Visual distractions (such as mobile drilling rigs and production platforms) are considered to be impact-producing factors. . . . It is possible that their presence could affect tourism expenditures due to decreased interest in the coastal areas because of the altered viewscape."

Translation: Tourists might not pay $150 for a waterfront room just to watch the sun go down between a couple of Shell Oil derricks.

However, the government promises that very few of these platforms will be visible from the beaches. Furthermore, it says, the negative economic aspects of offshore drilling are outweighed by the positive—even if a mishap occurs.

The report states that any loss of tourism revenues resulting from an "environmental incident" (meaning oil spill) should be balanced against the "beneficial effects resulting from expenditures made by research and media personnel and curious onlookers."

Using this ingenious logic, perhaps we should arrange a massive gooey oil slick once every year, in the off-season. Fill up all those empty beachfront hotels with reporters, scientists and biologists.

The Interior Department goes on to definitively shatter the myth of the Florida tarball.

I, for one, had always assumed that the appearance of sticky black gobs along the sand was a bad sign, and that it suggested something harmful was in the water. Not so.

"A matter of personal taste," reports our government. "The effect of tarballs on the beach is primarily an aesthetic one."

It goes on to say that, while "chronic tarball accumulation could have a significant effect on tourism," sporadic outbreaks of gunk on the beach have virtually no impact.

The feds admit that oil drilling creates other inevitable risks and damages. Under the proposed Eastern Gulf plan, the areas facing the greatest threat are the shores of Everglades National Park and Monroe County.

Back in October, when Interior Secretary Donald Hodel came to Miami, Sen. Bob Graham asked him to take time out for a tour of the Keys—just to see what was at stake.

Unfortunately, Hodel was just too darn busy attending Republican fundraisers and prayer breakfasts. At Gov. Bob Martinez's urging, a Keys visit is now planned for next month.

So come on down, Donald. Enjoy the viewscape before it's altered, before you have to tiptoe through the tarballs.

July 22, 1988

NATURALLY, THE GOVERNOR IS ALL WET

Governor Martinez's new Spoil Our Coast program got another boost Thursday when a state panel voted to make it easier for developers to mangle the wetlands.

The Environmental Regulatory Commission weakened and deleted important rules that would have encouraged developers to build around—not over—sensitive mangroves. The vote is considered a victory for Dale Twachtmann, chief of the Department of Environmental Regulation.

Since his appointment by Martinez, Twachtmann has loyally promoted the pro-development philosophy. Despite all his gushing over the glory of reefs and rivers, the governor is still a man whose heart (and campaign fund) throbs at the sight of concrete condos rising from the estuaries.

While the Department of Natural Resources reports directly to the Cabinet, the DER answers to the governor. No other watchdog agency so clearly reflects his views.

Under Reubin Askew and Bob Graham, the state at least went through the motions of defending coastal habitats, sometimes with significant results. Under Martinez and Twachtmann, the DER is being made user-friendly for big-time developers. One of the first directives was that staff members start treating permit applicants as "clients."

"DER had always taken the position that their client was the environment," says Thomas Reese, a St. Petersburg lawyer who has been fighting to keep the coastal protection rules intact.

Another clear signal of Martinez's sympathies was his choice of appointments to the seven-member Environmental Regulatory Commission, the rule-setting arm of DER. Three of Martinez's four selections have backgrounds as builders or developers.

Except for a slight hitch, it would have been four-for-four. One of the governor's original choices came from a family whose building firm turned out to be in trouble with DER—allegedly for illegal dredging and filling. Even Martinez recognized this as a potential public relations problem.

Thursday's vote focused on whether developers should be forced to redesign their projects to preserve sensitive coastal acreage. Also at issue were rules of "mitigation"—how much, if any, replanting and repairing of wetlands should be required of developers.

Last year, DER adopted rules that favored applicants who made an effort to preserve mangroves and to work around them. This year, Twachtmann wanted that section deleted. He also didn't think it was necessary for developers to have to replicate the wetlands they planned to destroy.

How very considerate. But what can you expect from the same folks who recently unveiled a plan that will make it easier to poison Florida's bays, lakes and rivers?

Twachtmann doesn't like the current Outstanding Florida Waters program, which is supposed to offer 200 state waterways the strictest protection from pollution. Now the DER wants to establish three classes of waters with varying degrees of regulation: local, state and national significance.

Incredibly, Twachtmann has decided that all Florida waters fit into the first two categories—in other words, we have no nationally significant waters deserving of the highest protection. Not at the Pennekamp Coral Reef, not in the Everglades, not Biscayne Bay, not even the Keys. A whole state surrounded by water but none of it a national resource.

The U.S. Environmental Protection Agency thinks Twachtmann's plan stinks. The agency is already on Florida's case for allowing the flushing of sewage, chemicals and agricultural runoff into state waters.

The only people who think the current rules are too tough either work for the governor or for developers. Twachtmann insists that the new DER programs will valiantly protect Florida's vanishing coastline and keep our waters safe. No way.

What we are witnessing is the systematic dismantling of the Askew-Graham environmental legacy. In November 1990, Gov. Martinez might learn just how popular that legacy is.

May 31, 1989

WE MUST END THE CALAMITIES ON OUR COASTS

The mass of humanity that swarmed to the great outdoors last weekend was a powerful reminder of how much we rely on water, not just for sustenance but for peace of mind.

The beauty of Florida's coasts is the state's prime attraction. Witness the never-ending quest to pave, plat and condominiumize every square centimeter of waterfront. Each new development removes one more piece of the natural treasure, and the small part that's left is in deepening trouble.

The Wilderness Society has issued a report on America's coastal preserves, and the future it paints is not bright. One reason for gloom is the Alaskan oil spill; some of the gunk has now migrated 500 miles from Valdez and is fouling the beaches and killing the wildlife at two national parks.

No such catastrophe has struck Florida's shores, but the Wilderness Society warns of "a distressing variety of threats" that could bring destruction:

- The beaches of the Canaveral National Seashore near Kennedy Space Center are shrinking from erosion, while garbage from freighters and cruise ships washes up on shore. In addition, the waters of its Mosquito Lagoon are contaminated and closed to shell fishermen after heavy rains.
- Fort Jefferson National Monument, off Key West, is less than two dozen miles from a proposed oil-drilling site that had been scheduled for leasing in March 1990. The sale of the lease, covering a boggling 14 million acres, is now postponed while a task force studies potential hazards.

  The old fort is located in the Dry Tortugas, a pristine sprinkle of islets that are home to turtles, sea birds and a variety of reef fishes. A blowout at an oil derrick could devastate the area.
- In Biscayne National Park, water quality is being degraded by runoff from Dade County's urban canals and bay-front developments. Increased boat traffic is chewing up the seabeds, clouding the water and damaging the reefs. Another threat is bilge waste, tar gobs and garbage dumped by commercial ships as they pass offshore.

  The park comprises more than 173,000 acres, most of it submerged, in the southern part of Biscayne Bay. The boundaries also take in a few privately owned islands in the Ragged Keys, where developers are again talking about building a village of luxury homes on stilts—a project that could radically disrupt the tranquillity of the tidal flats.
- Everglades National Park, regarded as one of the pure gems of the park system, is jeopardized by just about everything. Polluted drainage from sugarcane fields, dairy farms and orange groves flows steadily from Loxahatchee south toward the park. Ditches and dikes built long ago to benefit Big Agriculture divert precious water flow away from key areas of the glades.

We don't usually think of Everglades National Park as a seashore, but a big part of it is. The water that filters south through the sawgrass eventually empties from the mangroves into Florida Bay, the vast estuary at the state's southwestern tip. When water levels in the Everglades are made to fluctuate, the results are felt all the way to the Keys and up both coasts.

Last year, according to the Wilderness Society, high water resulted in the deaths of all newborn wood storks and 50 percent of the park's alligator eggs.

Yet the park is much more than a wildlife refuge, it's a key link of South Florida's ecology.

If something goes wrong in the glades, it usually goes wrong in a big way. For example, when the rain-swollen C-111 canal in South Dade was emptied into Barnes Sound, the surge of fresh water annihilated marine life for miles.

No one disputes the gravity of the crisis. U.S. Attorney Dexter Lehtinen has sued state water managers for failing to prevent the pollution of the park. Last week, a collection of biologists, water planners, environmentalists and farmers assembled to begin work on an Everglades rescue plan. Meanwhile, Florida's congressional delegation is pushing bills that would expand the park by more than 100,000 acres, most of it as vital watershed.

Maybe somebody is finally paying attention. To lose any of our coasts, whether slowly or in a sudden black tide, would be to lose everything.

April 11, 1990

GLIB SURVEY OBSCURES RISK OF OIL SPILLS

President Bush says he opposes a permanent ban on offshore oil exploration around Florida, but would prohibit drilling in some environmentally sensitive areas such as the Keys.

The president is no dummy. He likes to go bonefishing in Islamorada, and it's difficult enough to spot the critters in crystal-clear water. You'd stand no chance in a greasy black oil slick.

Many were hoping the administration would ban oil drilling everywhere off the South Florida coasts, but evidently that won't happen. A signal came when the Interior Department declined to release the findings of its vaunted task force—the one whose hearings established that most Floridians would rather catch rabies than see oil rigs in the Gulf.

In its muddled mission, the government actually commissioned a Virginia research firm to ask tourists if they'd be bothered by an oil mishap off Florida. The answer would seem obvious to most rational people, but nothing is obvious to the U.S. government.

The tourist survey didn't offer the most authentic picture of an oil accident. For example, it suggested that a major spill could be contained to a small area of coastline, and that the unsightly effects would disappear within six months. Folks in Alaska would regard this scenario as wildly optimistic, if not delusional.

The survey also asserted that a minor spill would affect "only a small section of one of many local beaches"—and didn't mention possible catastrophic damage to reef life, grassy shallows and mangroves.

The staff of the Interior Department probably was trying to do us a favor by playing down the potential impact of a spill. They didn't want to frighten off any of our tourists.

I haven't seen the whole survey, but I was trying to imagine what kind of questions were asked, and how coyly they must have been phrased. . . .

As a tourist, would it bother you to look out your hotel window and see an oil derrick on the horizon?

a) Depends on the size
b) Depends on whether or not it's on fire
c) Depends on how much I'm paying for the room

How many oil-encrusted sea birds would have to wash ashore before you'd abandon your vacation in the Keys?

a) Three or four birds
b) A flock or two
c) Several hundred real yukky ones

In the event of an accidental spill, what's the largest tarball you could tolerate before fleeing the beach in disgust?

a) A tarball as big as a quarter
b) A tarball as big as a cantaloupe
c) A tarball as big as Bergen County, New Jersey

As a tourist, would it bother you to look out your hotel window and see an oil slick covering the beach?

a) Depends on the size
b) Depends on whether or not it's on fire
c) Depends on how much I'm paying for a cabana

If a tanker disaster occurred during your stay in the Sunshine State, which of the following recreational activities might interest you?

a) Beach Hosing Contest
b) Oil Polo

c) Dead Flounder Frisbee Toss
d) Nude Wrestling in Turpentine

On a list of disappointing vacations, which of the following would rate worse than an oil slick in Florida?

a) Earthquake in San Francisco
b) Hurricane in Bermuda
c) Nerve-gas leak in Tehran
d) Long stoplight in Bergen County, New Jersey

In the event of an oil accident, many Florida restaurants would stay open to accommodate tourists. Which of the following entrees should not be added to the menu?

a) Snapper de Amoco
b) Blackened stone crabs
c) Quaker State lobster
d) Gulf shrimp sautéed in tanker bilge

Since a minor oil spill would affect only a small section of one of our many gorgeous beaches, wouldn't you stay in Florida and make the best of it?

a) What exactly is a "minor" spill?
b) What exactly is a "small section" of beach?
c) What exactly did you pay for this stupid survey?

August 6, 1990

LAUDERDALE SHOULD FIGHT FOR ITS STRIP

In fine Florida tradition, the city of Fort Lauderdale is preparing to deliver its famous public beach into the hands of private hotel developers. This is to be achieved, believe it or not, by physically moving State Road A1A away from the water.

It's a scheme so naked in arrogance that it's a cause for marvel: the moral equivalent of moving the Blue Ridge Parkway out of the mountains. The Strip in Fort Lauderdale is one of South Florida's last stretches of open beachfront—a place where you can actually drive down the highway and see the ocean from the window of your car.

This, of course, is totally unacceptable. The prevailing philosophy is that the Atlantic is there to be exploited; to give visitors a free, unobstructed view violates every basic tenet of waterfront development.

Miami Beach is a good example of what happens when you surrender the shoreline to hotels and condos. There, among concrete high-rises, you can drive for miles without a clue that there is an extremely large ocean nearby.

Sharp-eyed tourists, cruising slowly and peeking between buildings, sometimes catch a lucky glimpse of the azure surf. Many, however, are forced to check into hotels and trudge down to a delineated section of beach—a beach that is, true to form, phony.

The real Miami Beach washed away ages ago in tides that threatened to consume the precious hotels as well. Consequently, a fat "renourished" beach was created by dredging up marl, coral shards and broken seashells, and packing it all down with heavy machinery. Most tourists, bless their soles, never complain.

Fort Lauderdale still has a natural sandy beach, and you don't have to walk through an air-conditioned lobby to get there. Just drive up, park and dash for the waves.

Not for long. The city is moving parking to the side streets. Tired of traffic jams, local voters also approved a plan that shifts one part of A1A a few blocks west to Birch Road.

But the coup de grâce is the city's "beach redevelopment" plan that envisions a teeming Yuppie hellswamp of luxury hotels, bistros, town houses and what are coyly called "promenades" (translation: really big sidewalks).

Nine firms have entered the bidding. They are fuzzy on blueprints and financing, but most agree on one point: Nobody will build a resort hotel unless A1A is moved away from the beach. Developers insist that hotel guests don't want to cross the road to reach the water—a short pilgrimage with a long tradition.

What's really at stake is control of the beach: The hotels want the frontage for themselves. They don't want a highway separating their handsome cabana concession and lovely tiki bars from the sunbathers.

Admittedly, the Strip is tacky, peeling and, at night, crime-ridden. Since Spring Breakers were encouraged to party elsewhere, the commercial ambience along A1A cannot be described as thriving.

But the problem isn't the road, and it's certainly not the beach. Rather than restrict or divert public access, the city should be expanding it. Why not try to revitalize the existing shopping and hotel district without malling the beach?

Fort Lauderdale's sense of history is such that only one city leader, Vice Mayor Jim Naugle, has dared to speak out against rerouting A1A. He wants to put the issue on a ballot, a move for which there is little support on the commission. When it comes to grabbing up waterfront property, the electorate's view is not usually welcomed.

But last week another powerful voice joined Naugle in protest. U.S. Rep. E. Clay Shaw, a former mayor of Fort Lauderdale, said he'll fight any attempt to move the avenue known as A1A.

"The people will never vote to give up the beach," Shaw said. "They certainly don't want it hidden behind a wall of condominiums and hotels. That would be crazy."

It's worse than crazy. It's highway robbery.

October 16, 1994

YOU CAN HELP BAN PLUNDER OF SEA LIFE

At long last, voters can shut down the rapacious commercial netting operations that are wiping out Florida's sea life.

California, Texas, Georgia and South Carolina have already taken similar action, with impressive results. It should have happened years ago here, but nobody in Tallahassee had the guts to stand up to the commercial fishing lobby.

So nearly half a million Floridians signed a petition putting a net ban on the November 8 ballot. It will appear as Amendment 3.

The law would prohibit the use of entanglement gill nets in state waters. These are the devices that nearly decimated the redfish and kingfish stocks a few years ago. Indiscriminate netting is the big reason that the world's principal fisheries are either dead or in drastic decline.

Lobbyists for the netters blame pollution and foreign competition for their disappearing catch. Most marine biologists blame the nets. Where gill netters arrive, the fish eventually vanish.

Whatever becomes tangled in the mesh dies—not just the desired commercial stock, but also game fish, bait species, endangered sea turtles and bottle-nosed dolphins. The unwanted dead, known as "bycatch," end up as garbage or chum.

In the old days, netting was a father-and-son operation with smaller nets and small boats. Today the nets are vast. The boats are far-ranging and sometimes aided by spotter planes. As a result, whole schools of breeding or migrating fish can be obliterated in a morning's work.

On one day in 1985, a single commercial boat in upstate Florida illegally netted nearly 36 tons of redfish. That type of plundering is what inspired the anti-net petition drive.

Very soon, expensive media advertising will be launched to convince Floridians that a ban on gill nets will drive up seafood prices, and throw many thousands of hardworking folks out of their jobs. It will do neither.

The snapper, grouper, tuna and dolphin that you order in restaurants are caught by hook, not nets. Menu prices won't be affected by one cent.

According to the Texas Parks and Wildlife Department, sales at seafood restaurants actually have risen 8 percent since gill nets were outlawed there in the late 1980s. Meanwhile, improved sport fishing "has led to an economic boost in tourism . . . with an estimated impact to the state of over $2.5 billion."

As for the loss of fishing jobs, you'll hear some outlandish figures. In truth, Florida has fewer than 1,000 full-time gill netters, and they are most endangered by the increasing scarcity of fish.

If Amendment 3 passes, they can change jobs or change gear. Most offshore purse seines, cast nets, and small shrimp trawls will remain legal. So are hooks and lines.

The gill net industry portrays itself as an essential provider of domestic seafood, yet much of its catch goes overseas. The media scare campaign is bankrolled partly with money from Taiwan, a lucrative market for black mullet—a prized quarry of Florida netters.

The eggs of the mullet are a delicacy in Asia, where processed roe sells for up to $400 a pound. It doesn't take a Ph.D. to figure out that harvesting the eggs can seriously jeopardize the survival of a species. Already stocks of black mullet—an important food of eagles, osprey and game fish—are shrinking.

Roe season is just beginning. This week, residents of Green Cove Springs awoke to find the St. Johns River sprinkled with gutted female mullet and dead redfish—the "bycatch" of a massive gill-netting expedition.

It's time to end the wasteful slaughter, as other coastal states did. To let it continue ensures a barren future for Florida's marine life, and all those who depend on the sea.

November 19, 1995

UNCLE SAM'S SAND CASTLES INSURANCE CO.

You hear it everywhere: If there's one thing Florida needs, it's more high-rise condos in flood zones.

Leading the charge is U.S. Rep. Tillie Fowler of Jacksonville. She advocates lifting the ban on federal insurance for several low-lying areas that include some extremely prime beachfront, when it's dry.

Most insurance companies aren't stupid enough to write flood policies for these tracts, so the developers want the U.S. government to assume the risk.

Fowler is on the case. The hurdle is the 1982 Coastal Barrier Resources System, enacted to prevent imprudent building in undeveloped flood zones.

The CBRS discourages construction by denying government flood insurance and other subsidies, including funds for rebuilding after a storm.

The law was written to make sure public money isn't used to pay for damage whenever a beachfront project gets swamped by high water. Among the areas all or partially blacklisted from U.S. flood protection are Cedar Key, Hutchinson Island, Sanibel and Ponce Inlet, at New Smyrna Beach.

Ponce Inlet is of keen interest to Rep. Fowler. A 19-story condominium has risen there, but the developers are having trouble getting private insurance (what with all the hurricanes and such).

Fowler has filed a bill that would allow the Ponce Inlet property and other coastal acreage to receive federal flood policies. She says construction in these areas started before the CBRS became law, so the parcels shouldn't have been listed as undeveloped.

Last year she tried the same argument and Congress disagreed, deciding that work had commenced after 1982. But Fowler isn't giving up. Her bill is winding through the House.

If it passes, the landscape and seascape of Florida's remaining shorelines will change drastically. Hotel and condo schemes that previously would've been laughed out of the banks will quickly find themselves financed.

Insurance is the key. Without it, it's tough to get a mortgage.

The only thing more idiotic than building in a flood zone is bankrolling the project—unless it's insured. And who's the biggest pushover with the cheapest premiums?

Uncle Sam. The U.S. flood program covers about $250 billion worth of residential and commercial property, most of which will never be under water.

Then there's Florida—1,300 miles of beaches, bays and coastlines that are perpetually vulnerable to high tides, storm surges and sudden tropical deluges.

It took a while, but the U.S. government finally figured out that Florida was a very wet place, and that it probably was a bad idea to encourage folks to build and settle in the soggiest, most flood-prone areas.

Moreover, it was hard to justify making American taxpayers finance the roads, sewers and foolishness of a few heedless real-estate speculators. That's why the CBRS was adopted.

Rep. Fowler's plan to poke holes in coastal protection isn't especially well timed, coming on the heels of a hectic and costly hurricane season. Opal alone ripped up the Panhandle to the tune of $1.8 billion.

Mother Nature has scared insurance companies into canceling thousands of policies, or fleeing the state entirely, but Fowler and her colleagues in our congressional delegation are undaunted.

They want government to do what the private sector won't—provide cheap flood insurance and storm relief for condo kings.

But don't dare call it a handout. We're not talking about homeless shelters or free health clinics; we're talking about nineteen-story oceanfront high-rises.

Let's keep the priorities straight.

September 19, 1996

NETTERS, PANEL SABOTAGE THE WILL OF VOTERS

Seldom have Florida voters spoken so emphatically as they did two years ago when, by a 72 percent majority, they outlawed the use of large commercial gill nets in coastal waters.

Ever since then, some netters have been scheming ways to dodge the law and resume the indiscriminate harvesting that once brought redfish, kingfish and other species to the brink of collapse.

The newest scam is, believe it or not, giant tarpaulins.

In anticipation of next month's mullet season, netters in the Panhandle have stitched together huge tarps made from plastic and parachute nylon. In the center of each is a patch of net just small enough to squeak under the 500-square-foot limit mandated by the ban.

Tarp seines might be cumbersome, but they function much like their all-mesh counterparts, engulfing vast schools of mullet—and anything else unlucky enough to be trapped inside the perimeters. That includes protected game fish and tons of small but important forage fish, which are discarded dead as unwanted "bycatch."

You don't need to be a NASA engineer to figure out that a 10-acre underwater tarpaulin is basically a net without holes. And you don't need a degree in marine biology to understand the damage it will do.

So you'd think the state would have no trouble recognizing the tarps for what they are, and put a stop to them immediately.

That's what the Florida Marine Patrol would like to do, but it cannot. A higher authority, the state Marine Fisheries Commission, decided that the plastic contraptions technically don't violate any current laws.

So the MFC has proposed a new rule outlawing the tarpaulins for mullet harvesting, which has in turn prompted another lawsuit by the commercial fishing industry. It could be a long time before the issue is settled, which means Florida waters might be shimmering with plastic in the months ahead.

This is precisely the sort of rapacious behavior that precipitated the landslide Save Our Sealife referendum in 1994. Since then, fisheries have rebounded impressively.

For the state to allow tarp seines is to sabotage the net ban, and thumb its nose at the 2.8 million people who voted for it. We're not just talking about breaking a law, but defying a constitutional amendment.

Ironically, the amendment itself would have been unnecessary had the state done its job and properly regulated the netting industry years ago. In fact, if the MFC weren't so hamstrung and the commercial fishing lobby weren't so bullheaded, there would still be a netting industry today.

The MFC has been miserably slow to protect marine resources because it's designed to be. The panel of political appointees is unable to adopt the simplest regulation without a lengthy administrative process, followed by approval from the governor and Cabinet (who are not well-known for standing up to special interests).

That's why there's a growing push for a new statewide referendum that would sensibly unify freshwater and saltwater wildlife management under a single agency—one that could take decisive action without meddling from politicians.

Such solid authority would be useful now, as the netters prepare to cloak bays and shoreline waters with killer garbage bags, some a half mile in length.

The MFC isn't completely helpless to take action. If they conclude the threat is serious enough, the commissioners can pass an emergency rule temporarily blocking the use of the plastic tarps.

That option undoubtedly will receive great support at an October 7 public hearing, at which Floridians will get a chance to remind the MFC why it exists.

December 6, 1998

BROKEN VOWS BY THE BAY

The Miami City Commission stands poised to put a luxury-home community on the last splinter of open bayfront land in Coconut Grove.

Known as Commodore Bay, the 6.3-acre tract lies between Peacock Park and the Barnacle State Historic Site. The property—a ragged vestige of a lush hammock—was once to have been purchased and turned into a park.

That was the trade-off the city made in 1985 with the state for permission to put a shopping mall—Bayside Marketplace—next to another park, Bayfront.

Now, 13 years later, it's obvious the Commodore Bay swap was little more than a paper expedient. Negotiations for the Grove property flagged, it never got bought and developers never stopped trying to exploit it.

It appears they finally will. Plans call for 41 houses up to four stories, tennis courts, a pool and a clubhouse—pretty much the opposite of what Miami officials promised would be there.

While the project is opposed by some environmental and civic groups, the commission seems inclined—and, some say, legally bound—to approve. The proposed density actually is less than the zoning allows.

The culprits in the Commodore Bay fiasco aren't the current developers or even the current commission. The prime land is and has been privately held; the city's assent to acquire it was suspect from the start.

Somebody cooked up the idea back when Bayside fever gripped City Hall, and it was annoyingly pointed out the sprawling new mall would encroach on property strictly designated for public use.

That acreage, on the edge of Bayfront Park, had been deeded by the state with the stipulation that the city could never surrender it to private interests and that it would be used "solely for public purposes."

In other words, no Hooters was envisioned there.

Miami commissioners appealed to Gov. Bob Graham and the Cabinet, which ultimately granted a waiver that cleared the way for Bayside. In exchange, the city agreed to devote almost 18 percent of its net revenues from the new mall toward buying lands along Biscayne Bay and the Miami River.

The plan theoretically would have created more public recreation areas. First on the list of priorities was Commodore Bay.

The state agreed to put up half the money, and positioned the tract for acquisition by the Conservation and Recreational Lands program. It even offered to advance Miami its share of the purchase cost.

The trade made the Bayside machinations more politically palatable, and almost everyone signed on. Only then-Secretary of State George Firestone piped up to inquire what could be done if Miami failed to follow through and buy the waterfront lands.

"We sue them," declared an attorney for the Cabinet. "We get a court to order them to do it."

Well, it sure sounded good.

Needless to say, the state hasn't filed any lawsuits, or made scarcely a peep about Commodore Bay. What happened during the last 13 years is that the property got much more valuable, while the city got scandalized and went broke.

What seemed like a noble idea at the time now looks like a sham, a bargaining ploy to grease the Bayside shops project.

There is no waterfront park at Commodore Bay, and no prospects for one. Most of the commissioners who cut the deal are gone, Bob Graham is in Washington, and on Tuesday the current City Commission will vote on a gated subdivision for the property.

For what it's worth, the developers have vowed not to chop down too many native trees. Let's hope their word, and their memory, is more reliable than the city's.

April 2, 2000

THE CASE OF THE MISSING MANGROVES

A few weeks ago, a state biologist patrolling John Pennekamp Coral Reef State Park was sickened to find a long stretch of mangrove shoreline laid bare, the lush trees hacked to stumps.

It looked as if some supernatural scythe had shorn a hole in the forest, but it was just a tree-trimming outfit hired by rich landowners at the sprawling Ocean Reef Club in North Key Largo.

Between two and three acres of red, white and black mangroves, some taller than 50 feet, had been chopped down illegally to provide future home sites with a view of the Atlantic Ocean—every speculator's dream.

In a matter of days, a thick tropical canopy that had weathered more than a half century of hurricanes and flood tides had been reduced to dump fodder, all in the name of greed. No one called authorities to report it.

Mangroves are the most essential component of Florida's coastline ecology, a nursery for marine life and a buffer against storms. Trimming of the trees is strictly regulated.

The massacre in North Key Largo is one of the worst violations ever documented in South Florida.

"It's a horrible sight," said Capt. Carl Nielsen, a law-enforcement officer with the Department of Environmental Protection. "I've been doing this for a lot of years in the Keys and I've never seen a mangrove-cutting case this egregious."

Investigators were hardly surprised that the incident had occurred at the Ocean Reef Club, a gated winter haven for the wealthy, prominent and politically connected.

For decades, Ocean Reef has been the scene of the most prolific and defiant violations of environmental laws in Monroe County. The place is notorious for midnight dredgings, raw sewage dumpings and mass removals of native trees.

After-the-fact fines are nonchalantly paid as the cost of doing business when expanding waterfront development. But even by Ocean Reef's standards, the mangrove annihilation along Coral Lane was exceptionally brazen.

That's because those who ordered it didn't mangle just their own trees. The only way to gain an uncluttered vista of the ocean was to attack the tall old mangroves lining the shore, within the boundaries of Pennekamp itself.

Which, believe it or not, is exactly what they did. The tree cutters entered park grounds, cranked up their chain saws and went wild.

"It's just so incredibly stupid," said Allison DeFoor, a former Monroe County judge and now the environmental policy chief for Gov. Jeb Bush. As a private attorney, DeFoor represented some Ocean Reef lawbreakers.

"It's been 20 years since anybody in the Keys tried something like this," he said.

The state has assigned extra investigators to find out who ordered the cutting, but the trail isn't easy to follow. The property's owners, who include some residents of Ocean Reef, are cloaked in layers of corporate paperwork.

The lots are held by a company called O. R. Golf Partners, Ltd. No officers are named in Florida business records, but the resident agent is listed as RKF Holdings.

Records show the president of RKF Holdings is Miroslav Fajt, a Manhattan attorney. Fajt has a home at Ocean Reef and owns other land there. He didn't respond to two requests for an interview.

Ironically, the site of the destruction is part of a tract once designated to be condemned, purchased and preserved by the state as protection for Pennekamp. Unfortunately, the property was never acquired.

The previous owner of the Coral Lane parcels was Driscoll Properties, which in 1997 obtained a state permit for limited mangrove trimming on three lots.

Under the terms, no tree shorter than 10 feet could be cut. Those taller than 10 feet could be trimmed, but no more than four feet of height or 25 percent of foliage was to be removed each year.

Specifically, the permit forbade touching any trees below the mean high-water line, which is park property. There was, obviously, no authorization to invade Pennekamp, a boating and diving mecca that is Florida's most popular state park.

Driscoll didn't cut the mangroves. Instead, it sold the three lots and several others on Coral Lane to O. R. Golf Partners in June 1999. The price: about $2.9 million.

The trimming permit transferred to the new owners, but "it was useless," DEP's Nielsen said, because it couldn't achieve the desired effect. There would still be mangroves standing between the property and the blue waters of Pennekamp.

And those mangroves were below the mean high-water line, inside the park.

Messages left for Fajt, O. R. Golf Partners' resident agent, were returned by Robert Smith. He is a former county biologist who has been hired as a consultant by the company.

Smith conceded that the mangrove wipeout on Coral Lane was the largest he'd ever seen. "A fiasco," he said.

But he said the illegal cutting resulted from confusion over how much trimming was allowed by the Driscoll permit, and where it was supposed to occur. "It is very vague," Smith added.

However, the law is anything but ambiguous when it comes to razing mangrove fringe inside a state park. It's a crime, period, and everybody in the Keys knows it—landscapers, tree cutters, property owners.

Once the incursion was discovered, Pennekamp officers asked the Ocean Reef security staff to inform them immediately if the culprits returned to the scene.

But when a ranger revisited Coral Lane a few days later, he was dismayed to find the tree trimmers back at work, hacking away. To get there, the trucks had to have passed through Ocean Reef's security gates—yet no one at the club alerted the park.

Biologist Smith said the principals of O. R. Golf Partners fully comprehend the seriousness of the situation. He said they want to repair the buzz-cut shoreline, and might offer to improve other disturbed habitat on the island.

"They want to make amends. They want to do whatever it takes to make it right," Smith said. "That was the directive I was given."

But restoring the shore to a natural state is problematic; many of the sawed-off red mangroves are dead or dying. And nurseries don't sell replacements for rare 50-foot black mangroves.

Pennekamp biologists will soon begin the depressing task of counting stumps and adding up the costs. Where damage is severe, mangrove violators may be fined a minimum of $4 for each square foot of cutting.

In this case, the total could surpass $500,000—a sum hefty enough to make an impression even at Ocean Reef.

That's not all. It's a third-degree felony to destroy trees in a state park. It's also a felony to unlawfully destroy so much canopy that a habitat is changed—obliterated, in this instance.

Each crime carries a maximum $50,000 fine and five years in prison, which would be getting off light.

It'll take ten times as long for those mangroves to grow back the way they were.

(*Herald* researcher Elizabeth Donovan contributed to this report.)

August 6, 2000

GREED FUELS THE STAMPEDE TO HURRICANE ALLEY

August marks another queasy anniversary of Hurricane Andrew, the costliest natural disaster in the country's history.

If a storm of similar magnitude hammers the coast this year, the results likely will be even more catastrophic and deadly.

Hundreds of thousands of potential new victims have migrated to the Atlantic and Gulf shores since 1992, when Andrew creamed parts of Florida and Louisiana.

Despite the well-publicized increase in hurricane activity, oceanfront real-estate sales are booming. Never before have so many people so blithely placed themselves in harm's way.

It's not only the lure of the sea but the promise of future reimbursement that brings newcomers. Government policy fosters development on high-risk coastal zones, wetlands and barrier islands by essentially subsidizing those who, in the face of dire predictions, elect to live there.

The U.S. Army Corps of Engineers, for instance, spends about $80 million a year replenishing beaches that nature nibbles away. Artificial beach restoration enhances property values, which in turn spurs more coastal construction.

The closer you get to the ocean, the more you pay for land. Meanwhile, ironically, the ocean is getting closer to you.

From New York to Key West, sea levels are rising steadily to reclaim the shore inch by inch. The Federal Emergency Management Agency (FEMA) estimates that about 30,000 single-family homes and condos are on coastal tracts that will be submerged by 2030.

One could reasonably argue that anybody who lives on a beach is surely aware of the risks, and is free to take a chance against weather, erosion and rising oceans.

The government goes farther than that. It compensates homeowners who fall victim to their own arrogance, ignorance or misplaced optimism.

The program is national flood insurance, and it's sold to those who live in such imminent danger of being swamped that no private insurer will go near them.

Many folks with government flood protection never report a claim. Others file again and again. According to a recent series in *USA Today,* one piece of property in Houston has been the subject of 16 federal flood claims that so far have paid out $807,000.

Remarkable, for a property valued at only $114,480.

FEMA officials have fought to curtail beach replenishment and sharply limit development that ruins crucial natural drainages. Congress has repeatedly refused to act.

Huge money is at stake. Banks, land speculators, builders, highway contractors—all of them get rich off waterfront projects, and all have clout with politicians.

Witness the fierce struggle required to pass a minimally sensible building code here in Florida. At issue was nothing less than the safety of millions of families, yet industry lobbyists came disgracefully close to gutting the law.

National flood insurance has been tightened in recent years, but not enough. It's absurd that fellow taxpayers must bail out those of us, like myself, who've chosen to live on a flood zone in hurricane alley.

Cutting federal flood benefits won't happen, though. It would discourage banks from financing oceanfront property, which would slow coastal building. Profits always win out over common sense.

Those now stampeding to America's shorelines figure the move isn't so risky. If a hurricane comes, Uncle Sam will pay up to $350,000 to rebuild their splintered dream home, which they will have safely evacuated in advance of the surge.

Or maybe not. So densely populated is the U.S. coastal hurricane corridor that some experts believe evacuation might be more perilous than riding out the weather.

Last year, three million people across the South headed inland to escape Hurricane Floyd. The wild exodus gridlocked interstate highways, leaving some evacuees stranded in traffic for 18 hours.

If the storm had veered ashore, many would have died in their cars.

No wonder the mood among hurricane experts is one of glum resignation. Disaster is inevitable. Those who should have listened didn't.

People's mad dash to relocate at the ocean's edge—and lawmakers' cowardly refusal to curb it—shows how quickly Andrew was forgotten.

Consequently, the most destructive storm in history is destined to become the second most destructive. The big question, as always, is when.

3
THE LAST DAYS
OF FLORIDA BAY

June 18, 1986

MIGHTY TARPON SHOULD BE FISH THAT GETS AWAY

I remember, as a kid, going into just about any restaurant in the Keys and see-ing pictures of the great Ted Williams on the wall. In almost every photo The Kid was holding a fishing rod and standing next to a gaping dead tarpon. The tarpon was hung from a hook and, as big as Ted Williams looked, the tarpon always looked bigger.

The pictures were reminiscent of Ernest Hemingway, a great angler who loved to kill big fish. One season in Cuba, Hemingway caught 64 marlin and killed every one. He also loved to shoot his initials into sharks with a machine gun. Hemingway, though a splendid writer, was not exactly a charter mem-ber of the Cousteau Society.

In fact, Ted Williams has caught more than a thousand tarpon and killed only a few, but those few photographs have been spread around the Keys as a recurring tourist curiosity. You still see them taped up all over the place.

Williams continues to pursue the tarpon, probably the most spectacular game fish in the world, but he never kills them, just lets them go. You can't eat them, and these days most taxidermists don't even use the carcass. If you want a tarpon mounted, you only need to pick up the phone and order one by size. The mounts come in plastic molds.

So there's really no point to killing the fish, except to show off what you killed. Or win a trophy.

This week in Islamorada some of the world's top fishermen are gathered for the Gold Cup Invitational, a tarpon tournament that Ted Williams helped to start many years ago. The Gold Cup is elite because the anglers must use, of all things, a fly rod. A fly rod against a fish that often weighs 100 pounds, and sometimes twice as much.

Lately the debate at high-stakes tarpon tournaments has centered on the need to slaughter this magnificent silver fish. Some contestants say the only way to tell the true weight of a tarpon is to kill it and bring it in; others argue that the poundage can be computed from the length and girth, and the fish can be turned free.

One prestigious tournament, the Hawley, will switch to an all-release format next season. In the Gold Cup, anglers still must kill at least one big tarpon, a "weight fish," to have a chance at the grand prize. The killing is done with an enormous steel gaff.

Whether this seriously depletes the population is debatable, but it's true that today there are fewer tarpon, and fewer big ones, to catch. All during Florida's famous spring tarpon season—from Haulover to Boca Grande— fish are killed for the sake of a third-place trophy or a Polaroid picture. As Thomas McGuane has noted, "When you hang a tarpon up at the dock, it will suck the gawkers off the highway like a vacuum cleaner."

But dead fish look slack and pallid; alive they are all radiant muscle. Once off Long Key I fought one for four hours and 30 minutes, and vowed to stuff it for the living-room wall if I ever got it to the boat. The fish heard me. It broke the line.

Thankfully, some of the top guides and anglers refuse to kill tarpon. Some won't even do it in a tournament; others dread the prospect.

My friend Bob Branham, a guide, has an arresting way of satisfying a client's trophy lust: He hoists the tarpon into the skiff, lays it across the angler's lap and takes a photograph. Then he swiftly lowers the fish into the water and revives it. I do not casually recommend this method, for an angry seven-foot tarpon is an explosive package to have in one's arms.

I told Bob that one day he's going to kill a customer like this. He says it's better than killing the fish.

John Donnell, another tarpon guide, gaffed a fine fish Monday during the Gold Cup. "The first one I've ever killed," he told me. Though he was leading the tournament, he didn't sound completely on top of the world.

The mighty tarpon had been hung at dockside, weighed, measured, photographed and admired. Then a crab fisherman came by in a truck and hauled it away for bait.

July 28, 1986

CONTROVERSIAL LAND-USE PLAN TO SHAPE KEYS

The sloganeering to "Save Our Keys" hits a crescendo this week when the Florida Cabinet considers a controversial land-use plan for Monroe County.

This agenda item is of interest only if you happen to cherish what's left of the Keys and prefer not to see it dredged, filled, paved and condominiumized.

The state and county have collaborated on a master plan that purportedly balances environmental concerns, the rights of property holders and the economic needs of the Keys. The process has been contentious, confusing and excruciating, like giving birth to a porcupine. The result is just about as lovable.

As now written, the Keys' growth plan is seriously flawed—1,400 pages of good intentions, and loopholes as big as the Seven Mile Bridge.

Take the maps, for instance. The land-use maps were supposed to designate what kind of development is permitted in each region of the Keys. The idea was to promote growth while protecting vital wetlands and hammocks, to set strict rules about where "destination resorts" and other high-density projects should be allowed.

Sounds good, except that the maps have been gerrymandered into a high-priced coloring book for hotel and condo developers. One by one, their attorneys appeared at public hearings to ask for teeny-weeny exemptions.

A few acres here, a few more there—so now the maps actually contradict the land-use plan. And guess what: The state wants to go ahead and approve both. Sort out the whole mess later, OK?

This type of bureaucratic boobery brings tears of joy to a lawyer's eye. It plainly opens the door for legal challenges by any project planned in a disputed region. While it would seem an obvious solution to make the maps conform to the plan, the state Department of Community Affairs apparently has no time for such trivial detail.

This isn't to say the whole plan is worthless, because it's not. Finally the possibility of order looms in Monroe County, legendary for its zombie zoning department and haphazard growth policy. Some Keys officials remain bitter that the state intervened; they love to take Tallahassee's money, but they hate to take its advice.

All sides want to get the battle over with, but nobody is really sure what the new land-use plan would mean. Even environmental groups can't agree. George Kundtz of the Izaak Walton League has called the document "stranger and uglier than any kind of fiction."

Yet Charles Lee of the Florida Audubon Society has said the county's plan was "60 percent" acceptable, and thought it could be salvaged with a few important amendments. He had high hopes until last week, when the DCA not only ignored his suggestions but further watered down some key regulations.

Consequently, the plan presented to the Cabinet on Tuesday leaves unresolved the issue of the mystery maps.

In addition, language that would have ensured the continuity of hammocks and pinelands on some of the islands has been diluted. In the same vein, a rule to protect the habitat of endangered species has been sufficiently fuzzed up to allow multiple interpretations.

In short, the land-use plan as amended last week is now unacceptable to the Audubon Society, too. If it passes in its present form, Charles Lee warns, it means that "the state has laid down its arms and surrendered the Florida Keys."

The plan's supporters, including aides to the governor, say it's the best compromise possible, a big step forward. Yet if it's such a grand design for preserving the essential Keys environment, why are so many environmentalists upset? And why are the hotel and condo developers so subdued? This is known as a clue.

The "Save Our Keys" crusade emanates from Gov. Bob Graham himself, and he would leave no finer legacy than to make the slogan come true. It won't happen unless somebody fixes the sloppy leaks in this plan, starting with the land maps. You can't save what you can't find.

August 25, 1986

STATE MUST TAKE BOUGAINVILLE WHILE IT CAN

In the Friday the 13th slasher movies, Jason the disfigured ghoul invariably gets stabbed, shot, mushed or beheaded in the final scene.

When this happens there's always an audible sigh of relief from the audience, yet it doesn't last long. Everyone in the theater knows that Jason is not really dead. He'll be back for the sequel.

In the Keys, Jason goes by another name: Port Bougainville.

Twenty-eight hundred future condos and hotel rooms to befoul the waters of the John Pennekamp Coral Reef State Park.

Last Friday the Monroe County Commission wisely and bravely slammed the lid on this monster's coffin. By a 4–0 vote, the commissioners refused to extend a construction deadline that was part of Port Bougainville's controversial development order signed in 1982.

The vote means that all building permits for the bankrupt mini-city will expire October 26, and that any effort to revive this shambling beast will have to be attempted from scratch.

Dormant for years, Port Bougainville is in physical and financial ruin, an irreparable scab on the landscape of North Key Largo. A reasonable person might assume that the county commission's action is a death sentence, but this is not necessarily true. If you listen hard, there's still a noise from the coffin.

Hovering nearby are many gifted specialists whose expertise is legal CPR. Their task is to keep Port Bougainville alive, if not in fact then at least on paper.

This is the treatment prescribed for many extravagant coastal developments, and the reason they change hands so often. The true value of such schemes is not in the real estate, but in the development order—the piece of paper that says you can crank up the bulldozers. If the project sours or stalls, this magical piece of paper simply gets peddled by one entrepreneur to the next. In this way the project is kept alive.

To hear the lawyers tell it, Port Bougainville is a gold mine waiting to be salvaged, a radiant 400-acre vein through the last unspoiled stretch of the Keys. It sounds too good to be true, and of course it is. The project has been a gobbler from day one, a bad idea propped up by a risky loan from a failing bank.

The idea now is to unload it—or at least convince the state of Florida that somewhere out there awaits an eager developer with real money to pay for it.

Why the charade? Those with a stake in Port Bougainville claim it has sucked down $50 million, and they'd like to get some of that back.

Everybody knows the state wants to buy the property and preserve what hasn't already been blown to rubble. Naturally the court-appointed receiver wants his clients to extract every possible penny from this transaction.

Unfortunately for them, without any building permits the value of the Port Bougainville tract plummets. The magic piece of paper is about as precious as a Kleenex, and less useful. With canceled building permits you can forget the brochures and the floor plans and the architect's pretty pastel drawing; all you've got is a ghost town with a few rancid rock pits.

Which presents the amazing possibility that the state might actually end up paying a fair price for it.

Don't expect the lawyers to sit still for such a notion. Already there are stern promises to appeal the county commission's vote, opening yet a new round of legal battles for this, the most litigated development in South Florida history.

Now is the ideal time for the state to make an offer, a decent one.

The only way Florida can save the struggling Pennekamp reef is to save

North Key Largo, and the only way to do that is to buy up as much as possible.

The alternative is more developments like the sewage-dumping Ocean Reef Club, whose lucrative growth came on the crest of an unprecedented environmental crime wave.

This is one nightmare we should learn from.

This is what happens when Jason lives.

March 11, 1988

MARINA LIFE, MARINE LIFE: UNFORTUNATE BEDFELLOWS

Bernard Russell was only 17 when the Labor Day Hurricane of 1935 wiped out the Upper Keys. Today he's asking himself the same question he asked during that terrible storm: "What are we going to have left?"

A developer is on the verge of poisoning another bountiful marine estuary. And once more, the state and federal agencies that are supposed to guard our natural resources are on the verge of caving in.

This time the target is in Islamorada, where developer Arthur Choate wants to extend a canal about 3,000 feet through a hammock, dredge out a 95-slip marina and build something (probably condominiums) on the land. The project is located on the bay side of U.S. 1, near Papa Joe's restaurant at Mile Marker 80.

On an incoming tide the canals and marina would empty boat gunk, oil and effluent directly into the Lignumvitae Aquatic Preserve. On a falling tide, the slop would be sucked into the Atlantic Ocean, right out to the reef line.

In a recent letter to the U.S. Army Corps of Engineers, University of Miami marine biologist Dr. Samuel Snedaker warned that "the proposed design (of the marina) will effectively shunt the introduced wastes and pollutants into the open shallow waters of the Florida Keys, where pollution is already an insidious problem."

How does such a dangerous project get approved? Technically the Monroe County land-use plan prohibits most dredging, but politics often prevails. The state Department of Environmental Regulation reversed an earlier denial and approved the project, saying that water quality inside the marina system should meet acceptable standards.

No wonder, since all the bad water will be flushed out across the flats and mangroves.

Strangely, the DER also issued its permit heedless of the fact that the Choate group doesn't even own all the property it wants to dredge. At least two of the other landowners have said that they don't want anybody digging a channel through their lots. The Army Corps might want to consider this little obstacle before granting Choate a permit.

As usual, the developer has lined up certain well-connected planners and Tallahassee lawyers, who insist (as they always do) that their client would do nothing to disturb the delicate ecology.

Opponents have won support from the Izaak Walton League, Marjory Stoneman Douglas, Ted Williams and local sportfishing guides, whose livelihood depends on the abundance of tarpon, bonefish and permit in the Lignumvitae basin.

"You're talking about turning it into a desert," says Capt. Mike Collins. Hank Brown, one of the most respected captains in the Keys, told the Army Corps that the planned marina would be "devastating" to the Islamorada fishing grounds.

Of all the folks you don't want to get ticked off, flats guides are second on the list. Full-blooded Conchs are first.

Bernard Russell stayed in the Keys even though the '35 Hurricane killed his mother, sister and 48 other relatives. There were so many bodies that they had to be destroyed in mass cremations. One of those burn sites was the land on which the Choate condo-marina is planned.

But that isn't the reason Russell is upset about the project.

"It's just plain common sense," he says. "In my life I've covered every inch of shoreline around this island, and I know what they've done to it. It's fast disappearing.

"You just can't keep pressing and pressing and pressing . . . or else all the things that I stayed in the Keys for, and all the reasons people like to come here, will be gone."

Keep fouling the water and watch the marine life die out. And with it go the tourists and prosperity.

So Bernard Russell and the others are waiting for the Army Corps, DER, DNR and all the other alphabet-soup bureaucracies to answer the question: "What are we going to have left?"

November 26, 1990

THE KEYS' LAST STAND: A TOLLBOOTH

The proposal to put a 50-cent tollbooth at the entrance to the Keys has generated the usual bellyaching in Monroe County, where politicians love to blame the state for interfering in "local affairs."

It's crazy to think that 50 cents will discourage a single carload of tourists from visiting the islands. In fact, you could easily charge a buck per person and still not lose any business.

The toll idea is part of a broad plan hatched by the Department of Natural Resources as a desperation effort to raise funds for the protection of the coral reefs and marine resources. Other suggestions include tougher controls on trapping and spearfishing, and making endangered sections of the reef off-limits to divers and anglers.

One of most intriguing suggestions—and one that makes too much sense to be adopted—is requiring boaters in Monroe County to pass a test for an operator's license. That would instantly eliminate several thousand certifiable morons who can be found, on any given Sunday, catatonically motoring across the shallow sea-grass beds.

The entire state would benefit from licensing boaters, but politically it's a tough measure to push through the Legislature. The entire DNR package will eventually need legislative approval; if it gets past the Cabinet this week, it will undoubtedly change many times before becoming law.

Resistance to the 50-cent toll is more symbolic than substantive. Many folks in the Keys are fed up with what they see as meddling by state and federal authorities. They rail against the infernal bureaucracy and see every new regulation as a threat to economic survival.

But the biggest threat to the economy in Monroe County is the stark decline of its once-breathtaking aquatic resources. These days people cheer when they spot a school of porpoises; the sight of a roseate spoonbill is cause to break out the champagne.

The main reason people go to the Keys is to fish, sail and dive. When the reefs die and the water is fouled, you can kiss tourism goodbye. And without tourism, you've got no legitimate economy down there.

It's not a mystery why the Keys gets so much outside attention on environmental matters: Monroe County has done a consistently disgraceful job protecting the waters that sustain it. Local authorities cannot be trusted to resist developers and make tough decisions that might ultimately preserve the delicate ecology.

The next logical question is: If you lived in the Keys, would you rely on the geniuses in Tallahassee to solve your problems? Only if you were on some type of mood-altering chemical.

The 50-cent toll is only justifiable if the funds really go back to the Keys for conservation, enforcement and education. The DNR says turning the islands into a marine reserve—the goal of the new plan—would generate about $10 million annually in fees. But the money will be wasted if it's spent on more agencies and task forces and bureaucrats.

What the Keys really needs, for starters, is about two dozen more Florida Marine Patrol officers on the water. Nobody who visits the place is going to gripe about 50 lousy cents to make that happen.

For some locals, though, the DNR plan is simply more proof that the Keys gets singled out. Well, it is singled out, and with damn good reason: There's no place else like it—no other living reef, no other Florida Bay, no other tropical archipelago.

People don't come from all over the world to see Gadsden County in the Panhandle, but they do come to snorkel at Pennekamp. Try to find a single soul who believes that the coral is healthier, the estuaries are cleaner, the fish and the wading birds are more bountiful than they were even 20 years ago. They're not. They're dying off.

A tollbooth won't reverse the process, but it might help pay for our last stand. The sad truth is, they should've thought of it a long, long time ago.

And put one on the Florida-Georgia border.

February 24, 1994

BAY PROMISES: EASY TO MAKE, HARD TO KEEP

The secretary of interior took a tour of Florida Bay last weekend. It was Bruce Babbitt's first trip to the dying estuary, and he was appropriately awed.

Said Babbitt: "One thing that is a certain, good investment is to restore natural conditions as much as possible."

That sounds vaguely like a promise. We'll see.

When it comes to conservation, everything the U.S. government says must be taken with hard-bitten skepticism. Remember, the feds are the ones who screwed up Florida's natural watershed in the first place.

They "straightened" the Kissimmee River, diked and channelized the Everglades, and allowed farmers and ranchers to flush dirty fertilizers into public waters. Those waters eventually empty into fragile Florida Bay, between the Keys and the southwestern tip of the mainland.

Meanwhile, so much fresh water has been diverted for urban development and agriculture that the bay is now dangerously salty, gagging on algae and dead sea grasses. Thousands of square acres, once gin-clear, now are a milky shade of bile.

A child of 6 can see something is horribly wrong. Scientists hold several views about what should be done, but most agree that, as a start, massive re-plumbing is necessary to boost freshwater flow across the southern Everglades into Florida Bay. That's what Babbitt is talking about.

The problem is, we've heard such talk before.

Years ago, the Bush administration sent its interior secretary, Manuel Lujan, to Key Largo. There, Lujan hopped in the ocean with then-Gov. Bob Martinez and went diving on a magnificent coral reef.

The press dutifully covered the photo opportunity, though it was apparent that Lujan was uncomfortable. To his credit, Gov. Martinez used the moment to stress his opposition to offshore drilling, citing the grave hazards that an oil spill would pose for Florida's delicate reefs and estuaries.

Lujan nodded and smiled, smiled and nodded. When a microphone was put in his face, he agreed that the Keys was a place of rare beauty that deserves special protection. Then he flew back to Washington and promptly resumed making speeches in support of coastal oil exploration.

Lujan's boss, George Bush, spent vacations on the shallows of Florida Bay. He professed to love the place. Folks in the Keys were excited to have a bonefisherman in the White House. Finally, something would be done to save the bay.

The president's fishing guides made a special point of taking him across the bay's so-called Dead Zone, where algae has suffocated the sponges, and the sea bottom has turned to fetid muck.

One guide even scooped up handfuls so the president could see it and smell it. Turtle grass once grew here, the guide told him, and now it's all dead.

Bush manifested genuine concern. He promised to speak to his people at Interior. The flats guides and crawfishermen who depend on Florida Bay for a living were optimistic. After all, the president was on the case!

They waited. And waited. Nothing happened.

Politics got in the way. Enforcing clean-water laws would have cost Big Sugar dearly, and Big Sugar had been generous to the Bush campaign. Likewise, more water for the Everglades meant less for farmers and developers, also major GOP supporters.

In the end, George Bush, Mr. Outdoorsman, didn't lift a finger to help save the waters he fished upon.

Bruce Babbitt comes to the Florida Bay crisis with superior credentials, and what appears to be a solid grasp of the science. He's saying all the right things, but that's easy.

The hard part is making it happen.

March 26, 1995

THE FLORIDA KEYS: SOMETHING PRECIOUS IS FALLING APART

My father first took me to the Keys when I was 6. He was a passionate deep-sea fisherman, and had decided that I was old enough to join the hunt for blue marlin and sailfish.

The invitation was thrilling, but I had secret doubts about my suitability for big water. I suspected—correctly, it turned out—that I had not inherited my old man's cast-iron stomach.

But I wanted fiercely to experience the Keys. I'd wanted it since the day I'd seen an old photograph of my father, struggling to lift an amberjack that seemed nearly as tall as he was. The picture was taken in Key West around 1938, when my father was 13. He wore a white shirt and khaki pants, and with long tanned arms hoisted the fish for the camera. He looked as happy as I'd ever seen him.

Over the years, my father and grandfather told me so many stories that the Keys had become in my young mind a mystical, Oz-like destination: a string of rough-cut jewels, trailing like a broken necklace from Florida's southern-most flank—the water, a dozen shades of blue and boiling with porpoises and game fish; the infinite churning sky, streaked by pink spoonbills and gawky pelicans and elegant ospreys. This I had to see for myself.

On a summer morning we headed down U.S. 1, which was (and remains) the only road through the Keys. Although we lived in Fort Lauderdale, merely a hundred miles north, it might as well have been Minneapolis. The drive seemed to take forever. From the backseat I watched fruitlessly for evidence of paradise, but all I saw were trailer parks, gas pumps, bait shops, mom-and-pop diners, bleached-out motels and palm-thatched tourist sheds that sold spray-painted conch shells. My restlessness took the form of whining, and from the front seat my father and grandfather instructed me to settle down and be patient. The farther south we go (they promised), the better it gets.

We passed the charter docks at Bud n' Mary's, where the great Ted Williams occasionally could be found, and suddenly blue water appeared on both sides of the Overseas Highway. To the distant east was the full sweep of the Atlantic, deep indigo stirred to a light, lazy chop. To the near west was Florida Bay, glassy and shallow, with knots of lush green mangroves freckled with roosting white herons. At the time I didn't know the names of these islands, but they were Shell Key, Lignum Vitae, the Petersons, the Twin Keys, the Gophers—places where I would spend, in coming years, hundreds upon hundreds of hours, none wasted.

The Keys never looked so enchanting as they did on that morning. As soon as we got to the motel, I grabbed a spinning rod from the car and made straight for the pier. Standing at the brim of those velvet horizons, gulping the sharp salty air, I understood what my father and grandfather meant. This was an honest-to-God wilderness, as pure and unspoiled and accessible as a boy could imagine. On my first trip to the Gulf Stream, I caught no marlin, only a bonito, but it pulled harder than anything I'd ever felt. It was a great day, made better by the fact that I'd managed to hold down my lunch.

The deep-running Atlantic was undeniably impressive, but the calm crystal flats of the backcountry intrigued me the most. To wade the banks was to enter a boundless natural aquarium: starfish, nurse sharks, eagle rays, barracuda, bonefish, permit and tarpon, all swimming literally at your feet. The flats rippled with unique tidal energies—sweltering, primeval, seemingly indomitable.

This was around 1959, and nobody considered the possibility that the shoals of the Keys might be destroyed and that it might happen within a single human generation. Unimaginable! Life flourished everywhere in this tropical embrace, from the buttonwood hammocks to the coral reefs. The sun was so warm and constant, the waters so wide and clear, the currents so strong. Destroyed—how? By whom? Over centuries the Keys had survived droughts, floods and the most ferocious of hurricanes. What was there to fear from man?

The worst, as it turned out. The population of Miami exploded during the next three decades, and urban blight metastasized straight down Highway 1, bringing crowds, crime, garbage and big-city indifference to the Keys. The quaint and casual opportunism of the islands was replaced by an unrelenting hunger to dredge, subdivide, pave, build and sell. It was tawdry, sad and probably inevitable. By the 1980s, southeast Florida was home to 4 million souls, increasingly frenetic and determined to recreate at all costs. Where else would they go but the Keys?

I was one of them. A few years ago I bought a stilt house in a hammock near Islamorada. It's significant to note that Ted Williams, his timing still flawless, had already sold his place and fled Monroe County. The stampede of humanity was too much for him. My own friends gingerly questioned why a person would move to the Keys at a time when smart people were bailing out. Maybe there was a sentimental component to my decision—why, after all, does one sit with a dying relative? Duty? Guilt? Nostalgia? Maybe there was more.

Certainly I had no illusions about what was happening. As a journalist, I've written plenty about the rape of the Keys and the fast-buck mentality that incites it. On Big Pine, for instance, the federal government is doggedly buying up land to save the diminutive Key deer from extinction. Pro-growth forces have retaliated with lawsuits, high-powered lobbying and old-fashioned venom. Road signs that alert motorists to deer crossings are routinely defaced—crosshairs painted over the emblem of a leaping buck.

As dispiriting as such cretinous behavior might be, the Keys also breed a devoted and tenacious species of environmentalist. About 10 years ago, the hardwood forests and coral shores of North Key Largo were in danger of being bulldozed and dynamited into a series of huge condominium resorts. If completed, the developments would have brought as many as 60,000 residents (and their speedboats) to a narrow belt of hammock situated between a national wildlife refuge and North America's only living barrier reef. You'd have been hard-pressed to find a more catastrophic location for a massive condo village. But local conservation groups banded together in opposition, and dragged slow-moving regulatory agencies into the battle. One by one, the seaside resort projects collapsed; today, much of North Key Largo has been purchased by the state for preservation.

That was a rare victory, but it made many of us believe that what was left of the Keys could be saved. To give up would be unthinkable, cowardly, immoral.

So I arrived to find the stores, tackle shops, restaurants and highway jammed, even in the deadening heat of summer. This depressing state of affairs also applied to the bonefish flats and tarpon lanes. Raging and cursing, I've managed to cope; friendly fishing guides generously help me avoid congested waters, and I've marked a few hidden spots of my own. There are still plenty of fine fish to be caught.

Of course it's not the same place I knew as a boy. The best of it is gone forever. But if one knows where to look, and which tides to ride, it's still possible to be the only human in sight, to drift along crescent banks while schools of bottle-nosed dolphins roll and play ahead of your bow. These luminous moments become more rare with each tick of nature's clock. The Keys are in desperate trouble.

Not long ago I drove south past Bud n' Mary's and, on both sides of the Overseas Highway, the water was the color of bile—algae, emptying from Florida Bay to the sea. A foul stain has settled around Shell Key, Lignum Vitae, the Petersons; on the falling tides it bleeds through the channels to the ocean. At the fishing docks, the talk is of little else. The old guides are sickened, the young ones are angry; and all of them are frightened for tomorrow. Wherever the cloud of algae appears, sea life vanishes. That which cannot flee dies. Already the baby lobsters have disappeared from Florida Bay, spelling future disaster for commercial crawfishermen.

Smaller blooms are not uncommon in the summer months, but the water ordinarily clears as soon as temperatures drop. Not in recent years. The chilliest days have failed to stop the spread of the milky green-brown crud. As I write this, about 450 square miles in the heart of the bay, Everglades National Park, is essentially dead. From the air, the sight is heartbreaking. If the algae continues to spill out to sea, it will smother the coral reefs, which require sunlight to survive.

For years, bureaucrats and politicians beholden to Big Agriculture have insisted that the "decline" of Florida Bay is unconnected to the egregious flood-control practices that have transfigured the lower Everglades. But this much dirty water was impossible to ignore. The algae bloom in Florida Bay became so vast and unsightly that tourists began to complain, prompting Florida's leaders to exhibit the first official signs of alarm. From Tallahassee to Key West, establishment voices demanded swift action to replenish the bay, preferably before the next winter's tourist season.

As if it was as easy as turning a spigot. It's not. Florida Bay historically was a brackish estuary, fed by a dependable, unimpeded flow of fresh water from the Everglades. As the state's population grew, the water from the glades was purloined and diverted through a network of deep man-made canals. This was done exclusively to benefit farmers, developers and newborn cities, with no thought whatsoever to the profound long-term consequences. To this day, the golf courses of South Florida are more assiduously tended than the Everglades. Nature's plumbing has been rejiggered so that farms and cattle ranches can tap into the Everglades at will, use the water, then dump it back as waste. Florida's famous river of grass is being used not only as a fountain, but as a toilet.

The high-tech siphoning of the Everglades begins below Lake Okeechobee, at the sugarcane fields, and continues down to the tomato farms and avocado orchards of southern Dade County. The capture is so efficient that only 10 percent of the fresh water naturally destined for Florida Bay ever gets there. Many scientists believe this is why the bay is so sick. Without a seasonal flow from the East Everglades, the bay water has gotten saltier and saltier.

Several years of drought accelerated the transformation from estuary to hypersaline lagoon. By the mid-1980s, rich beds of turtle grass had begun to die and decompose, leaving bald patches on the bottom. The rotting grass became a nutrient for aquatic algae, which bloomed extravagantly in the salty, overheated pond. The algae, in turn, blocked so much sunlight that it killed the sponges and other marine organisms. The bay started turning to mud. Each year it looks worse.

Now (at this writing) it's early spring and the algae continues its spread. A steamy summer promises an eruption of new growth; airplane pilots and boat captains already report that bilious mile-wide puddles of the stuff have drifted out of the bay toward the pristine Gulf banks of the Lower Keys. Meanwhile, in the Upper Keys, floating clumps of dead sponges can be found from Flamingo to Long Key.

What can be done to save Florida Bay? Many experts say the most urgent priority is reviving the freshwater flow through Taylor Slough, which drains from the Everglades into the northeast part of the bay. A new trickle has been promised; getting more water will require taking it from Dade farmers and developers, who have powerful political allies in Tallahassee. And restoring flow is only part of the prescription—the water coming to the bay also must be free of phosphates and pesticides, and its arrival must be timed for the dry winter months. Too much fresh water can be just as lethal as too little, especially during the rainy season.

It doesn't take a marine biologist to know that tropical waters aren't supposed to look like bean soup, or smell like rotted mulch. These are not signs of a healthy ecosystem. Maybe the algae will die naturally, drowned by heavy summer rains, or blown out to the Gulf of Mexico by tropical storms. Yet even if we awake tomorrow and the stuff is gone, it's only a temporary reprieve. For the killer algae is but one symptom of many threats to the Florida Keys, each resulting from the uncontrolled invasion of man.

Runoff and sewage from high-density condos and hotels poison invisibly. Offshore, rusty freighters plow into the reef, while pleasure boats drag heavy anchors across the delicate corals. In the backcountry, manic water bikers and macho speedboaters frighten wading birds from their nests in the mangroves, disrupting centuries-old breeding patterns. Turtle-grass beds—a crucial nursery of the marine life chain—are gouged, shorn and crisscrossed by propeller ditches.

This is not what I wanted to show my son.

I first brought him here when he was a youngster, and I probably spent too much time telling him how splendid it used to be, before the greedy bastards ruined it. My boy listened but he also kept his eyes on the water—and fell in love with the place, prop scars and all. He got his first bonefish at age 7, and a big tarpon on fly at age 16. He spends every spare moment here, including precious vacations. On a recent spring morning when many of his pals were slugging down Budweisers on the beach at Daytona, my kid was wading the flats of Long Key, scouting for tailing fish.

Battered, ragged and long past their prime, the Keys continue to enchant and seduce. I can't blame my son for his weak heart, because there's still nothing as gorgeous as a calm dawn at Ninemile Bank, or a sunset in the Marquesas. The truth is, I always wanted him to love the Keys as much as I did, and as much as my father and grandfather before me. But if my son was to grow up fighting to save this place, he also needed to feel the sorrow and anger that come with watching something precious be destroyed.

He does feel these things, deeply, and that gives me a jolt of hope. The kid is damn angry about what's happening down here. Maybe even angrier than his old man.

Copyright © Carl Hiaasen. Reprinted from "Heart of the Land," edited by the Nature Conservancy and published by Pantheon Books

February 13, 1997

FLORIDA KEYS AN IRONIC TARGET FOR MISSILES

Dr. Strangelove is alive and well, and planning to shoot off missiles in the Florida Keys.

It's no joke. The same government that's spending millions to protect the Keys from destruction wants to use it for a missile test range—"test" being the key word.

The Department of Defense says a military launch pad isn't incompatible with a marine sanctuary. Unarmed drones would blast off from the Lower Keys and be shot at by warships cruising the Gulf of Mexico, or by rockets fired from Eglin Air Force Base in the Panhandle.

If you think Jet Skis are noisy, wait'll you hear a 44-foot, 13-ton Hera missile.

Each one will carry 13,748 pounds of fuel and use two booster rockets, which are supposed to tumble harmlessly into the water, far from innocent Key deer and tourists.

The Air Force and the Ballistic Missile Defense Organization say there's no cause for worry. They say the launches will be rigidly controlled, and will pose no danger to reefs, wildlife or humans.

That's assuming all drone missiles leaving the Keys (and all the live ones streaking downrange from Eglin) will go more or less where they've been aimed.

Which isn't exactly what happened during Desert Storm.

Ironically, the Air Force invokes the Persian Gulf experience to justify its proposal to hold launches at Cudjoe Key or the Saddlebunches. Officials say these are the best locations to try out mid-range defense missiles of the type used against Saddam Hussein.

White Sands, the vast and desolate test area in the desert Southwest, was deemed too small for the operation. An alternative range in the Pacific was rejected as too large.

So Eglin was chosen, the plan being to shoot down the Heras safely over the Gulf of Mexico. But accidents do happen.

Let's concede that a few places in the Keys might benefit, aesthetically, from a misguided missile strike. Even locals privately acknowledge that a smoldering crater would be a big improvement over some of the rattier T-shirt shops and tiki bars.

Still, public reaction to the missile plan is as vocal and unified as it was on the issue of offshore oil drilling. Bearing videos and visual aids, military officials visited Monroe County earlier this month to make their pitch. They were met by outrage and incredulity.

The timing of the presentation was dreadful, coming just as the state Cabinet was approving the National Marine Sanctuary plan, a topic that had bitterly divided the Keys.

It has always been a place where sentiment toward the government ranged from innate distrust to gibbering wild-eyed paranoia. But even the most moderate residents were struck by the incongruity—some would say hypocrisy—of the missile scheme.

On the one hand, the islands of the Keys are such a fragile treasure that they deserve a vigilant federal stewardship. On the other, it's the ideal spot for war games!

Even if the missile trials posed a minimal risk, the audacity is what angers people, and threatens to destroy whatever credibility the government earned for itself in the recent sanctuary negotiations.

Hera launches aren't due to begin until the Air Force completes an environmental-impact study, and holds more hearings.

Meanwhile, another arm of government continues to watch over the Keys, aiming to conserve and protect. On February 2 a wayward containership slammed a reef near Key West. Divers from the National Marine Sanctuary are still mapping serious damage to the corals and sponges.

Dummies in ships—and, now, dummies with dummy missiles. Even in paradise, there's no escape.

4

THE BEARDED ONE

January 11, 1988

"INVADERS" ARRIVE WITH A PRIVATE TELEVISION CREW

The invasion of Elliott Key took place January 3, a blustery Sunday morning. A garbage crew was the first to notice something ominous.

Eight people, all dressed in black, hopped out of a boat. Several carried rifles.

The attack zone was a small slice of beach near the University Docks on the bay side of the island. On a prettier day, the area would have been packed with swimmers, sunbathers and children. On E-Day it was not so crowded.

Still, the maintenance men thought they'd call the rangers and let them know what was happening. Elliott Key is part of Biscayne National Park; national parks have strict rules when it comes to firearms.

Within minutes a patrol boat slowed to a stop off the island. The ranger studied the scene, noted the black commando outfits, counted the guns and promptly radioed for help.

Soon other park rangers arrived. Metro-Dade police, the Florida Marine Patrol and U.S. Customs were notified of a possible emergency on Elliott Key.

"We approached it as a high-risk situation," said Ranger J. T. Flood. "It was so unusual in our experience . . . even the drug smugglers don't storm the beaches."

Several sailboaters spotted the heavily armed men on the shore, and also the surveillance by armed rangers. Without further inquiry, the sailors hastily weighed anchor.

Shortly after noon, the men in black got back in their boat. Ranger Flood decided to move in, before they could get away. Eight park rangers in two speedboats swiftly surrounded the commandos.

Flood took no chances. When he boarded the other craft, he aimed his revolver directly at the intruders. He saw they were wearing caps with an insignia for Alpha 66, the anti-Castro paramilitary group.

The park rangers gathered the weapons: a handgun and five semiautomatic rifles—three .308-caliber H-and-K Model 91s, a .223 Springfield and a .223 Colt. At least two of the rifles had live bullets. "Particularly imposing," the ranger recalled.

The commandos—seven men and one woman—said they were staging an assault exercise for a visiting television crew from WBZ in Boston. From a distance the rangers had not seen any cameras, but the TV crew (not dressed in black) verified the story—and began to film the commandos being frisked by the park rangers.

In Spanish, Ranger Flood explained that it was illegal to have loaded guns in a national park. The Alpha 66 members said they were unaware of such a law and didn't know they were in a national park. Flood said he found this difficult to believe.

"They were very cooperative," he added. "The situation defused very quickly." No shots were fired. The guns were seized and the commandos were issued citations. A court hearing is set for February 12.

Jose Jiminez, the officer in charge of training for Alpha 66, said the group has run into this problem before. "It's always the same procedure—we pay a fine and get our guns back."

Jiminez, who did not attend last week's exercise, says he doesn't know why the men brought live ammo to the park. "We didn't have a great amount. Maybe 40, 50 rounds maximum."

He said Alpha 66 uses Elliott Key frequently. "Matter of fact, that's been our training site, our landing area for the last year and half," Jiminez said. The trip to Biscayne Bay is more economical, gas-wise, than driving to remote staging zones in the Everglades, he explained.

Usually the commandos try to arrive at the island by dawn and be gone by 10 A.M., when the boat traffic picks up. Jiminez said the January 3 maneuver was late because one of the equipment trucks had a flat tire.

After the incident with the park rangers, Alpha 66 made a policy decision. "The only time we're going to carry rounds is in an actual situation, like down in Cuba, or at the practice range," Jiminez said. "We learned a lesson."

March 13, 1989

A LITMUS TEST FOR 1990'S CALLE OCHO

(Overheard at the early auditions for Calle Ocho 1990:)

"Quiet, people! Before we start, let me introduce myself. I'm the Grand Kluglehorn of the Little Havana Kiwanis Club, and I'll be in charge of talent for next year's festival. Naturally we want to avoid repeating the embarrassments of this year, so we ask your cooperation. Now, you've all got your loyalty oaths in front of you, so repeat after me: "I am not now . . ."

"I AM NOT NOW . . ."

"And never have been . . ."

"AND NEVER HAVE BEEN . . ."

"A member of the Communist Party, the Socialist Workers Party or the Downtown Elks' Lodge."

"A MEMBER OF THE COMMUNIST PARTY, THE SOCIALIST WORKERS PARTY OR THE DOWNTOWN ELKS' LODGE."

"Excellent, people. Now let's see the first act. Your name?"

"Jose Lopez."

"Mr. Lopez, can you sing?"

"Nope."

"Can you dance?"

"Not really."

"Have you ever been to Cuba?"

"No."

"Great! You're hired. Next?"

"My name is Emilio Gomez."

"Mr. Gomez, have you ever sung a Cuban song?"

"Never!"

"Danced a Cuban dance?"

"Well, maybe once. But it was an accident! I glanced down and my feet were moving."

"Ha, that's what they all say. Get out of here. Next!"

"My name is Juan Hernandez."

"Mr. Hernandez, have you been to Cuba lately?"

"No, sir."

"Ever smoked a Cuban cigar?"

"Er, I'm not sure."

"What do you mean, 'not sure'?"

"Well, I've smoked many thousands of cigars. It's possible that one or two might have come from Cuba."

"You didn't personally inspect the tobacco leaves?"

"Not every one, no—"

"Next! Yes, you. Have you been to Cuba?"

"No."

"Ever grown a beard?"

"What?"

"Don't play coy with me, señorita. We have ways of getting the truth."

"But this is absurd."

"Ever drank any Cuban rum?"

"Well . . . I must confess, yes. Once I had some Havana rum in a planter's punch. Somebody had scraped the label off the bottle."

"A likely story! Get out of here."

"But I want to sing. It's not fair!"

"Quiet! How dare you challenge the Grand Kluglehorn! I could have you banned from any authorized Kiwanis function in the free world!"

"You're full of beans, Kluglehead. If you keep kicking people out of Calle Ocho, you're going to wind up with a street but no festival. None of the top entertainers will want anything to do with you."

"Nonsense. Just look at some of the great acts we've already lined up for next year. Jerry Vale. Rich Little. The Irish Rovers."

"The Irish Rovers? But this is supposed to be a Latin festival."

"Ah, you should hear 'Guantanamera' in a brogue. It's enough to make you cry."

"I'll bet. Don't you have any Hispanic acts?"

"Of course we do. Don't tell me you've never heard of the Hialeah Sound Machine!"

"Wait a minute. What happened to the Miami Sound Machine?"

"Ah, a most unfortunate incident. We were all ready to extend an invitation when we discovered that their ex-drummer's second cousin's gardener once went to Cuba to visit his dying grandmother. Naturally, we had to ban the whole group forever."

"Unbelievable. And not a single member of your club or any of their relatives have ever gone to Cuba to visit loved ones?"

"That's different! We're not musicians. Now, get out of here, young lady, before I give your name and address to the radio stations. Now bring on the next act!"

"Hullo. Uh, I'm listed down there as Schwartz, Lenny. But my real name is Iglesias. Yeah, that's it, Jules Iglesias. And I never been south of Staten Island, I swear."

"Perfect! Our new Grand Marshal!"

February 3, 1994

CASTRO, BEWARE: OUR BAD GUYS ARE BADDER THAN YOURS

In a disturbing echo of Mariel, Cuban authorities last week took three men out of prison and launched them in a small boat toward Florida. One of the men was wanted for murder in Miami.

The official U.S. response was one of cautious concern—the same as on the eve of the chaotic boatlift of 1980. That's when Castro removed thousands of hardened criminals and mental patients from prison and forced them to board Florida-bound vessels. The mayhem that followed will never be forgotten.

It doesn't have to happen again. If we weren't so busy condemning Castro, we might seize this golden opportunity to learn from him.

With one of history's most diabolical intellects only 90 miles away, it's foolish not to filch one or two of his most sinister ideas—especially for retaliation.

Suppose Castro moves ahead with a mini-Mariel, planting dangerous convicts among the rafters escaping from the island. Instead of hollow rhetoric, a more effective American reaction would be to unload our own undesirables on Cuba.

In a battle of felonious rafters, the United States would win in a breeze. Our criminals are bigger, tougher, more experienced and better nourished than any of Castro's scrawny thugs. Here's the way it would work:

Castro sends us a purse-snatcher. We send him a carjacker.

He sends us a mugger. We send him a smash-and-grabber.

He sends us a burglar. We send him a home invader.

He sends us a pot smuggler. We send him a crack dealer.

For every murderer he sends us, we send him two.

For every corrupt government official he sends us, we send him three.

Fidel wouldn't know what hit him. In no time, he'd be whining to the United Nations and the Organization of American States about a ruthless new imperialist aggression against his country.

A counter flotilla would accomplish two things: It would inflict devastating political humiliation on Cuba, while simultaneously easing the prison crowding here in the United States.

True, a few logistical problems stand in the way of a reverse Mariel program. The most serious obstacle is the Gulf Stream, which, unfortunately, flows north. Convict-laden rafts setting off from the Keys are more likely to wind up in Hilton Head, South Carolina, than in Havana.

But what better occasion to call on the Coast Guard! Launch the rafts from a cutter in the Windward Passage, between Haiti and the eastern tip of Cuba. Prevailing winds and currents should deposit our seafaring felons directly at Castro's back door.

Out of decency, the first wave of outlaw rafters should be a mild warning. It's only fair to include some of the several hundred Mariel felons still occupying U.S. prison cells.

If that doesn't get Fidel's attention, then we start shipping homegrown talent. That's when things get nasty.

Castro might think he's got some badasses locked up over there, but he's never been to Raiford or Sing Sing. He's got no concept of the vast pool of criminal talent available for export by the United States.

Let's say Cuba manages to dredge up a local serial killer, and drops him on a raft. Our response should be swift and emphatic:

Mr. Castro, say hello to Mr. Jeffrey Dahmer. And we strongly recommend a private cell.

Or suppose a dinghy drifts into Key West harbor carrying Cuba's version of a homicidal cult leader. The United States should answer with heavy artillery that goes by the name of Manson.

Old Charlie's just loony enough to volunteer for a free raft ride to Santiago. And guess what, Fidel? There's plenty more where he comes from.

July 20, 1995

REBOREDO TOE THUMBS NOSE AT TAXPAYERS

I propose a tribute to Pedro Reboredo's toe.

As everybody knows, the toe was lost last week in the name of democracy. The Metro-Dade commissioner was aboard a Miami boat that entered Cuban territorial waters in a peaceful protest flotilla. His toe got smushed when Cuban gunboats rammed one of the Miami vessels.

What a heroic toe it was, and expensive.

Dade County dispatched its only available air-rescue helicopter to Key West on a $3,000 dash to transfer the commissioner to Miami's Jackson Memorial Hospital, renowned for its emergency toe-trauma team.

Since then, Reboredo has spent the week in the hospital—more time than some heart-attack victims—recovering from the removal of the martyred toe and the repair of two others.

Some folks are griping about the commissioner's treatment, muttering such impertinent questions as: What was he doing in that foolhardy situation, anyway? How'd his foot wind up between two moving boats?

Aw, lay off. If it were Pete Stoyanovich whose tootsie got hurt, don't you think Shula would've mobilized an air rescue? And here was a toe with a nobler mission than kicking footballs. (For all we know, Castro himself could have ordered the attack on the commissioner.)

The most controversy involves the helicopter trip. Here the story does get fuzzy. County Manager Armando Vidal originally said he sent the chopper because he didn't know if Reboredo was seriously hurt. He said he'd heard sketchy reports of spinal cord damage.

Critics note that the incident off Havana occurred at 2:30 in the afternoon, and was highly publicized even before the six o'clock news. Details of the commissioner's injury were well known, as local journalists were aboard the same boat when the collision happened.

Moreover, Reboredo felt well enough to give TV interviews afterward. Nonetheless, Dade's only rescue helicopter was sent to the Keys at 9:16 P.M., and returned with the commissioner at 11:41 P.M.

Under further questioning, Metro officials said the chopper was requested by the Key West doctors who'd examined the damaged toe. Authorities there denied it. They said they're well trained to amputate toes and other small appendages, even those belonging to politicians.

On Wednesday, Reboredo's supporters offered to reimburse the county for the helicopter trip. The commissioner himself said he was merely a patient following orders.

OK, let's say he did get special treatment, whether he asked for it or not.

Imagine yourself in the county manager's dilemma—forced to choose between the toe of a commissioner and the life of a police officer who might get shot, or a toddler who might fall into a pool, or car crash victim, or any other emergency that might occur between 9:16 and 11:41 on a Thursday night.

Who gets the helicopter? Vidal picked the toe.

But not just any toe: the second one on Reboredo's right foot.

Had it been Pedro's baby toe, or even the toe next to the baby toe, I'm confident Metro wouldn't have splurged on the chopper, or a police guard for the commissioner's hospital room. I also doubt that Jackson Memorial Hospital would've kept the commissioner for six days of observation.

No, obviously this was an important digit—one worthy of special attention and, now, commemoration.

A statue of honor would be fitting—a gleaming bronze likeness of Pedro's toe, erected in Key West's Mallory Square and pointed symbolically toward Havana. The next best thing to giving Fidel the finger.

January 18, 1998

TV GODDESS' CUBA VISIT BRINGS A RAFT OF TROUBLES

An absolutely true news item: CBS is sending arts-and-crafts goddess Martha Stewart to Cuba for the upcoming visit of Pope John Paul II.

Her first report:

Hello, Paula. As you can see, I'm on a gorgeous tropical beach not far from historic old Havana. Working like busy bees behind me are five actual Cubans—go ahead, fellas, wave to the camera. . . .

Well, I guess my new friends are a bit shy. As a matter of fact, they asked me not to mention their real names (just as well, since I can't pronounce 'em anyway!).

This morning, I'm going to do something I've never done in any of my books, TV shows, home videos or interactive CD-ROMs. I'm going to show you how to build a raft!

Now, when my friends back in America think of a raft, they probably think of something that goes in the swimming pool, something with an inflatable headrest and a handy cup holder.

But here in Cuba, Paula, people actually use rafts to escape to the United States!

I couldn't believe it, either. Then I found out from the pope that Cuba is some kind of communist dictatorship, where there's no freedom of speech or even catalog shopping. The people I've met don't seem to have enough money for food or new clothes, much less interior design.

Many Cubans try to reach Florida, which is only 90 miles that way, straight where I'm pointing. What? Oh, OK, *that* way. Anyhow, it's a treacherous journey across rough water, and lots of people actually die trying to make it. The rafts need to be quite sturdy.

Now, if I were back home in Connecticut, I'd march myself over to the Home Depot and pick up whatever I needed for a top-notch homemade float—coolers, cushions, a nice big umbrella. But, Paula, there are no Home Depots here in Cuba. Or Builder's Squares, either.

That means everything's gotta be made from scratch. So my friends here are putting their raft together with all kinds of interesting odds and ends. All I can say is, they must be incredibly desperate to get off the island. . . .

See this? It's an inner tube from the tire of a 1959 Buick Roadmaster. (Apparently antique car-collecting is the big hobby in Havana, because you see these old beauties everywhere.)

And here we've got a piece of ordinary bed linen—judging by the low thread count, some sort of inexpensive, nondesigner muslin. But, heck, it'll do just fine as a sail!

For the mast, we'll be using the rusty drive shaft from an old Russian tractor. Personally, I'm not a fan of Eastern-bloc farm equipment, but my friends here never heard of John Deere. Don't worry, boys, we'll make it work.

Oops, they're signaling me to keep my voice down. I almost forgot that Cuba's got a very tough law against raft-building. People actually get tossed in jail for it!

Speaking of which, where do you think we got the straps to hold our snug little vessel together? It's common, everyday concertina wire, and it came off the fence of a prison where political dissidents are held, not far from here.

I'm not exactly positive what a political dissident is, but they must be pretty dangerous characters—look how sharp this is! Morty, can you get a close-up?

Always remember: When building a raft, be very careful not to let the straps or nails puncture your rubber inner tube. It's a long swim to Key West, and the hotels aren't cheap.

Just look at this creative touch—genuine bamboo! My rafter friends are using it for cross-bracing, but wouldn't it be dreamy as patio furniture? Or an armoire for a summer home?

Honestly, Paula, it's sad enough to make a person think twice about moving here. If this is what communism is all about, then count me out.

Tomorrow: Spicing up those black-market vegetable gardens! From Cuba, this is Martha Stewart reporting.

August 2, 1998

DEATH WISHES FOR CASTRO

Apparently Cuban President Fidel Castro isn't afflicted with a potentially fatal brain disorder, as was recently reported.

So now we add hypertensive encephalopathy to the list of ailments that have been rumored to be killing Castro during the past 39 years. Typically these reports turn out to be hoaxes, fed by the politics of wishful thinking.

The president-for-life is a much-hated figure in Cuban exile communities, and thousands would exult at news he was dying. While some feel he deserves a miserable end, others would be satisfied to see him punch out quickly and get it over with.

Death wishes and Castro go way back. The CIA schemed to kill him in the '60s, with no luck. Other plotters have failed, too; even the Mafia couldn't find a way to bump him off.

As the chances for a successful assassination faded, hopes rose for a natural solution to the Castro problem.

Time and again the Cuban leader was said to be suffering from a galloping inoperable cancer. Initially these rumors dwelt on the ghastly symptoms associated with a heavy cigar habit, but Castro's lips, tongue, and nose remain intact to this date. (He has, however, given up stogies.)

On other occasions a dreaded disease was whispered to have invaded Fidel's intimate hydraulics, setting the stage for a finale that's not only excruciating but emasculating, too.

But, so far, the man refuses to die of anything. In fact, his usual reaction to lethal-disease rumors is to stand up and give a five-hour speech so boring that everyone in the audience wishes they were dead.

The latest ailing-Castro yarn, which raised the possibility that his brain was turning to Brie, developed instant credibility problems. Under questioning, the "doctor" who claimed to have treated Fidel at a Havana hospital couldn't produce an authentic medical diploma.

Cuban officials said she wasn't a doctor at all, but rather a nursing-school dropout. Other details of her story appeared similarly at odds with known facts.

Meanwhile, Castro departed on a whirlwind tour of the Caribbean, where he appears as feisty and long-winded as ever, and in full command of basic motor skills.

Intrigue has always swirled around the health of communist leaders. This is because they usually will not retire or flee discreetly into exile, leaving death as the only hope for political change.

Communist regimes also are inherently secretive, provoking wild speculation whenever the top banana isn't seen in public for a spell. Leonid Brezhnev was out of sight for weeks before his demise was acknowledged by Soviet authorities—who knows how long the old hard-liner had been packed on ice.

Viewers in exile communities such as South Florida and New Jersey watch closely whenever Castro is on television. Recently commentators have been heard to observe that he appears thinner or grayer than before, or a bit unsteady. The slightest hint of tremor or fatigue is reported with thinly concealed hopefulness: Maybe, just maybe, Fidel's time is near!

That his time is nearer there can be no doubt. Castro is 71, an age at which the male body provides few cheery surprises. Two glum questions of aging are: What'll go wrong next, and will it be the final straw?

Perhaps Fidel's prostate will get him. Or maybe the ultimate betrayer will be his digestive tract, grim payoff for years of gastronomic excess. But just as likely it'll be something ordinary, a stroke or a heart attack, and he'll drop like a sack of cassavas.

Quick or slow, mundane or exotic, something is surely going to kill Castro one day. But wishing, obviously, won't make it happen any sooner.

September 20, 1998

COMRADES, SPYING DOESN'T PAY BILLS

The Hard Life of a Cuban Spy:

COMMUNIQUÉ 1: Greetings, comrades in Havana! This confirms my safe arrival in Florida. I patriotically await further orders.

COMMUNIQUÉ 2: Greetings, brother workers! This is to inform you that I have successfully penetrated the Boca Chica air base, and secured employment in the top-secret "public works" department! Please send money for cameras, eavesdropping devices and—most important—rent.

COMMUNIQUÉ 3: Greetings, fellow Marxists in the motherland! I spent today watching F-16s take off. Impressive, but the wasteful imperialists refuel these puppies every single day—not just in March and December, like our brave and frugal Cuban Air Force.

To answer your inquiry: Yes, comrades, I'm certain my surveillance activities are unnoticed. The fools have given me wide-open access to vast outdoor areas of the base, and the elevated seat on my riding mower affords an excellent vantage for spying.

COMMUNIQUÉ 4: Salutations from behind enemy lines! Alas, while I proudly and humbly serve mother Cuba, I must again raise the sensitive issue of funding. Today my landlord threatened to cut off my electricity if I don't pay the rent by Friday.

True, electricity is a luxury in our homeland, but I've become somewhat accustomed to it here—especially this amazing device known as the "room air conditioner." Without it, I fear, the heat will sap my strength so severely as to hinder my important espionage enterprises.

COMMUNIQUÉ 5: My first act of sabotage! After infiltrating an anti-Castro rally, I snuck into the parking lot and (following your expert instructions) let the air out of the tires of several cars. Needless to say, I didn't wait around to see the ensuing chaos—but it must've been wild! ¡Viva Fidel!

COMMUNIQUÉ 6: Subdued but hopeful greetings from the bowels of the capitalist beast. Once again I must raise the ugly topic of finances. Finally I received your money order, drawn on the Community Bank of Guadalajara, which I was able to cash (after much haggling) at a retail liquor establishment.

I'm not unappreciative, but you should be aware that $475 is scarcely enough to bankroll "operation John Deere" for another two weeks, max. I know things are tough at home, but I sacrifice, too—in lieu of paying rent, I'm now mowing my landlord's lawn, and also those of his step-uncle and parents. This leaves me little time for spying.

COMMUNIQUÉ 7: Chastened tidings to my abstemious revolutionary colleagues across the Straits, and apologies for the mix-up with that computer disk. Originally it contained the names, addresses and horoscopes of all fighter pilots assigned to Boca Chica—highly classified stuff, I assure you!

Who knows what happened. Certainly I didn't intend to send you "The Best of the Penthouse Forum Letters." It was probably a downloading mishap, and one that could have been avoided if only you'd sent enough money for one lousy extra box of diskettes!!!

COMMUNIQUÉ 8: Hello, Havana, guess who. Per you orders, I successfully infiltrated a "freedom flotilla." The boat ride itself was uneventful, but the box lunches were fantastic! Hoagies, fresh fruit, hard-boiled eggs—it was the best meal I've had since arriving as a spy, thanks to my dire financial crisis, of which you are tiresomely (though unresponsively) aware.

COMMUNIQUÉ 9: Adiós, you miserable cheapskate commies. Happy now? The bank repo'd my Sunbird, the landlord evicted my revolutionary butt, and the check I wrote to Spy World bounced like a bad guava.

And guess who shows up today at Boca Chica! The FBI. That's right, my tightfisted Fidelistas, now I've gotta hire me a lawyer. Any brilliant ideas?

December 12, 1999

DEBATE OVER ELIAN ABOUT POLITICS, NOT FAMILY

The battle over Elian Gonzalez has dissolved into dueling absurdities:

In Miami, a swarm of lawyers declares they'll fight to prevent the tiny Cuban rafter from being returned to his natural father, on the grounds that the 6-year-old could face "political persecution" upon his return.

Meanwhile in Havana, Elian's face blazes from a highway billboard, a tribute usually reserved for Che Guevara and Fidel himself. The boy's photograph has even been silk-screened on T-shirts—what next, red berets?

In the midst of the madness are a child and his father, neither in control of the grotesquery swirling around them. They're both bewildered, and they're both being used.

A boy watches his mother and stepfather die, then clings alone to an inner tube until he is somehow spotted, a bobbing speck off the Florida shore. Back in Cuba, a father is told of the miracle rescue.

Then frenzy: Reporters and TV crews arrive. Soon the politicians loudly weigh in. Demonstrators take to the streets. On either side of the Straits, the scenario looks curiously similar.

Because it is. In Miami and Havana alike, the debate over Elian and Juan Miguel Gonzalez is about politics, not a tragically broken family. It's about Fidel Castro, and those in exile who have waited 40 years for his downfall.

This is just one more standoff; one more shouting match across the water.

Elian didn't leave Cuba because he is opposed to communism; he left because his mother was leaving—and little kids want to be with their mothers.

Although Elian's parents were separated, by all accounts Juan Miguel Gonzalez has stayed close with his son. Even Elian's legal team isn't challenging the father's character.

For a judge to deny custody of a child to a fit, sole surviving parent is almost unheard of. Anything can happen, though, because in Florida judges must run for office. They read the papers and watch the news.

Elian's cousins in Miami believe he should stay. Certainly he would enjoy more freedom and opportunity, a brighter future by every measure but one: He wouldn't have his father.

What might that do to the boy, emotionally?

It's one of many heavy questions that can't be answered until the tent is folded on this two-ring circus. The press should back off, politicians should shut up and serious people should be allowed to meet with Elian and his father, separately and together.

Who knows when that will happen? Even as the mood quiets in Miami, Castro continues to milk Elian's plight for all it's worth—speeches, rallies, photo ops with the boy's father.

I feel sorry for Juan Miguel Gonzalez. Although there's no indication he wants to emigrate to the United States—many Cubans don't—his options clearly have been narrowed. When Fidel wraps his arm around your shoulder, it usually means you're not going anywhere.

Just like his son, Gonzalez has unwittingly been turned into a political symbol. Here, Elian and his lost mother are portrayed as victims of Fidel's oppressive rule. In Cuba, Elian's father is held forth as a victim of heartless Yankee imperialism.

When U.S. immigration officials finally decided to inform Gonzalez of his parental rights, the reaction from Castro was reported as chilly.

He doesn't want the furor to end too soon. Inflaming anti-American sentiments is one of the Cuban leader's favorite diversions, and the "kidnapping" of Elian Gonzalez gives him an ideal platform to rant.

So Havana isn't the place to turn for sensitivity, or for a compassionate compromise. The best hope for humanely resolving Elian's custody case lies with the boy's relatives here, who themselves are under tremendous pressure.

They say Elian wants to stay. Maybe he does. Maybe he doesn't.

Shower any 6-year-old with new toys and feed him scrumptious birthday cake, and what do you think he'll say when asked if he's happy?

Now tell that little boy he's never going home to his father, and ask him the same question.

These are the very deepest bonds of the heart, and it's obscene to reduce them to billboards, campaign quips and TV insta-polls. Unless the nonsense abates, there is no chance of reuniting Elian and Juan Gonzalez, even for a day.

Until those two are allowed to see each other again, nobody—least of all, columnists, talk-show hosts and politicians—can possibly know how the boy and his father truly feel, or what's best for them.

April 5, 2000

PENELAS HAD BETTER PRAY FOR PEACE AND SANITY IN MIAMI

If violence erupts in Little Havana this week, Miami-Dade Mayor Alex Penelas can say good-bye to all his national political ambitions.

Thanks to his brainless remarks last week—and his frenetic backpedaling ever since—the rest of the country now views Penelas as an irresponsible, rabble-rousing twerp.

From coast to coast, he is being mockingly compared to Gov. George Wallace of Alabama, the virulent bigot who defied federal integration orders in 1963.

Penelas wouldn't be in such a jam if he'd been content merely to express strong disapproval of the government's handling of the Elian Gonzalez immigration case.

But since he's up for reelection against a strong Hispanic opponent, the mayor felt inspired to take a stab at Miami-style demagoguery. As we saw, it's not his strong suit.

Of U.S. authorities, Penelas squeaked indignantly: "If their continued provocation, in the form of unjustified threats to revoke the boy's parole, leads to civil unrest and violence, we are holding the federal government responsible and specifically Janet Reno and President Clinton."

It takes a special breed of jackass to invoke the specter of rioting in advance, and then announce that your own police force won't lift a finger to help federal law-enforcement officers do their jobs.

And it takes a special gall to make that declaration in a community that repeatedly has turned to Uncle Sam with open palms, begging for relief during some unforeseen crisis—race riots triggered by police-involved shootings, the Mariel boatlift, Hurricane Andrew.

Next time I guess we won't be calling the National Guard, right, Mr. Mayor?

Who knows what Penelas was thinking. Maybe by turning on Clinton, on whose behalf he has raised much campaign money, Penelas was hoping to score points with Miami's hard-line exiles. Certainly that's what Al Gore was doing when he flopped over like a bad omelet on the Elian issue, saying he now supports a half-baked Senate bill that would give the whole Gonzalez family residency status.

Unfortunately, the family hasn't asked for residency status, but never mind that.

Gore is tight with Penelas, who undoubtedly urged him to perform a public waffle—two great minds at work. The result was a twin bungle of memorable proportions.

The vice president's peculiar change of heart won him exactly zero votes in Miami-Dade and probably cost him thousands throughout the rest of the country, where sentiment is strong that Elian belongs with his father.

Meanwhile Penelas, once a rising star of the Democratic party, in one short week has managed to recast himself nationally as a loose-lipped lightweight and—worse—a pawn of the fanatical anti-Castro fringe.

If an election were held today, poor Alex couldn't get elected dogcatcher north of County Line Road.

The scope of his miscalculation became evident quickly. To all who'll listen, the mayor now insists his remarks were "misinterpreted," and that he'd never instruct the police to sit back and allow the community to be engulfed in violence.

But Penelas's speech was not misinterpreted. It was broadcasted fully and in context, and almost everyone who heard it had the same reaction: Is that guy nuts? I heard the question repeatedly during a trip to California last week.

The mayor isn't nuts, but neither is he the sharpest knife in the drawer. Maybe next time he ought to rehearse his little tirade in the bathroom mirror before cutting loose on CNN.

Because of his own ominous phrasing—"If blood is shed . . . I will hold them responsible"—the burden of preventing violence shifted to Penelas himself, away from Reno and the agents assigned to carry out the orders of the Justice Department.

Penelas should hope and pray that not a single rock or bottle gets thrown in the streets of Miami; that not a single demonstrator goes whacko outside the home of Elian's relatives.

Penelas better pray that not a single U.S. marshal is harmed in the line of duty.

He better pray, in other words, for peace and sanity.

Because the whole world is watching.

If things go crazy and somebody gets hurt, Penelas will be seeing himself again on national TV, that boneheaded press conference replayed over and over against a video backdrop of sirens and tears and chaos.

And he will be forever known as the mayor who invited a riot.

April 19, 2000

LET'S DISCUSS CHARACTER ISSUES

After months of saying the opposite, the Miami relatives of Elian Gonzalez now are accusing his father of being an unfit parent.

The tactic is as predictable as it is desperate. Faced with the imminent removal of the child from their client's custody, attorneys for Elian's great-uncle Lazaro are playing their last sleazy trump card: the character smear.

Well, since they brought it up, let's talk about character. But unlike

Lazaro's ace legal team, let's not toss around vague, half-whispered rumors. Let's stick to facts.

Let's talk about the DUI convictions of Lazaro and the drunk-driving accidents of Delfin Gonzalez, Elian's other attending great-uncle. Let's talk about how such incidents reflect upon their fitness to care for a 6-year-old child.

Is there an ongoing problem with alcohol abuse in the household?

A judge certainly would be curious.

And as long as we're on the character issue, let's talk about Lazaro and Delfin's twin nephews, who visited the house and played with little Elian in the days after his rescue at sea.

One of those fine upstanding citizens, Jose Cid, has a record for grand theft, forgery and violating probation. The other, Luis Cid, most recently was arrested for allegedly robbing a tourist in Little Havana.

Why were they allowed to go anywhere near Elian?

A judge surely would have the same question.

As long as we're debating character, let's look at the most damning piece of evidence pointing to the unfitness of Elian's Miami kin: That repugnant, 40-second snip of homemade propaganda released to the media last week.

Let's talk about what kind of irresponsible people sit a little boy in front of a video camera at 1 A.M. and coach him to speak out against his own father—a father they won't even let him go see.

Let's talk about exploiting an exhausted child. Let's talk about brainwashing. Let's talk about mental abuse. It's all right there in living color, Exhibit A.

Some have remarked upon the videotape's dismaying resemblance to old POW footage from Vietnam. Instead of a weary soldier you see a weary kid, being prodded to denounce a political system he cannot possibly comprehend.

How could anyone with a conscience put a child in such an impossible position?

A judge would be most interested to know.

Finally, let's talk about Juan Miguel Gonzalez, or what we know of him. He has a real job, a wife, a baby and some political beliefs with which his uncles—and many in Miami—disagree.

Yet, until lately, the uncles had nothing bad to say about Elian's father. Only when the Justice Department began closing in did Lazaro accuse Juan Miguel of being an abusive parent.

A judge would demand proof—and an explanation for why the Miami family waited until the last minute to make such serious charges.

A judge might also ask why, if Juan Miguel is such a terrible father, does he have the unflagging support of Elian's maternal grandmother, whose daughter gave birth to the boy and later died on the ill-fated voyage to Florida.

This much is certain: The longer the case drags on the harder it is on the child, and the more difficult the reunion with his father will be.

The video plainly reveals what's been happening inside the house in Miami. No wonder Juan Miguel is frantic.

Each day among the great-uncles and the restless demonstrators means more emotional damage to the child—not because they don't care about him, but because they're too selfish and self-important to let go.

Yes, let's talk about character, which means sacrifice and compassion. It means putting concern for others above self, ego and politics.

So let's talk about what kind of people would prolong a child's separation from his only living parent, when the law is clear and the outcome is inevitable.

Forget about negotiating with Lazaro Gonzalez. He had his chance to ease Elian's transition, but instead chose a standoff. That the boy might now be caught in a volatile street confrontation doesn't seem to worry his loving great-uncles.

Once all the judges are done with this mess, Janet Reno needs to end it swiftly.

Close the show, fold the tent and return the son to his father, while there is still a son left.

April 26, 2000

AND SO, ELIAN WAS TAKEN "BY FORCE"

On April 12, shortly after meeting face-to-face with Attorney General Janet Reno, Lazaro Gonzalez made the following declaration about his great-nephew Elian:

"Our position is we will not turn over the child—anywhere," he said. The government "will have to take this child from me by force."

Thus, Lazaro Gonzalez and his handlers set the scene for what happened in the pre-dawn hours last Saturday. By their own obstinance, they brought INS agents thundering into that house as surely as if they'd sent out engraved invitations.

By force. Lazaro's words, not Reno's. "Force" doesn't mean saying please, pretty please, open the door. It means large, impatient men with badges and guns—a harrowing three minutes for Elian and everyone inside that house.

And they're right: It didn't need to happen. Up until the final hours, Lazaro and his family could have avoided the whole ugly mess.

The contention that Reno acted just as negotiations were reaching a last-minute breakthrough is not borne out by correspondence released in the raid's aftermath.

What's plainly evident is Lazaro Gonzalez's resistance to budge on two key demands of the Justice Department:

That the reunion between Elian and Juan Miguel Gonzalez be held in the Washington, D.C., area, and that the boy be physically transferred into his father's care before the two families settled into a joint living arrangement.

Hours before the raid, Lazaro and his relatives continued to insist that Juan Miguel come to Miami and move with them into a neutral dwelling until all legal appeals were exhausted.

"We understand that you have transfered temporary custody of Elian to his father," family members wrote in a fax to Reno. Significantly, however, they didn't specifically agree to turn over Elian to Juan Miguel.

The bottom line: They refused to let go of a child they loved, but to whom they had no legal claim.

Armed with a ruling from U.S. District Judge K. Michael Moore, the U.S. government had revoked Lazaro's temporary custody. A state judge had agreed that the case belonged with the INS, not in family court.

"Elian Gonzalez's physical presence in this country is at the discretion of the federal government," ruled Miami-Dade Circuit Judge Jennifer Bailey on April 13.

In tossing out the lawsuit filed by Lazaro Gonzalez against Juan Miguel, Bailey also said that, under Florida law, a great-uncle was too distant a relative to petition to keep Elian.

The later ruling by a U.S. appeals court ordering the child to remain in the country dealt solely with the Miami family's request for an asylum hearing—not the issue of custody.

After Lazaro refused to give up the child, Reno was legally empowered to act at any time. Many people think she went too far: I think she waited too long.

One thing is certain: Lazaro Gonzalez had plenty of opportunities to avoid that traumatic pre-dawn confrontation.

Weeks ago, he and his family were given a chance to accompany Elian to Washington, D.C., and reunite privately with Juan Miguel Gonzalez. Lazaro said no.

Soon afterward, Reno flew to Miami and personally reiterated a similar offer, and again Lazaro refused. He was then given another deadline to comply with the INS order and voluntarily deliver the child. He rejected it.

To fervently adhere to one's principles can be noble, unless the result is willfully placing another man's child in harm's way.

That's what Lazaro did to Elian, and it was both reckless and unnecessary. He'll be lucky if Juan Miguel lets him visit his great-nephew again.

Lazaro and his family can't credibly claim to be surprised by Reno's raid because they basically dared her to do it. They knew she would; everybody did. The whole neighborhood was on alert, which is why the agents came heavily armed.

Even Miami Mayor Joe Carollo figured it out. After speaking to Reno on April 20, he said, "They are serious about doing this . . . it's just a matter of when."

The eleventh-hour negotiations, conducted by earnest intermediaries, had no chance of success as long as Lazaro wouldn't agree to transfer Elian into his father's care.

Reno could have waited longer, and set more deadlines, but the standoff was always doomed to end the way it did.

By force.

Exactly how it was scripted, in Lazaro's own words.

Part

2

5

TAX DOLLARS AT WORK

January 10, 1986

FOR $10,700, THAT DESK OUGHT TO BE DRIVEN

Former County Manager Merrett Stierheim already was cleaning out his desk by the time we learned that the darned thing cost $10,700, including credenza.

Everybody just shrugged this off, so it must be perfectly acceptable for a public servant to buy such fancy furniture with taxpayers' money.

Personally I've never seen a $10,000 desk, and I can't imagine why Stierheim needed one. I wish instead he would have used the dough to fix the exhaust pipes on some of the county buses.

Officially, we are informed that the Stierheim Desk is merely made of mahogany and shaped like a rectangle, and that the credenza is nice but unremarkable. I don't buy this for a minute.

For that much money a desk has to be something straight out of Steven Spielberg. The Stierheim model probably is made of high-grade plutonium, and equipped with tiny little turbochargers so that Merrett could zoom up and down the halls. Maybe it even has a Magic Fingers slot where you put in a quarter and the whole thing starts to vibrate.

Or perhaps it is simply a magic desk, where wishes come true.

At any rate, for $10,700 you might do better with a condo. If every county manager in Florida had Stierheim's taste, taxpayers would be out $717,000.

It's true that desks don't come cheap. For instance, the desks here in the newsroom cost about $700, including four drawers that are painted orange. One could make a good argument that nothing painted orange is worth $700.

Even in this era of office computers, it's not easy to find a $10,000 desk. I tried.

Bova Furniture said its best model carries a $1,000 price tag.

At Levitz, a salesman named Pepe said his finest desk goes for $699. It has a cherry veneer with a Formica-type top that measures six feet, which seems plenty.

At Jaffe Stationers, a salesman confided, "I never heard of a $10,000 desk." His top-of-the-line model goes for $599.95 (with locking drawers), although a deluxe version can be had for $700. This is a very large desk, six-feet-by-three, and it's hard to imagine why a county manager would need anything larger.

An old pro of the desk business, Joe Rosso of Desk-Mate Products, offered an inside view: "They go up as high as $3,000, $4,000 retail. Burlwood top, burlwood sides. That's good stuff. Locking pedestals in the desk and a center drawer that locks the whole desk. And you get your pullout tabs."

When I asked Joe how any desk could be worth $10,000, he laughed and said, "It would have to be gold plated." Twenty-five years in the business and he'd never seen one.

Finally, in the Design District, I tracked down an expert on extravagant desks. Winston Lippert of Richard Plumer Design reported that corporate honchos occasionally spend $5,000 to $10,000 on a custom desk. "The buzz-word now is *systems*," he explained. "Nobody buys just a desk."

Nonetheless, Lippert was surprised when I described the Stierheim System. He said he doesn't sell many $10,000 desks to county employees.

One of the most expensive desks I located turned out to be the most interesting. The bronze-trimmed beauty costs $5,500 and, according to furniture dealer Joseph Gilbert, is a replica of the desk upon which President Woodrow Wilson signed the Treaty of Versailles in 1919. Gilbert calls it "The Peace Desk."

I like the idea of a county manager sitting at a "Peace Desk," but it's too late now. Stierheim's successor, Sergio Pereira, has already picked out a brand-new desk and two tables for $9,400—which, I suppose, we should celebrate as a veritable spasm of frugality.

The new desk is round and made of aqua marble. It could always be cut up for tombstones if Pereira gets fired.

Meanwhile, the $10,000 Magic Vibrating Turbocharged Stierheim Desk has been given to Deputy County Manager Dewey Knight. If I were him, I'd immediately trade it in for something sensible, like a Subaru.

February 26, 1988

IN MIAMI, THERE'S NO SUCH THING AS A FREE ERRAND

Emergency memo to: *All Miami taxpayers.*
From: *The General Services Administration.*
Re: *Various important tasks and errands for the city commissioners.*

This week there has been some extremely nasty publicity about certain costs incurred by the GSA in performance of its lawful duties of running a world-class city.

Because of the innuendo and misinformation put out by the vultures in the local press, we feel obliged to explain some of these expense items and put your minds at ease.

- Admittedly, two car washes for Commissioner Victor De Yurre's Cadillac did cost $203.50. This was due to the fact that our highly trained GSA Car-Wash Engineers accidentally sprayed down the commissioner's vehicle with 17 gallons of Aramis cologne.

   This was an unfortunate error, but it will not happen again. From now on, Mr. De Yurre's Cadillac will be washed with a more reasonably priced men's product, such as Brut, or maybe Old Spice.

- Admittedly, a 39-cent battery for Commissioner J. L. Plummer's beeper did wind up costing taxpayers $42.09. But this is only because a GSA Motor Pool Specialist had to actually go out and get the battery and then deliver it safely to Mr. Plummer.

   Security for the mission was airtight, due to anonymous callers who threatened to hijack the GSA car and steal the commissioner's beeper battery. For this reason, several "decoy" batteries were purchased and transported to City Hall in different GSA vehicles. Luckily, the threats proved to be a hoax.

- Regarding the $28.25 it cost to move six boxes from Commissioner Miller Dawkins' office to the basement: The per-box cost of the mission was only $4.70, a bargain when you consider that these weren't just any old boxes, but "magic boxes."

   Each of them had to be carried downstairs one at a time by a highly trained GSA Box-Hauling Specialist and then placed in a special four-point configuration by a GSA Box-Stacking Supervisor.

- Regarding the $203.50 it cost to return former Commissioner Joe Carollo's leased Volvo to the dealership, we can explain.

The reason it required two motor pool employees to drive the car back is simple. As any automotive expert knows, the Volvo is an extremely complicated vehicle to operate. In fact, it isn't even built in America! To avoid any possible problems, we assigned one Foreign Car–Return Specialist to the brake pedal and another to the accelerator.

The reason it took 2½ hours to return the vehicle is that the two GSA specialists apparently became so engrossed in operating the car that they took a wrong turn and wound up in Key Largo, where they had a very brief lunch of pompano almondine and drove straight home.

• Regarding the $339.71 it cost to install a new battery and wash and wax the Oldsmobile of Mayor Xavier Suarez, this is also justified.

Keep in mind that, in the past, the mayor has experienced certain security problems involving his automobile and its contents. This time we decided to take extra precautions.

Working nonstop for almost 19 minutes, a GSA Battery-Replacement Engineer (Oldsmobile Division) welded the mayor's new battery to the frame of his car and then installed an adorable little cast-iron burglar cage around it. You should see it, really.

Much has been made of the car-washing costs and the fact that the GSA charges $40.70 an hour for this labor. Some have even suggested that Mayor Suarez and Commissioner De Yurre would do the taxpayers a big favor by washing their own city vehicles.

We would caution against this, as it is an extremely difficult task that would consume hours and hours of a commissioner's valuable time. Furthermore, in the hands of an amateur, a simple car-washing tool can become a deadly weapon.

In conclusion, we here at the GSA feel strongly that—even more than our beloved commissioners—we are best qualified to do the hosing in this town.

March 15, 1989

TAXPAYERS, TOO, MAY FEEL SHARK'S BITE

Great Moments in Jurisprudence:

Jonathan Popper went surfing off Haulover Beach. He got chomped by a shark. He says it's the lifeguards' fault, and now he's suing. He wants the county to pay his medical bills, lost wages and an undetermined amount for pain and suffering.

Why? Because the county "had knowledge that at least one shark was in the general vicinity of the bathing public, that a shark had been hanging around the general vicinity for approximately one month, and that the shark had made at least one attempt to attack a human being during that past month."

Yikes.

Since the taxpayers are footing the bill, it's only fair that they should get a glimpse of the drama unfolding in the courtroom of Dade Circuit Judge Mario Goderich.

At issue are the events of May 21, 1983. On that day Popper got bit on the right foot, probably by a blacktip shark. In itself the event was not unique—sharks and surfers have clashed ever since the sport was invented. Usually it is the shark who triumphs.

Indeed, Popper's foot was badly lacerated. Gory color photographs of the wound were introduced as exhibits. Though Popper resumed surfing within months after the accident, he claims a 25 percent permanent disability, including nerve and toe damage. Needless to say, the shark escaped unpunished.

Popper's lawyers asserted that Metro-Dade lifeguards should have posted a warning that day. They said that other sharks had been lurking within weeks of the attack. The lawyers said another surfer had gotten the fin chewed off his surfboard by "something with strong jaws" (presumably by a shark), and that one of the beasties had even scared a fisherman from the water.

All this, said lawyer Jay Rothlein, conclusively demonstrated "heightened shark activity" off Haulover Beach. Popper, he said, should have been warned.

You might suppose that anyone with nine years of surfing experience would assume the occasional presence of sharks, and be aware of their traits. They are prolific, predatory and hopelessly primordial. When a shark spots a paddling surfer, its tiny eye relays this information to a tiny brain, which sometimes says: FOOD!!!

This doesn't happen often. In fact, during the 10 years prior to 1983, not a single documented shark attack had occurred at Haulover. The question for the jury: Should lifeguards have foreseen the Popper attack?

Called as a witness: one John Fletemeyer, age 38, newly appointed supervisor of beaches for the Town of Palm Beach. Fletemeyer makes about $17 an hour at his lifeguard job; as an expert witness for the plaintiff, he charged $150 an hour. (Is this a great country or what?)

Fletemeyer testified that he would have posted a public warning at

Haulover, given the previous episodes with the frightened fisherman and the chewed-up surfboard. But when told that there was no sworn testimony that those incidents happened on the day that Popper was attacked, Fletemeyer seemed to soften his opinion.

He admitted that shark sightings are common off South Florida beaches and that the surf is seldom cleared of bathers for very long. Under further cross-examination, Fletemeyer agreed that he wasn't an expert on sharks at all. Most of what he knew about the Popper incident came from Popper's lawyers and newspaper articles published at the time.

Assistant County Attorney Ron Bernstein asked the Palm Beach lifeguard what he does when sharks are sighted near the beaches in his control. Fletemeyer said that his staff alerts bathers through a bullhorn, and then posts a notice on an information board.

"In most cases, instead of writing SHARK, we put DANGEROUS FISH," he explained. The reason: When you use the word *shark,* people tend to panic.

Then Bernstein asked if swimmers really pay attention to the danger warnings.

Fletemeyer said no, people go in the water anyway.

Jurors did not appear shocked by this testimony. Their verdict is expected today.

February 23, 1990

BROWARD TAKES ITS BUREAUCRATS ON A FIELD TRIP

The vast and mystical bureaucracy of Broward County is embarking on an interesting plan to make itself more efficient.

The Personnel Division is taking top administrators on training sessions away from the office. The other day they went to a planetarium. Everybody had a good time.

A memo said the field trip was intended to help bureaucrats "develop an appreciation for the size of the universe, our place in it—a relative sense of perspective."

Before you scoff, remember: This is the same county that gave us the Sawgrass Expressway and the Port Everglades scandals. These folks do need perspective. Lots of perspective.

Critics might say that a trip to the planetarium is superfluous, because whoever is running Broward County is already lost in space.

But Phil Rosenberg, director of personnel, believes that the 50 or so people who manage the county's 6,000 employees will benefit from such informal excursions.

He says they can provide agency chiefs with valuable lessons about interacting with clients. He even wants some of the managers to exchange jobs for a day or two.

To give him credit, Rosenberg didn't go out and hire one of those high-priced consulting firms that specialize in touchy-feely corporate "retreats"—you know, where all the big shots sit around cross-legged and sing "Kum Ba Yah."

Instead, Rosenberg organized the training sessions without a New Age consultant and without a big budget. "Scrounging," he said. It cost only $450 to take his managers to the planetarium. (By contrast, the Port Everglades Authority probably would have bought the place.)

Other planned expeditions (yes, these are real):

- "At the Zoo—Coping with Pressure, Confinement and Constraint."

  During this session a zoologist will lecture about the behavior of different types of animals (predators vs. herd mammals, for example), followed by a discussion of bureaucrats with similar personality traits.
- "At the Art Museum or Concert Hall—Developing the Art of Management."

  On this trip, a live dance or musical performance would be used to illustrate "the human relations aspects of management, including effective employee relations, grievance prevention, etc."
- "At the Hospital—Diagnosing and Curing Problems."

  Here, free physical exams would be given to any bureaucrats who want them. A physician will be on hand to discuss "the feedback techniques" used in medicine and how similar techniques "also can apply to the diagnosis and treatment of organizational 'illnesses.'"

In theory, each seminar is designed to give managers a broader view. A few noteworthy omissions come to mind ("At the Grand Jury" might have been useful, for instance), but overall Rosenberg seems to have touched all the bases.

He has not, however, touched the hearts and minds of all his troops.

Upon receiving Rosenberg's memo, one division director, Dr. Ronald K. Wright, wrote back: "I respectfully decline to participate in this frivolity.

"To expend tax dollars to give highly paid bureaucrats free trips to the zoo, the planetarium, the art museum or a concert hall while they are on the clock, in my view, approaches criminality. You might as well go to the logical extreme and have them explore the 'management of alcohol and drug abuse' at the Pink Pussycat."

Wright is the medical examiner for Broward County. Most of his clients are deceased and do not require much personal interaction.

As for his management style, Wright is known as an opinionated fellow of very high intelligence. "The kind of warp-speed brain that we need to participate," says Rosenberg, who wishes that the doctor would go along with the program.

Says Wright: "I like going to the zoo, all right? But not on company time."

On the whole, he says, he'd rather be doing autopsies.

He also has grave reservations about the job-exchange portion of the seminar.

December 22, 1991

METRO DOESN'T GIVE HOMELESS A SPORTING CHANCE

On the same day Metro commissioners pledged to spend $3 million on the homeless, they gave out $48.5 million to such worthy causes as a professional tennis center, an auto race, a golf course and a baseball stadium.

Thank God they've got their priorities straight. What's more important— new dorms for the Cleveland Indians, or food and shelter for poor families living on the streets?

Commissioners would point out that there's tons more money available for sports than for homeless people, and that's true. It's exactly the way they planned it.

Funds for the homeless would come from a slight increase in Dade's restaurant tax, which still needs approval of the Legislature. The money for sports comes from a 1 percent hotel tax, which passed last year.

Given the rotten economy, everyone understands the plight of the homeless and the need for humanitarian relief. It's harder to comprehend the plight of the Miami Grand Prix or the Lipton tennis tournament, and why it's necessary to give such events millions of dollars in glorified welfare payments.

We're told the Lipton and the Grand Prix attract hordes of free-spending tourists to Dade, but the true numbers are difficult to nail down. The allegedly massive "economic impact" is based on whimsical extrapolations that no serious economist would accept. County commissioners, however, are pushovers.

Let's say thousands of tourists flock to Miami just to see the Lipton. And let's say they spend several hundred dollars each on T-shirts, corn dogs and sunblock. Does that justify a massive tax subsidy for a glitzy new tennis center?

Once, Lipton promoters promised that no tax dollars would be spent building the Key Biscayne tennis complex. Today they're in line for 16.5 million free smackers. What happened, guys? Every year you tell us what a smashing success the tournament is, yet every year you come quietly begging at the public coffers.

It's enough to make one long for an independent audit—an audit that's not arranged by either the county or the promoters.

You get the same song-and-dance with the Grand Prix. When the event was inaugurated, the city of Miami paved a public park so the race cars would have a place to run. Now Metro wants to spend $9 million on a "permanent" track. Incredibly, promoter Ralph Sanchez was seeking twice as much.

A sensible taxpayer might think: Gee, if the race is such a huge hit, why can't Sanchez afford to buy his own speedway? Excellent question. Maybe one of these days the Metro Commission will ask.

Other dubious beneficiaries of the sports tax include the Golf Club of Miami, into which Metro already has sunk about $8 million. Last week commissioners voted another $7.5 million for old debts and a new clubhouse.

Bailing out a country club is a code-one emergency, but why? Is there a shortage of golf courses in South Florida? Are stranded foursomes wandering the turnpike median? Then there's the Homestead stadium, which wouldn't even exist if the city of Miami Beach had been paying attention. One day somebody noticed that tourist-tax dollars were building this ballpark down among the potato fields. . . . By then it was too late.

In a poetic union, the Cleveland Indians adopted the Homestead site for spring training. Though the stadium is brand spanking new, it suddenly needs $500,000 to $1.5 million for new dormitories. What will next year's wish list be? And the year after that? It sounds like the beginning of a beautiful friendship.

You can't blame sports promoters for asking Metro for free money, because Metro pays up. Ask for anything in the name of tourism, and it's yours. No questions asked.

The county can't afford a shelter for its homeless, but by golly there's $16.5 million to spare for a tennis stadium. Maybe the Lipton folks will open it as a soup kitchen, once the tournament is over.

May 4, 1995

COST OVERRUNS PUT SPEEDWAY IN THE FAST LANE

Even before it's open, the Homestead racetrack is gaining a reputation for speed. It has turned into a money pit faster than you can say "Ferrari!"

In three years flat, the price tag has accelerated from $14 million to $51 million, prompting Homestead to come begging again to the Metro Commission.

Already the county has committed $31 million from bond sales backed by the county's tourist bed tax. You remember the bed tax? That's what built Homestead's baseball stadium, which sits as empty as a tomb.

That was the handiwork of ex–City Manager Alex Muxo, who was also instrumental in soliciting the dough for the racetrack. In 1992 he and promoter Ralph Sanchez convinced Metro that a big-time speedway would (in contrast to the annual Grand Prix) actually turn a profit.

Unfortunately, they slightly underestimated the cost—by $37 million.

The overruns officially are blamed on the price of building materials and expensive design features demanded by NASCAR and other racing authorities. It's a puzzler why these groups weren't consulted before the track was budgeted.

Sensing trouble, Homestead last summer borrowed $18 million from Barnett Bank. The loan was guaranteed by (of all things) utility revenues. Unfortunately, the city utility is losing money.

So Homestead is frantic. The track is supposed to open in November with the aptly named Jiffy Lube 300, to be televised by CBS. The city says it needs lots more money for:

Landscaping ($1 million), a grandstand ($5.8 million), bleachers ($4.2 million), "tire shacks" ($100,000), shops and food court ($350,000), new offices for Sanchez's company ($500,000), mitigation ($1.8 million), "fees" ($600,000) and "contingency" ($800,000).

Dade already has spent $11 million, with another $20 million promised from bonds. If that's doubled to $40 million, Homestead officials say, they can pay off Barnett and finish the speedway on time.

As always, it is fervently vowed that taxpayers won't get stuck with the tab. Fasten your seat belts.

Homestead plans to cover the first two years of bond payments with revenues from the racetrack and the city utility. The fanciful assumption is that one or both will make money.

Ever since Sanchez brought auto racing to South Florida, public funds have subsidized it. Not one event has paid for itself.

Now we're to believe that things will be rosier in Homestead. Maybe it'll be easy selling 65,000 seats for a Grand Prix in South Dade. Maybe cats will grow antlers, too.

Homestead acknowledges that, if revenues fall short, the bond payments will be taken from the general fund. So what you've got is the ingeniously irresponsible scheme of using public utilities as collateral for a privately operated racetrack.

Naturally, Metro commissioners would be enlisted as partners, given their historic willingness to suck up to sports promoters.

Never mind that there are wiser, better uses for the bed tax. Sanchez is banking that commissioners, having poured millions into the track, are too red-faced to shut off the faucet.

There's no reason to think the speedway's price tag won't soar above $51 million, well beyond Homestead's modest capacity to cover the bonds. Then look for Metro to take over.

While a few commissioners seem perturbed by the runaway racetrack budget, most will probably vote to bail out Sanchez yet again. When it comes to sports giveaways, politicians can always find the money, and never find the brakes.

Those who vote more taxes for the speedway deserve to have a tire shack named in their honor.

May 2, 1999

A WORKER OF MIRACLES

And you thought your car was a gas hog.

Consider the Jeep Grand Cherokee driven by Miami Commissioner Tomas Regalado, and paid for by city taxpayers.

Between February 1998 and March 1999, Regalado supposedly pumped 2,355 gallons of gas into this parched pig. Every drop of fuel was purchased at the same Amoco station on Coral Way, using a city credit card.

To explain the staggering $2,652 gas bill, Regalado said he "drives a lot" for his city duties. In fact, his motoring habits challenge the bounds of credulity, the laws of physics—and even basic arithmetic.

A Grand Cherokee holds 23 gallons. Yet, according to Regalado's receipts, on a dozen occasions he miraculously managed to pump more gas into his vehicle than it's designed to hold. Makes you wonder what he could do with five loaves of bread.

Then there's the mileage discrepancy. The EPA says the 5.9-liter Grand Cherokee averages about fourteen miles to the gallon. Regalado says his gets a measly 9.

Using either the high or the low figure, based on documented gas consumption, Regalado's odometer ought to show between 3,200 and 16,000 more miles than it does. What explains this mystery gap?

Perhaps the commissioner cruises his district while driving in reverse, thereby taking mileage off the odometer.

Or perhaps somebody else in his family is borrowing the city's Amoco card for their own vehicle—a suggestion Regalado strongly denies. He says he's the only one who touches the credit card.

So we are left to contemplate this astoundingly thirsty Jeep, which (if Regalado is being truthful) required four fill-ups last August 26th. Jeff Gordon could get through a whole Daytona 500 without that many.

Regalado's total payload that day: 65.7 gallons.

Depending on which mileage estimate you believe, that's enough gas to take a Cherokee 600 to 900 miles—all of it supposedly racked up in an area only 31 blocks long and 58 blocks wide. Maybe he got really, really lost.

Regalado, a popular news broadcaster, said he spends about two hours every day driving through his district. One of his chief missions, he said, is scouting for holes that need to be repaired. (An excellent place to look would be the bottom of his gas tank.)

According to credit receipts, on eight different days the commissioner made multiple pit stops at that same service station—57 gallons one day, 52 another, and so on. He spends so much time there, Amoco ought to bronze one of the high-octane hoses and dedicate it in his honor.

Speaking of hosing, it now costs Miami taxpayers about $800 a month to keep Regalado on the road—almost $200 for fuel, and another $598 monthly to lease the Cherokee.

That's still less than the flat $900 car allowance paid every month to his fellow commissioners, who can spend it any way they choose. But only Regalado has city gas privileges, and the records don't lie: Somebody's using that credit card to pump a pondful of petrol.

The Miami-Dade state attorney's office is investigating, but in the meantime there's an easy remedy: Unload the gas guzzler.

A city struggling back from the brink of bankruptcy can't afford a car that gets only 9 mpg, which is not much better than Willie Nelson's bus. So dump the Jeep and put the commissioner behind the wheel of a thrifty Honda or Escort.

Something he can drive around all day if he wants—backward or forward—and not be throttled by the bills.

June 14, 2000

HOME, WET HOME

Tomorrow the South Florida Water Management Governing Board might finally decide what to do about the so-called 8½-Square-Mile Area, a swampy puddle in west Miami-Dade where 450 or so people have chosen to live.

Many conservation groups say acquiring the tract is necessary to restore freshwater flow through the Everglades—a position once favored by state water managers. But many of the property owners want to stay and are asking for $40 million in drainage projects to help dry them out.

The new SFWMD board, appointed by Gov. Jeb Bush, seems inclined to let folks remain in the 8½-Square-Mile Area, with improved flood protection paid for by you and me.

Subsidizing the foolhardiness of others is nothing new in Florida, but in this case it would make more sense just to hand out mops and wish them all good luck. Because the 8½-Square-Mile Area is doomed to be wet, no matter what. That's the nature of a wetland.

The battle is a circus of absurdities. The 8½-Square-Mile Area is situated west of the L-31 levee, meaning there's no flood control. This was hardly a secret to those who invested there.

Letting them stay and fend for themselves seems reasonable. But the Army Corps of Engineers and state water managers fear lawsuits from soggy property owners if the Everglades replumbing spills even more water into the 8½-Square-Mile Area.

The Corps has presented the SFWMD governing board with nine possible solutions. Of all the options, a complete buyout would have been best.

And it might have happened eventually if it weren't for the Miccosukee Indians, of all people, who joined the legal fight on behalf of the landowners unwilling to sell.

The tribe says it will take too long for the government to purchase the 8½-Square-Mile Area parcel by parcel, and in the meantime Miccosukee lands are being ravaged by high water that has nowhere to go.

The tribe favors one option that would leave residents of the 8½-Square-Mile Area in place and provide a new dike and canal to ease flooding. To bolster its case, the tribe has hired a stellar list of experts who say a buyout isn't crucial to nourishing Everglades National Park.

Park officials disagree, as do many environmental groups. But the obstacles to a successful buyout are formidable: time, money and lawyers. Enriched by gambling profits, the Miccosukees have plenty of dough for lawsuits and for lengthy appeals.

The question is: Can we surrender one small but important piece of the Everglades and still achieve the larger goal of saving the whole system?

The Miccosukees say Yes. If the SFWMD governing board caves in and agrees, it will be gambling with the future of the national park.

There's another risk, too. Providing the tract with its own dike opens the door for more development. Believe it or not, some greedy fools have visions of a bustling subdivision, and that can't be done without federal flood protection.

With that guaranteed flood protection comes the ability to sock Miami-Dade taxpayers for road and drainage improvements that could cost more than $200 million.

Even then, the 8½-Square-Mile Area would still be under water when the rains come. It's ridiculous to believe that any dike or ditch can prevent it.

Eighty landowners who'd hoped to sell recently got a kick in the shins from the Miami-Dade Commission, which voted 5–4 not to set aside $25 million for property purchases. The commissioners said they didn't want to appear to be supporting a government land grab.

Some property owners actually charged that the buyout proposal was an ethnic attack, since most of them are Hispanic. (So, by the way, are many of the landholders who would like to be bought out.)

So the debate over the 8½-Square-Mile Area has degenerated in all the predictable ways. The right move is to condemn and acquire the whole tract and pay every landowner a fair price. That's not, unfortunately, the expedient move.

Haggling would take years, a delay the Everglades cannot afford. Those who wish to stay in the 8½-Square-Mile Area should stay, but not one more human being should be allowed to settle there.

And not a penny should be wasted on digging a moat around that swamp, because it won't spare anybody from getting soaked—especially Miami-Dade taxpayers.

August 16, 2000

WHERE DID 3,232 TREES GO?

First they were shrinking. Now they're vanishing.

Strange things keep happening to trees grown at Manuel Diaz Farms.

The latest mystery involves more than $1 million worth of coconut palms and other species that were supposed to be planted on Key Biscayne. Nobody can find them.

It's a riddle that goes back to 1994 and 1995, when the county used federal hurricane-relief funds to purchase 14,376 trees from Diaz Farms in Homestead. It was part of a plan to restore the gardens of Crandon Park at the old zoo site on Key Biscayne. Over time the project's landscape architect swapped some kinds for others, so it became a chore to keep track of the new vegetation.

Finally, in 1998, the parks department took drastic action. It sent someone out to count the trees. The tally came up shy by 4,232. Of those, officials said, as many as 1,000 could have been mistakenly planted elsewhere.

That still left 3,232 trees missing, and an ugly $1 million hole.

The man who signed all but one of the 28 receipts from Diaz was Parks Director Bill Cutie. He was suspended and has since been charged with official misconduct.

Miami-Dade officials suspect the trees were never delivered, and prosecutors have commenced a criminal investigation.

Manny Diaz, the owner of Diaz Farms, insists the trees made it to Key Biscayne. He says bumbling county workers lost them.

Even for the Penelas administration, misplacing a couple thousand trees wouldn't be easy. But it's a more plausible theory than the one heard four years ago from Diaz, when another one of his tree deals came up short. Literally.

Then it was revealed that he'd sold the county hundreds of palm trees that were considerably smaller than what had been ordered.

On Kendall Drive, for example, trees that were supposed to stand between 28 and 30 feet taped out at only 22 to 24 feet. Along Southwest 152nd Street, 11-foot date palms were planted where 14-to-16-foot trees were supposed to be.

Even more forlorn were hundreds of Diaz-grown tabebuias that wound up in Homestead. Instead of the 15-to-17-foot trees it had paid for, the county got 8-to-12-footers.

Taller trees cost more than shorter ones, so the disparity resulted in a hefty six-figure overpayment to Diaz Farms. Then as now, Diaz claimed he'd done nothing wrong.

His spokesperson offered an extraordinary scenario: The trees were the correct height when Diaz delivered them—then they shrank! Cold weather and transplant shock were blamed.

The Incredible Shrinking Tree Hypothesis was received with what might charitably be called skepticism. Some horticulturists failed to suppress the giggles, as nobody had heard of a palm tree spontaneously losing six feet in height.

To settle the shrunken-tree dispute, Diaz Farms gave the county a

$250,000 credit. And if the scandal shook the public's confidence, it didn't shake that of commissioners, whose friendliness was well fertilized by campaign donations.

Currently a fight is under way over Diaz trees that turned up dead in public parks. The county says the company is obligated to replace the deceased trees. Diaz says Miami-Dade broke the contract last year when it stopped buying live ones.

Since 1995, Diaz Farms has sold the county more than 49,000 trees at a cost of almost $10 million. It's not known how many of those 49,000 trees actually got delivered, but perhaps somebody should check on that.

And perhaps in future dealings with Diaz and other nurseries, the county should try a radical new policy. Perhaps somebody should count the trees before writing the check, instead of the other way around.

Meanwhile, the mystery of the vanishing palms lingers. Maybe they got treejacked on the Rickenbacker Causeway. Or maybe they were abducted by coconut-craving aliens. Or maybe, as Manny Diaz says, the county simply mislaid them. For all we know, all 3,232 could be out at the airport, sprucing up the runways.

The public can help. If a suspicious-looking forest suddenly appears in your neighborhood, call Crime Stoppers. Whatever you do, don't try to approach these trees yourself. Especially with a tape measure.

6

WHAT ARE FRIENDS
(AND RELATIVES) FOR?

April 21, 1986

MAYOR SUAREZ'S GRAND GESTURE CAME TOO LATE

Once more it's roll-over-and-play-dead time at Miami City Hall.

This week's travesty is an alleged $130 million development for Watson Island, proposed by a collection of investors that includes business pals and political bedmates of Mayor Xavier Suarez.

The story of how this extravaganza suddenly got the needed votes might be amusing, if it were not such a shame. Center stage in the charade is Suarez himself, who's nearly talked himself hoarse in his proclamations of skepticism.

Amazingly, the only city commissioner who seems to comprehend (or at least acknowledge) what's happening is Joe Carollo. While it's seldom possible to agree with anything that spills out of Carollo's mouth, in this case he's dead right. The Watson Island proposal stinks.

Oh, the artist's painting is pretty, but paintings don't file for Chapter 11.

Among the features of the proposed Miami Marine Exposition Inc. (which, we are assured, will hugely benefit all mankind) are a 300-room hotel, 90,000 square feet of shops and restaurants, slips for 299 boats and a 500,000-square-foot marine marketplace. Oh yes, and a boardwalk to take your mind off all the concrete.

The artist's fancy rendering shows the bayside project bustling beneath a vast tentlike structure, imbuing the island with all the charms of a Benghazi flea market.

Where did it come from? That's what the commission wondered a few weeks back. Here was this enormous project and no one could get a straight answer about who was putting up the dough.

Then a funny thing happened. On April 9, the day before the commission was to debate the development, a list of a dozen prominent investors was finally released, and with fanfare.

The group included Antonio Zamora, the mayor's former law partner; Pepe Hernandez, a law client and heavy contributor to the Suarez campaign; Jorge Mas Canosa, one of the mayor's top political buddies; and former United Nations Ambassador Jeane Kirkpatrick, whose son works at the mayor's firm.

Decreed Suarez: "They are not going to get a bargain out of me just because they are friends of mine."

They got more than a bargain; they got a reprieve.

During the April 10 meeting, the developers were grilled about the details of the marine mart. How, it was asked, could the city be certain that the project wouldn't turn into another bankrupt fiasco?

The commissioners wanted to know exactly who was putting up money and how much to start. The answer to the second part was $24 million cash, but the answer to the first part was very fuzzy.

The commissioners seemed unimpressed, and two of them (Carollo and J. L. Plummer) wanted to bring the issue to an immediate vote. Two other commissioners, Rosario Kennedy and Miller Dawkins, sought to delay the decision.

The swing vote was Mayor Suarez, and guess what? After professing so much doubt and displeasure about the project's vague financial innards, the mayor voted to put it on hold. The marine mart stayed alive.

Of course Suarez should never have voted at all. With his deep and inextricable connections to these investors, the mayor shouldn't even have showed his face during the debate.

Challenged on this, Suarez said he checked it out and concluded that there was no real conflict of interest.

That was then. This is now.

And now the mayor says he'll abstain Tuesday when the Watson Island project comes up for a vote. By amazing coincidence, Commissioner Plummer has suddenly had his doubts allayed, so it looks like the development will pass 3–1.

Now that his vote isn't needed, the mayor bravely abstains. Not only is the Watson Island exploitation approved (making all his investor-buddies happy), but Suarez can also claim that he properly removed himself from the fray.

You can judge for yourself why he didn't make the same noble gesture two weeks ago, when it mattered.

July 23, 1986

CAJUN COOKING MAKES REDFISH POACHERS' PREY

The governor's pal is in trouble again.

Gene Raffield, the commercial fishing titan from Port St. Joe, was charged in another ghastly redfish slaughter last week.

This time the damage was 85,534 pounds, the worst case in the history of the state. Worse even than the illegal 71,041- pound catch racked up last November by Raffield's son Randy.

In the latest episode, federal and state marine officers followed three tractor-trailer rigs from a dock in Louisiana to the Raffield fish processing plant in the Florida Panhandle. There 42 tons of redfish were confiscated, and Raffield was charged with unlawful possession of food fish caught with a purse seine net.

It should be amusing to hear his explanation for how all those fish got so dead. A longtime political booster of Gov. Bob Graham, Raffield got a break last time when his son Randy was fined a whopping $619.50—a penalty that struck utter indifference into the hearts of poachers everywhere.

Even under fire Gene Raffield claims to speak for the commercial fishermen; if this is true, they've got a stinking PR problem.

The man is not only a menace to the environment, he's a slow learner. It was only two months ago that he quit the Marine Fisheries Commission in the embarrassing fallout from his son's escapade. To avert losing his dealer's license, Raffield donated some money to a marine biology program and promised never again to violate the redfish laws.

State prosecutors say he broke his promise, stupendously. Raffield says he didn't do anything that other big wholesalers don't do.

The laws have been toughened because the redfish, a favorite with weekend anglers, is in trouble. As improbable as it seems, a big part of the crisis is the Cajun cooking craze that has popularized a dish called "blackened redfish."

While nine out of 10 restaurant customers couldn't tell a charred redfish from a carp, the fad has been a windfall for commercial fishermen. Big net boats, such as those owned by Raffield, have been encircling and devastating the huge breeding schools that congregate in the Gulf of Mexico.

So far this year an estimated 10 million pounds have been netted, compared with 210,000 pounds in all 1983. The situation is so critical that U.S. Secretary of Commerce Malcolm Baldrige has issued an emergency order putting a cap on the redfish catch in federal waters.

Next week the state Marine Fisheries Commission meets in Orlando to vote on making redfish a game fish. This would effectively take the species off Florida food markets, and protect it from commercial plunder in state coastal waters.

It's a good idea, and long overdue. As a further measure, Commerce Secretary Baldrige should place an indefinite moratorium on all commercial redfish harvesting.

The alternative is obvious. If nothing is done, the net boats will decimate the redfish as avariciously as they did the kingfish and mackerel populations, taking tons upon tons that wind up as chum or chowder, or a $15 entree in some fancy French Quarter bistro.

Before long there will be no redfish for our kids to catch—not on the flats of Flamingo, not on the oyster bars of the Ten Thousand Islands, not in the surf off Sebastian.

For this we'll be able to thank not only Gene Raffield and his cohorts, but the state and federal agencies that stood by and let the extermination continue.

As for Raffield himself, he faces a laughable $500 fine if convicted of the possession charge. Fortunately, the case doesn't have to stop there. The state Department of Natural Resources could also move to revoke Raffield's commercial dealer license and shut him down.

The sooner, the better.

Take away his killer nets and give him a fishing pole. Let him try the old-fashioned way, one fish at a time.

June 17, 1987

ROWING CLUB HELPS DEVELOP POLITICAL MUSCLE

I once thought of rowing as a Spartan and solitary endeavor that demanded too much pain and endurance. A more sensible way to cross Biscayne Bay, it seemed, was by fuel-injected Evinrude.

After reading about this Miami Rowing Club, though, I've changed my opinion. Suddenly it sounds like one heck of a fun sport, one that requires less actual exercise than I thought.

Somehow the club persuaded the Miami City Commission to lease it a scenic chunk of Virginia Key waterfront for the incredibly reasonable sum of only $100 a year. Ostensibly, the idea was to give morning rowers a safe wedge of shoreline from which to launch their shells.

That was back in 1977, and since those modest beginnings life around the old rowing club certainly has changed. A luxurious, 11,000-square-foot club-house with a banquet room and bar, a boathouse and an Olympic-sized swimming pool have sprouted on three-quarter acres of city property not far from the Marine Stadium.

I never realized that rowers were such party animals. After a tough turn at the oars, I guess nothing soothes the muscles like a dip in the pool, a cookout and a cool mango daiquiri.

The *Miami News* revealed that the club's layout is so comfy that it's been raking in thousands by renting the place out, even though the lease forbids such deals without prior approval of the commissioners. In 1985, the non-profit organization listed $147,000 in revenues, including $61,000 in "benefits paid to or for members."

Reverse dues? That's my kind of club.

Good thing the city has a soft spot for these rowers. When the club recently found itself in need of storage space, the city gave the club permission to fence off 10,000 square feet of adjacent property. Very convenient.

And for years the city has known (and done nothing) about the fact that the rowing club carries only half its required $1 million liability insurance.

It can't hurt that the city manager, Cesar Odio, is a former president and free lifetime member of the rowing club. Or that its current president, Juan Portuondo, was until last month one of Odio's top aides.

By astounding coincidence, Portuondo's replacement at City Hall, Carlos Smith, is also a former officer of the club. In fact, Odio has hired other rowing club members to city jobs.

And in another astounding coincidence, Commissioner Joe Carollo's private company once provided security there, according to members.

A VIP lease is a nifty arrangement, if you can get it.

Not everyone can. Down the road from the Miami Rowing Club is another club, the Casino Espanol, which got stuck for $5,000 a year. Similarly, the Miami Outboard Club on Watson Island pays $13,120 a year, while the Coconut Grove Sailing Club pays the city a minimum annual rate of nearly $20,000.

The rowing club's lease runs through the year 2000, and nobody at City Hall seems particularly concerned about Cesar's Palace.

Word is that, besides Odio, quite a few city workers are members. We don't know for sure because the rowing club refuses to make public its membership rolls (interesting, since Carollo demanded such a disclosure from Casino Espanol).

When confronted by the revelation that the club has been leasing out its digs, city commissioners decisively vowed to mull over the problem. Apparently they are still mulling.

Next week they will discuss whether or not to take the radical step of making the rowing club actually adhere to its lease, or alter the terms to accommodate the group's bustling social agenda.

Right now it's too good to be true. Take a slice of city waterfront, fence it off as your own private hideaway on the bay—all for $100 a year, with no property taxes. At rates like this almost any of us could start our own club.

All we need is some bargain beach.

January 30, 1992

BEAR-HUNTING COMMISSIONER A REAL DANGER

Does a bear go in the woods?

Ask J. Ben Rowe. Last November he enjoyed a big day of hunting in Columbia County. A pack of dogs chased and cornered a 315-pound male black bear. Rowe stepped up and shot it dead.

Killing a bear usually doesn't cause a fuss in that neck of the north Florida boonies. This time was different.

Ben Rowe isn't just any old hunter. He's one of five members of the Game and Fresh Water Fish Commission, the state agency charged with protecting wildlife.

Since 1974, Florida has listed the black bear as a "threatened" species. Once plentiful, the animal long ago vanished from most of South Florida. A few dozen struggle for survival near Naples, but the only healthy populations are in the state's northern forests. Bear hunting is legal there during a brief season.

Animal rights groups are trying to convince the Game and Fresh Water Fish Commission to ban the annual bear hunt because there aren't enough bears left. It was alarming, then, when a commissioner went out and blasted one.

If Rowe's timing was lousy, his explanation was worse. He said he went on the bear hunt to learn what it was like. He said it would help him decide how to vote on the issue.

In an article in *Florida Environments* magazine, Rowe said: "At some point along the line, I'm going to have to make a decision about this. That's why I went out there. If I'm going to take something away from people, I'm going to see what it is."

Having inserted his boot into his mouth, Rowe then attempted to swallow it: "There may not be any (bears) in Dade County, but, boy, there's a bunch of them in Baker and Columbia County . . . The bear hunter in the South, probably in America, is a lot more endangered than the bear."

And it's not hard to see why.

Most public officials, having said something unbelievably insensitive, try to recoup as best they can. They do this by issuing a "clarification" of their previous dopey remark.

But last week, as the Fund for Animals called for Rowe's resignation, the commissioner gave the following statement: "I participated in a black bear hunt only for educational purposes. I wanted to obtain firsthand knowledge about an issue I must consider as a member of the commission."

In other words, he had to kill a bear to see if they were worth protecting. What an interesting approach to conservation! What next, Ben—speargunning for manatees?

Rowe, a Gainesville newspaper publisher, was selected for the Game and Fresh Water Fish Commission by the governor. Such appointments are traditionally political, which translates: Those with scientific expertise need not apply. You don't see many wildlife biologists making wildlife policy.

The fact that Rowe is an avid hunter isn't the issue; plenty of concerned conservationists also hunt. Rowe's problem is failing to separate his outdoor hobby from his public duty.

Given the furor over the black bear—and his own future role in deciding its fate—a prudent fellow would've found something else to shoot. If Rowe's mission was really "educational," he could've learned more about bear behavior from a live one than from a carcass.

Experts say 500 to 1,000 black bears remain in Florida, but that's only a guess. Forty-six were shot legally last year by hunters, and about the same number was known to be killed by automobiles and poachers.

All 21 members of Florida's congressional delegation recently asked the U.S. Fish and Wildlife Service to give federal protection to the black bear. The agency agreed that the animal is in danger, but placed it on a waiting list behind 150 other threatened species.

I'd name them all here, except I don't want to give Commissioner Rowe any more sporting ideas. The elusive St. Andrews beach mouse would make quite a trophy.

April 16, 1992

WITH FRIENDS OF THE COURT LIKE THIS . . .

What a busy little beaver Ted Mastos is!

Dumped by voters, the ex-judge returned to court as a humble private attorney in 1989. Fellow judges took pity on their de-robed colleague and showered him with court-appointed cases.

During his first week in the real world, Mastos billed the county for more than 83 hours of defense work—about $3,500. Not bad for an upstart. In his first full month, Mastos raked in $52,345 from court appointments.

Records show that Mastos worked at a superhuman pace. Twice he charged the county for more than 24 hours of legal work in a single day! Perry Mason, eat your heart out.

Apparently Mastos' cronies on the bench saw nothing fishy about his alleged work habits, as they approved his hefty fees without question. Trust is a wonderful thing.

Mastos is one of five private lawyers who charged taxpayers $2.3 million for legal "work" over the past three years. This week, a *Miami Herald* series revealed a pattern of brazen overbilling and outright cheating in a system that's become a very expensive joke.

Many attorneys haven't cashed in. They take court-appointed cases at less than their usual fees, and file honest bills for the hours they work. The other way is easier and sleazier.

Judges routinely accept campaign contributions from private defense lawyers. Some judges repay these favors by giving court-appointed cases to those lawyers, then rubber-stamping their exorbitant bills. In legal parlance, this would be known as a clean rip-off.

The recent Operation Court Broom indictments allege that some corrupt judges got cash kickbacks from the inflated fees they approved—a symbiotic cycle of corruption, large greed feeding on small greed.

Mastos hasn't been indicted, just embarrassed. He blames his overbilling on sloppy bookkeeping and a lack of supervision by the courts. He apparently is too busy being a legal wizard to be bothered with simple arithmetic. What else explains billing 30.5 hours in a 24-hour period?

Another ex-judge who eased smoothly into the private sector is Arthur Huttoe, inhaling $1.4 million in court-appointed fees since departing the bench. Most of Huttoe's cases came from old pals, particularly Judges Al Sepe and Ellen Morphonios. Together they gave Huttoe scores of cases worth hundreds of thousands of taxpayer dollars.

Usually, Huttoe didn't even do the work. He farmed the cases to other lawyers, and divvied up the fee. Still, case after case got assigned to him. Friendship is a wonderful thing.

Today, the Art Huttoe Relief Fund has dried up. Sepe is indicted and Morphonios is retired. Since other judges aren't so magnanimous, Huttoe must now make his own living, like thousands of other attorneys.

But don't get the wrong idea—new court appointments are given every day. Private lawyers receive almost $7 million a year to represent fewer than 7,000 indigent clients. For less than half that money, the Dade Public Defender's Office could hire enough staff to handle 7,500 new cases.

The newspaper's revelations have sparked the predictable chorus of outrage and indignation. The Dade state attorney and the Florida Bar have braced the controversy in their usual timely fashion, with the usual after-the-fact vow to seek out wrongdoers and punish appropriately. Don't hold your breath.

The last time reforms were promised, Dade judges approved a new fee policy with major loopholes: High-volume attorneys could charge the county about five times more than directed by law. And no one checked to see if they'd really done the work.

Professional courtesy is a wonderful thing.

June 10, 1993

PSC FOLLOWS PARTY LINE TO DISNEY WORLD

The Public Service Commission is going to Disney World, and you're picking up the tab.

Is that so bad? The commissioners and their staffs work hard all year, deciding what you should pay for electricity and telephone service.

Besides, the Disney excursion is no vacation, or so they say. It's a conference of something called the Southeastern Association of Regulatory Utility Commissioners. You probably didn't know there was an association of utility commissioners, much less that they'd divided themselves into geo-specific subgroups. The purpose of this is to increase the number of conventions that must be attended at theme parks.

In any event, Florida's PSC members will be a busy bunch. On Sunday they've got a welcoming shindig at the Disney Yacht Club Resort. On Monday afternoon, it's golf or tennis (take your pick) with old pals from various utility companies. Tuesday night is a Beauty-and-the-Beast party for the kiddies, while grown-ups feast at a banquet.

In between, the commissioners plan to attend several actual business meetings.

The disgrace of the Disney jaunt isn't the money—as boondoggles go, this one is relatively cheap. Taxpayers will spend about $9,000 to send four of the five PSC commissioners.

A more disturbing problem is the guest list. Utility customers, who have the greatest stake in PSC decisions, aren't even invited to share in the festivities. Yet, lobbyists for the utilities are packing their golf clubs and heading for Disney, as are company executives.

PSC members will spend three days drinking, eating, sporting and schmoozing with the very industries that they're supposed to regulate. Taxpayers are being told there's nothing screwy about the arrangement, and are assured that the integrity of the commissioners cannot be compromised by harmless socializing.

Except it's not so harmless—it's at the very core of what's rotten with state government. Special interests get special access, while the public gets shut out.

The Disney convention comes at a time when the PSC can't afford new credibility problems. Commissioner Tom Beard is already in hot water for dating two Southern Bell employees he met at other conventions.

Beard is entitled to a private social life, but taxpayers are entitled to unclouded representation. A commissioner with a romantic attachment at a utility firm obviously should abstain from voting on matters affecting the company and its customers.

But Beard says he's got no intention of recusing himself. He claims he and his dates never talk business. Sure, Tom.

Among Beard's pals is PSC economic analyst Tom McCabe, who coincidentally dates a woman in Southern Bell's regulatory office in Tallahassee. McCabe and his girlfriend often attend cookouts and parties given by phone company bigwigs and lobbyists. McCabe's PSC bosses say they were unaware of the relationship, and recently ordered him off all Southern Bell cases.

True love is grand, except when it affects our telephone rates. Perhaps Beard and McCabe truly don't discuss PSC business with their Southern Bell girlfriends, but the appearance of impropriety is glaring.

It's also noteworthy that the phone company has taken no public steps to discourage intimacies between its employees and state utility regulators. Gee, I wonder why.

Who knows what new romances will bloom next week under Disney's sultry skies. When regulator meets regulated, watch out for the sparks.

And watch out for your wallet.

September 29, 1994

EX-GIRLFRIEND ON PAYROLL: IT LOOKS SUSPICIOUS

Local Leaders on Parade (continued):

Now comes Eladio Armesto-Garcia, representing District 117 in the Florida Legislature, to explain why he put a former mistress on the state-payroll:

"Please know that each and every member of my staff, without exception, has been hired strictly on the basis of their experience, skills and dedication. . . ."

We can only imagine. Here's Armesto's story, and he's sticking to it:

In May 1993, the Republican legislator hired a woman named Dulce Espinosa as "executive secretary" for his district office. Her salary: $1,623 a month.

Armesto says he violated no laws against the hiring of relatives, since he and Espinosa are not married.

However, Armesto failed to share with his constituents the fact that Espinosa is an ex-girlfriend with whom he had a daughter in 1976. Three times in the 1980s, Armesto was summoned to court for missing $25-a-week child-support payments. Armesto says his hiring of Dulce Espinosa "had nothing to do with my daughter."

When asked about Espinosa's specific duties, Armesto said she prepared his daily agenda. He insists that she worked every day for which she was paid.

Yet a former employee has stated that Espinosa spent lots of time out of the office. Armesto said she was working on "special projects" and visiting constituents. He said he sometimes sent her to the library on errands.

Interestingly, Espinosa left the staff temporarily during the legislative session. Armesto said he didn't want her in Tallahassee, for fear people would accuse him of keeping a girlfriend. "It was a matter of appearance," he explained Wednesday.

Apparently he had no such concerns about employing her here at home.

Espinosa's employment ended June 17—one day before her and Armesto's daughter turned 18, and he was no longer required to pay child support.

Pure coincidence, said Armesto. He says he continues to pay for his daughter's private schooling.

Long-ago love affairs ordinarily have no bearing on a person's fitness for office. Armesto, who's been married to the same woman for 39 years, is free to handle his personal responsibilities as he sees fit.

But voters should be alarmed if a candidate's private obligations are paid with public monies.

Armesto says he'd never stick the citizens of Florida with his family expenses, but the circumstances of Espinosa's employment are mighty suspicious.

While he lists a net worth of $481,000, Armesto has money problems. He owes $21,000 in unpaid property tax, plus he's being sued for delinquent mortgage payments.

Putting Espinosa on the state payroll undoubtedly helped support his daughter, although Armesto indignantly denies that was his intention. Instead we're expected to believe that he hired an ex-girlfriend, and mother of his child, purely because she was the most qualified for the job.

On balance, it would be nice to report that Armesto has distinguished himself in Tallahassee. He hasn't. One claim to fame was an ill-fated bill that would have legalized simulated bullfighting, which Armesto perceives as a potential boon for tourism.

With the election less than a week away, he can take solace in the fact that many voters are forgiving, indifferent or oblivious. Rep. Carlos Valdes was re-elected last month, despite being caught on videotape vandalizing a West Dade condominium with a marker. If Armesto is returned to office, he shouldn't assume that constituents approve of his employment practices. It's not wise to hire old flames to whom money is due.

A matter of appearance, to quote the candidate himself.

October 13, 1994

DAWKINS: A STRONGMAN'S BEST FRIEND

I hereby nominate Miller Dawkins as Ambassador to Mars.

The Miami commissioner, famous for brainless flubs, has outdone himself again.

Since early this year, Dawkins has ardently cultivated a friendship with, of all people, Lt. Gen. Raoul Cedras in Haiti. The two men have met, exchanged letters and obviously bonded.

Dawkins even visited Cedras in Port-au-Prince. Miami taxpayers paid for the commissioner's plane fare, as well as the gift he presented to the general.

Shopping for that special military strongman in your life isn't easy. Dawkins hasn't said what he picked out for Cedras, but records show it was purchased from Burdines for $275.84.

Undoubtedly it was something elegant yet practical—perhaps a mono-grammed truncheon.

Upon returning from Haiti, Dawkins spoke against the U.N. embargo, and asked the Congressional Black Caucus to meet with his misunderstood friend Raoul. The caucus declined.

The commissioner was strangely unbothered by the fact that Cedras and his cohorts had overthrown a democracy, and had since ruled over the bloodiest era in recent Haitian history.

Shortly after American forces landed, Dawkins consoled his beleaguered pen pal: "Those who do not understand the Raoul Cedras I know, will never understand nor appreciate the stress and sacrifices suffered by you and your wife, to get Haiti to this turning point in history. . . ."

Yeah, coups can be a real bitch.

Don't be surprised if the newly exiled Cedras doesn't receive a Hallmark card from his old buddy in Florida:

So sorry to hear that your junta collapsed. Our thoughts are with you in your time of need. . .

One might suppose that Miami's only black commissioner would be especially sensitive to the feelings of thousands of Haitians living here. Many have fled the savage grip of that country's military, and had relatives who were tortured or killed.

But Dawkins is no ordinary politician. Insensitivity is his trademark. Once, when an AIDS information center was proposed for Overtown, Dawkins vowed to block the project "if I have to break the law and get the brothers out there and burn it down."

Another time he accused a black job candidate of not really being black, and made the man produce a letter attesting to his ethnicity.

What attracted Dawkins to Cedras remains unclear, for the commissioner refuses to discuss his role as self-appointed envoy. One of his letters to the general suggests compassion for Haitian children, who were suffering terribly under the trade embargo.

That certainly would be a worthy concern. But it doesn't explain why Dawkins also corresponded with Lt. Col. Michel Francois, the dreaded police chief of Port-au-Prince and the architect of the 1991 coup.

It was Francois, along with Cedras, who established the terrorist squads that have murdered hundreds, many of them supporters of ousted President Jean-Bertrand Aristide.

Astoundingly, Commissioner Dawkins praised Col. Francois' "efforts to bring about a safe, free and independent Haiti." He added: "The progress made by Gen. Cedras, you and others towards finding a solution to the problem, is beginning to work."

No kidding, Miller. Things tend to roll along pretty smoothly after you assassinate those who disagree with you.

Now that Francois and Cedras have been driven from power, Dawkins must be scouting for new diplomatic missions, and new friends abroad.

Perhaps a trip to Havana or Baghdad is next on the commissioner's busy agenda. Armed with only his wits and a Burdines shopping bag, Ambassador Dawkins flies high.

Jimmy Carter, eat your heart out.

April 20, 1997

NAMING POACHER TO COMMISSION A BIRD BRAIN IDEA

Only in Florida could a convicted poacher be appointed to the agency that regulates hunting and fishing.

His name is Joe Bruner, and he's a buddy of Gov. Lawton Chiles. He and the governor go bird shooting together, and the governor has kept a horse on Bruner's Panhandle spread.

Last summer, Chiles named the Destin amusement park owner to fill a vacancy on the Game and Fresh Water Fish Commission. The five-member panel makes and enforces the rules for hunters and fishermen.

Bruner certainly brings a unique insight to the job.

On January 7, 1989, he and three other men were arrested on a hunting foray in Louisiana. They were charged with taking birds after legal hours, and hunting with no license.

Poaching, in other words.

Bruner pleaded guilty. U.S. Magistrate Roy S. Payne gave him a $1,500 fine and a suspended sentence. In January 1990, Bruner was placed on a one-year unsupervised probation "with [the] condition that he not engage in the hunting of any species of bird covered by the Federal Migratory Bird Act."

When the episode came to light last June, Bruner said he couldn't recall being convicted in Shreveport, although he did remember paying a fine there.

A spokesperson for Chiles said the governor had been aware of Bruner's arrest, but not of the subsequent conviction. Didn't Chiles wonder (or ask) about the outcome of the case against his hunting pal?

Maybe he didn't care. In a letter last fall, he portrayed Bruner as "an individual of high caliber . . . and one who has the best interests of the outdoor resources of Florida at heart."

Which might be absolutely true. But surely there are others equally dedicated who don't have a rap sheet for poaching.

If Bruner's background qualifies him for any role in wildlife management, it's as a consultant—like the reformed safecracker who advises banks on security.

Confirmation hearings for Bruner will soon begin before a committee headed by Sen. Charlie Crist of St. Petersburg. Crist is concerned not only about Bruner's hunting record, but about other complaints that have surfaced recently.

The game commission has received reports that Bruner illegally set bait for birds in a public forest, and ran other hunters off state land.

A Crestview cattle rancher says he tried to get Bruner to leave his property in November, but the commissioner drove over his fence and threatened him with arrest.

"You can't close a gate on a game commissioner!" the rancher quoted Bruner as saying.

Other files allege that Bruner was abusive to wildlife officers who stopped him to check his hunting permits.

Bruner has said the accusations are groundless, and stem from competitors jealous of his success in training bird dogs. He wasn't charged in any of the incidents, and never has been convicted of a wildlife crime in Florida.

Nevertheless, Bruner's reappointment is strongly opposed by some conservation groups, including the Florida Wildlife Federation.

Its president, Manley Fuller, wrote to Senate President Toni Jennings: "We believe that Floridians' confidence in our stewardship of fish and wildlife requires that those who serve on Boards like the [Game and Fresh Water Fish] Commission be free of fish and wildlife violations. . . ."

It would seem the minimum qualification.

Chiles is torn between friendship and common sense. Either that, or he has had one too many bird guns go off near his head.

Putting a poacher on the game commission is like putting a hit-and-run driver in charge of the highway patrol.

September 17, 1998

GETTING PAID TO SPEND MONEY

Forget law school, med school, business administration. Kids, here's what you want to be when you grow up: the spouse of a big-shot lobbyist.

It's a sweet gig, especially in Miami-Dade, where politicians are as lavish in dispensing taxpayer dollars as they are hazy in recollecting why they did it.

Maritza Gutierrez, the wife of political operative Armando Gutierrez, owns a company called Creative Ideas Advertising. Five years ago, commissioners awarded the firm a very unusual—and lucrative—contract.

Creative was hired to do marketing and advertising for Metrozoo, Vizcaya and other county attractions that needed a boost.

County staff had recommended awarding the individual marketing jobs to the lowest-priced bidders, but commissioners had a different idea: Make Creative the lead agency for all the work.

It was a peculiar move, considering the Gutierrez firm was ranked below its four competitors. Even more peculiar was the decision to pay Creative a $50,000-a-year "management fee"—something never before offered in a county advertising contract.

And the commissioners' generosity didn't stop there. Most government contracts set a cap on costs, but this one called for mandatory minimum spending of $900,000 annually, to be split among Creative and three subcontractors. For its share, the Gutierrez firm would get 15 percent in commissions.

Quite a deal: The county promises to spend nearly a million bucks a year, whether it needs the services or not. As it turned out, officials constantly had to scramble to spend that much money promoting the zoo and Vizcaya—and still wound up owing $163,393.

To understand why commissioners were so nice to Maritza Gutierrez, it's useful to know their relationship with her lobbyist hubby, Armando.

He was a key campaign guru to Bruce Kaplan, the ethically challenged commissioner who was run out of office earlier this year. Kaplan was a big supporter of the Creative Ideas contract.

Another booster was then-Commissioner Alex Penelas, who went on to employ Armando Gutierrez (and his wife's advertising firm) in a successful run for mayor three years later.

Both Kaplan and Penelas have denied that their political connections to Armando had anything to do with voting for the sweetheart deal given to his wife's company.

Penelas says he can't remember why the contract included a $50,000 fee and a $900,000 annual minimum expenditure. But he concedes (five years and $4.5 million later) that the arrangement might not have been in "the best interest" of the public.

The Creative contract expired in July, and won't be renewed in its previous form. Incoming County Manager Merrett Stierheim was mighty displeased when he learned of the terms—a sentiment echoed by an audit released this week: "The management fee does not provide any specific benefits to the county."

What a surprise. Auditors also criticized the county for requiring flimsy or nonexistent documentation of Creative's billings.

The firm says it has done a good job, and earned all the money it's made. While Metrozoo said it's satisfied with the firm's marketing efforts, Vizcaya administrators have had some complaints.

Among the audit's findings was that Creative's creativity was riddled with mistakes, specifically "an abnormal amount of grammatical and spelling errors."

Unfamiliarity with dictionaries can be a drawback in the writing business, but it didn't hinder the fortunes of Mrs. Gutierrez's advertising company. County commissioners either didn't notice, or didn't care.

Now, kids, can you spell "boondoggle"?

February 13, 2000

FLUSHING OUT CORRUPTION IN MIAMI

One memorable night last week, Miami police encountered a city employee hidden in a bathroom stall. They said he was standing on the toilet so his feet wouldn't be visible under the door.

The man was clutching a bag of city-owned files and computer diskettes, which he handed over to officers. He conceded that he had purposely deleted material from the disks.

The man's name was Vikas Surana. If it sounds familiar, it should. He's the nephew of a notorious crook, former Miami Finance Director Manohar Surana, whose sticky fingers were on the throttle as the city augered toward bankruptcy in the mid-1990s.

Aside from creative bookkeeping, Surana is best known for squeezing kickbacks out of contractors, a criminal scheme that included former City Manager Cesar Odio. Surana, who cooperated with the FBI, is now waiting to see how much prison time he'll do—if any.

Meanwhile, nephew Vikas has problems of his own. He works for a city agency improbably named the Bayfront Park Management Trust.

You probably didn't know that Bayfront Park was managed by a trust. In fact, if you've been to the park—located downtown next to the Bayside Marketplace—you might be surprised to learn that anybody gets paid to do more than mow it.

The executive director of the Bayfront Park Management Trust is Ira Marc Katz. No fooling—the park has its own "executive director." He makes about $80,000 a year. He also spends a lot.

On what? you might ask. Good question. City auditors wanted to know the same thing.

It turns out that the trust had purchased primo tickets for basketball games, hockey games, the Orange Bowl—even a Rolling Stones concert. Katz once got reimbursed for a $108 lunch at Joe's Stone Crab and other pricey meals.

Auditors were bothered because so many expenses submitted by Katz included no explanation for why he was billing the trust, or what it had to do with running the park. (Maybe he rounded up all the rats and took them out for stone crabs.)

One item was especially suspicious: The trust paid lobbyist Rosario Kennedy $6,750 for her expertise in obtaining building permits for a new sidewalk.

Even by Miami standards, this was egregious. As City Manager Donald Warshaw lamented, "The city basically paid for the city to pull a permit from itself."

Worse, it paid Rosario Kennedy.

This is the same woman who, as a city commissioner, blithely blew $111,000 of taxpayer money to refurbish her office. Later, she would become engaged to Metro Commissioner Joe Gersten, before he got implicated in a crack-house scandal and fled to Australia.

It's amazing that Kennedy is still around, lapping at the public trough for $150 an hour. But that's what happens in South Florida: Elected officials who are lucky enough not to get indicted usually become lobbyists. It's easier than getting a real job.

The $6,750 question: Was it Katz's idiotic idea to hire Kennedy for the sidewalk permits, or was he pressured?

Since its inception, the Bayfront Park Management Trust was overseen by longtime City Commissioner J. L. Plummer, who lost his seat last fall. Plummer and Kennedy have known each other for eons, so one might wonder if he nudged the dubious lobby deal in her direction.

You've also got to wonder about other things that went on inside Bayfront's so-called trust—for example, who ended up with all those choice concert and sports tickets?

Remarkably, much of this nonsense took place over the last two years—after Miami's epidemic corruption had been exposed, and after the state had stepped in to try to save the city from fiscal ruin.

In light of those multiple scandals, the toilet seems an appropriate place for police to have found Vikas Surana when they came to collect financial records of the Bayfront trust.

Surana says he wasn't really hiding; he says he got locked in the bathroom. He also insists he erased only personal files from the trust's computer diskettes.

Perhaps Vikas will stick to his story. Or perhaps he'll follow his uncle's footsteps and turn snitch, to save his own hide. Meanwhile, executive director Ira Marc Katz has been suspended from the trust, with pay.

Something tells me that Bayfront Park can survive without his stewardship, or his expense account.

7

LUCKY YOU

March 21, 1986

BOND ISSUES ARE GOLD MINE FOR LAW FIRMS

Dade County commissioners have a chance to turn off the taps on law firms that have been collecting a fortune on simple bond issues.

The sooner this happens, the better. Never have so many been paid so much for doing so little.

As it stands, five local law firms get juicy pieces of county bond work; all have affiliated themselves with national firms more experienced in bond deals. The logic behind this piggybacking is perplexing. In its incalculable wisdom, the county must figure: Why pay one law firm when you can pay two?

The negotiated fees are often based on a percentage of the deal; the more bonds issued, the higher the lawyers' payoff. It doesn't seem to matter that a $50 million bond package might require no more legal scrutiny than one a tenth as large.

Since 1981, $8.9 million in fees has been doled out this way, and guess where it has gone: big-name law firms with heavy political connections; firms that contributed $73,750 to the most recent election campaigns of county commissioners.

Can the public conclude anything but that the bond business has become a nifty way to pay back political favors? The reward is outlandish fees, and the source is your pocketbook.

The main job of a bond counsel is to make sure the bonds are validly is-sued and tax-exempt under state and federal laws. To hear members of "The

Favored Five" law firms tell it, this service demands legal genius and presents a daunting risk to the firm.

But, privately, many bond lawyers agree that the work usually is prosaic, and that the actual risk is minimal because the bonds are validated by a court. In reality it's the court—not the law firm—that guarantees the safety of investors' money.

Percentage-based fees are totally out of line. An hour's worth of outside legal work might cost IBM $150 an hour, but right now the same 60 minutes is costing Dade County thousands.

There's a simple way to end this outrage: The county ought to pay lawyers the same way corporations do—by the hour.

"Paying them a percentage of the deal is insane," says attorney Dan Paul, who has done bond work. "It's routine—really garden-variety legal work."

As you might expect, the idea of hourly billing is not a big hit with the firms that have prospered so handsomely under the current system. A shift to hourly billing would reduce fees dramatically in many cases. Would the law firms starve? Hardly.

Morgan Lewis & Bockius, a respected national firm with a local office, uses hourly billing in its bond work for the city of Miami Beach. "Bond issues ought to be billed hourly like everything else law firms for large corporations do," says Paul Levine, a partner in that firm.

Incidentally, of all the firms doing county bond work, Morgan Lewis was the only one that didn't hook up with an out-of-state law firm for help. Its reward? In November, the county dropped Morgan Lewis in favor of Broad and Cassel, the firm that pays a salary to County Commissioner Barry Schreiber. If you believe this is mere coincidence, then you also believe in the Easter Bunny.

In a few weeks the County Commission will consider important reforms to the bond counsel system. This is the perfect time to implement hourly billing, and to require law firms to submit not only time sheets but a detailed account of exactly what work they did while the taxpayer's clock was running.

You can bet this proposal will cause the Favored Five to kick and whine and clutch spasmodically at their wallets. At least one firm even has a lobbyist to slither around and whisper into commissioners' ears.

The question is, do the commissioners have the spine to stop this rip-off? After all, why should citizens get stuck with legal bills that no private corporation would tolerate?

"It's a gravy train, that's the problem," says attorney Dennis Olle, who specializes in corporate finance. "It's an absolute joke."

An expensive joke, too. On us.

April 1, 1987

THE DIARY OF A NEW COUNTY CODE INSPECTOR

Dear Diary,

This was my first day on the job, and people were so nice! I rode with one of the other building inspectors to several sites, and was so impressed by the cordial attitude of all the contractors. Some of them insisted on shaking my boss's hand five or six times during the inspection. Who said this isn't a friendly town!

Feeling Welcome,
Yours Truly

Dear Diary,

Today I met more new friends on my travels, and they all seemed so interested in my personal life—what kind of cigars I smoke, what brand of bourbon I drink, what kind of golf balls I use. My boss even suggested that I write up a list of all my relatives' birthdays and anniversaries, because many of the contractors enjoy sending cards. Isn't that the sweetest thing you ever heard? Boy, I think I'm really going to like it here.

Feeling at Home,
Yours Truly

Dear Diary,

Well, today was the big day: my very first solo inspection, at a small West Dade apartment building. At first I thought there was going to be big trouble because—unless I was seeing things—the walls appeared to be made of Saltine crackers. Then the builder (a very nice man, by the way) explained that this was the latest trend in lightweight plasterboard. Boy, did I feel silly.

And guess what! When I got back to my car, I found a $10 bill stuck in the windshield wiper. A gust of wind must have blown it there—the builder said it happens all the time.

Feeling Lucky,
Yours Truly

Dear Diary,

More gusty weather! This time, two $20 bills on the windshield!

Feeling Flush,
Yours Truly

Dear Diary,

Today I had to get tough after finding a nest of bad wiring at a big con-dominium project. When I tried to turn on the lights, 10 city blocks blacked out. The contractor was most apologetic, though, and promised to get the situation straightened out.

Then the strangest thing happened. When I went back to where I'd parked my car, it was gone! The builder explained that one of his dump trucks had accidentally backed over it, and he gave me a brand new one right on the spot—a 1987 El Dorado! With cruise control! When I got back to the office, a bunch of the guys looked really jealous.

Feeling Like a King,
Yours Truly

Dear Diary,

Something disconcerting happened today. While I was inspecting an apartment complex, the roof suddenly buckled and caved in, trapping sev-eral construction workers in the debris for hours. Luckily, the builder pulled me out of the way just in the nick of time. I didn't know how I could ever thank him, but he shrugged it off and said he'd settle for a sim-ple certificate of occupancy. Well, it seemed the least I could do, consider-ing he saved my life.

Feeling Pretty Darn Lucky,
Yours Truly

Dear Diary,

A sad day at work, as one of the other inspectors was injured in a freak accident. Seems he was struck in the chest by a huge wad of $50 bills as he was leaving a construction site, and had to be airlifted to the hospital. My boss says this is the third time something like this has happened this year—boy, I didn't know this job was going to be so dangerous!

Feeling Blue,
Yours Truly

Dear Diary,

Today I learned a lot about plumbing in South Florida. A contractor showed me how he had spelled out his children's initials with a set of kitchen drainpipes. We shared a laugh over this. Later in the afternoon, the bank called to say that someone had opened an IRA account in my name. What a nice gesture!

Feeling Better,
Yours Truly

Dear Diary,

Disastrous news! One of the other inspectors turned out to be an undercover policeman, and now all my new friends are getting arrested for bribery. I guess this means I better send back my tickets to the builders' association talent show. Geez, I'm beginning to think I should have kept my old job with the New York parking bureau.

Feeling Homesick,
Yours Truly

January 31, 1990

LET'S GIVE TO THIS GUY TILL IT HURTS

Dear friends: A small voice cries out for help.

His name is David. David L. Paul. He lives far, far away at a place called La Gorce Island.

Those who've never been there can't appreciate the hardships and pressures of daily life for somebody like David. Burglar alarms shorting out at all hours of the night. Teakwood decks peeling in the harsh sun. Mildew assaults on the Parisian linens.

This is David's world, and it's about to get even meaner.

He's head honcho of a savings and loan called CenTrust, which is bleeding like a stuck hog and on the verge of federal takeover. The grave situation has called into question David's judgment and reputation.

Regulators say he treated CenTrust "as if it were his own personal piggy bank." They say he was a very naughty boy, using customer deposits to live like a sultan even as the S&L was hurtling toward the cosmic Dumpster.

David says he's not bad, only misunderstood. He says he did nothing wrong.

One time he threw a fancy party. He flew in six famous French chefs and invited many of Miami's richest and most overdressed people to chow down. Then he billed CenTrust $122,726.20 for the gala affair.

Later, when investigators started snooping around, David paid the money back. That's the kind of guy he is.

Now they want to take his savings and loan away—the S&L that paid him $4.8 million in salary and benefits between January 1, 1988, and September 30, 1989.

The S&L that loaned him $6.1 million to buy his house on La Gorce, and paid $257,784 annually for his life insurance.

The S&L that shelled out $456,591 for security at his estate.

The S&L that bought $29 million worth of famous paintings and let David hang some in his home.

The S&L that leased for his use a Mercedes-Benz limo and a corporate jet.

The S&L that last October paid him a $310,000 bonus, even as it was dissipating into fiscal insolvency.

How can they take all this? Without an S&L at ready disposal, where's a person such as David supposed to get the kind of money it takes to scrape by in his world? Who eats the $84,000 tab next time the executive dining room runs out of Baccarat crystal?

We can't look the other way, because someday what's happening to David could happen to us. Like when hell freezes over.

Heartless regulators have been joined in their inquiries by the Securities and Exchange Commission and the U.S. attorney's office. There are allegations that more than $150,000 worth of items billed to CenTrust are actually being used by David in his home. These include a refrigerator, a deep fryer, dehumidifiers, intercoms and various high-tech security gadgets.

One former employee has sworn that in 1987 she was told to use CenTrust funds to pay for David's garbage pickup and lawn service. She said CenTrust maintenance workers went out to David's home every month to varnish the wooden boat dock.

David says everybody's getting worked up over nothing, and that the government is out to nail him. He says it's just like Germany in the 1930s.

The good news is: We can help. By contributing to the Save-A-Dave Relief Fund, we can keep the CenTrust chairman living in the manner to which he is accustomed.

By giving only $2,003 a day, you can make the mortgage payments on David's mansion.

For only $706 a day, you can pay the premiums on David's $6 million life insurance policies.

For only $91 a day, you can pay for the telephones in his cars and home.

For only $1,700 a day, you can pay David's hotel bill when he goes to New York.

If you can't afford to give now, don't worry. If CenTrust is taken over by the government, we'll all get to pitch in and pay for David's things.

Whether we want to or not.

May 16, 1990

FOR DAOUD, IF THERE'S A WILL, THERE'S A WAY

Miami Beach Mayor Alex Daoud is in line for some big bucks if the courts uphold a will signed by the late Peter Clayton.

The circumstances of the bequest are in dispute, but certain facts are not. In 1987, the flamboyant socialite left nothing to Daoud. A year later, a new will provided $5,000.

In the ensuing months, Clayton must have become totally dazzled by the mayor's charms: A 1989 will increased the bequest to $210,000, and named Daoud as one of two personal representatives of the estate—a potentially lucrative role for a lawyer.

By March 30 of this year, the ailing Clayton allegedly approved yet another will. A document bearing that date reduced Daoud's share of the estate to $85,000 and gave him no role in administering the estate.

Even if the most recent will is ruled valid, the embattled Daoud will make out nicely. Eighty-five grand isn't peanuts.

And it sure beats schmoozing a few thousand here and there from elderly society types, a scheme at which the dapper mayor obviously excels. From the late philanthropist Nancy Greene he received $8,000 cash in the same year he awarded her the city's medal of honor. From Egmont Sonderling the mayor got $3,000 after voting to let Sonderling's wife build a private driveway on city property.

It's more discreet to concentrate on fund raising from the deceased.

Loyal supporters of Mayor Daoud must be reading about the Peter Clayton arrangement and saying to themselves: What a great idea! Let's write the mayor into our will!

It's a perfect way to thwart those fussy campaign laws, which limit the amount you can contribute to a candidate. After you're dead, there's no limit to how much you can give, and no constraint on how the mayor might use the dough. It's his money, after all.

Should he wish to spend it on political bumper stickers, no problem. Or if instead he chooses to buy a new three-speed Jacuzzi for his patio, that's fine, too. He's a nice young man, and he should live well.

This is such a novel plan that it could catch on. I wouldn't be surprised if wills all over Florida are being rewritten to make instant heirs of other local officeholders. What better way to reward bold political leadership! You don't even have to leave money—Metro Mayor Steve Clark, for example, probably would be thrilled to get an old pair of golf shoes.

Like all fund-raising tactics, though, this one could be abused. Among politicians, the competition for future posthumous contributors could get tawdry—especially on Miami Beach, where there are so many senior citizens. Soon the streets could be crawling with smooth-talking city commissioners and probate lawyers.

If you're thinking about changing your Last Will and Testament to include Mayor Daoud, the best advice is to keep it simple and straightforward:

"I (your name), being of sound mind and body, upon my death do hereby bequeath to Mayor Alex Daoud the sum of (whatever you can spare). This bequest is made without encumbrance and may be spent in whatever manner the beneficiary chooses—including but not limited to campaign expenses, home improvements, legal fees, or, if necessary, bail bondsmen.

"In the event this document should become a subject of inquiry by the Federal Bureau of Investigation, Internal Revenue Service or any other agency, I hereby declare that this bequest is being made voluntarily, and with no coercion from the beneficiary. While Mayor Daoud occasionally may have voted in a way that (insert favor) on my behalf, this was merely coincidental and is in no way connected to the bequest described herein.

"In the further event that the beneficiary is indicted before the terms of this will can be executed, the full sum of this bequest shall immediately be placed in an interest-bearing offshore trust account in (tax haven of your choice). The full balance of this account shall be made available to the beneficiary immediately upon his acquittal, or upon completion of his sentence."

August 27, 1990

GIVE TO THE UNITED WAY—AND ITS EX-BOSS

They say charity begins at home, but this is ridiculous.

The Dade County United Way gave $225,000 to its former president in exchange for a promise that she won't sue the agency on her way out the door.

As part of the settlement, Tanya Glazebrook also gets a company car, 36 months of health benefits and membership in a private club until the end of the year.

Not a bad deal for somebody who was demoted only eight weeks ago.

Glazebrook put in many years with the United Way, and accomplished some good things. Yet her bossy management style brought complaints about high turnover and low morale. Moreover, for three straight years the United Way has fallen short of its fund-raising goals, and recently cut allocations to many organizations.

Given all the agency's problems, it's hard to figure why Glazebrook deserves such a lucrative farewell package.

People who give money to the United Way do so with the expectation that it's going to a worthy cause—the elderly, the homeless, abused children, the mentally ill. No place on your donor card does it say: "CHECK HERE IF YOU WANT YOUR CONTRIBUTION USED AS A GOLDEN PARACHUTE FOR EX–UNITED WAY BIGSHOTS."

Nor is any such overhead mentioned in the agency's annual booklet, "Here's Where Your Money Goes." A review of the Dade United Way's other financial commitments puts the $225,000 Glazebrook Relief Fund in perspective:

- It's about $75,000 more than the United Way gives annually to the Miami Bridge, which offers housing and counseling for homeless and physically abused teenagers.
- It's about $113,000 more than the United Way gives to the Epilepsy Foundation of South Florida, which provides epileptics with medical, educational and vocational support.
- It's about $112,000 more than the United Way gives to the Mental Health Association of Dade County, which organizes support groups for victims of mental illness.
- It's about $123,000 more than the United Way gives to the Deaf Services Bureau, which provides special telephone services and interpreters for the hearing impaired.
- It's about $159,000 more than the United Way gives to the Health Crisis Network, which counsels AIDS patients and their families.
- It's about $178,000 more than the United Way gives to the St. Vincent Adoption Center, which offers prenatal care and counseling to pregnant single teenage girls.
- It's about $194,000 more than the United Way gives to the Catholic Services to the Elderly, which arranges at-home visits and meals to the aged and handicapped.

The Glazebrook going-away giveaway couldn't come at a worse time. Because of slack fund raising, 34 of the 73 agencies receiving United Way funds will get less this year than last.

Still, Glazebrook's attorney was able to get a sweet settlement. That's because the United Way was afraid of a lawsuit if it canned her. Only months ago the relationship was all hugs and kisses: The board persuaded Glazebrook not to pursue a job in California, then gave her a raise and favorable review in April.

The sudden change of heart—marked by the demotion in June—was embarrassing and problematic. An extravagant severance payout might have seemed expeditious, but someone should've considered its potentially devastating effect on new fund-raising efforts.

The sad irony is that most of the hard work done by United Way is performed by thousands of volunteers. Glazebrook was paid $150,000 a year—and getting rid of her is costing a small fortune.

Whether she's a victim or a villain doesn't really matter. Mother Teresa couldn't cut a deal like this.

The cash, the car and the health benefits are only part of it. The United Way will also pay Glazebrook for training "to maintain her professional skills," whatever that means. And when she lands a new job, the United Way will reimburse her moving expenses.

Oh well. You probably didn't want your donations going to some dreary old soup kitchen in Homestead, anyway.

May 15, 1991

JESCA NEEDS MORE THAN ANOTHER LOAN

Cross your fingers.

The United Way is loaning $250,000 to the scandal-plagued James E. Scott Community Association. If the loan is guarded diligently, the money literally could be a lifesaver for poor families.

But if the money is handled the way some JESCA funds have been handled, United Way would do better to scatter the cash from low-flying airplanes. At least then it might reach some of those who truly need it.

The oldest social service agency in Miami is in terrible trouble—its leadership disgraced, its finances in chaos. JESCA owes creditors about $1 million, including an IRS debt of $250,000 to $400,000. Last year things were so bad that 300 workers got laid off.

Meanwhile, JESCA President Archie Hardwick was awarding himself a $50,000 raise and doubling the salary of fiscal officer George Thoroman. If that wasn't generous enough, Hardwick and Thoroman removed $100,000 more from agency accounts. In seven lively months, they cashed 96 JESCA checks made out to themselves.

What for? The answers changed from day to day. At first Hardwick said he cashed the checks to repay himself for covering an IRS lien against the agency. Later Hardwick said that wasn't true, and admitted backdating a fake memorandum to support his story.

New version: He dipped into the agency's accounts to repay himself for out-of-pocket expenses. Investigators can't wait to see the receipts.

News of Hardwick's check-cashing habits startled JESCA's board of directors, who put the president on a paid leave of absence. Hardwick says he's done nothing wrong, but wisely has retained a criminal defense lawyer.

The Dade state attorney's office has subpoenaed JESCA's books going back several years, and the mess is worse than anyone imagined. To say there were "irregularities" is like saying the *Hindenburg* had a slow leak.

The George Thoroman escapade is a prime example. If it weren't so disgraceful, it would be funny: JESCA's chief financial steward cashed an agency check and bought himself a new $12,000 Plymouth Sundance. He claimed it was promised as a job perk. Yet when he learned that the *Herald* would be writing about the car, Thoroman promised to give it back to JESCA when he quit work.

Days later, Thoroman left town. He sold the Plymouth to a pal for $3,000.

To appreciate the damage from the Hardwick-Thoroman shenanigans, remember that JESCA is the main provider of crucial social services for Liberty City and other neighborhoods. It offers job training, day-care centers for working parents and meals for the elderly.

JESCA operates on an annual budget of $7 million in both private and public contributions. Last year it got $600,000 from United Way, and owes another $130,000 on a previous loan.

You don't have to be Price or Waterhouse to see the risk in trusting one more nickel to JESCA. Yet it would be disastrous to abandon the estimated 8,000 needy people whom it serves every day. The new $250,000 "loan" is contingent on several key changes in the way JESCA runs its affairs. To receive the bailout, the agency must find an interim chief executive "with communitywide credibility," appoint a new fiscal officer within 60 days and complete an audit by the end of this month.

More importantly, the new funds won't be given to JESCA in a lump sum, but dished out in increments as needed. Now if only they can find someone who can balance a checkbook.

Keeping JESCA afloat is one challenge. Restoring its image is another. Archie Hardwick's long years of service can't mitigate the outrageous liberties of this past year; as long as he's around, donors will be reluctant to open their wallets.

Hardwick should be dismissed immediately and a new president should be found—someone who won't use JESCA as his own personal ATM machine.

March 18, 1993

EX-REP. SMITH GETS BIG HELPING FROM CONGRESS

Former U.S. Rep. Larry Smith of Hollywood recently got an $18,624 contract to spend two months comparing the restaurant operations in the House of Representatives with those in private business.

News of the contract has prompted some people to wonder if, in times of a national deficit crisis, Congress is still dishing out financial favors to strapped ex-colleagues and chums.

Smith decided not to seek re-election last year after it was revealed that he'd bounced 161 checks at the House bank. More questions arose about $10,000 in campaign funds that were funneled through his former law office; part of the money was used to pay a gambling debt in the Bahamas. Recently the Florida Bar reprimanded Smith for keeping his name on the law practice, while asserting he had no connection to it.

So the popular Democrat has had a rocky time lately. When *Roll Call* newspaper revealed the terms of Smith's new deal with the House, cynics grumbled that it was nothing but a giveaway disguised as a consulting contract. After all, what qualifies an ex-congressman as a $9,000-a-month expert on food services?

Admittedly, it sounds fishy. But, according to Smith's resume, he is well experienced in the field—operating a snack bar at age 13, waiting tables in college, and working later as a bartender and catering manager for his father. He knows food.

Heidi Pinder, special counsel for the Committee on House Administration, said Smith "is surveying (food) operations with an eye to comparing them to the real world to see whether we are deficient in any way."

While Smith's probe of Congressional restaurants is two weeks from completion, sources have leaked some raw findings—preliminary, but tantalizing. As you can tell, this wasn't some hokey, featherbedded job. The man sunk his teeth into it:

MARCH 15. Breakfast at the House cafeteria.

Raisin bagels hard as rocks. Omelette zesty but overcooked. The cheese is glue-like (real cheddar, or processed?). Pancakes fluffy and light, but the syrup selection is better at IHOP.

MARCH 15. Lunch at the House dining room.

Disaster! Got a bad anchovy in my Caesar. And what's with the scampi—eight measly shrimps. Who put Jenny Craig in charge of the kitchen? I mean, geez, would it kill 'em to throw a few jumbos on the plate? Maybe it's time I dragged Tom Foley to the Red Lobster.

MARCH 15. Dinner at the House dining room.

Soup of the day: A feisty crab bisque (though it could stand an extra drop or three of sherry. Who would know?). Steamed veggies were so-so, but the steaks were a pleasant surprise. Tried the rib-eye, filet and 14-oz. strip sirloin. Mmmmm, Sizzler, eat your heart out. My only gripe: Why just one stuffed potato per person? Who makes up these stupid rules?

MARCH 15. Evening snack at the House cafeteria.

Some wiseacre at the frozen tofu machine: "Sorry, Mr. Smith, but the almond chocolate is reserved for sitting congressmen only. How about vanilla instead?" Here, punk, vanilla this.

MARCH 15. Late-night snack at the House coffee shop.

Pathetic. Three of four microwaves still on the fritz, and that bozo Gingrich is hogging the good one. Like he's the only guy in the entire Capitol who loves popcorn!

MARCH 15. Midnight snack at the House dining room.

Brief struggle over the apple crisps. Rent-a-cop tells me to beat it, says they've had lots of complaints. "You wanna loiter," he says, "try Mister Donut." So I get right in his fat face and say, "Is that any way to talk to Mr. Dante Fascell?" He backs off real quick, and I get my pick of the crisps. Which, by the way, could use another egg in the batter.

January 28, 1996

EASTER SEAL MERITS LICKING FOR LETCH DEAL

This season's Bonehead Charity Trophy goes to the Easter Seal Society, for giving congenital skirt-chaser Larry Hawkins a $400,000 send-off after he was accused of sexual harassment.

Yes, again.

Hawkins was president of Dade's Easter Seal operation until he resigned last week. A prominent Miami law firm hired by the charity turned up "credible" testimony that Larry the Letch was insulting female employees with lewd remarks.

What a shock, huh? Two years ago, voters booted Hawkins off the Metro Commission after several women complained about his priapic predisposition. Allegations, dating to 1988, include:

Poking one woman in the breast with a pencil; asking another to rub him with liniment; and purposely dropping a bullet on the floor so he could peer down another woman's blouse when she bent to pick it up. A smooth operator, that Larry!

Last month, the state Ethics Commission, which is not famous for tough sanctions, fined our Packwood wannabe $5,000 after a judge decided Hawkins had harassed staffers "for his own sexual gratification."

The ex-commissioner insisted the women had misunderstood him, citing a lie-detector test as proof of his pure heart. He also claimed he was the target of a political conspiracy.

Now with two meaningless polygraphs to back him up, Hawkins says the new charges come from a spurned lover and an angry secretary, among others. And, oh yes, the conspiracy is even larger than we thought!

Workers tell it differently. Easter Seal secretary Lynn Solte said Hawkins handed her a $5 bill when she came to work in a jacket and a tapered skirt. "Women who dress like this usually get paid," she quoted him as saying.

Unchastened by his humiliation at the polls and public rebuke by the ethics panel, Hawkins either cannot help behaving like a rutting pig, or doesn't think it's wrong. His actions aren't nearly as surprising as that of Easter Seal.

Instead of flatly firing Hawkins, the board chose to pay him off once he resigned. The deal is indefensible: a $100,000 lump severance, plus a $30,000 annual pension for 10 years.

Hey, chumps, does the name Tanya Glazebrook ring a bell?

Back in 1990, Dade's United Way wanted to dismiss Glazebrook as president after an internal squabble. To discourage her from suing, the charity kissed her good-bye with $225,000, the use of a car, health benefits, a club membership and moving expenses.

As soon as the details hit the headlines, donations to United Way plummeted. Local companies hastily offered to chip in and pay for Glazebrook's golden parachute, but the charity still suffered. It took a long time to regain the public's trust.

Ironically, Hawkins has been credited with helping pull Easter Seal out of financial muck. This exorbitant severance package could kick it back in the sinkhole.

About the charges against Hawkins, Easter Seal Chairman Ron Dresnick told a reporter: "It's a perception problem. . . . I don't think Larry understands for the most part that what he's doing is unwanted and unappreciated."

So let's give him $400,000. That'll teach him.

Unfortunately, it's also $400,000 that won't be available for disabled children, whom Easter Seal's dedicated workers spend so much time helping.

The kids don't need to hear about the Hawkins scandal, but the charity's donors might demand an explanation.

Talk about a "perception problem." Who'll write a check to Easter Seal if they perceive that one thin dime will end up in the sweaty palms of Larry the Letch?

September 8, 1996

CHASING VERMIN IN CITY HALL'S BRIBE FACTORY

They're coming to bury Cesar, and none too soon.

They being federal prosecutors, and Cesar being Cesar Odio, Miami's soon-to-be-unemployed city manager.

A corruption indictment is expected within days. Meanwhile, Odio has been trying to work a plea that would allow him to keep his lucrative pension.

That's the least we could do, no? Everyone facing felony charges deserves a comfy retirement financed by soft-hearted taxpayers.

The FBI investigation centers on alleged shakedowns of contractors. In addition to Odio, agents are focusing on City Commissioner Miller Dawkins, lobbyist Jorge de Cardenas and others. Former Finance Director Manohar S. Surana secretly has been cooperating with the feds.

Among the evidence are surveillance tapes, the quality of which might determine whether Odio and the others cop a plea or go to trial. In any case, the lid is temporarily coming off the bribe factory known as Miami City Hall.

It's impossible for anyone who follows local politics to be flabbergasted by the headlines. The only surprise is that it's taken the FBI so long to throw a net over the vermin. How big a net remains to be seen.

Bet on this: Some serious names around town are praying that Odio doesn't start blabbing everything he knows. Undoubtedly he has received private beseechments to this effect.

Ironically, he was about to lose his job for reasons having nothing to do with the FBI probe. Odio is detested by new Mayor Joe Carollo, who's been lining up the votes to dump him.

The pugnacious Carollo had begun scrutinizing Odio's expenditures from discretionary accounts. By law, the city manager is allowed to spend up to $4,500 a pop without notifying the full commission.

In this convenient fashion, money has quietly gone to Odio's pals, political allies, even friendly radio personalities. Commissioners themselves were not averse to dipping into Cesar's slush fund.

A few weeks ago, *New Times* published a damningly exhaustive account of Odio's casual generosity with taxpayer funds.

From January 1993 through April 1996, for example, he approved the purchase of $11,500 worth of tickets to events sponsored by the Cuban American National Foundation, a group hardly hurting for cash. However, Chairman Jorge Mas Canosa is a close chum of Odio's.

Another, Juan Amador of Radio Mambi, got checks up to $4,000 each for (according to Odio's records) assisting the city with press releases. Talk about an easy gig.

The city manager was similarly magnanimous toward ex-Commissioner Victor De Yurre, one of Odio's strongest supporters. While in office, De Yurre's American Express bills for meals and foreign travel were paid from Odio's budget. Heck, what are friends for?

Undoubtedly Odio's office also gave money to charities and causes whose neediness was beyond question. But it's equally clear he squandered "emergency" funds on favored hacks and cronies.

How about that $4,500 contribution to the Latin Builders Association magazine? Meanwhile, the city is so strapped for funds that hundreds of jobs are being cut.

Odio says many of the controversial payments were requested by individual commissioners. If that's true, he should be able to document each one and defend the others. He hasn't yet.

This isn't a guy to be trusted with the city's checkbook. Regardless of what the FBI does, Odio deserves the ax. And, even if he manages to stay out of prison, he doesn't deserve a golden parachute.

What he deserves is a big fat bill.

April 17, 1997

MONEY APPEARS IN HEAVENLY WAY FOR PORT BOSS

This is the story of a man who's been touched by an angel.

The man's name is Carmen Lunetta, and he's the director of the Port of Miami.

The angel's name is a great big secret, although he or she currently is operating as the Ayoka Holding Ltd. The company is registered in the British Virgin Islands, which is quite a popular place with anonymous offshore angels.

You wouldn't ordinarily think of Lunetta as a fellow in need of heavenly intervention. As boss of Florida's largest seaport (budget: $74 million), he is powerful, politically connected and well compensated.

Which just goes to show that angels watch over all of us, not just the downtrodden and meek.

As a sideline, Carmen Lunetta has a private construction business with brother Carl. Together they wanted to build one of those lovely new subdivisions in Southwest Broward—theirs was to be called Somerset Shores.

But, before they could get started, they needed loans totaling about $1.8 million.

Yikes! thought Carmen. That's a lot of dough. He says his brother "put the word on the street that we needed additional financing."

And the word traveled to a faraway place, where the aforementioned angel happened to be listening. The angel appeared to the Lunettas in the form of Ayoka Holding, which pledged a $500,000 standby letter of credit toward the development of Somerset Shores.

The commitment proved crucial to the two brothers, who used it to secure a big loan from Totalbank in Miami. The Lunettas recently have started buying raw lots in Miramar, and anticipate putting up 120 homes.

If the project sells out, the brothers' construction company stands to make at least $15 million. What a heartwarming success story!

But what a shy and enigmatic angel, too. Never once showed his face. Never descended upon a swirling pink cloud into Carmen Lunetta's office. Never personally graced the brothers with his beatific glow.

Instead, the angel used an intermediary to carry out his good deed. The terms of the $500,000 transaction are confidential and will remain that way, according to the Lunettas.

To this day, Carmen insists he doesn't know the identity of those who helped get Somerset Shores off the ground. His lack of curiosity is peculiar, considering the embarrassing possibilities.

Offshore holding companies sometimes are used by non-angelic types for the purpose of laundering money. Drug cartels, white-collar swindlers, terrorist groups and corrupt despots have all been known to move ill-gotten cash through shell corporations in the islands.

One would think that a person of Carmen Lunetta's position and experience—a high-profile public official—would be much more cautious in his private dealings. One would imagine he'd want to know exactly who was backing him, and why.

Otherwise, people might begin to wonder.

They might wonder, for instance, if Lunetta's mystery benefactor could be someone who has or wants a lucrative contract with the soon-to-be-expanding Port of Miami; someone who figures that a $500,000 letter of credit is one way to get on Lunetta's good side, or to repay a favor.

In which case, you could easily understand why the angel behind Ayoka Holding chooses to remain anonymous, and why Lunetta himself wouldn't be particularly eager to see the name in print.

The next time he got touched by anybody, it might be an FBI agent.

NO CONFLICTS HERE!

October 18, 1985

THIS COLUMN FOR RENT

What a deal.

Two columnists for the *Miami Times* got paid $6,000 to serve as "consultants" for Mayor Maurice Ferre's re-election campaign.

Just by coincidence (or so we're to believe), the same duo proceeds to write column after column lambasting Ferre's opponents, including a particularly vile attack on Marvin Dunn.

When questioned about this suspicious affair, the two journalists said that their Miami Info column is "objective" and provides vital information to readers. They insisted that Ferre's six grand had no influence on the content of their articles.

The best part is, they said all this with a straight face.

I don't know what these folks were up to, but they sure opened my eyes. All this time I'd thought columnists were supposed to be irascibly independent, ready to sink their fangs into any deserving politician or scoundrel.

Now I see all sorts of possible angles to this "consultant" racket. As I understand it, not only could you write snide and venal things about candidates, but you actually could be subsidized for it!

I checked Miami Info for hints on technique. In a mere 16 paragraphs, the columnists manage six times to mention the fact that Marvin Dunn, a black candidate, has a white wife. What this has to do with Dunn's qualifications to be mayor I can't imagine, but apparently relevancy is no concern.

It sounds so easy. A little magic on the pocket calculator tells me that after a few of these "consultant" gigs, I can dump the Oldsmobile and start thinking BMW.

From now on this column is for rent to the highest bidder.

Let's say you work for the Committee to Re-Elect Mayor White, and you want to read something disgusting about your opponent, Candidate Green. Here's a price list and a sample of what you might get.

(a) The $25 column (Fashion and Footwear):

Candidate John Green is a sartorial disgrace. His lapels are too narrow, his neckties are too wide and his trousers are too short. He couldn't get elected mayor of Dogpatch, much less Miami.

(b) The $100 column (Marital Scandal):

Not only is John Green a tacky dresser, he's married to a wild floozy who neglects her small children and steals her elderly housekeeper's Social Security checks to buy champagne. She also dances on tabletops to Barry Manilow's hit "At the Copa."

(c) The $1,000 column (Religion):

Satanic candidate John Green, well-known cuckold and fashion disaster, belongs to a bizarre religious sect that gathers in a cornfield on the first full moon of autumn to chant erotic mantras beneath a Styrofoam likeness of H. R. Haldeman . . .

(d) The $5,000 column (Mental Problems):

Johnny "Meet Me at Bellevue" Green, heretic, philanderer and fashion scarecrow, has a long history of dangerous psychotic behavior. He once terrorized a college campus by climbing to the top of a 12-story clock tower and hurling live hamsters down on innocent passersby . . .

(e) The $10,000 column (The Works):

Mafia chieftain John Green kicked off his mayoral campaign today by calling for the legalization of drugs, pornography and "some forms" of manslaughter. Flanked on one side by his parole officer and on the other by his wife, Suzy, a former snake dancer, Green promised voters "a slot-machine in every high school, a brothel on every block . . . "

This rent-a-column thing is a nifty setup. Whenever you don't know what to write or who to write about, just open the mail and sort the checks. Let your bank book be your guide.

I probably ought to run this idea by my boss, just in case. They've got a name for this kind of thing—I heard it once down on 79th Street, but I just can't remember what it was.

January 17, 1986

CONFLICT LAW REALLY AMOUNTS TO A MOCKERY

Several new developments on the Conflict-of-Interest Front:

- Metro Commissioner Barry Schreiber says he will no longer vote on matters affecting the law firm that pays him a big fat salary. He avers that while there's nothing improper about these votes, he won't do it anymore. Doesn't want to give the "appearance of conflict."

  (In political terminology, a "conflict of interest" is when you get away with it. An "appearance of conflict" is when you get caught.)

- Mayor Steve Clark has appointed one of those blue-ribbon panels to write a new conflict-of-interest ordinance. Among those chosen are blue-ribbon Bob Shevin and blue-ribbon Reubin Askew, who both work for blue-ribbon law firms that get work from the county.

  Why choose independent legal scholars to draft an important law when you can find ex-politicians, with a financial stake in the issue, to do it for you? Thus the mayor has clumsily turned the conflict-of-interest committee into a brand new conflict of interest.

- The Dade state attorney's office has decided the law was not violated when Metrorail contractors spent thousands wining and dining top county officials.

The vouchers in this case are enough to gag a buzzard—food, football tickets, flowers, fruit baskets and fishing trips. One company, Westinghouse, spent $13,059 entertaining county commissioners and transportation administrators.

These people don't just eat, they pig out; maybe this explains why Metrorail runs where it runs. I'm amazed nobody tried to run a spur out to Joe's Stone Crab.

No cheap date, Mayor Clark and three businessmen gulped down a $241.50 dinner at the Ginger Man restaurant. Two Metrorail administrators joined contractors at the Grove Isle Club for a $395 soiree. In all, $39,000 was spent this way; having eaten their fill, several of these Metrorail officials have since departed the county.

The best item is from December 1983. County officials were upset about the late delivery of some Metrorail cars. Instead of just picking up the phone ("Hey, where the heck are those cars!"), the county manager, two county commissioners and two Metrorail supervisors hopped on a plane, flew to

Philadelphia and chowed down on a $225 dinner with the train's manufacturer.

Unfortunately, the commissioners did not bring the finished Metrorail cars home with them.

Obviously we need a new conflict-of-interest law, and we don't need a bunch of downtown lawyers to write it:

It shall be illegal for all county commissioners, administrators, department heads and second-bananas to:

(a) Drool, grovel or otherwise prostrate themselves before any firm offering to do business with the county.

(b) Accept any item of value, including (but not limited to) stocks, bonds, jewelry, clothing, shoes, funny hats, automobiles, ski boats, golf clubs, video recorders, indoor carpeting, hot tubs or fondue pots.

(c) Claim that any trip to Paris, Bermuda, Cozumel or San Francisco is for "business," when everybody knows it's just for goofing off.

(d) Accept free meals, or eat anywhere besides an inexpensive salad bar that shall be installed around the dais of the new commission chambers. Commissioners who travel shall be allotted $7.25 per diem for food, which sum shall be closely held by a chaperone until needed.

(e) Accept any free tickets to sporting events, except for mud-wrestling matches and USFL football games, which by law are not considered things of value.

(f) Vote on any matter in which he or she, or any friend, neighbor or relative (no matter how distant or estranged) has a financial interest, or the remotest chance of making one lousy nickel.

(g) Embarrass voters by begging for tips, colorful trinkets or other goodies. It shall be assumed that all such gifts, no matter how small, are intended to influence or corrupt the employee, because this method has worked so well in the past.

April 14, 1989

WRIGHT STUFF FILLS POCKETS, BORES READERS

A big ethics debate in Washington centers on whether congressmen should be allowed to accept lucrative speaker's fees from lobbyists and special-interest groups. These honoraria are viewed as a way in which members of Congress can be quietly enriched without breaking the law.

There's another scheme for elected legislators to get extra money from rich campaign contributors, a scheme far more diabolical and coldblooded: Write a book.

Politicians love to see a book with their name on the cover. These volumes are invariably dull, disingenuous and self-serving, but it doesn't matter. Politicians have the power to make people buy their book, regardless of how bad it is.

Look at the case of embattled House Speaker Jim Wright. In 1985, Wright wrote a book called *Reflections of a Public Man.* Actually, Wright didn't write it himself. He got one of his staff members (whose salary was paid by tax dollars) to put the book together.

You probably never read Jim Wright's masterpiece, or even heard of it. Most people didn't. Yet the Texas Democrat made good money from it, about $55,000 in royalties. How?

Easy. The trick was clever marketing. Wright sold his book—in bulk—to the only people on this planet (besides his immediate family) who had the slightest motive to buy it: lobby groups and fat-cat political supporters.

The special counsel for the House Ethics Committee has concluded that Wright arranged mass sales of the book to his supporters in order to get around laws limiting a congressman's outside income. Speaker's fees, for example, are capped at a certain amount. No such restrictions affect book royalties.

Wright denies doing anything wrong. It's all a nasty Republican vendetta, he says.

Reflections of a Public Man was only 117 pages long and sold for $5.95. The book was touted as a collection of Wright's great speeches and wry musings. Reviewers widely ignored it. So did most bookstores.

Technically this is called a "bomb." Authors customarily do not make much money when this happens. Of course, most authors cannot turn for help to lobbyists and financial contributors, who apparently purchase their books by the boxcar.

Wright must have had one terrific agent. While most contracts offer the author a royalty of 10 to 15 percent of sales, the royalty rate for Wright's book was 55 percent. Most writers would kill for this kind of a deal.

Of course, Wright had a friendly publisher. Very friendly. The publisher later received more than $250,000 in printing fees from Wright's re-election committee.

The Democrats haven't cornered the market on boring books. A Republican congressman named Newt Gingrich cajoled 21 investors to put up $5,000 each to publish a Gingrich epic called *Window of Opportunity.* Maybe seven people in the whole country ever read it. The publisher lost money, the investors got a tax write-off, and most of America still doesn't know why Gingrich's parents named him after a salamander.

With all this recently exposed, Congress ought to pass a law prohibiting members from publishing any books while in office. If nothing else, it surely violates the littering ordinance. And the term "cruel and unusual" does not begin to describe the practice of pressuring anyone—even a lobbyist—to purchase a politician's memoirs.

In the old days, a payoff was simply a payoff. The bribers didn't get stuck with boxes and boxes of worthless books.

If Wright squirms off the hook, it will give new life to a horrifying trend. Elected officials at all levels of government will feel impelled to sit down at the typewriter to share their wit and wisdom.

A couple years ago, a work-in-progress by Miami Mayor Xavier Suarez was stolen from his car, along with a handgun. Many of us expected the burglar to turn up dead of a self-inflicted gunshot wound after foolishly attempting to read the mayor's manuscript.

It didn't happen then, but it could someday. Stop this torture. Stop the presses.

January 17, 1990

ETHICS PANEL MAY TAKE AWAY OFFICIAL'S GUSTO

In a time when many politicians conceal their skulduggery behind slick lobbyists, intricate land deals and impenetrable blind trusts, it's refreshing to find an elected official who's not afraid to reach out and grab for the gusto.

Such a fellow appears to be Coral Springs City Commissioner Jim Gordon who, according to a state ethics investigator, has done everything but hang a "For Sale" sign around his neck.

An excoriating 35-page report to the Florida Commission on Ethics says Gordon repeatedly violated the law by using his position to benefit himself and special interests, particularly developers.

The pleasant North Broward community of Coral Springs is one of the fastest growing in the country, and Commissioner Gordon dearly loves growth. His problem seems to be a chronic inability to comprehend the term "conflict of interest," or the laws governing it.

Gordon has denied any wrongdoing, and said the charges stem from a political vendetta. Not the most novel defense, but there's little room to be inventive when the report is so devastating.

In 1985 Gordon voted to approve the city's purchase of an empty Morrison's Cafeteria building. At the time, he was working as a real-estate salesman with a firm that brokered the deal. A conflict? Naaah. Not for Commissioner Gordon.

Another time Gordon got a $30,600 fee from Waste Management Inc. for setting up a scholarship program. The ethics investigator found the fee "excessive" for a service that any PR man could do for practically nothing. In fact, a reasonable person might wonder why the 30 grand wasn't deposited into the alleged scholarship fund instead of into Gordon's pocket.

As you might have guessed, Waste Management holds the garbage contract for the city of Coral Springs. A conflict? Naaah, not for Commissioner Gordon.

Over a two-year stretch he also accepted nearly $52,000 in private "consulting fees" from Coral Springs Cable TV, a firm regulated (surprise, surprise!) by the city commission. A conflict? Naaah, not for Commissioner Gordon.

Being the helpful chap he is, Gordon once used his title and city stationery to promote a breakfast symposium held by Nova University. For these efforts, Nova rewarded Gordon with a $33,000 fee. According to the ethics report, Gordon's actions were a clear violation of law.

But what a versatile guy! One day he's a real estate whiz, the next he's a cable TV consultant, then he's a scholarship organizer, and before you know it he's doing promotional work for academia. It's amazing.

Gordon saved most of his energy for developer pals. He allegedly once phoned an assistant city attorney "and began yelling at her about a plat waiver for Pulte Homes." According to the attorney's account, Gordon complained that the city was "giving the developer a hard time."

In another case, the ethics investigator concluded that the commissioner "misused his position" to help the developer of a commercial property called Royal Lands (a parcel sold by Gordon's business partner for a fat profit).

When the developer wanted the city to buy a utility company, it was Gordon who allegedly pressured the city to speed up the deal at an inflated price. When the developer wanted a variance for a Kmart sign, it was Gordon who leaned on city officials to approve it.

And when the developer's plan to be annexed by the city hit a snag, it was Gordon who allegedly raised hell to try to get special exemptions. Said the ethics report: "His action and intent were inconsistent with the proper performance of his public duties."

Inconsistent is a polite word for it. The guy acts like he learned civics from Professor John Lomelo.

Assistant Attorney General Craig B. Willis found evidence that Gordon broke the law in nine instances. If the Ethics Commission agrees, the commissioner faces a fine, a reprimand or (egads!) removal from office.

Talk about lowering the boom. You take away a man's stationery, you strip him of all dignity.

Harsh punishment for a fellow who's simply trying to make the most of his opportunities.

September 24, 1990

SCOTT SHOULD HAVE TO PAY FOR FREE TRIPS

A bad case of jet lag has caught up with State Sen. Jim Scott of Fort Lauderdale.

The Florida Commission on Ethics is investigating whether Scott and several other state lawmakers broke the law by not reporting trips paid for by lobbyists.

Scott says that free trips aren't really gifts, so they needn't be revealed under Florida's gift-disclosure law. The ethics commission, toothless wonder that it is, has drafted an opinion saying that all trips worth more than $100 must be reported.

Lawmakers have been mooching freebies off lobbyists forever; it is a time-honored tradition in Tallahassee, where the term "conflict of interest" is foreign to the political vernacular. The current stink arises mainly because Scott wants to be president of the Senate, a position that carries great prestige (and enormous potential for more free trips).

According to a complaint filed with the ethics commission, Scott and fellow Republican Tim Deratany of Indialantic journeyed to Mexico in 1987, courtesy of Southeast Toyota Distributors. The purpose of the mission remains murky—perhaps the senators were testing four-wheel drives on the Baja.

Two years later, Scott and Deratany, who chairs the Senate Tax and Finance Committee, visited France at the invitation of two insurance lobbyists. By a wild coincidence, the Legislature shortly thereafter passed two laws pushed by the insurance industry.

Scott says he paid his share of the France trip, although he has provided no details or receipts. He has not publicly discussed, or shown slides of, the Mexico adventure.

The most interesting trip, however, was a hunting expedition paid for by Gulf Power Corp. in autumn 1988. Lobbyists reported hosting Scott and four other legislators. Scott says he wasn't there, but another Republican, former State Rep. Dale Patchett, says he talked to Scott on the trip.

Only three possibilities could explain this strange discrepancy:

a) Scott is telling a fib.
b) Patchett has a rotten memory.
c) The man who spoke to Patchett wasn't really Jim Scott. It was an evil twin.

Interestingly, Scott's colleagues in both parties present the dilemma as one of fuzzy laws, not twisted ethics. If the disclosure act were more specific, they say, they'd be happy to list all those free trips as gifts.

Of course they're dodging the point. Legislators have no business going anywhere or doing anything paid for by special interests. Merely reporting each junket on a disclosure form doesn't diminish the obvious conflict; the trips should be outlawed.

When it comes to stuffing a politician's pocket, what's the difference between an airline ticket and cold cash? It's not a "gift," it's payola.

From a lobbyist's point of view, why would any sane person round up a group of Tallahassee legislators and take them to France? Is it because their cosmopolitan charms make them delightful travel companions? Hardly. The trips are grease, pure and simple. You show them a nice time in the hope that they'll vote your way next time around.

And from the legislator's point of view, does Scott or any of his globe-trotting buddies truly believe that lobbyists for utility companies or auto dealers don't expect something in return for their generosity? Do they seriously think voters are dumb enough to believe that a lawmaker won't be influenced just a teeny bit by a free trip to Europe?

A city commissioner would be strung up for such antics, but it's accepted social behavior in Tallahassee. The juicing and seducing of legislators is a vast industry, though the seamy details are usually shielded from the public's delicate eye. People shouldn't be surprised by what Scott did; most of his colleagues do the same thing.

That's why free trips haven't been outlawed by the Legislature. The stalwart public servants who should be passing tough ethics laws don't want to give up their fun.

November 21, 1990

REAL ETHICS BILL WOULD RUIN FUN OF LEGISLATORS

It's hilarious whenever the Legislature "tackles" the topic of ethics.

The debate never lingers on the issue of whether it's right or wrong to accept gifts from special interests. No, sir, the big question is: How much free stuff can we take without getting in trouble?

For a long time lawmakers considered it an obligation to grab everything in sight. Then some of the jackals in the press started writing about it, and there came a cry for "reform"—meaning, they had to do something to save their butts.

So reluctantly they passed "ethics" legislation, which was largely a farce but looked pretty darn impressive in the headlines. They even appointed a state Ethics Commission, which was largely impotent but had a really tough-sounding title.

And then the lawmakers quietly went back to grabbing everything in sight, until they got caught again this year and their antics appeared in the newspapers.

So on Tuesday the Legislature, meeting in special session, again "tackled" the problem of ethics reform. And quite a problem it is, for in order to reform one's ethics, one must vaguely comprehend what the word means. A large contingent of legislators don't.

With a straight face they'll tell you there's nothing wrong with accepting free trips and goodies from a utility firm or a developer or a phosphate mining firm, and then voting on legislation that affects that company's financial future. These lawmakers will feign indignation at the suggestion they could be influenced—even compromised!—by such modest attention.

A reasonable person might say that officeholders shouldn't take anything from anybody, lest it appear they are prostituting themselves to special interests. But to outlaw freebies would dismantle a grand Tallahassee tradition of mooching and schmoozing and partying.

For some politicians, this is the main reason to run for office. Were they ordinary citizens, who would buy them stone crabs or send them bottles of wine or invite them on fishing trips? Getting free stuff ratifies one's sense of importance; it makes you feel like a big shot.

Recently, though, the Legislature has been embarrassed by disclosures that some members failed to report free hunting excursions and European vacations paid for by lobbyists. The lawmakers insisted that such trips are not technically gifts, and shouldn't therefore be reportable to the public.

The Leon County state attorney began investigating the matter, subpoenas were issued and orifices throughout the capitol began to pucker. Of course these legislators had a perfectly valid reason for not reporting the trips—they didn't want the voters back home to find out.

And now all this unseemly publicity!

In reaction to the Leon County investigation, incoming Senate President Gwen Margolis and House Speaker T. K. Wetherell on Tuesday pushed through yet another ethics reform bill, a package affecting thousands of local officeholders as well as state lawmakers.

The bill bans gifts worth more than $100 from political action committees, lobbyists and their employers—but allows gifts worth more than $100 from companies that don't have lobbyists. That's the kind of loophole for which the Legislature is infamous, and the main reason that Florida's ethics rules are the sham that they are.

As an example of how dearly the lawmakers cling to their Tallahassee lifestyle, the new "ban" on $100 gifts will specifically not apply to meals and drinks consumed at one sitting. Apparently, there is widespread fear that legislators will starve if they ever have to pick up the tab themselves.

The best ethics law would be the simplest: Once elected to office, you accept nothing from anybody. No hunting trips, no presents, no booze, no food, not even a beer nut.

Never in a million years will these spineless blobs pass such a law. It would take all the fun out of their job.

November 13, 1994

KAPLAN, WHOM DO YOU THINK YOU'RE FOOLING?

Local Leaders on Parade (again):

Now comes Metro Commissioner Bruce Kaplan, who unabashedly sought a juicy plum of a job from American Airlines.

It wasn't your typical employment application. It was a bungled shakedown.

Kaplan sits on Dade's aviation committee. The panel has authority over American's $1 billion expansion at Miami International Airport. With so much at stake, the airline needs to maintain friendly relations with members of the committee.

Earlier this year, Commissioner Kaplan, an aviation lawyer, wrote American to share a brainstorm: Why not hire him to be the company's representative in Latin America?

Executives at American were taken aback because a.) no such job existed, and b.) they didn't expect such a brazen request from an elected official with oversight responsibilities at the airport.

The term "conflict of interest" instantly sprung to many minds—except, apparently, that of Commissioner Kaplan.

He says he cleared the job idea with the county attorney. The county attorney says Kaplan never mentioned American Airlines by name, or even hinted that he desired employment with a company doing business with Metro.

To its great credit, American politely said no to the commissioner's grossly inappropriate proposition. Then a peculiar thing happened.

Two months later, at the aviation committee, Commissioner Kaplan lashed into American's airport expansion plan and accused the company of tricking Metro into backing the project.

Kaplan says his harsh words against American had absolutely nothing to do with the fact that the airline had rebuffed him for the job.

Don't worry, Bruce, we believe you! We also believe that Elvis is alive and well, and running a Jenny Craig franchise in Zolfo Springs.

No one seriously expected Kaplan to be a paragon of clean ethics. Last year he won his commission seat with a vicious and dishonest campaign. His attacks on opponent Conchy Bretos set a rancid new standard by which all future political slime will be judged.

It was only a matter of time before Kaplan showed his true colors again. The only surprise is the ham-handed way he did it. As he demonstrated in the 1993 race, Kaplan's strong suit isn't subtlety. Even so, you'd think a lawyer could cook up a smarter scheme.

Soliciting American Airlines in the midst of its negotiations with the county was only slightly shy of pure stupidity. The company didn't get to be a major international air carrier by allowing itself to be ripped off by small-time local politicians.

Had American created a dream job for Kaplan, it would have exploded into a public-relations nightmare. Such arrangements do not remain private for long. Ask former Commissioner Larry Hawkins.

Kaplan claims his letter to American wasn't a job request, but rather a "broad" outline of business opportunities. However, airline officials interpreted Kaplan's words as a direct request to be hired.

American declined to release the letter. Kaplan says he threw out his copy. He says he abandoned the idea of working for American after the state Ethics

Commission issued an opinion restricting outside work by public officials who are also lawyers.

A politician who makes a living as an aviation attorney shouldn't sit on the committee that regulates the airport. The conflict would be obvious to a ninth-grader, but evidently not to the Metro Commission.

Kaplan undoubtedly will try to cash in on his position again. The only mystery is when, and how much he'll want next time.

November 19, 1998

A BABY STEP ON STATE ETHICS

Governor-elect Jeb Bush has established a "code" of ethical conduct for members of his transition team.

They must sign a promise to refrain from lobbying any state agencies with which they interact between now and inauguration day. The celibacy period is supposed to last a year after Bush takes office.

Wow. One whole year of keeping your fingers out of the pie. Talk about sacrifice. Talk about selflessness.

This isn't just an "ethics code." It's a call to sainthood.

You're probably thinking: What the heck's going on? Of course a governor's buddies shouldn't be allowed to do business with the same agencies they once helped staff and organize. It would be such an obvious, indefensible conflict of interest. . . .

Obvious to you and me, maybe, but not to everybody at the Capitol. By Tallahassee standards, Bush's modest rules of conduct are positively draconian. The Legislature usually responds to the notion of "ethics reform" much as a vampire responds to the sight of a crucifix.

For instance: In 1994, the Senate—realizing it was widely viewed as a sty of craven, butt-kissing moochers—barred its members from accepting free booze and food from lobbyists.

To the average citizen, the rule seemed anything but radical. In fact, it seemed like common sense. A politician who gets extravagantly wined and dined by special interests might be unduly influenced by such hospitality—or, at least, perceived to be.

Moreover, the unfettered food-for-all made it difficult for Joe Constituent to compete with deep-pocketed lobbyists for a coveted supper slot on a senator's busy calendar. The fair thing to do was to level the playing field by banning free meals and bar tabs.

It was a good idea, but now it's a dead one.

While you and I have to buy our own meals, it's clearly too much to ask of elected officials. The Senate's no-freebies edict caused so much social upheaval and gastronomic deprivation that it has been quietly scotched.

So it's party time again in Tallahassee! Senators can rejoin their well-fed colleagues from the House of Representatives—who ignored the folly of ethics reform—at that ripe, bountiful smorgasbord known as government.

The law that prohibits lawmakers from accepting gifts worth more than $100 conveniently doesn't apply to food and liquor slurped down at a single sitting. Even as you read this, your elected representatives could be sipping mimosas and nibbling eggs Benedict paid for by cigarette makers or sugar tycoons or trial lawyers or even some H. Wayne Huizenga wannabe.

It would be lovely to believe that, as Senate President Toni Jennings and others assert, most legislators cannot be compromised by a free meal—even a five-star meal. It would also be lovely to believe that all citizens have the same opportunity as an NRA lobbyist to take their senator out for dinner or drinks, to bend his or her ear for an hour.

Unfortunately, it didn't work that way when the Democrats held power, and it probably won't work that way under the Republicans. Ruling parties generally aren't too gung-ho on reform. It takes the fun out of being in charge.

Jeb Bush's advantage is to arrive as a newcomer, with broad popular support. He appears to have a genuine distaste for the way deals have been done—and undone—for so long in Tallahassee.

But it's easy to impose a code of conduct for a temporary transition team. Pushing for new permanent ethics standards throughout state government would be a tough battle. We'll see if the new governor has the appetite for it.

We already know about the bottomless appetites of legislators.

February 4, 1999

MORE RELIEF FOR CROOKED POLS?

Financial disclosure is an acid test of an elected officeholder's honesty, and therefore a source of high anxiety to some politicians.

A Senate committee is considering a way to cripple Florida's financial disclosure law by rendering it so vague as to be worthless. If the plan goes through, any crooked councilman, commissioner or legislator could double his or her net worth in twelve months—and not be required to divulge it, much less explain it.

Paradoxically, the same plan proposes toughening the current disclosure law in other ways—such as requiring elected officials to state exactly what kind of business they're in. You'd be amazed at how many of them aren't sure.

But extracting a plausible occupation is pointless if they no longer have to list dollar amounts for net worth, assets and liabilities. Believe it or not, that's the plan.

Lame as it is, the current law at least compels officials to provide specific monetary figures. And in rare cases—such as that of former Miami-Dade Commissioner Bruce Kaplan—it has actually helped rid voters of a slippery eel.

Not surprisingly, some politicians want to go back to the days when they could legally conceal suspicious windfalls. The Senate Ethics and Elections Committee on Wednesday began discussing a new financial disclosure form that would require public officials only to mark broad categories, not write down exact numbers.

For instance, someone whose net worth was $250,001 would check off the same box as a person whose net worth was $500,000. The next category would be $500,001 to $1 million, then $1,000,001 to $2 million. All officials worth more than $2 million would check the same box. The benefit to bought-off politicians is vast. They could feather their nest eggs by 100 percent (or more), and still be entitled to mark the same box as the previous year. That means their bonanza would remain secret from both the media and the voters.

What an invitation to crooks—and we've got more than a few in office—who would blithely take cash, stock or other goodies from those needing a favor. And what a smooth way to hide it.

Nobody with the exception of Donald Trump enjoys having their personal finances published for the world to see. It's one of the most uncomfortable, intrusive demands of public service.

But the reason we need full financial disclosure is that some of the people we elect turn out to be bums who enrich themselves unlawfully, or at least questionably, while in office.

Voters want, and deserve, the details. It's important to know if the senator leading the charge against tough tobacco taxes owns stock in Philip Morris, and precisely how much his or her holdings are worth.

Politicians who call that an invasion of privacy don't belong in the public arena. Once elected, financial privacy is lost, a casualty of epidemic corruption and conflicts of interest.

If everyone who sought office was candid and forthcoming, we wouldn't need financial disclosure. What do those disclosure forms show? That, with few exceptions, the net worth of politicians tends to increase handsomely, the longer they're in office.

Some are probably just real good at their occupations, whether it's real estate or law or mobile home sales. Others undoubtedly work extra hard despite the drain of time for civic duties. And others . . . well, maybe they lucked into a juicy inheritance, or won the Publishers Clearinghouse sweepstakes.

Whatever their good fortune might be, the circumstances are of demonstrable interest to those who elected them. Honest politicians put it all on paper, every dollar.

Others check the box marked "weasel."

June 25, 2000

IT'S A DE-CORRUPTION CONSPIRACY!

A bunch of stuffed shirts and party poopers is conspiring to take all the fun out of local corruption.

Calling themselves the Alliance for Ethical Government, a coalition of 190 business leaders, educators and civic activists has proposed a host of reforms that could make it more difficult to buy, influence or compromise elected officials.

If adopted, these radical measures might discourage future thieves, scammers and deadbeats from running for office. That would mean substantially less employment for prosecutors, FBI agents, criminal-defense lawyers and, of course, journalists.

It's a disquieting prospect. In South Florida, politics without crooks would be like Biscayne Bay without *e. coli*.

For starters, the alliance wants a law prohibiting county commissioners from voting on any issue that would benefit businesspeople or lobbyists who contributed more than $1,000 to the commissioner's election.

Who're they kidding? The only point of giving that kind of dough to a politician is to purchase his or her fealty—I write a check to your campaign, you vote to give my firm the next big county landscaping contract, or whatever.

Eliminating that cozy quid pro quo defeats the whole purpose of big-money donations. It's the most cherished method of legalized bribery in our entire political system, and now some big-shot do-gooders are trying to thwart it!

The group even wants municipalities to require companies seeking government contracts to swear to an ethical "code of conduct." The code would be modeled on one used by the Greater Miami chamber of commerce: "We will not, directly or indirectly, offer to give a bribe or otherwise channel kickbacks from contracts awarded to government officials, their family members or business associates. We will not seek or expect preferential treatment on bids based on our participation in political campaigns."

That's just great. No bribes. No kickbacks. No bid-rigging. What next, no sleazy backroom lobbying?

Yup. The alliance says lobbyists should be required to report the fees they get paid, in addition to providing lists of all clients and what those clients hired them for.

Now we're into the realm of genetic tampering—asking a lobbyist for full public disclosure is like asking a cockroach to crawl out in broad daylight. It's an unnatural act.

But the anti-corruption crusaders apparently will settle for nothing less than squeaky-clean government. How else to explain their heartless scheme to restrict the role of county commissioners in awarding $1 million-plus contracts.

Talk about a swift kick in the scruples. The only reason some of these hapless boobs run for office is to get their paws on taxpayer money, doling it out giddily to cronies, in-laws and incompetents.

Who can forget when the county bought all those palm trees that turned out to be munchkin-sized versions of what was ordered? Nobody bothered to measure the darn things.

Or how about the time those silly dolts paid for miles and miles of road striping that never was done? Nobody bothered to drive out and eyeball the asphalt!

And it's fair to say that Miami International Airport wouldn't be the frantic free-for-all it is today if politicians and their lobbyist pals hadn't been allowed to diddle around with the vendor contracts.

If the coalition gets its way, even politicians who figure out a new way to steal will find it harder to hide. They'd be forced to explain any unusual jumps in their net worth and to file financial disclosure statements for three years after leaving office (in case they're getting bribed on the installment plan).

The ethics alliance obviously is aware of the hardships these laws would impose on dishonest officeholders. It recommends boosting the annual salary of Miami-Dade commissioners to $76,200 from $6,000, presumably to compensate for lost payoffs and kickbacks.

I trust the current commission to see through this hollow gesture and dispense with the coalition's "reform" agenda accordingly. To do any less would besmirch the shining legacy of Jim Burke, Joe Gersten, and Barry Schreiber, not to mention all those who didn't get caught.

Sure, honest government has its good points. But there's a tradition here in South Florida, and traditions should never be abandoned lightly.

9

SICK PUPPIES

April 25, 1988

GOVERNOR NEARLY FOOLED US WITH STAND ON ECOLOGY

He almost had us fooled, the governor did.

Several times in recent months Bob Martinez has energetically joined sides with conservationists to speak out for the preservation of Florida's natural treasures.

Remember when he squashed the reborn scheme to build a big jetport in the Everglades? And when he pushed for the state acquisition of thousands of acres in the environmentally sensitive East Everglades?

He even went skin diving on the Pennekamp reef with the Secretary of Interior, and rightly took some of the credit when the government scaled back its plans for oil drilling off the Florida Keys.

These crusades got the governor lots of good print at a time when he sorely needed it. He now understands what his predecessors—Bob Graham and Reubin Askew—figured out a long time ago: Floridians do care about conservation.

Privately, though, Martinez is acting like the same good old boy who puts political favors ahead of the public interest.

Last month, he nominated a fellow named Jerry Sansom to the South Atlantic Fishery Management Council, a federal board with regulatory powers over coastal fishing for Spanish mackerel, kingfish and other popular offshore species.

Sansom is the head of the Organized Fishermen of Florida, the main lobby for the same commercial netters whose multitonnage plunders nearly wiped out Florida's kingfish migrations. Using spotter planes and miles of mesh, commercial boats were able to annihilate whole schools of fish, leaving few for recreational weekend anglers.

As a lobbyist for these net boats, Sansom is sharp and effective.

Back when the state Marine Fisheries Commission acted to preserve our dwindling redfish stocks (also devastated by commercial boats), it was Sansom who fought against giving the species the protection of game fish status. Ignoring his own experts, the governor sided with the netters.

Martinez's faith in the industry's ability to safeguard the fish population is baffling. Even with tough emergency limits, some netters continue to demonstrate a firm commitment to depletion. This year, they managed to haul in 300,000 pounds of Spanish mackerel during the closed season—this, thanks to an inexcusable loophole in state regulations.

The clout of the commercial lobby extends to the federal level. The same fishery council to which Sansom is nominated refused to ban destructive fish traps and long-lines from Dade County's artificial reefs. Why? Because a handful of commercial boats load up on these sites.

As recent crises have demonstrated, no resource has been more poorly managed or more greedily exploited than our fisheries. The idea that Martinez would now appoint a fish-industry lobbyist to such a key position is a disgrace.

Does he really expect us to believe that Sansom will act impartially? If so, it would be the first time.

Lobbyists are paid to lobby for a private cause. They have no business in the management of public policy. In the Sansom case, the conflict of interest is so egregious that we can only assume that Martinez just doesn't care.

Odd, because recreational divers and anglers overwhelmingly outnumber the commercial netters and pump millions more into Florida's economy. If sportsmen ever got together and voted in their full numbers, the governor would have a whale-sized problem.

When he was running for the office, Martinez actively courted conservationists by promising that all nominees to the marine commissions would be free of personal or financial conflicts.

So here is another forgotten pledge, not the first for this particular governor.

Martinez can talk all he wants about the rapture of the Everglades and snorkel over the reef to his heart's content. Lots of Floridians would like to believe that he's sincere, but stunts such as the Sansom nomination make you wonder how much of the governor's newfound nature-loving is just an act.

July 28, 1989

GOP LEADER NOT ASHAMED OF HUD SCAM

What a proud week for the Republican party.

A fellow named William L. Taylor sat in front of a congressional committee and matter-of-factly described how he got more than $500,000 in cash and equity for acting as a "consultant" to some developers. The developers were trying to do business with the U.S. Department of Housing and Urban Development during the Reagan administration.

Mr. Taylor was a lobbyist for the city of Jacksonville and the former Republican state chairman of Florida. He is currently one of two state representatives to the Republican National Committee.

And his testimony was so disgusting and devoid of remorse that it inspired this comment from Rep. Christopher Shays of Connecticut: "I'm a Republican and you're a Republican, and I wish you were a Democrat. . . . Instead of representing your party, you cashed in on your party."

Taylor replied that, at the time, he didn't think he was doing anything wrong. Lots of Republican big shots were groveling for HUD goodies while President Rip Van Reagan dozed.

This is how the scheme worked. If you were a GOP muckety-muck with friends in high places, you would present yourself as an expert consultant to developers who wanted government housing subsidies. Upon receiving an obscenely large fee, you would promptly drop a chatty little note to one Deborah Gore Dean.

As the top aide to HUD Secretary Samuel Pierce Jr., Ms. Dean was the Vanna White of Washington—only instead of turning letters, she rubber-stamped them. Today the giveaway queen is so modest about her generosity that she invokes the Fifth Amendment rather than answer questions. Luckily, the testimony of others paints a detailed picture.

Take James Watt, one of the lowest vertebrate life forms ever to inhabit a Cabinet office. After embarrassing Reagan (no easy task), he resigned from the Department of Interior and entered the lucrative world of high-powered Washington lobbyist/consultants. Having no background in housing matters didn't prevent Watt from peddling himself as a person of influence.

And apparently he was. He made a few calls to Pierce, and three low-income projects were steered to the developers who had paid Watt about $400,000 in fees. In recent testimony before a House subcommittee, Watt admitted that he knew practically zero about housing but said he was very proud of his efforts lobbying HUD.

William L. Taylor, the Florida GOP honcho, was even less subtle. Time and again he wrote to Pierce and Dean using Republican National Committee stationery to tout his private clients. "I did it because I wanted Mr. Pierce to know that Bill Taylor is the national committeeman from Florida," Taylor explained.

Again, it worked like a charm. For his labors on behalf of five HUD-related projects, Taylor said he got $130,000 in fees and a 10 percent ownership in a housing development worth about $400,000. Taylor's smugness prompted one congressman to say he wanted to "upchuck."

Influence peddling is a nauseating part of how government works, and it is always the party in power who passes out favors. But you've got to marvel at the hypocrisy of Republican stalwarts trying to slime a fast buck off a program designed to help the poor—a program created by Democrats.

The plan for a Cabinet-level housing agency was developed by John F. Kennedy and implemented by Lyndon Johnson. The idea was to provide decent urban living conditions by giving subsidies and loan incentives to private builders. The idea was not to make people like James Watt wealthy for doing nothing but picking up the telephone.

That's what happened to HUD under Reagan. It was a gravy train, and all the smart little doggies got in line. William L. Taylor's lack of conscience before Congress was revealing. In defending himself, he said, "Lobbying is probably the second-oldest profession."

To use the term loosely.

October 31, 1991

GANGSTERS NEED NOT WORRY OVER LATEST GUN LAW

Snipers and drug gangsters, take heart. You've got allies in Washington.

Say thanks to Rep. E. Clay Shaw of Fort Lauderdale and 246 other congresspersons who voted to keep it legal for any bozo off the street to buy a semiautomatic assault rifle.

A ban on the manufacture and importation of several super-lethal models had passed the Senate, but was killed October 17 by Shaw and colleagues, who shunned the pleas of law enforcement groups.

The gun lobby had fought the ban with a persuasion lubricated by campaign money. Straight-faced NRA lobbyists insisted the semiautomatics in question were grand sporting weapons and that unrestricted ownership was essential to the integrity of the Constitution.

However, most firearm reference books don't list these models as sporting arms—the *Shooter's Bible* classifies many as paramilitary. The Uzi, with its 4½-inch barrel, is scarcely ideal for hunters or serious target shooters. Same goes for the Intratec TEC-9, manufactured proudly right here in Dade County. These babies are available with a 3-inch barrel and a 20-round clip; no wonder they're a big favorite of crack gangs nationwide.

Apparently Rep. Shaw even found sporting attributes in the venerable MAC-10, which was designed as a lightweight combat weapon. Undoubtedly a MAC could kill a moose—32 moose, if you bumped into a herd at close range.

Other guns receiving the Congressional Seal of Approval were the Armscorps FAL, the Israeli-made Galil ("battle proven" and outfitted for infrared scopes), the M1 Thompson, the Beretta AR-70 ("crafted from the toughest materials in modern arsenal technology"), the Colt AR-15 and CAR-15, the Fabrique National FAL and FNC, the AK-47 (used in the massacre of students in Stockton, California), the Springfield SAR-48, the Steyr AUG and the whimsically named "Street Sweeper," a semiautomatic shotgun prized by gangs and dreaded by police.

All these weapons fire scores of high-caliber rounds in rapid succession. No self-respecting game hunter would be seen with such guns, but they boast a large and loyal following of violent criminals.

"We've got vaults full of 'em out here," says Bruce Snyder, spokesman for the Bureau of Alcohol, Tobacco and Firearms in Miami. Finding lawfully purchased assault rifles in the hands of criminals, he says, "is an everyday thing."

The congressmen who so love these instruments of carnage seldom get to view the results firsthand. None of them were at the schoolyard in Stockton. None were at the Suniland shopping center in South Dade when seven FBI agents were shot down, two fatally, by bank robbers with a Ruger Mini-14.

John Hanlon, one of the agents who survived Suniland, was pleased to see the Mini-14 on the list of assault rifles to be banned. But he was bitterly stunned when Congress turned yellow and struck the measure from this year's anti-crime bill. "I was completely amazed," said Hanlon, now a Broward felony prosecutor. "What does it take?"

The ban would have done nothing about the many assault rifles already in private ownership, but it would have prevented future generations of psychopaths from shopping over-the-counter.

Most South Florida lawmakers listened to the agents, police officers and prosecutors who wanted the new restrictions. Dante Fascell, Ileana Ros-Lehtinen, Bill Lehman, Larry Smith and Harry Johnston all voted to outlaw the importation and manufacture of the Mini-14 and other cop-killers.

Clay Shaw, as usual, listened to the NRA.

He should have been at Suniland that spring day five years ago, when agents Ben Grogan and Jerry Dove lay dead in the grass, when John Hanlon and four others were carried off with shattered bones and exploded arteries.

Maybe it was a sporting event for the bank robbers with the Ruger. If they were alive today, they'd be grateful to see that Congress is still protecting their rights.

October 22, 1995

LOBBYIST HAS HOST OF ANGELS IN HIS POCKET

Do you believe in angels?

Lobbyist Ron Book should. He's got one at the Dade state attorney's office.

Book got caught systematically funneling illegal campaign checks to state and local politicians. He was allowed to plead guilty to four penny-ante misdemeanors, pay a small fine and donate $40,000 to charity.

On the day the plea was announced, lots of elected officeholders burped a sigh of relief. They'd been spared the pain of taking the witness stand to try to explain why Ron Book got money for them—and what they had to do in return for it.

Book is one of Florida's most powerful persons, handsomely paid to lobby for private interests and local governments. He's in the business of doing big favors and asking for them.

Agents nailed him good. They wanted 80 criminal charges.

But, demonstrating its long-standing allergy to politically sensitive cases, the state attorney's office caved. The cops who had built the case against Book weren't even consulted about the plea bargain, and it's no wonder.

The deal is a stinking disgrace—so bad that the Florida Department of Law Enforcement has decided to ignore it and pursue its investigation of Book's boiler room.

The operation was textbook sleaze. Politicians all over Florida would phone Book for $5,000 to $20,000 in campaign dough. Ronnie would promptly hit up his corporate clients.

If he needed more money, he'd tell his office workers to write personal checks, then reimburse them from his own pocket—deliberately subverting a law that caps individual contributions at $500.

Ronnie scarcely was a master of deception. Secretaries earning less than $20,000 a year were "giving" $10,000 in campaign donations. For Book, the crimes were flagrant, premeditated and completely routine.

Funds were channeled to many candidates, including Gov. Lawton Chiles, Broward Sheriff Ron Cochran and U.S. Attorney Kendall Coffey, a former Senate hopeful.

Those who took the money naturally say they didn't know how Book got it—though it would have been intriguing to see if they'd say the same thing under oath.

Before the whistle blew, everybody was happy. Politicians got their cash. Book and his clients got a bigger lever on the politicians. Voters, meanwhile, remained safely in the dark.

A trial would have dragged the whole rancid mess into the open, and nobody—not Book, those who hired him, or the politicians—wanted that to happen. Plea bargaining commenced at a breakneck pace.

So fast, in fact, that one group of Book's most influential clients—specifically, the companies held by H. Wayne Huizenga—didn't have time to deliver subpoenaed documents. Prosecutors said shucks, they didn't need the stuff anyway.

Angels. That's what they were.

Some guys are blessed. Back in 1986, Book phonied an insurance claim on a stolen car. He later pleaded no contest to a misdemeanor, and a kindly judge withheld adjudication.

This time around, Ronnie gets a criminal record, which can only be a big boost for his lobby business.

But he's also a lawyer. No joke—the man has a law degree. You wouldn't know it from his chronic befuddlement about the criminal statutes, but it's true.

So, just for giggles, the Florida Bar announced it will review Book's latest shenanigans to see if punishment is deserved.

Ronnie's not losing much sleep. Lawyers are disciplined only slightly more often than Halley's comet appears in the sky.

The Bar is just one more friendly choir of angels. Like I said, some guys are blessed.

May 23, 1996

FLORIDA ADRIFT IN PROMOTING BOATING SAFETY

Florida lawmakers paid no attention to recreational marine mayhem until a tourist crashed his water bike into Gloria Estefan's 33-foot cruiser last year.

If he'd smashed into a non-celebrity or even another tourist, Tallahassee's

Gomer Brigade once again would've been able to snuff all attempts to make our waterways less perilous.

But thanks to a steadfast campaign by Estefan and her husband, Emilio, legislators finally passed the state's first boating safety bill. Gov. Lawton Chiles signed it Monday.

The law doesn't go nearly far enough, but it's a start. Beginning in October, powerboaters 16 years old and younger will be required to pass eight-hour safety courses before taking the helm. The age limit rises to twenty-one by 2001.

Significantly, the water biker killed in the accident with the Estefans was no youngster. He was 29. In fact, most serious boating mishaps involve grown-ups, not kids.

Why, then, didn't the Legislature do the sensible thing and require boaters of all ages to learn water safety and navigation? For the same reason the fine for violating the Estefan law is a measly $50.

Politics. For a decade, lobbyists for some marine and resort interests have successfully blocked attempts to pass boating-safety measures.

Consequently, any fool with money can drive a speedboat or a Jet Ski that goes as fast as a car, but without the brakes to stop it. Sometimes these guys end up with their brains splattered on bridge abutments, but more often they send innocent victims to hospitals and morgues.

On any sunny weekend, there might be half a million pleasure vessels on the water. Too many are piloted by novices or incompetents who don't know their aft from a hole in the ground.

That's why this state is the most dangerous in America for boating. In 1994, there were 1,193 accidents and 74 deaths. Last year the toll rose: 1,337 accidents and 78 deaths.

The water biker who died wave-jumping around the Estefans' boat was not a statistical anomaly. Statewide, 37 percent of last year's marine accidents involved Jet Skis, Waverunners and other "personal watercraft."

According to the Florida Marine Patrol, 72 percent of the boat operators involved in collisions had received no prior safety training. That doesn't surprise experienced skippers.

Still, some say boating licenses wouldn't keep the worst maniacs off the water, any more than driver's licenses keep rotten drivers off the highways.

While that's probably true, a strong law could help beach chronic offenders. And no harm can come from the minor inconvenience of a classroom safety course. Most people would learn something, and the result would be fewer accidents and fatalities.

Opponents say that even the most simple, undemanding licensing process would scare off potential boat buyers and tourists—a cynical hypothesis, but embraced by Tallahassee nonetheless. In a contest between private profits and public safety, guess who wins.

The upcoming Memorial Day weekend is traditionally one of the most treacherous afloat. Prime viewing areas are along the Intracoastal Waterway in Broward, Hobie Beach off the Rickenbacker Causeway in Dade or practically any bridge in the Keys. You won't believe what you'll see.

Even more unbelievable is the state's unwillingness to confront the reality that a speeding Donzi can be just as lethal as a speeding Camaro.

But unless one happens to plow into another celebrity—say, Jimmy Johnson's sportfisherman, or a yacht carrying Madonna—no new boating laws are likely to be passed. The death and maiming of nonfamous Floridians don't seem to count.

May 16, 1999

BUILDERS' PLAN REEKS OF GREED

Remember Hurricane Andrew? Well, get over it.

That's the message from Florida's construction industry, which is lobbying for a statewide building code that would wipe out virtually all the lifesaving reforms put in place after Andrew steamrolled South Florida in 1992.

It's no joke. Exactly such a dangerous proposal has been drafted, and some version will reach the Legislature next year.

The audacity is boggling. Andrew left nearly $30 billion in damage, most of it caused by cheap materials, inept construction and sloppy code enforcement. Thousands of lives torn, thousands of families left homeless—and now, perversely, the building industry asks for your trust.

The reforms went too far, some builders say. The price of new homes was driven too high.

Hurricane shutters? Who needs 'em! Same goes for those nails in your shingles—heck, staples work just fine . . . well, most of the time. And code inspections? There are just too darn many.

Right. These are some of the same craftsmen who slapped together the crackerbox subdivisions that disintegrated in Andrew's weakest winds; some of the same geniuses who couldn't strap down a roof, or hit a truss with a nail; some of the same cheapskates who built exterior walls with particleboard, which is only slightly more weather resistant than a Triscuit.

Why is anyone even listening to these people? Because they have money, and politicians listen to money.

Scandalized by Andrew, the building lobby lost some of its clout in South Florida. So it turned to Tallahassee, which is always sunny for special interests bearing hefty campaign donations.

A plan was hatched to undo the tough post-Andrew reforms adopted in Broward, Palm Beach, Monroe and Miami-Dade, and to make sure no other counties would ever take such bold action. A compliant Legislature created the Florida Building Commission.

Mission: Write a statewide building code to supplant local ones.

The panel was stacked heavily with members of the construction trade. And guess what they came up with as a first draft? A code that's actually weaker than the one in place when Andrew struck.

The strategy is notable for its casual disregard for human life and safety. This is about money. This is about making it easier to crank out cheap houses under minimal scrutiny.

Builders' lobbyists claim mandatory shutters and wind-resistant materials hike the price of new homes too high for some buyers. That's big-hearted logic—better to sell some sucker a house that's likely to blow apart, instead of no house at all.

Say a set of storm shutters adds $5,000 to the cost. Amortized over a 30-year mortgage, it's a bargain—and a lot cheaper than what you'll pay extra in homeowner's insurance on a place with no window protection.

Speaking of insurance rates: If you think they're painful now, grab your ankles. Once this disgraceful excuse for a building code passes, insurance costs will explode.

On Monday, the building commission holds its first public hearing. It starts at 3 P.M. at the Broward Convention Center.

Someone will probably ask the commissioners what on earth they're thinking—trying to gut building codes in a state in which nobody, not a single soul, isn't vulnerable to a hurricane.

Another hearing is set next month in South Dade. At first, the commission had no plans to convene down there, but residents objected. They mentioned something about a big hurricane, a few years back.

Seems they haven't forgotten.

TIME TO GROUND JETPORT SCHEME

The rich guys who want to turn South Dade into another Hialeah have hired heavyweight Washington lobbyists to beseech the Clinton administration.

Listen to the violins, courtesy of the law firm of Verner, Liipfert, Bernhard, McPherson & Hand: "There is a deep, fundamental unfairness here which has resulted in the unabashed denial of justice to the people of Homestead."

This unabashed crapola appears in a contorted 20-page letter sent by Vernon Liipfert to Attorney General Janet Reno, and obtained by the *Herald*'s Cyril T. Zaneski.

At issue is the redevelopment of Homestead Air Force Base, trashed in 1992 by Hurricane Andrew. Afterward, much of the property was to be conveyed to Miami-Dade County.

And who can forget what the county commission did: They gave away the whole enchilada to political insiders who didn't know diddly about building an airport.

In a scandalous no-bid deal, the Homestead base was leased to a group known as HABDI, led by Carlos Herrera, a honcho with the Latin Builders Association and a big Democratic campaign donor. Many South Dade residents protested, but to no avail.

Grand plans were announced for a new commercial jetport, hotels, shops and warehouses. But the real gold mine lay in the subdivisions that would sprout around the airport complex. Bankers, builders, landowners—everybody was in a fine drool.

Then came the snag. It was pointed out that the jetport described in the original environmental impact study bore only a passing resemblance to the one being touted.

A few minor details had gone unmentioned—an entire second runway, for instance. And the ground-shaking projection of an eventual 236,000 flights a year, or about 650 a day.

This was noteworthy because the jetport site is between the Biscayne and Everglades national parks, neither of which are thriving under urban pressures. Soon, conservation groups got involved.

In December 1997, the FAA and the Air Force ordered a new environmental study, to be based on more complete information. It was bad news for HABDI supporters such as Sen. Bob Graham and Miami-Dade Mayor Alex Penelas.

Now Vernon Liipfert has been hired to goose the White House, though no one is saying who's paying the fee. I'd bet it's not Haitian Community Radio or the Greater New Covenant Missionary Baptist Church, both of which are suspiciously listed in the "coalition."

Developers need those names on their letter to Reno, because they contend that the federal studies now delaying the jetport amount to discrimination against "the poor and minorities" who need jobs.

Get this: HABDI boosters actually claim to be fighting not to enrich their own bank accounts, but to protect (among others) Haitian and Hispanic farmworkers. Yet if the jetport gets approved, there will instantly be less agriculture in South Dade—many farmers can't wait to unload their cropland to builders.

It's indisputable that Homestead and Florida City haven't fully recovered from Hurricane Andrew. But to blindly put the area's future in the hands of HABDI would be a foolhardy and unfixable mistake.

There are ways to develop the air base without jeopardizing the community's character, not to mention its two largest tourist attractions, Biscayne Bay and the Everglades.

Unfortunately, desperation politics breeds bad judgment. Look at the motor speedway, built at taxpayer expense and hyped as a godsend to South Dade's battered economy. Wrong.

Plenty of people made money, but not the ones who needed it most; not the ones who write their own letters, and can't afford to hire Washington lobbyists.

August 9, 2000

PENELAS LOBBYISTS NOW HIS FUND-RAISERS

Every time a corruption scandal breaks, Miami-Dade Mayor Alex Penelas gets religion. He says county government must be reformed. He says lobbyists hold too much sway over elected officials.

Now the mayor is running for reelection, and guess whom he has chosen as his arm-twisting fund-raisers? The same lobbyists whose influence he purports to lament.

Penelas is like the guy who preaches abstinence from the balcony of a whorehouse. His credibility is somewhat shaky. Which is probably why he isn't answering questions these days about his $1 million campaign kitty. Such riches are embarrassing for a self-proclaimed reformer, especially when you consider the sources.

Leading the Penelas shakedown team are lobbyists Brian May, Rodney Barreto, Jorge Lopez and Chris Korge. All four represent business interests that hold (and hope to keep) huge county contracts.

Two of the men made news recently—Korge, a top Democratic fund-raiser and the mayor's longtime guru, and Lopez, who worked for Penelas when Penelas was a commissioner.

Both are part of the lucky lobbyist contingent that divvied up the concession jackpot at Miami International Airport. Korge's clients have been awarded more than $123 million in contracts at MIA, including duty-free shops and restaurants. Among Lopez's many MIA clients is the largest supplier of phone cards.

The Penelas connection came to light during the *Miami Herald*'s investigation of MIA, one of the country's most inconveniently operated airports—chaotic, debt-ridden and widely dreaded by passengers.

One reason for the mess is that Miami-Dade commissioners doled out lucrative airport deals to reward lobbyists who supported their elections. The result was a predictable circus of waste and ineptitude.

The revelations provoked the usual bleat of chagrin from the mayor, who seemed oddly unaware of the windfall reaped by his cronies at the airport.

Later Penelas drafted a law that would have removed county contracts from the grip of commissioners (and, by default, the lobbyists who control them). The commission hurriedly killed that idea as well as two tougher proposals from Commissioner Jimmy Morales.

Strangely, the mayor's discomfiture about the role of lobbyists doesn't extend to their influence over his own career.

Not only has he again recruited them to raise money, but the money is coming from big shots of companies such as Sirgany International and Host International—two of the largest vendors at MIA.

No wonder Penelas has got a case of lockjaw. It's hard to defend such actions without sounding like a hypocrite.

His spokesman says Penelas can't be compromised by campaign donations because the mayor by law isn't involved in deciding who gets county contracts. In other words, he's not worth buying off.

It's an amusingly strained attempt to inoculate Penelas against charges that he's exploiting a system he professes to detest.

He might not have a vote, but he's got a veto, a formidable weapon. Moreover, he's a dominant force with commissioners, deploying lobbyists to raise money for those he likes.

The mayor knows that executives of Sirgany and other firms will cough up donations simply to please those lobbyists, whose connections they sorely need.

For example, if you wanted an MIA vending contract, you'd go to Korge or Lopez. And if you got the contract, you'd conclude that you had hired the right guys. And if they later came and asked for donations for candidate Joe Blow, you'd say: "Sure, whatever makes 'em happy."

Penelas understands the insider game. By using those same wheeler-dealer fundraisers, he benefits directly from their clout—and client list.

His opponent, Commissioner Miguel Diaz de la Portilla, has raised only $245,000, a fourth as much as the mayor. Like Penelas, Diaz de la Portilla has accepted campaign funds from lobbyists representing companies that have (or are seeking) county business. And, like Penelas, Diaz de la Portilla has called for reform. He actually voted for it, too.

Theoretically, even a mayor without a vote is supposed to be a leader. But on this issue of government integrity, so important to a scandal-weary public, Penelas has spent less time leading than talking.

And now he's not even doing that.

10

ZONED OUT

VOICE OF REASON MUFFLED IN KEYS AS ZONERS QUIT

The Monroe County Zoning Board did not meet this week. It's tough to get a quorum when four of five members resign.

Even in the Ringling Brothers atmosphere of Keys politics, this act of protest was astounding. It came at a crucial time, as Monroe County finally gets down to the business of choosing a land-use plan that will govern its growth.

Those who quit the zoning board are hardly wild-eyed radicals—a real estate agent, an attorney, a League of Women Voters leader and a retired U.S. Secret Service agent. "They are people of the highest integrity," laments activist Dagny Johnson. "They will never have this kind of board again."

Publicly the ex–zoning board members aren't discussing why they quit; they want Gov. Bob Graham to appoint a special commission. Privately they are frustrated and disenchanted. They feel that the county commission has thwarted key zoning decisions and bent itself into pretzels to help developers skirt a countywide building moratorium.

Much of their ire is focused on County Attorney Lucien Proby, a former judge who has issued numerous opinions favorable to developers. Whenever Loophole Lucien seems muddled on zoning issues (which is often), he turns for advice to his old pal Fred Tittle, a lawyer who represents most major developers.

Call them old-fashioned, but the zoning board members didn't think it was kosher to have their procedures co-authored by the developers' lawyer. But what else is new?—this is the Keys, after all.

Some things have changed for the better. The revamped planning department shows signs of actual competence, even expertise. Once upon a time its inspectors could not accurately count the number of floors in a given building.

There is optimism, too, because conservationists have never had stronger voices on the county commission than John Stormont and Alison Fahrer, though Fahrer has alienated some of her old allies by supporting the building of a Kmart plaza in Key Largo.

Emotions run so strong on each side of the development issue that compromise is often seen as treason. This attitude is unfortunate but understandable, given the shameful blight evident along U.S. 1.

If you don't live in a community, it's much easier to carve it up and divvy it out to your pals. Key West commissioners have been doing this to the rest of Monroe County for decades. This is why the state intervened, why there now is a building moratorium, and why the proposed county land-use plan is so controversial.

Tonight, in Plantation Key, the county commission meets to consider approval of this complicated new plan.

Among its features are allowances for "destination resorts"—a benign euphemism for big fat condo projects. At 20 to 30 units per acre, several of these elephants are slated for the Marathon area, including one at the pristine Crane Point Hammock.

If you've driven past Vaca Cut lately, you can appreciate the absurdity of these schemes. Years of mindless zoning have given Marathon the tackiest strip of highway in the islands. As a "destination resort" it has all the aesthetics of Bakersfield, though the fishing is better.

It's amazing. After years of failures, developers still hallucinate about making a killing in the Keys. Heading south, you see one turkey project after another that has changed hands, changed names, changed paint, changed prices, and changed concepts.

No one ever says the obvious: that the future of Monroe County is not condo clusters because the market isn't there. Most developers and bankers don't want to hear this because it pains them. Sensible, low-density residential projects are not the fast-money machines they like to ride.

Regardless of what happens to the land-use plan, the planning process could be changed critically by this week's mass resignation. In the Keys, voices of reason are as precious as the land and water itself.

June 24, 1987

BUILDERS' CLOUT WINNING WAR ON LAND RUSH

Get ready for the big West Dade land grab.

It happens Thursday at the Metro Commission meeting, and all the heavy hitters will be sitting up front—developers, landowners, their lawyers and lobbyists. You might not know all their names, but the county commissioners certainly do.

Two years ago, they obediently approved 15 of 19 changes to the master plan, and thus sent a ringing message to development interests across the county: Come be our pals. We'll treat you right. Forget zoning, forget the master plan, we'll work things out.

And they have. Most recently the commission has been busy rezoning West Kendall to make way for more sprawling shopping malls. Just what they need out there, too.

How do such things happen? Easily, for the developer who hires Stephen Ross or Dusty Melton as his lobbyist. And for his lawyer: Bob Traurig or Tom Carlos, who has become the new Yoda-figure—on zoning matters the commissioners seem in awe of his wisdom, and vote accordingly.

Thursday promises another display of naked political power. In most cases the deciding factor won't be the will of the voters, but the developers' campaign money and the clout it buys.

The commission meeting itself is mostly a formality, since the lobbyists will have already lined up the necessary votes. The commissioners will make a brief show of listening to opponents of the land rush, but that's about all.

The big-shot developers need the commissioners because they need the rules changed. They want the master plan hacked up to open western tracts for new industrial and residential projects. This year there are 30 requests for amendments to the master development plan. Some are not so bad, and some are preposterous.

The magic number on many of these applications is six homes per acre, which is ideal for people who don't like to mow their lawns. One batch of proposed subdivisions off the Tamiami Trail would cram 9,564 new houses between Southwest 137th and 157th avenues. Sounds like paradise, doesn't it?

Developers contend that building more homes (up to 45,000, under this year's requests) keeps prices down so that average folks can afford to move in. Planners say this isn't what really happens.

In fact, lots of land already zoned for development remains untouched, and there's a good reason: The need hasn't caught up.

For all county residents much is at stake here—police and fire protection, schools, sewage, transportation and, most significant, the quality of our drinking water. All could be severely impaired by slapdash growth and over-building.

Some of the land being lusted after is located in environmentally sensitive wetlands, such as the Bird Road–Everglades Basin. A lonely voice of sanity, the county's planning department has strongly recommended against bulldozing these areas, which feed the Biscayne Aquifer.

"In my opinion it makes no sense to add more land in the wetlands," says Planning Director Reginald Walters.

The U.S. Army Corps of Engineers recently blocked construction of a school in the Bird Road basin until environmental impact studies can be completed, and it is likely that the agency would do the same to other projects.

"It's time to call a temporary halt until we find out what we're doing, instead of blazing ahead to say development at any cost," Walters says. "That's not responsible local government."

An example of the blind voracity is the push to open two square miles of South Dade agricultural lands to residential development—this, despite county studies that show a 19-year supply of single-family homes already exists in the area.

The planning department has recommended that the commission unconditionally deny 20 of the 30 requests pending this week, but don't hold your breath.

This particular commission doesn't pay much attention to the advice of its planners. After all, what do they know?—they're only the experts.

March 25, 1988

COMMISSION: ZONING LAW IS REVOLTING DEVELOPMENT

A tragedy of Vesuvian proportions has struck county government: no more shopping centers in unincorporated Dade.

I know what you're thinking: What did we do to deserve this? How could it happen here?

It's a grim saga indeed. A state appellate court recently ruled that the County Commission can't rezone land for commercial use without approval from the people who live in that neighborhood.

Whoever heard of such a radical notion—allowing mere citizens to decide if they need a handsome new Kmart across the street?

Traditionally, the county has merrily ignored its "neighborhood area studies" and butchered the master development plan on a whim. Take away this power, and you take away the commissioners' ability to pay back the developers for all those juicy campaign contributions.

No wonder they're apoplectic. Since the day the new court ruling was explained by the county attorney, paramedics have hovered near the commission chambers, ready to rush in and give CPR if necessary.

"A disaster for our community," moaned Commissioner Jorge Valdes, who darkly compared the moment to the day after a nuclear holocaust.

"A hammerlock," lamented Commissioner Harvey Ruvin.

Even Mayor Steve Clark attempted a denunciation: "We're trying to do our best to circumvent the albatross that's killing us here." Well said, Mr. Mayor.

The specter of no more slapdash shopping malls also sent high-priced zoning lawyers into spasms of hyperbole. "This community comes to a screeching halt as of today," intoned Stan Price.

Lawyer Alan Gold: "We are put in the very definite position of not being able to do our communitywide business . . ."

Lawyer Al Cardenas: "This will bring an economic crisis to the county."

And zoning czar Robert Traurig, whose ring all county commissioners must kiss, added to the pall with these remarks: "Obviously there is a great chagrin that the normal processes have been thwarted by this."

The normal process being to ignore the neighbors and throw up a cheesy-looking mall wherever your clients want. This is what made South Florida what it is today, the shopping-center center of the free world.

And though you won't find anybody putting up a Zippo Mart or a Mr. Bagel in Bob Traurig's ritzy waterfront neighborhood, he and his lawyer colleagues are defending an important principle: the rights of all property owners to triple their worth by fiddling with the zoning laws.

In fact, the county's master land-use plan had been carefully designed to allow the maximum abuse with the minimum of public input. This system proved ideal for both developers and commissioners, who cling together like lovebugs at election time.

Disaster came in the form of a lawyer named John Fletcher and pesky homeowner groups in Kendall and Southwest Dade. These uppity folks decided they'd had plenty of commercial development in their neighborhoods, and sued to make the county quit.

For some reason, the Third District Court of Appeal sided with these lowly taxpayers—thus temporarily thwarting the commission's dream that every West Dade family will someday have its own personal shopping mall.

So, because a few hundred people happen to like ranches and farms more than Laundromats and pizzerias, progress in Dade County has come to a grinding halt.

The gloom is palpable. Despair is in the eyes of everyone you meet on the street, and on the faces of the little children. What do we tell them when they ask, "Daddy, when is that beautiful new strip mall going to be built next to the elementary school?"

We tell them the truth, that the fight is never over and the dream is never dead; that as long as we have courageous leaders like Steve Clark, we'll surely find a way to circumvent this albatross.

June 10, 1988

COMMISSION PROVES IT'S HOPELESSLY ZONED OUT

Here's what bad government does to good ideas:

Metro Commissioner Harvey Ruvin had this radical notion that he and the other commissioners ought to find out who really owns a property before granting lucrative zoning variances.

The advantage would be avoiding gross embarrassments such as then–County Manager Sergio Pereira's secret connection to property that had once come before the commission for rezoning.

In the fallout, Ruvin had sought a stricter law requiring trusts, corporations and partnerships that want zoning variances to publicly identify their owners. The measure would also require the disclosure of anyone who had contracted to buy the land once it was rezoned.

All Ruvin wanted to know was: Who benefits? Who's really behind XYZ Corp.? Who's waiting to grab the land once the zoning gets changed? If you think these are sensible questions, think again.

The Greater Miami Chamber of Commerce, bastion of image-polishers, declared war on the disclosure ordinance. The chamber said it would have a "chilling effect" on foreign investors.

What kind of high-class investors are they looking for—the kind who're afraid to have their names attached to a land transaction? Just what we need: an open invitation to bury your dirty dollars in Dade County real estate. We don't care how you got it or who you are.

An example: Last December, the U.S government seized about $20 million of South Florida property—ranches, apartment buildings, condos—

owned by members of the Colombian cocaine underworld. These gentlemen operated namelessly behind dummy corporations, never once listing "Medellin Cartel" on the deeds.

Maybe the chamber feels we don't have enough of these sleazeballs pulling deals around here. God forbid that we should make it tougher for them by requiring that they actually put down their real names!

Then there's the Disney argument, a classic. During the debate over zoning disclosure, a real estate man took the microphone and declared: "Gentlemen, if this ordinance was in Orange County as proposed, we would have no Disney World."

Sounds pretty dramatic. Too bad it's malarkey.

The legendary secrecy with which the Disney interests purchased Central Florida land back in the mid-1960s had nothing to do with variances or rezoning. The property—marshes and cattle land—was acquired quietly to avoid huge price hikes by landowners.

Disney's people never went to Orange County and asked to put up a Kmart or a condo. They didn't have to; the Legislature gave them self-rule over all development on the property.

Nothing in Ruvin's proposal affects the simple purchase of property or discourages legitimate investors. None of the principals would become known until they approached the county for a zoning variance.

There's a good reason for this. Zoning is a matter of important public concern. Changes affect traffic and commerce, police protection and utilities. It can alter the whole face of a neighborhood.

And the people who live there have a right to know who stands to gain from the vote—whether it's a county employee with hidden shares, a Fortune 500 conglomerate or a Bolivian coffee baron.

Unfortunately, secrecy has served the system too sweetly. Monkeying around with zoning is the biggest money game in town, and all kinds of important people are up to their armpits in it. Most of the time they would rather you didn't know their names—and the county commissioners are absolutely delighted not to ask. That's what got them into trouble on Pereira.

It's a smoke screen to say Ruvin's ordinance would have scared off foreign investors. What it really would have done is lay bare the connections between those who vote and those who profit, and expose the zoning process for the incestuous racket that it is.

Naturally, the County Commission voted it down.

August 18, 1989

DADE TO GET ANOTHER STRIP OF URBAN STRESS

The quest to make suburban Dade County the most unsightly, congested hellhole on the continent got a small but significant boost recently.

On July 27, the Metro Commission approved a zoning change that will allow a strip shopping center to be built at the corner of Southwest 97th Avenue and Miller Drive.

The vote didn't even make the local section of this paper, probably because it's a relatively small tract (10 acres), and also because the Metro Commission caves in so regularly that the event no longer qualifies as news.

Homeowners in the area had presented a petition with 1,853 signatures protesting the project. They said they needed another shopping center like they needed a nuclear dump.

But the developer had hired a Big Cheese Zoning Lawyer named Tom Carlos. Carlos is on a first-wink basis with the commissioners, and he persuaded them that a strip shopping center is exactly what's needed on Miller Drive, no matter what the residents say.

The 5–2 vote was pathetically easy to call. Mayor Steve Clark endorsed the project, along with Commissioners Carey, Gersten, Schreiber and Valdes. Only Larry Hawkins and Charles Dusseau took the side of the homeowners.

Carmela Pinto McIntire was so angry that she wrote a letter to the Metro Commission. It is a literate and incisive commentary, so there is scant hope that the commissioners could understand it, or appreciate the damage they've done:

"I travel Miller Road daily to get to my job at FIU; I shop frequently at all the businesses already available to me. I've long rejoiced that compared to Bird Road and Sunset, Miller is relatively free of congestion; it's even possible to see some green space.

"But no more. It will be solid shopping centers from 102 Avenue (with more at 107 Avenue; did the commission check any maps?) to 92nd Avenue. Who needs it? Once again Metro Commission has shown that all it's interested in is the picture of Miami as developers see it. Money! Shops!"

McIntire is no screeching bug-eyed radical. She is an English professor at Florida International University and the mother of a young daughter. She says, "I never lived in a place where you could see this happening before your eyes."

She wrote to the commission: "Multiply this zoning change by five or six, and you can easily see why county residents, including me, are so utterly cynical about living here. In the scheme of county government, we matter least. Our quality of life erodes daily; our exposure to stress, in the form of traffic congestion, crowds and urban ugliness, increases tenfold."

Obviously McIntire has done some driving in Southwest Dade. As she passed shopping center after shopping center (noting all the vacancy signs) she must have wondered why in the world we need any more of these tacky eyesores.

This is a question that the Metro commissioners can't answer. Most have only recently discovered the depth of voter fury on the issue of overdevelopment. What precious little courage the commissioners have managed to summon, they save for bigger and more controversial projects.

In the meantime, folks such as Carmela McIntire watch nice neighborhoods clot up with U-Tote-Ems and lube shops and coin laundries, and they start looking for a new place to live.

To the commission she wrote: "I've lived in Dade County eight years and watched the dubious effects of growth, saddened by much of it. . . . My family and I would like to leave, and the disappearance of any chance for a decent urban life is the main reason.

"I love Dade's ethnic diversity; my husband and I have both lived abroad, we both speak Spanish, and we will miss the cultural mix. But I won't miss the traffic snarls, the ugliness of one strip shopping center after another, and people who are so angry and afraid of urban life that they carry guns in their cars."

Everything she says is true. Now, if you really want to be sick, think about the future.

And think about who's in charge now.

January 21, 1993

CHANGE LOOMS FOR METRO'S POWER ZONE

The rabid scramble for Dade's 13 new commission seats has begun. For the next two months, an assortment of lightweights, grifters, slackers and kooks likely will enter the campaign.

They'll be joined by a precious handful of bright, decent, honest candidates who are running for the right reasons.

It could be a while before we know if the expanded, resectioned Metro Commission is an improvement over the Gong Show that now passes for county government. In the meantime, another issue facing Dade residents could shake up the back-room power structure even more radically than the redistricting.

Soon voters will have the chance to strip the Metro Commission of its zoning authority. This is your basic chain saw vasectomy—indelicate but effective.

Zoning is political power in Florida. It's the clout that puts an all-night liquor store in a quiet subdivision. Or turns farmlands into warehouses. Or puts a flea market next to a cemetery.

The "variance" is a grand old tradition. In return for caving in to lobbyists, politicians are rewarded with juicy campaign donations. Sometimes they're rewarded in other ways, too. Former Hialeah Mayor Raul Martinez is facing prison for bartering zoning favors.

The Metro Commission is in charge of zoning for unincorporated Dade, which explains why unincorporated Dade is the tacky, congested, ramshackle mess that it is. Flagler, Bird Road, Kendall Drive—take your pick of nightmares.

A coalition of citizen groups called Protect Our Communities says the county can no longer be trusted with zoning decisions. This is like saying Hannibal Lechter can no longer be trusted with the Crock-Pot.

One would think the damage is already done; every Dade intersection seems to have the obligatory half-empty strip mall. By air, though, one can see lots of raw acreage still ripe for exploitation.

The homeowners' coalition wants to give all future zoning decisions to eight regional boards, comprised of locally elected members. As you might imagine, builders and developers aren't ecstatic about the idea. Neighborhood representatives are likely to be more sympathetic to the wishes of residents, and less susceptible to political arm-twisting.

Originally, Metro commissioners agreed to put the zoning reform amendment on the ballot. Then they chickened out. The backlash was so hot that Protect Our Communities quickly collected nearly 100,000 signatures. Now the commission has no choice but to let the public vote, possibly as soon as March.

The strongest support for zoning autonomy comes from long-suffering Kendall and Coconut Grove, which has been threatening to secede from the city of Miami. (The POC amendment makes it easier for neighborhoods with 5,000 or more residents to form their own city.)

Voters in fast-growing areas have become disgusted by zoning abuse. Several current Metro commissioners won election as "reform" candidates, ousting old-timers who were painted as pawns of the special interests. But as time has passed, it's become clear that developers, lobbyists and their lawyers still have an iron grip on the system.

Arguments against local boards raise some valid concerns. Neighborhood goals sometimes clash with those of the county as a whole; when Dade needs a new landfill or a prison, which region will nobly volunteer to take it? Probably none.

As for the issue of integrity, there's no guarantee that locally elected boards will be more pure or selfless than the County Commission. Whether they'd do a better job of zoning is unknown. It's hard to imagine how they could possibly do worse.

May 7, 1995

HOMEOWNERS LEAST PROTECTED UNDER NEW LAW

The so-called "property rights bill" passed by the Legislature is really the Land Speculator's Relief Act.

By weakening local control over zoning and planning, the law will make it harder for homeowners to shape and preserve their neighborhoods.

Most Florida municipalities need no additional incentives to placate developers and wealthy landholders. This masterfully vague law, now on its way to Gov. Chiles' desk, gives politicians a splendid new excuse.

Landowners who believe they are "inordinately burdened" by new government regulations may seek compensation. Translation: Any rezoning that lowers a property value can result in a lawsuit. Taxpayers will bear the cost.

Many cities and counties haven't got the stomach, or the budget, for a court battle with developers. It's easier to back off and let them build that mall or high-rise or parking garage, even if the people don't want it.

The "property rights" propaganda says government should get off the little guy's back. Yet it wasn't the little guys who hired all those lobbyists and lawyers in Tallahassee; it was big business—the same forces pushing similar legislation in Congress.

Landowners whose property is substantially reduced in value by the act of a government agency deserve fair compensation—and they can usually get it, under current laws.

To be sure, there are horror stories about small landowners being crushed by arcane regulations. Though relatively rare, these incidents have been portrayed as everyday atrocities.

In truth, the new law wasn't written to prevent ordinary citizens from being screwed. It was written to intimidate government from doing its job.

Cities historically have had the right to make, change and enforce zoning. That's why you don't often see a porno theater next to a kindergarten.

Similarly, local governments have always passed land-use rules to answer residents' concerns about air pollution, water quality, traffic and other growth-related problems. The school shortage in West Dade is prime evidence of the need for smart, courageous planning.

Clearly the property-rights bill could have a chilling effect. Imagine the cost to the public of litigating routine zoning and land-use decisions. Imagine the fresh clutter on the court dockets.

Ironically, politicians have seldom been shy about rezoning to benefit developers, industry or agribusiness. Yet these interests still complain, sometimes justly, of bureaucratic meddling.

A key target of the property-rights movement is environmental regulation that blocks or restricts land use. Out West the bugaboo is the spotted owl; in Florida it's the panther or the Key deer—extreme and special cases, each one.

Writing in the *New York Times,* Dan Gordon of Philadelphia decries the notion "that landowners have the right to do whatever they want with their property regardless of the impact on others."

He predicts homeowners will be the real victims of property-rights legislation, because they'll lose control of their neighborhoods. Gordon's opinion is noteworthy because he's a developer.

You'd think that a "property rights" law would hold the rights of homeowners above those of speculators. Not this law.

A community might decide it has enough shopping plazas, or miniwarehouses, or boatyards—but it won't matter if its elected officials are too afraid of lawsuits to act.

Ask yourself if your house would be worth more, or less, with a Kmart next door, a Chevy dealership down the block and an RV park across the street.

Now whose rights are being trampled—and what's fair compensation for the "inordinate" burden of watching your neighborhood crumble?

July 13, 1995

COURT ZONES OUT THE REAL EXPERTS—RESIDENTS

Kendall needs malls like a toad needs more warts, but plans roll ahead for two new mammoth retail complexes near the Dadeland Mall.

A longtime resident of the neighborhood wrote to share his reaction, upon learning of the projects: "It made me sick to my stomach. . . . Don't we have enough all along South Dixie Highway and on Kendall Drive?"

That kind of frustration roils from one end of Dade to the other. It's a big reason why some neighborhoods want to incorporate as cities, and break away from a county government seen as unresponsive.

People are sick of getting malled, and sick of being rebuffed from the planning process. Though homeowner groups have gained clout and savvy in recent years, they're still often out-muscled by politically connected developers.

And the zoning game, which has always been tilted in favor of monied interests, recently got more lopsided.

Last month, an appeals court upheld a ruling that Metro was wrong to deny rezoning for a 360-apartment complex called Devon Lakes, slated for 20 acres near the turnpike in West Dade. According to the judges, commissioners shouldn't have given weight to objections from a neighborhood activist, because he wasn't an "expert" on zoning.

The witness in question was Morgan Levy, head of the West Dade Federation of Homeowner Associations. Levy contended that, at 18 units per acre, the density of Devon Lakes was too high. Area residents feared it would degrade property values and create more traffic problems.

But, in a 2–1 vote, the Third District Court of Appeal said Levy wasn't qualified to testify on "zoning matters." The decision could affect anyone who wants to get involved in his or her neighborhood's planning.

If all zoning hearings were restricted to "expert witnesses," those folks most affected by a proposed high-rise or shopping mall or auto dealership might not be allowed to give testimony.

Instead, they'd be forced to hire top-gun experts to compete against those retained by the developers. Few grassroots civic groups can afford to do that.

Attorneys for developers say the court's decision isn't radical. They say it simply bolsters earlier rulings that "quasi-judicial" proceedings ought to revolve on facts and law, not emotions.

Zoning hearings can get hot. Both sides are capable of making wildly exaggerated claims. Part of a county commission's job is to winnow the debate. In his dissenting opinion on Devon Lakes, Appellate Judge Gerald D. Cope said: "The citizen testimony in this case was fact-based, and perfectly proper."

It doesn't require a doctorate in urban planning to know a neighborhood changes when you shoehorn 360 new apartments on 20 acres. So, who rates as an "expert" on zoning? The court offers little guidance.

A commuter who spends hours sitting in traffic each day would seem superbly qualified to testify about worsening gridlock. Likewise, a parent whose kids are crammed into overcrowded classrooms would seem a very credible witness on the issue of neighborhood growth.

Land-use attorneys say homeowners' testimony probably won't be excluded from zoning hearings as long as they present facts and observations—

and don't draw conclusions. In other words, be prepared to document your concerns. (I would recommend, as Exhibit A, a videotaped tour of Kendall Drive. No narration would be necessary.)

Actually, it's still demanding too much. People are entitled to speak out about their neighborhood's future, and they should be able to do so without "expert" credentials. Living there makes them the experts.

April 25, 1996

OFFICIALS STAR IN OWN VERSION OF PRICE IS RIGHT

The secret videotapes from the aborted corruption investigation into Dade zoning practices offered no surprises, only a stark confirmation:

The system in 1989 was every bit as rotten as you thought. And if you think it's different today, you're right: It's worse.

True, the transaction of vote selling probably was simpler a few years ago. It had to be, in order for a dunce like Jorge "No Visible Means of Support" Valdes to grasp it.

Then a county commissioner, Valdes had a starring role in the undercover tapes compiled by the Florida Department of Law Enforcement. At one point he garrulously expounded on his policy of taking cash only "under the table" so there's no trace.

(Confronted with his own words, Valdes now claims he was merely acting.)

Valdes' chief role on the Metro Commission was to do whatever the Latin Builders Association told him to do. On zoning votes, he and Steve Clark were the LBA's most loyal toadies.

It therefore was entirely logical for then-LBA Executive Director Jorge Abril to serve as the liaison between developers seeking favors and commissioners who gave them.

The tone of Abril's taped discussions about bribing county politicians is straightforward and matter-of-fact. That an LBA big shot was immersed in such slime isn't earthshaking news to anyone who follows local politics.

Nor is the taped performance of zoning lawyer Tom Carlos, casually explaining how his clients must be prepared to "work" the Metro Commission.

Add to this luminous cast Mr. Pablo Valdes, a home builder once spotlighted on the cover of the LBA's magazine. That was before it became known Pablo bankrolled his developments with laundered cocaine money.

It was he who, in exchange for leniency, agreed to help authorities blow the lid off Dade zoning corruption.

The best part? While an informant, Pablo was allowed to continue build-ing houses in Hialeah Gardens. The source of his capital, and his scummy past, were kept secret from creditors, colleagues and customers, some of whom found their lots flooded after it rained.

Questions about Pablo's character, and bickering among law-enforcement agencies, eventually doomed the 1989 bribery probe. It's a shame because prosecutors lost a chance to purge the county of some congenital crooks, and to save the master land-use plan from becoming a sham.

Over the years, corrupt zoning in South Florida has ruined neighbor-hoods, paralyzed traffic and nearly exploded the school systems. Locking up a few thieving politicians might have scared the others into behaving, at least for a while.

Since the Pablo Valdes case fell apart, little has changed at the Metro Com-mission except a few of the names.

Steve Clark mercifully departed to become mayor of Miami, while Jorge Valdes was booted out of office by disgusted voters. But among new commis-sioners the LBA has found trusty lapdogs in Bruce Kaplan, Natacha Millan and others.

The group has lost none of its clout. Exhibit A: Metro's recent giveaway of the Homestead air base development rights to the HABDI group, led by LBA President Carlos Herrera.

(Imagine the pang of nostalgia felt by ex-Commissioner Valdes when that rich Homestead deal went down, and he wasn't there to vote on it.)

With undeveloped land vanishing fast under concrete, the stakes are even higher now than in 1989. Every zoning vote is more valuable, and lawbreak-ers on both sides know it.

Ask any honest developer if things have gotten better in Dade County. The answer, wedged between expletives, is an emphatic no.

11

WHAT HAVE THEY
BEEN SMOKING?

February 19, 1986

MEALYMOUTHING SMOKING PERILS JUST WON'T DO

If you've picked up a pack of cigarettes lately, you might have noticed an important change in the Surgeon General's warning.

Instead of the familiar refrain that smoking is dangerous to your health, each pack now carries one of four new labels, to be rotated every several months.

The lamest of these: "SURGEON GENERAL'S WARNING: Cigarette Smoke Contains Carbon Monoxide."

This is supposed to scare the daylights out of smokers, particularly young smokers, but the sad truth is that many consumers don't know exactly what carbon monoxide is, or what it does. A more graphic and effective label would be: "WARNING: Smoking a Cigarette is like wrapping your lips around the tailpipe of a Trailways bus."

Unfortunately, nothing so blunt will ever come out of Congress, which remains politically enslaved to the poison peddlers at the Tobacco Institute.

The health industry began to push for tougher cigarette warning labels in 1982 when it became clear that the old one had lost its impact. "People didn't pay any attention to it whatsoever," said Matt Myer of the national Coalition on Smoking or Health.

Experts said detailed medical warnings would be more effective, but the last thing cigarette makers wanted to see on their product was names of actual diseases. Very bad PR.

A compromise was reached in Congress. The bad news is that the word *dangerous* no longer appears anywhere on cigarette packs. The good news is, the new labels leave no doubt what happens when you light up:

- "Smoking Causes Lung Cancer, Heart Disease, Emphysema, and May Complicate Pregnancy."
- "Quitting Smoking Now Greatly Reduces Serious Risk to Your Health."
- "Smoking by Pregnant Women May Result in Fetal Injury, Premature Birth, and Low Birth Weight."

While the wording certainly is specific, it's also dull and clinical—no match for splashy billboards showing lithe young tennis players sucking down a Vantage after three grueling sets.

Matt Myer, who helped write the new warnings, said they aren't as strong as he would have liked, but are the best "within the realm of what is politically possible."

Whether they work or not is another matter. Studies show that few of America's 55 million smokers bother to read the warning labels. The hard-core nicotine freak is no different from any drug addict—the carton could feature a picture of a hollow human skull, a Marlboro stuck in its mandibles, and it still wouldn't do any good.

Every adult has a right to lock himself in a room and privately pollute his body with carcinogens. The question is, should government help?

Taxpayers shell out millions in price supports to tobacco growers at a time when that industry, according to *Forbes* magazine, produces the second highest return-on-equity of any in the country. There's something morally despicable about paying farmers to grow a product that puts one thousand Americans into coffins every day.

It is equally despicable how magazines and newspapers (including this one) editorialize so piously against the evils of cocaine and marijuana, yet gladly accept millions to advertise cigarettes—which kill roughly 100 times more people than all illegal drugs combined.

While college students and adult men are smoking less, other demographic groups are puffing more. The best ways to curb this would be a mass education program and a ban on all cigarette advertising—distant fantasies as long as Jesse Helms is alive.

So, for now, the chief weapon against Big Tobacco's $2 billion advertising orgy is that tiny label on each pack of cigarettes.

Too bad it can't simply say: "WARNING—Cigarette smoking is a lethal addiction that turns your lungs into asphalt, your arteries into pasta and your spouse into a beneficiary."

That's what it ought to say, but don't hold your breath. Assuming you still can.

February 19, 1990

TOBACCO FIRMS PEDDLE POISON TO NEW MARKET

The R. J. Reynolds Tobacco Co., one of the world's largest peddlers of killer narcotics, is vigorously denying that it's marketing a new brand of cigarettes toward young, white women with no college education.

Documents leaked to the *Washington Post* indicate that Reynolds is specifically aiming "Dakota" cigarettes at 18- to 24-year-old white females—the only demographic segment in the United States that's smoking more, and not less.

As are so many marketing schemes, this one is unabashedly crass. It is code-named "Project V.F."—with the initials standing for "virile female." Translation: Potential new smoker.

What exactly is a virile female? Can she arm-wrestle? Field-strip a Harley Davidson while blindfolded? Spit wads of Red Man for both distance and accuracy?

The Chicago firm that's promoting Dakota cigarettes paints the typical "virile female" in more passive, if not equally condescending, hues.

According to the strategy report, she has no education beyond high school. She likes jeans and sweaters and all-male music groups.

Her favorite TV personalities are Roseanne Barr and soap opera "bitches" such as Joan Collins. Her spare time is spent "cruising" and partying.

Her dream date is going to a hot-rod show or a "tractor pull."

If you fall into the virile-female category, the tobacco companies want your business. Their market research says these young women are a gold mine.

More of them are taking up smoking in spite of the highly publicized health threats. Tragically, it's this same group that faces the gravest medical risks associated with tobacco use—cancers and cardiovascular disease.

Reynolds officials won't admit that Dakotas will rely on the "V.F." marketing strategy. They say they're simply trying to compete with Marlboro, currently the brand of choice among young adult women.

You can understand the company's fervor. In these fitness-conscious times it's not easy selling a product that's both poisonous and addictive. Millions of Americans have struggled to quit smoking, and those who haven't must be wooed ardently.

The folks who promote tobacco now concentrate on blue-collar workers, young adults and minorities. A few weeks ago, Reynolds sheepishly canceled plans to test-market another new cigarette. This one, aimed at blacks, was stupidly called "Uptown"—which is only slightly less demeaning than if they'd named it "Hey Bro!"

Imagine: Squads of bright young advertising people getting paid big bucks to peddle something they know is fatal to the public. What's even more contemptible is aiming at customers in specific high-risk groups, such as minorities and women.

Think of the greedy little Madison Avenue yuppies who came up with the idea for "Uptown" cigarettes—knowing that blacks are especially vulnerable to high blood pressure, and that smoking can dangerously worsen that condition.

You've got to wonder what the folks at R. J. Reynolds and Philip Morris tell their kids when they go home at night. Are they actually proud of what they do? In a single year they kill and cripple hundreds of thousands more people than the most vicious international drug rings. Mortality-wise, cocaine is practically therapeutic compared with cigarettes.

Still, the U.S. tobacco cartel is dedicated (with the help of our government) to saturating foreign countries with this narcotic. Meanwhile, at home it has spent billions (with the help of tax breaks) in an unrelenting campaign to make nicotine addicts out of America's young people.

A little puffery is necessary; nobody's going to buy a pack of "Wheeze" brand cigarettes, so you go for a softer, more pastoral name like "Dakota."

Next time you're at a tractor pull, offer one to your favorite virile female. Maybe she'll tell you to blow it out your John Deere.

June 27, 1993

BIG TOBACCO'S MEDICAL ADVICE IS LAUGHABLE

America's worst drug pushers are getting desperate. They're suing the Environmental Protection Agency.

Philip Morris USA, R. J. Reynolds Tobacco Co. and other cigarette makers are trying to discredit an EPA report that links passive tobacco smoke to lung cancer. The industry says that the EPA study has accelerated the nationwide campaign to ban smoking in places open to the public.

Cigarette peddlers claim the EPA's conclusions about passive smoke are based on faulty science. Considering the source, the criticism is laughable. Getting a medical lecture from the tobacco industry is like getting tax advice from Willie Nelson.

It's been 29 years since the Surgeon General determined that cigarettes cause cancer, but the tobacco pushers still refuse to admit the connection. What every major health organization accepts as irrefutable medical fact, the cigarette makers absurdly dismiss as coincidence.

But they haven't banded together and sued the U.S. government, until now. Fear has set in because new no-smoking laws are being enacted across the country. Many cities, such as Coral Gables and Lauderdale Lakes, recently banned smoking in city buildings. Other ordinances go even farther.

Last week Los Angeles outlawed smoking in all restaurants except bars, nightclubs and outdoor cafes. The controversial move faces a legislative challenge, but the vote still sent a shock down the spine of the tobacco lobby.

True, the industry isn't exactly wheezing, financially. While smoking is declining overall in the United States, cigarette makers are successfully luring new addicts, particularly young women. Meanwhile, exports of tobacco products are booming, as Uncle Sam promotes homegrown toxins abroad.

But the issue of passive smoke is a threat to the cigarette industry. It's easy to defend the right of a consumer who willfully chooses to poison himself. It's not so easy to defend the poisoning of those around him, including children.

The Centers for Disease Control recently took blood serum from 800 Americans, aged 4 to 91. Every single person—nonsmokers included—had nicotine in their system. According to the EPA, at least 3,000 nonsmokers die annually as a result of breathing other people's fumes.

The agency concluded that secondhand smoke is a carcinogen, like asbestos. That ignited Big Tobacco's legal counterattack. What a country. Not only are our farmers subsidized for growing a lethal crop, they can use the money to sue the very government that's subsidizing them!

Tobacco companies face a hard task, trying to convince a court that secondhand smoke is harmless. The wisp off the end of a lit Camel is the same noxious gas that eventually kills the smoker. (I suppose exhaled smoke isn't quite as deadly, having been once-filtered through somebody else's lung tissue.)

EPA chief Carol Browner says the agency stands firmly behind its medical findings and will fight the tobacco lawsuit. In the meantime, other cities might follow Los Angeles' example by proposing tougher laws to rid the air of passive smoke.

If it comes down to a battle between good health and big money, bet on the big money. Cigarette makers have millions to spread around, and politicians aren't the only ones who take it. Every newspaper and magazine I've ever worked for has published cigarette advertising, and gladly cashed the checks.

Cigarettes kill many times more people than cocaine and heroin combined, but that's OK because the stuff is legal. If Pablo Escobar had been born here instead of Colombia, he wouldn't be a fugitive today. He'd be on the board of R. J. Reynolds.

Because in America, money doesn't just talk. It coughs.

April 17, 1994

THE FDA SHOULD CONTROL ADDICTIVE DRUG—NICOTINE

The nation's worst drug pushers got hauled in front of Congress last week. They wore expensive suits, not handcuffs. And they came in fear of the FDA, not the DEA.

Bosses of seven major tobacco companies went before a House subcommittee and swore that the dope they sell isn't really addictive. They said cigarettes are merely a casual indulgence, like soft drinks or ice cream.

Listen to William Campbell, president of Philip Morris: "I have a common-sense definition of addiction. I'm a smoker and I'm not a drug addict."

Spoken like a true junkie. Yeah, I shoot a little smack. But I'm not hooked! It's called denial.

Practically everyone who smokes knows that nicotine can be powerfully addictive. Now, finally, the FDA is considering regulating cigarettes the same way it regulates prescription drugs.

Since nicotine has few medical uses, the tobacco industry would be shut down if the FDA does its job. No wonder the cartel kingpins are apoplectic.

They trooped to Capitol Hill in a grimly unified front to argue their case. The core of their defense: We don't manipulate nicotine levels to ensure consumer addiction—besides, cigarettes aren't addictive, anyhow.

Then, for comic relief, the tobacco bosses stoically recited their long-standing position that no medical data conclusively links smoking to cancer, heart disease, lung disorders and birth defects. They actually stated this in public, under oath.

Under uncharacteristically tough questioning by House members, the cigarette pushers offered unassailable proof that their customers don't get hooked. How could smoking be addictive, they said, if 40 million people have quit since 1974?

With that kind of pretzel logic, you could argue that heroin, cocaine, Valium, speed and codeine aren't addictive, either. It's outlandish.

Addicts often kick their habits. It doesn't mean they weren't hooked; it means they got help. I've heard ex-junkies say that cigarettes were 10 times harder to quit than anything they ever smoked, snorted, swallowed or shot into their veins.

It's not that the corporate dope peddlers from Philip Morris and R. J. Reynolds are truly ignorant about the nature of biochemical addiction. They've got no choice but to say dumb things, because the truth is unspeakable.

When they boast of the 40 million who have quit smoking in the last 20 years, they don't mention the eight million estimated to have died of cigarette-caused illnesses during the same period, or the untold billions in health-care costs to taxpayers.

Last week, Gov. Lawton Chiles got the Florida Legislature to pass an important law enabling the state to sue tobacco companies. The goal is to reclaim millions of public dollars spent on medical treatment for poor people who smoke.

Instead of filing separate cases for each Medicaid recipient, the state can now pursue a broad claim against all cigarette makers, based on the total number of patients suffering from smoking-related diseases.

The bill, which passed unanimously, slipped by tobacco industry lobbyists late in the session. They're furious and will surely launch a counterattack.

Theoretically, the U.S. government doesn't need new legislation to crack down on nicotine. For the FDA, the issue isn't product liability or smokers' rights. It's a matter of science and law—how to regulate a known harmful substance.

If the job had been done 20 years ago, thousands who are dying today would still be healthy. If the job is done now, William Campbell himself might make it to a ripe old age.

Unless he finds a doctor to write him a prescription for Marlboros.

July 27, 1995

PUT THIS IN YOUR PIPE: CRACK AS NATIONAL DRUG

Imagine if George Washington had grown coca instead of tobacco.

Maybe crack would be legal, and cigarettes would be outlawed. The Cali cartel, not Marlboro or Virginia Slims, would sponsor NASCAR and women's tennis. Newt and Jesse would be raking in PAC money from cocaine combines, who'd be raking in lucrative farm subsidies.

History had a different plan. Tobacco became America's national drug, and today it kills many times more users than crack, heroin, speed and acid put together.

But its legal status is shaky. Earlier this month, the FDA (the D standing for "duh") decided nicotine should be regulated because it appears to be—brace yourselves—addictive.

Even more shocking: The tobacco industry has known for 40 years, and has been less than candid on the subject. Imagine that. Those rascals lied to us.

Documents leaked from cigarette giant Brown & Williamson, as well as Philip Morris, indicate the companies had more than an inkling that they were peddling hard drugs.

And in a confidential memo written in 1972 but recently slipped to the *New York Times,* an R. J. Reynolds researcher wrote that "tobacco products uniquely contain and deliver nicotine, a potent drug with a variety of physiological effects."

He went on to recommend that the firm promote its cigarettes not for their tar content or flavor, but as "attractive dosage forms of nicotine."

These documents are having a bombshell effect in Washington, the only place in the nation where there's still a debate about the lethality of cigarettes.

Except for a few marble-mouth congressmen from North Carolina and Virginia, the rest of America is keenly aware that cigarettes kill. That includes the millions of teens who've been lighting up in record numbers.

It's a choice people make—a dumb and self-destructive choice, but theirs nonetheless. The Tobacco Institute is right: As long as cigarettes are legal, people have a right to smoke.

However, now that the government admits nicotine is addictive, it has a regulatory obligation to do something. Nothing suggests that the FDA dares to be so bold as to ban it.

As a less ambitious strategy, the Clinton administration has set out to discredit the cigarette makers. It shouldn't be especially difficult. Nobody believes a word R. J. Reynolds says, anyway.

Nonetheless, the Justice Department has recently assembled a grand jury in New York to hear claims that the tobacco industry deceived regulators about the contents and known hazards of cigarettes.

A second grand jury will likely be convened to investigate whether seven top tobacco executives lied when they testified about nicotine before Congress. As if there was some doubt.

While indicting them for perjury might be appropriate, it's not necessarily worthwhile. The government's attentions would be more wisely focused on the deaths and diseases that cigarettes cause, not on the lame, predictable fibs of company big shots.

The FDA's most important job is to keep the public safe from harmful products, yet the most harmful of all will never be outlawed, because of greed and politics.

In one breath, Speaker Gingrich calls for the swift execution of dope pushers, and in the next he says the FDA has "lost its mind" for trying to regulate nicotine.

See, you can't mess with the national drug. The "dosage forms" are just too darn attractive.

The boys in Cali can only watch in amazement, and wish they'd gotten here first. If South American coca had beaten British tobacco to Virginia, today's young addicts might be digging Joe Llama instead of Joe Camel.

March 17, 1996

A GUTSY WOMAN JUST SAYS NO TO BIG TOBACCO

Until a few days ago, most people outside Hernando County didn't know who Ginny Brown-Waite was.

Now she's a hero. She clobbered Joe Camel in the chops.

In a perfect world, what the Republican lawmaker from Spring Hill did last Wednesday wouldn't have made headlines. In a perfect world, all elected officials would do what Brown-Waite did, on all important issues.

But it doesn't happen like that in Tallahassee, Washington, D.C., or anyplace else where laws are made. Public moments of courage and candor are rare.

Ginny Brown-Waite simply rose on the floor of the Senate and talked about right and wrong. If you saw it, you know how dramatic it was.

The Senate was on the verge of repealing a law that allows Florida to sue tobacco manufacturers to recoup the medical costs of treating smoking-related diseases. Senators tried to knock out the law last year, but were thwarted by Gov. Lawton Chiles' veto.

This time the veto was in danger of being overridden. In addition to showering lawmakers with campaign contributions, tobacco firms and their allies in the business community had hired 40 lobbyists—one for each state senator.

A razor-thin vote was expected, but the pro-tobacco forces were confident they had the edge. That's when Ginny Brown-Waite stood up and smoked 'em.

"I can't sit here any longer and play the tobacco game," she said.

It was impossible not to be moved when she spoke of losing her mother, father and sister—all smokers—to cancer. The political battle was over then, and everybody knew it.

Later, the governor said, "It was a great day for courage."

Yes, but people have reached the point where they're surprised—no, make that elated—by any show of spine in an elected official.

In this instance, that's what it took to defeat the tobacco companies and their hired toadies: just one person to stand up and talk about conscience, about losing sleep at night.

Here's the disappointing thing about what happened in Tallahassee: Each of those senators who was prepared to vote pro-tobacco could have taken the floor and made the same powerful point as Brown-Waite.

Like her, all of them have lost friends or relatives to smoking-related illnesses. The same is probably true for everyone reading this column. No lives are untouched by the tragic results of cigarette addiction.

That Brown-Waite stood so alone among her GOP colleagues is discouraging evidence that Big Tobacco's strategy is basically sound: Money smothers conscience almost every time.

It's true that the liability law wasn't a work of seamless perfection. Opponents voiced a legitimate concern that litigation could be expanded beyond cigarettes to other products and industries deemed harmful by the state.

To fix that loophole, the language was narrowed to focus on tobacco manufacturers. That should've turned the tide in the Senate, but it didn't—proving that, no matter what the opposing senators originally had claimed about their motives, their true loyalty was to Joe Camel.

Big Tobacco spent a fortune trying to win in Florida. Considering all the politicians who accepted campaign donations and all the lobbyists who pocketed big fat fees, it's hard to believe that Ginny Brown-Waite was the only one losing sleep.

But she's the one who did something about it, who spoke from her heart. "This is the vote that I am going to be proud of," she said.

She should. The rest of them ought to be sick with shame.

March 23, 1997

SHOUT IT: CIGARETTES ARE POISON!

In a symbolic surrender to candor, the Liggett company soon will begin using the term *addictive* in its promotions.

The overdue admission is part of a milestone legal settlement between the small tobacco firm and 22 states, including Florida.

Addictive is a strong word, and if there's one thing Big Tobacco doesn't want on its products, it's a strong public-health warning.

When first conceived, labels on cigarette packs and advertisements seemed like a bold initiative. But, over time, the warnings lost their novelty and some of their impact.

It doesn't help that they're purposely written to be dry and clinical. The effect is more of a whisper than a shout:

"WARNING: Smoking Causes Lung Cancer, Heart Disease, Emphysema, and May Complicate Pregnancy." Wow. Try not to get so worked up about it.

Or: "Quitting Smoking Now Greatly Reduces Serious Risks to Your Health." No kidding? Zzzzzzzz.

The labels are so deliberately dull that many chronic smokers, especially young ones, aren't taking notice.

Why mince words? "WARNING: NOT ONLY WILL YOU DIE FROM SMOKING, IT'LL BE A LONG, HORRIBLE, WITHERING DEATH."

For obvious reasons, tobacco companies are opposed to such blunt language. The feeling is shared in Congress, where (coincidentally) members of both parties accept large donations from cigarette makers.

That's not to say the government's warning labels couldn't be more eye-catching. In fact, they ought to be written with as much flair as the advertising pitch itself.

Macho Marlboros, for example, might carry this label:

"HEY, PARDNER, YOU THINK SADDLE SORES HURT. TRY A MALIGNANT STOMACH TUMOR!"

Or, for the menthol crowd: "REMEMBER ALL THAT VILE GREEN GUNK YOU COUGHED UP THIS MORNING? GUESS WHERE IT CAME FROM."

Granted, that's not the precise terminology preferred by doctors, but it is medically accurate. More upscale smokers, the Silk Cut bunch, might finally become alarmed if they were told:

"SMOKE THIS CRAP IF YOU WANT YOUR TEETH TO TURN BROWN AND YOUR BREATH TO STINK LIKE A DUMPSTER. ANOTHER BONUS: TONGUE LESIONS!"

For Virginia Slims and other women's cigarettes, the warning label could play off the industry's fashion-wise marketing:

"HEY, BABY, YOU'RE SOOOOOO HOT WITH THAT CIGARETTE DANGLING FROM THOSE LUSCIOUS LIPS. . . . OH, BY THE WAY, IN 20 YEARS YOUR FACE IS GOING TO LOOK LIKE A DRIED RHINOCEROS HIDE."

For teenagers, a booming segment of the tobacco market, a scolding tone probably won't work. Cop a cooler attitude:

"SMOKE ALL YOU WANT, DUDE. SO WHAT IF YOUR LUNGS END UP IN A MASON JAR AT A CARIBBEAN MEDICAL SCHOOL? IT'S ALL FOR A GOOD CAUSE."

There's always hip sarcasm:

"OK, LET'S SEE IF WE'VE GOT THIS STRAIGHT — YOUR NEW PERSONAL ROLE MODEL IS A CARTOON CAMEL NAMED JOE. THAT'S NOT PATHETIC. NOT MUCH."

At least it might grab their attention, which isn't happening now.

For Liggett to acknowledge itself as a pusher of narcotics is a good step. Unfortunately, its competitors won't willingly follow. Big Tobacco is too afraid that truth-in-advertising would do to its profits what cigarettes already do to its customers.

Poison is the word for it.

May 29, 1997

TOBACCO STOCKS DUMPED FOR THE WRONG REASON

Florida is finally dumping its $840 million of tobacco stocks, but not for the most pure and upright reasons.

Not because it's a disgrace for the state's largest retirement fund to own a stake in a product that kills so many people.

And not because it's hypocritical for the state to be earning hefty dividends from the same firms that it's suing for public-health costs and damages exceeding a billion dollars.

No, the reason given by Gov. Lawton Chiles and Insurance Commissioner Bill Nelson for divesting Florida's shares of RJR Nabisco, Loews Corp. and Philip Morris:

Tobacco stocks have become too "risky" an investment.

In other words, the main issue isn't the immeasurable human suffering caused by tobacco products, it's the money to be made or lost on stock fluctuations.

Ah, government with a heart.

In their defense, Chiles and Nelson were in a sticky spot. As members of the Board of Administration, which oversees the state's pension portfolios, they felt legally obliged to invoke fiscal grounds for selling off the tobacco holdings.

They didn't want to be accused of taking a rash or emotional action that might harm the retirement trust fund—a lofty but somewhat ironic concern, considering that thousands of the fund's beneficiaries are dying, or will die, of cancer and other smoking-related diseases.

I wonder how many of those folks would trade their lives for a 15 percent annual return.

The impetus to unload the tobacco shares came from the governor himself, and was initially resisted. Philip Morris and other cigarette firms have been exceptional performers in the stock market, and are a staple of most top mutual funds.

In fact, state Comptroller Bob Milligan voted in favor of keeping the cigarette stocks, based on their dandy record over the years.

Yet those shares represented but a thin sliver of the $60 billion package that covers 685,000 past and present state employees, many of them teachers. There are lots of other profitable stocks that can fill out the portfolio—preferably, stocks of companies not being sued by Florida.

The tobacco shares should've been dropped the day the attorney general marched into court. Even the most cold-blooded market hound can appreciate the state's indefensible position, attacking an industry in which it had a $840 million stake.

If Florida didn't get rid of the stock, attorneys for Philip Morris and RJR would've had a field day in front of the jury, come August. They still might.

That's the most pragmatic reason for Wednesday's decision.

Oh, Chiles and Nelson are right when they say cigarette stocks are shakier these days. They're shakier precisely because of massive class-action suits like the one filed by Florida.

If Big Tobacco gets whipped—the attorney general is seeking about $800 million plus treble damages—you won't need Smith or Barney to tell you how Wall Street will react.

Using the endangered-profits argument (and ignoring the state's role in it), bailing out of tobacco holdings makes some sense.

Still, it would have been refreshing if either Chiles or Nelson had stepped forward and briefly dropped the act. It would've been good to hear somebody say it's immoral for a state to invest in a lethal and addictive substance.

It would've been nice to hear them say the decision to sell off tobacco wasn't dictated by Wall Street advisers or trial lawyers, but by a genuine concern for people's health.

It would've been great for them to say they were dumping the stock not because of financial worries, but because it was the decent thing to do.

July 18, 1999

BIG LIE SINKING BIG TOBACCO

Finally the Big Lie is catching up to Big Tobacco.

In 1994, the heads of seven major tobacco companies sat before a Congressional panel and, to a man, asserted that cigarettes had not been proved to be either harmful or addictive. This they stated under oath.

Not since the Watergate hearings had America seen such well-rehearsed denial and deception. It was an arrogant, farcical performance—and it's coming back to haunt Big Tobacco.

The Miami-Dade jury that recently handed the industry its most shocking courtroom defeat sent a blunt message to cigarette makers: Nobody believes a word you say.

After eight months of testimony in a class-action suit filed on behalf of as many as five hundred thousand Florida smokers, jurors ruled that Big Tobacco engaged in "extreme and outrageous conduct" by knowingly marketing a deadly product, lying about its effects, and concealing vital health information.

Soon the same jury will decide how much money the industry should pay. Lawyers for smokers and their surviving relatives are seeking $200 billion.

Whatever the final sum, Big Tobacco will vigorously appeal, and has sought to assure Wall Street that the sledgehammer verdict will be overturned. (On the day the Miami-Dade jury announced its decision, the price of Philip Morris shares actually rose 37½ cents.)

But what happened in Miami was not a freak ruling, but rather an omen, as cigarette makers know. They fear juries because juries are made up of ordinary folks, not lawyers. Ordinary folks take offense when lied to.

What sank Big Tobacco here were its own words—not just the false claims and damaging secret memos, but the cynical marketing. Forty years of calculated lies, from the Marlboro Man to Joe Camel to the CEOs themselves.

Everybody knows cigarettes are poison. So big tobacco's strategy in the Miami case, as in others, was to mince around the unpleasant issue of its product's lethality, and focus instead on individual responsibility.

Yes, there are health risks, the tobacco lawyers said, but everyone who lights up knows that. Therefore, it's not our fault if they get sick and die.

That argument had been effective in other trials: This is America, where people are free to make their own choices! And smoking is a choice.

Lately, though, juries have been hearing experts testify that nicotine is highly addictive, and that cigarette makers not only know it but exploit it. The six Miami jurors—among them a smoker—must have sensibly concluded that a "choice" made by an addict isn't a free choice at all.

Big Tobacco insists nicotine can't be addictive, because people quit cigarettes every day. Lots of people manage to quit heroin, too, but nobody would dare claim it's not addictive.

So the industry has a serious credibility problem with the public—and therefore with potential jurors. Think about it. The only thing tobacco lawyers can forthrightly say about their clients' product is that it's legal.

During the Miami trial, one industry attorney conceded that "not smoking" probably was healthier than smoking. That's as close as he would get to the damning truth, which is that cigarettes kill many times more people than all illicit drugs combined.

Maybe the Florida Supreme Court will, as Philip Morris shareholders hope, overturn this month's scathing verdict.

Even if that happens, the case still opens the way for more class-action suits against Big Tobacco, more dicey trials and more astronomical judgments.

That's the price of living off a lie that kills so many. If you don't have a conscience, you'd better have some money.

March 26, 2000

THAT'S MONEY, NOT SMOKE, IN THEIR EYES

Just about everyone has been suing Big Tobacco. That's why cigarette makers are so conciliatory lately. They're running scared. Unlike politicians, juries usually can't be bought. And more and more juries are slamming the tobacco firms.

It's depressing to think that the future health of America's children depends on Congress, but that's what the Supreme Court said last week.

By a 5–4 margin, justices ruled that the most dangerous drug product in the country—cigarettes—cannot be regulated by the Food and Drug Administration. In other words, the agency that's supposed to protect the public from health threats is helpless to act against the most serious one.

The story was played as a victory for tobacco companies and their stockholders, and a defeat for the Clinton administration. Yet the big losers are our kids, who now will have greater access to cigarettes from vending machines and convenience stores.

Writing for the majority, Justice Sandra Day O'Connor capsulized the court's position:

"We believe that Congress has clearly precluded the FDA from asserting jurisdiction to regulate tobacco products."

Of course, the main reason the FDA finally tried to crack down on cigarettes is because Congress wouldn't. Too many senators and representatives hungrily accept campaign contributions from Big Tobacco, and vote accordingly.

Morally, it's no different than taking bribes from a cocaine kingpin or a heroin pusher. Cigarettes kill more than 400,000 Americans every year, many times more than all other drugs combined.

No single product has done more for the funeral trade than Marlboro.

The FDA would seem to have an obvious interest, given its mission to protect the public from harmful, lung-rotting substances. Justice Stephen Breyer, writing for the High Court minority, argued that very point.

The perils of smoking were acknowledged by the final ruling, which called it "perhaps the most single significant threat to public health in the United States."

Yet because cigarette makers don't boast of any health benefits from smoking, the FDA cannot step in without congressional action, the court said.

And Senate Majority Leader Trent Lott and House Majority Leader Dick Armey—both of whom pocket donations from Big Tobacco—say they've got no intention of expanding the FDA's reach.

So, with Congress compromised and the FDA neutralized, who's left for the cigarette makers to fear?

Lawyers. Busloads of lawyers.

Just about everyone has been suing Big Tobacco—smokers, families of deceased smokers, nonsmokers forced to work with smokers, states and even Uncle Sam. That's why cigarette makers are so conciliatory lately.

They're running scared. Unlike politicians, juries usually can't be bought. And more and more juries are slamming the tobacco firms.

No case has put more dread into the industry than the class-action suit filed on behalf of Florida smokers and their heirs. A six-member jury in Miami last summer found cigarette manufacturers guilty of "outrageous conduct" for selling a defective and lethal product.

Soon that same jury will set a dollar figure on the damages to be assessed. The sum will be boggling, and the consequences far-ranging.

Say what you will about personal-injury attorneys, but it's because of them that our kids aren't seeing so much of Joe Camel's face these days.

And it's because of those lawyers that tobacco executives are suggesting that they might accede, finally, to certain nicotine restrictions.

And it's because of them that Big Tobacco has settled $259 billion in health-care claims by many states, including Florida, and agreed to reduce teen-aimed advertising.

Cigarette makers are so desperate to appear reasonable that at least one, Philip Morris, has actually given up lying about the hazards of smoking. Last fall, after five decades of deceit and denial, the tobacco giant publicly admitted that its products are addictive and cancer-causing.

Either trait is enough to get any other substance banned from the shelves, but not cigarettes. Philip Morris' announcement caused scarcely a murmur among congressional leaders, thus confirming the necessity for outside litigation.

The lawsuits definitely have gotten Big Tobacco's attention and forced some promising concessions.

They've also made more than a few lawyers absurdly wealthy, but for that you can blame the tramps on Capitol Hill. They're the ones who wouldn't lift a finger to stop cigarette makers from hooking and killing people.

June 28, 2000

CONSCIENCE-STRICKEN "DOPE" DEALERS

The world's slickest dope peddlers came to Miami to plead for mercy.

"I do have regrets," admitted one of them, Nicholas Brookes. "I have sincere regrets that many of the things we are now embarked on doing could have been done sooner."

Brookes isn't a cocaine kingpin or a heroin lord. He is chairman of Brown & Williamson Tobacco Corp., a large manufacturer of cigarettes. He and other industry big shots are forsaking decades of denial and deceit to admit, at long last, that the product they sell is lethal and addictive.

This newfound candor isn't the result of sober moral introspection or spiritual enlightenment of any sort. It's purely a legal tactic, albeit a desperate one.

A Miami-Dade jury has already found that tobacco is addictive and causes lung cancer, emphysema and other fatal diseases. It ordered the industry to pay $12.7 million to three smokers in a marathon class-action suit that eventually could enlist 500,000 Florida smokers.

The trial recently reached the stage where those same jurors must decide how much money should be awarded in punitive damages, a sum that could surpass $100 billion.

Faced with a potentially ruinous judgment, tobacco makers suddenly heard the clarion of angels. Miraculously, their attorneys heard it, too.

The time had come to quit lying and tell the truth, even if the truth was ugly. So they journeyed to Miami to look jurors squarely in the eye and say: Yes, we admit it. We kill people for a living. Not exactly in those words, but close enough.

"Does smoking cause disease?" Brookes was asked.

"Smoking is a cause of lung cancer and other diseases," he replied.

"Is smoking addictive?"

"Yes," Brookes answered—the opposite of what he told Congress only two years ago.

Another tobacco executive, Michael Szymanczyk of Philip Morris, told the court: "My personal opinion is smoking is bad for your health." He said he wouldn't want his own kids to pick up the habit.

And Bennet Lebow, rebel owner of the Liggett Group, directly addressed smokers and their relatives: "There's nothing I can do to bring back your loved ones . . . there's nothing I can do to bring back your health. But I promise you I will continue to fight this war and win this war on tobacco."

Of all the executives to testify, only one—Andrew J. Schindler of R. J. Reynolds—cantankerously clung to the old party line. The most he conceded was that smoking carried a "risk factor" for lung cancer.

Schindler is the same genius who once breezily compared nicotine addiction to a fondness for carrots or chocolate. His appearance in court was a godsend for Stanley Rosenblatt, the smokers' attorney, who has been urging jurors to punish the industry for its arrogance.

Their decision is expected in July, though the appeals will drag on for years. In the end, there might be two historic milestones: how much the cigarette makers are forced to pay, and how much they were forced to say.

The specter of a financial and public-relations catastrophe is what made these guys drop their act and finally admit what everyone else has long known: Tobacco kills.

And whatever "regrets" Brookes and his colleagues might harbor, they are not so guilt-stricken that they would halt cigarette production. Like all dope peddlers, they put profits ahead of principles.

Nonetheless, the courtroom confessions were meant to suggest the dawning of a new era of tobacco-industry responsibility. Give us a chance, the CEOs seemed to be saying, and we'll behave as good citizens from now on. We'll stop marketing to hook teenagers, young women and minorities.

Whether or not this pitch worked on the jury remains to be seen, but it won't work on the public. Whatever its outcome, the Miami tobacco deliberations should be remembered not only for the unprecedented sums attached to culpability, but also for the first words of honesty to come from a cigarette maker's lips. All it took was a $100 billion attack of conscience.

12

BANG FOR THE BUCK

PRAISE THE LAW, AND QUICK, PASS THE AMMUNITION

Florida's new handgun law, also known as the Mortician's Relief Act, officially makes us the most dangerous state in America.

The same legislature and same governor who screwed up the taxes somehow also found the time to pass a law allowing any psychotic miscreant to pack a pistol in public. They nullified local gun ordinances and made it a cinch to get a concealed-weapons permit. Most amazingly, they made it legal to carry a gun in plain view.

More handguns on the streets means more dead children, more dead cops, more dead husbands and wives, more dead barroom buddies. Only gun dealers and the most radical of population-control advocates are celebrating today.

Meanwhile the state's gory reputation is being edified anew. Already *Nightline,* the *New York Times* and *Time* magazine have resurrected the Dodge City allusion and alerted millions of potential tourists to the drama that awaits.

Once upon a time, the word *Florida* evoked the image of a sun-drenched beach; now it's the Tamiami Gun Shop.

Imagine the officer who pulls over a motorist wearing a shoulder holster with a pistol. Does the cop draw his own gun, or simply ask to see a weapons permit along with the driver license?

"Absurd," says Florida Highway Patrol Capt. Rich Rossman of the new law. "What if I have a trooper stop somebody on Alligator Alley at 4 o'clock in the morning, and he's carrying a firearm and he's drunk? The trooper, if he takes the wrong action, can be prosecuted. If he waits, he can be buried."

On his way to work Wednesday morning, Metro homicide detective Al Singleton heard a snappy radio commercial for a gun dealer offering a quickie concealed-weapons course.

"Incredible," Singleton says. "It's a bad law. No matter how you cut it, it's legislators knuckling under to the NRA lobby. They did it for their own selfish interests."

Gov. Bob Martinez and the legislators, meeting this week in Tallahassee, say they are too busy to take up the task of fixing the new gun laws. This, despite a plea from Attorney General Bob Butterworth, who lost his son in a tragic handgun murder last year.

The last thing lawmakers want is a public referendum, because the public doesn't want more guns. Every reputable national poll in recent years has shown overwhelming support for stricter handgun laws. A 1986 Gallup survey showed only 8 percent in favor of relaxing handgun restrictions.

But, as usual, the Florida Legislature didn't let the will of the people get in the way of special interests—in this case, the NRA, operating under the laughable misnomer of Unified Sportsmen of Florida. Sportsmen, when was the last time you went duck hunting with a 9mm Beretta?

The notion that lenient laws make it easier for the average citizen to defend himself ignores decades of crime statistics on who kills whom. These guns won't be used on crooks, they'll be used against friends and loved ones. Or, more often, stolen by burglars.

"Scary," says Miami homicide detective Bill O'Connor. "It's going to be a nightmare. . . . You know, I've hunted my whole life, always had guns. But I'm so anti-NRA because of this. They don't see what I see—not just the murders, the suicides."

To illustrate how tough the new requirements are, one state official expects 130,000 concealed-weapons permits to be issued in the first year. Think about that next time you honk at some maniac who cuts you off on I-95.

The new laws don't worry Bob Martinez. He's got a chauffeur, and plenty of armed bodyguards. It might be instructive, though, if the governor spent one midnight shift on the streets of South Florida, riding with a cop.

The job was dangerous enough when a drunk's only weapon was a car. Just wait until he's got a pistol on his hip.

Says detective O'Connor: "People who want to carry their guns around better get used to having guns drawn on them . . . by police."

October 12, 1987

HANDGUN FORCES PERCEIVE SAFETY IN REVISED LAW

Leave it to our fearless leaders in Tallahassee to put the handgun fiasco in its proper, Florida-type perspective.

See, the trouble with the gun law wasn't that it allowed folks to swagger down the streets with a six-gun on their hips, or that it was marred by any particular legal loophole. The trouble, they tell us, was the perception of a loophole.

Rather than admit to their own sloppiness, the pro-handgun forces adopted this line: The law wasn't bad—rather, the public was simply "misinformed."

Gun lobbyist Marion Hammer, defending what has soured into a public relations disaster for the NRA, insisted: "Open carrying was not our issue. We did nothing to allow open carrying."

Nonetheless, the NRA's prepaid toadies in the state Legislature acquiesced last week and voted with the unanimous majority to change the law back, so that the open display of firearms is now a second-degree misdemeanor.

What finally got the lawmakers' attention? What was it that ultimately persuaded them to close a loophole that supposedly did not exist?

Could it have been the plea from the state attorney general, the protests from prosecutors, the anger from law enforcement and the fear from the citizenry—all screaming bloody murder? Probably not.

What really got them worried in Tallahassee was all the nasty national publicity. They simply couldn't sit still while yet another network news correspondent stood under the palm trees and talked about Dodge City, 1987.

This sort of thing is bad news, because it's bad for the tourist business.

As cynical as it sounds, many lawmakers weren't reacting to the thought of more dead bodies in the county morgue, but to the thought of empty hotel rooms at Disney World.

When Gov. Bob Martinez commented about the revised law, he didn't talk much about saving children's lives or protecting cops on the street. He talked about the perception that the handgun law was flawed, and pointedly noted how hotel and convention bookings were holding steady, despite all the bad publicity.

Only in Florida does tourism take primacy over human life.

I suppose we should be grateful that the Legislature finally agreed to fix the most dangerous gap in a hopelessly dangerous law. Much of the credit for this goes to Ron Silver, Mike Friedman and other South Florida lawmakers, who pushed the issue when their colleagues seemed reluctant.

Panama City Rep. Ron ("I think Florida is a safe place to live") Johnson actually wanted to have the ban on open pistoleros expire after one year, so the Legislature might "review" its necessity. Talk about a guy born in the wrong century.

With the Wyatt Earp loophole closed, the streets will be a little safer, but there is still no cause for a sigh of relief.

By this time next year, 130,000 Floridians are expected to hold permits for concealed weapons, most of them in South Florida. Some of these citizens will be responsible, well-trained and cautious. Others will be trigger-happy, drug-addled maniacs.

From a police officer's point of view, the newly "fixed" gun law is not much better than the original. Anything that puts more handguns out on the street creates a peril for the police—whether those guns are worn openly on the hip, or hidden in a pocket. Some cops would argue that a concealed weapon poses an even greater threat.

Revised or not, the new law is a bloody disgrace. It makes it quicker to buy a pistol, a joke to license one and legally chic to hide it in your boot, purse or cummerbund. With this kind of "regulation," Florida gets more dangerous every day.

If the governor and his accessories in the Legislature started paying as much attention to homicide statistics as they do to tourist bookings, they might get the message about handguns in Florida.

Like it or not, the rest of the country already has.

August 5, 1988

YOU'RE NEVER TOO YOUNG TO AIM HIGH

(*A true news item: The National Rifle Association has offered to help Florida schools teach special courses in gun education, beginning as early as kindergarten.*)

Sit down, boys and girls.

For today's NRA lesson, we're going to show you how to help mommy and daddy select the best handgun for your family. Yes, Billy?

"What about the snub-nosed Ruger, Mr. Rogers?"

Well, Billy, the Ruger Speed-Six Magnum is a nifty little weapon. I like it because it comes with a rubber combat stock instead of a walnut grip. Can any of you children tell me the disadvantages of a wooden stock on a small gun?

"It's a recoil control problem, Mr. Rogers."

You're exactly right, Maria. If daddy and mommy insist on buying one of these snubbie Magnums, make sure they trade the walnut grip for neoprene. They'll be amazed at the difference.

And, kids, while we're on the subject, who can tell me which Magnum bullet carries the most stopping power against a human target? Andrea?

"Um, I think it's the 110-grain factory load, Mr. Rogers."

No, Andrea, that's wrong. Remember last week's pop quiz on hollow points? Bobby, you've got your hand up.

"Yeah, Mr. Rogers. The 125-grain jacketed Magnum bullet has the most stopping power."

Good. But don't forget, boys and girls, there's one serious problem with the 125-grainers. Can you remember what it is? All together:

"MUZZLE FLASH, MR. ROGERS!"

That's right, kids. And why is muzzle flash so dangerous?

"BECAUSE MOST SHOOT-OUTS HAPPEN AT NIGHT!"

Correct. A white muzzle flash can blind you in the middle of a firefight, and we can't have that, can we?

"NO, MR. ROGERS."

Getting back to personal weapons, some of your mommies and daddies probably prefer something more substantial to hide in the nightstand. Jimmy, take your thumb out of your mouth and tell me about the Beretta 92-F.

"Gee, Mr. Rogers, I kind of like the 92-F. I mean it's OK, for a 9mm."

Jimmy, I'm very disappointed. Obviously, you weren't paying attention yesterday when we talked about the repeated slide failures being experienced with the 92-F by U.S. armed forces personnel. Until more testing is done, mommy and daddy would be better off with the standard Model 84, a .380 auto. What is it now, Jimmy?

"The Model 84 only holds 13 bullets, Mr. Rogers. My daddy says he needs at least fifteen."

Fine, Mr. Smartypants, stick with the 92-F. Only I suggest you tell your father to avoid using high-pressure loads and replace the slide mechanism every 3,000 rounds. Otherwise, he'll be picking hot shells out of his nostrils.

"Mr. Rogers, can we play with our crayons now?"

Yes, after lunch we'll practice drawing more bank-robber silhouettes. Only this time, no big red noses. Andrea?

"Mr. Rogers, was it Mark David Chapman or John Hinckley who used a Charter Arms .38?"

Oh no, you don't—that one's going to be on Monday's quiz. Look it up yourself. Bobby, you've got a question?

"Yeah, my dad wanted to know if he could borrow your MAC-10 converter kit this weekend."

I don't see why not. Be sure to remind him that he wouldn't even need a converter kit if those liberal wimps in Congress hadn't banned the sale of fully automatic machine guns a few years ago. By the way, you kids are still taking those petitions door-to-door, I hope.

"YES, MR. ROGERS!"

Great. Now, boys and girls, we all know what time it is.

"Oh no, not the pledge again, Mr. Rogers."

That's right. Everybody stand and repeat: The only way . . .

"THE ONLY WAY . . ."

. . . you'll take my gun . . .

". . . YOU'LL TAKE MY GUN . . ."

. . . is to pry it from my cold dead fingers.

"Aw, come on, Mr. Rogers. Do we have to?"

Say it!

". . . IS TO PRY IT FROM MY COLD DEAD FINGERS."

Very good, children. Now let's all take a little nap before target practice.

March 17, 1989

IMPORT BAN WON'T PRY ANY GUNS FROM HANDS

The government's temporary ban on importing AK-47s and other foreign assault rifles has worried the lobby wing of the NRA, but there's no cause for alarm.

Homicidal maniacs should have no trouble locating reliable domestic assault rifles, including the ever-popular MAC-10. More importantly, you should have no trouble buying one. The nice thing about many gun dealers is that they'll sell just about anything to anybody.

Ask Earl William Petit. On March 6, while awaiting trial on burglary charges in Broward County, he walked into a Service Merchandise store and picked out a Ruger .22-caliber semiautomatic rifle with a banana clip and a bipod for steady aiming. He also purchased about 400 rounds of ammunition.

Petit paid the cashier at 6:38 P.M.

At 8:20 P.M., two Pompano Beach police officers stopped a man approaching a public playground where Little League games were being played. It was Earl Petit. He was carrying his new rifle, the ammo, binoculars, a knife and assorted survival gear. He was dressed in an olive-drab hunting outfit, though police had a feeling that he wasn't looking for elk.

Petit is now in custody, awaiting a court hearing. If he is found to be sane, he will probably be released. After all, the only charges pending against him are for loitering and allegedly stealing a T-shirt out of somebody's truck.

Nothing will prevent Petit from buying another gun, maybe even upgrading to Ruger's Mini-14—the same beaut used by Michael L. Platt in the FBI massacre, the same one used by accused mass killer William Cruse in an attack on a Palm Bay shopping mall.

The new restriction on assault rifles probably won't put a dent in murder statistics, but police pushed hard for the ban on imports. Robert J. Creighton, special agent in charge of the federal Alcohol, Tobacco and Firearms bureau in Florida, says the ban won't affect the "huge vast reservoir of guns" already in the public's hands, but it is a step forward.

"The problem with guns now is the same problem with narcotics. There's got to be an attitudinal change," he says. "We're not talking about sporting uses. We're talking about a fascination with violence."

Only six Florida counties require waiting periods to buy guns, but the NRA believes that this is too many. Dade County's waiting period is three days, and of course the NRA believes that this is too long. Yet even facing such a time burden, many Dade Countians have been able to fully exercise their right to bear arms.

Last month, for example, a 15-year-old teen-ager in a housing project got a great deal on a .44 Magnum—only $40. Police say he used the pistol to kill one of his friends, accidentally.

Only Wednesday a young man was showing off a handgun when he shot both his girlfriend and himself. On March 10, a 16-year-old boy shot his mother to death with a .44 Magnum during an argument while riding in the car. On March 1, an elderly man allegedly murdered his bedridden wife with a .357 Magnum. On March 2, a 16-year-old South Dade boy was shot in the head by a 15-year-old companion while a group of teens played with a .25-caliber handgun.

On February 28, a Coral Gables man shot and killed his daughter's boyfriend. He told police he mistook the man for a burglar. On February 13, a lumber company owner allegedly pulled a .38 out of an ankle holster and killed a man during a dispute over a flat tire.

How can the NRA worry? Last weekend, guns were the weapon-of-choice in nine of the 10 murders committed in Dade County. Already this year there have been 70 homicides and 37 suicides by gunshot.

A waiting period might dampen the urgency to bear arms. This the NRA understands.

On Wednesday, a Pompano Beach man walked into a Kmart at lunch hour and bought himself a shotgun and some shells. The cashier rang up the items at 12:04 P.M.

Thirty minutes later police were called to the man's home. He had committed suicide with his brand new gun. The Kmart receipt was still in the trunk of his car.

October 18, 1989

NEW STATISTICS FIRE ANOTHER ROUND AT NRA

Once again, the flustered flacks of the NRA are circling the wagons.

Another study of violent crime has been published, another assault on their holy myth that guns are good, that guns save lives, that guns protect property.

Statistics from morgues and hospitals say otherwise. This newspaper studied a week's worth of gunplay in peace-loving Dade County, and the results were overpowering, chilling, indefensible. One week in the slow crawl of summer: 14 dead, 55 wounded. A shooting took place every three hours; an armed robbery 20 times a day.

This was not a remarkably extra-violent period. There wasn't even a full moon.

The gun episodes of July 9–15 weren't particularly maniacal: suicides, stickups, drug rip-offs and domestics. A man got shot by a 12-year-old vandal. A DEA agent was wounded by a drug dealer. A Miami Beach commissioner and his wife were robbed at gunpoint in their driveway.

When bullets were fired, the shooter often knew his victim. Typically, they had argued. Over cocaine. Over romance. Or money. Or clothes. Even a necklace.

Of all the findings that mock the NRA's propaganda, none is more telling than these: During that single week in July, 567 guns were used in crimes in Dade County. Guess how often a citizen used a gun to stop a crime? Three times.

Pitiful. You're better off with a large dog or a loud whistle.

The NRA insists that an armed home is a safer home; statistics show that nothing could be further from the truth. A home with a gun is a place where relatives are more likely to plug each other on the dumbest whim. Worse, a home with a gun is a burglar's dream.

NRA flacks say tougher laws are worthless because criminals will always be able to find more guns. What they don't tell you is where many criminals get their guns—from law-abiding folks who leave them in night tables and glove compartments.

In that one week in July, 92 guns were reported stolen in Dade County. Ninety-two handguns, rifles and shotguns delivered into the hands of crooks in just seven days. That's more than 4,700 new guns a year on the streets of one Florida county. Police say the actual number is higher, because many citizens won't report the theft of a weapon.

When the wimps in the Legislature gutted the handgun laws back in 1987, they ignored reams of crime studies just like these. They also ignored the pleas of top police officials who warned of escalating violence if guns were made more accessible.

The cops were dead right. Since the laws were changed, crimes involving handguns have shot up dramatically in all urban areas. By last July, Metro-Dade was reporting a 28 percent increase in robberies and a 22 percent increase in aggravated assaults over the previous year. Police say it's no coincidence.

South Florida has become a national showcase for mayhem, a bloody example of taking a terrible problem and making it worse. The NRA promised that liberalized gun laws would make us all safer, and just the opposite has happened.

The cost in human suffering is immeasurable, but there's another big ticket to pay. Our image as a tourist mecca and international business magnet can never be restored so long as outsiders think of us as the sun-and-gun capital of America.

Recently, *Fortune* magazine published a survey of major corporations that rated the most desirable cities for investment and relocation. Only New Orleans fared worse in the polling than Miami. Corporate leaders cited crime as their main fear.

Anyone who says the crisis is overblown isn't paying attention. Nothing about it is overblown or hyped.

Not when 14 people die and 55 are wounded in one week. Not when 31 assault rifles and 397 handguns are used against citizens. Not when a 6-year-old girl and her uncle are shot dead in traffic.

No wonder people want tougher gun laws. No wonder the NRA hates statistics.

November 6, 1989

NRA OFFERS GIFTS, COUPONS AND HYSTERIA

A surprise in this week's mailbox: an application to join the National Rifle Association!

How it came here is a wonder. Apparently the NRA screens its mailing list about as carefully as the state of Florida screens its concealed-weapon applications.

Rather than waste the postage, I decided to read through the membership material to see if it was more moderate than the bug-eyed ravings of paid gun lobbyists. It wasn't. According to NRA recruiters, the country is on the verge of collapse at the hands of anti-gun rabble-rousers.

What makes this hysteria so odd is that many NRA members are perfectly reasonable people with no urgent need for MAC-10s, no unnatural passion for armor-piercing bullets and no objection to imposing a sensible waiting period before somebody can purchase a handgun.

This is not the NRA leadership, though, and the leadership is in charge of finding new blood. Judging by the mail, times must be tough.

The pitch starts with a free decal, which can be attached to the windshield of your car, truck or tank turret. Even if you don't join the NRA, you get to keep the decal and are encouraged to display it as a warning to wimps and crybaby liberals.

Then come the mail-order goodies. By joining RIGHT NOW, you get an official NRA "shooter's cap" in either black or blue (the black one is snazzier because of the gold braided visor). You hardly ever see anyone wearing these caps in public, but they could become the new fashion rage in urban shoot-outs.

Next (but only if you sign up soon) you get a package of discount coupons for ammunition and hunting products made by Remington, Federal and Ram-Line, to name a few top brands.

Joining the NRA also qualifies you for this year's NRA Sweepstakes. The first prize is a gargantuan Winnebago, but there are plenty of others—outdoors expeditions, camping gear and your choice of five Browning weapons, from a nickel-plated .380 to a .22 Buck Mark varmint pistol.

I would guess that no other sweepstakes in America offers a varmint pistol as a prize. Those who resist this enticement are confronted by a leaflet that commands: "If you've decided not to join the NRA, STOP, read this crucial message. . . ."

Here's where the recruiters get down to business. A letter from J. Warren Cassidy, NRA executive vice president, begins like this:

"Dear Undecided Reader:

"On May 24, 1989, the governor of California signed into law a bill that stripped away a fundamental freedom of Americans guaranteed by the U.S. Constitution."

Reading on, you discover that the alleged anti-patriotic legislation was drafted to ban semiautomatic assault rifles, such as the one used by a madman to shoot down thirty children in a Stockton playground.

Because of this bill, the NRA honchos are outraged. One crummy little slaughter and those lily-livered Californians go and outlaw AK-47s!

As the indignant Mr. Cassidy exhorts: "So the choice is clear—and up to you. You can ignore the threat which is now spreading like a cancer from California outward . . . and perhaps suffer the loss of your gun rights, which have been a cornerstone of American democracy for years.

"Or you can join the NRA and do your part to hold on to your Constitutional right to own and use firearms."

Boy. Makes you wonder how the republic survived all those years before Uzis were invented.

The way the NRA sells it, joining up offers a double bonus. Not only do you get cut-rate ammo, you also get to save the Constitution from destruction.

As if that's not enough, members also receive (I swear) $600 in gun theft insurance. This allows you to replace a stolen pistol quickly. Unfortunately, it doesn't do anything for the unlucky guy who gets shot by the stolen gun.

Only one of the NRA's fringe benefits was not fully explained in the literature. It was the free $10,000 Accidental Death and Dismemberment Insurance. I can't imagine why they'd need it.

May 8, 1994

POLITICIANS AT LAST CATCH ON AND BAN ASSAULT WEAPONS

Frothing in defeat, the screamers of the NRA say the new federal ban on assault weapons won't do any good. They say criminals don't buy their guns at gun stores.

Tell that to the friends and loved ones of Jack Greeney III.

In late 1989, a man named Lancelot Armstrong walked into a Broward gun shop and purchased two handguns. About the same time, he bought a TEC-9 assault pistol, capable of firing 20 to 32 rounds without reloading.

When Armstrong made these purchases, he was wanted in Massachusetts on two counts of assault with intent to commit murder. That nasty business didn't matter here in Florida. He simply lied to the store clerk and got his new guns.

He still had the receipts two months later, when he and an accomplice decided to rob a Church's Fried Chicken. They were interrupted by Broward sheriff's cars.

From inside the restaurant, Armstrong ambushed the officers with a wild barrage of gunfire. Deputy Jack Greeney died in the parking lot. Another deputy was wounded.

The murder weapon wasn't found, but police concluded it was a semiautomatic assault pistol, such as a Tec-9. Armstrong claimed he didn't own one. He had no convincing explanation for the sales receipt that was folded neatly in his wallet. A judge sent him off to Death Row.

I thought of Jack Greeney last week when the U.S. House of Representatives narrowly voted to ban the Tec-9 and 18 other types of assault weapons. Had the law been enacted sooner, Armstrong might've been carrying a pistol instead of a military-style gun, and Greeney might still be alive.

It's also possible that Armstrong would have found another way to get his mitts on a Tec-9. We'll never know. What is certain, beyond doubt, is that a violent fugitive had absolutely no trouble buying lethal weapons from a licensed gun shop.

The new law is designed to prevent street thugs from legally arming themselves with heavy weapons. It's also meant to stop future hotheads and psychos from purchasing AR-15s, Uzis, MAC-10s or AK-47s to exact vengeance on employers, fellow motorists or humanity in general.

No, the law won't take the guns off the street. And no, the law won't reverse the crime rate. Nobody said it would.

Rep. Lincoln Diaz-Balart opposed the ban because, he said, it was "not serious crime-fighting legislation." The fact that every important police organization supported the bill failed to impress Diaz-Balart, who apparently thinks he knows more about crime than cops do.

The point is to save a few lives, period. The guns banned are styled for combat. They're not made to shoot deer and antelope. They're made to put multiple holes in humans, as expeditiously as possible. That's why gangsters like Lance Armstrong and losers like David Koresh like them.

Of the 214 congressmen who voted to keep assault weapons legal, few offered guidance as to where (or if) they would draw the line on private ownership. Machine guns? Bazookas? Stinger missiles? If it were up to the nutty NRA, anything with a trigger would be available over the counter.

Gun lobbyists lost touch with the public long ago. Finally they're losing some clout with politicians. In 1991, U.S. Rep. E. Clay Shaw voted against banning assault rifles. Last week he changed his mind.

Maybe he was just paying attention to his mail. Or maybe he was remembering Deputy Jack Greeney, or the ATF agents in Waco or those children on a California playground—all slain with legally purchased assault weapons.

Banning them wasn't an act of courage. It was an act of conscience, long overdue.

February 25, 1999

GUNS' DEFENDER MISFIRES

The desperation of the National Rifle Association has manifested itself in the person of an obscure buffoon named George Albright.

Albright is sponsoring a bill in the Florida Legislature that would make it a felony for local governments to sue firearms manufacturers. The retroactive measure is aimed at killing a lawsuit against 26 gunmakers filed last month by Mayor Alex Penelas on behalf of Miami-Dade County.

Here's what Albright, an Ocala Republican, had to say: "I look forward to Mayor Penelas, if he continues this lawsuit, being a convicted felon and being removed from office by the governor. And I hope you quote me on that."

With pleasure, George. It's a rare politician willing to stand up and unabashedly identify himself as a slavering lapdog of the NRA.

Things are going so poorly that apparently the gun lobby will take whatever can be dredged up in the way of help. Cities all over the country are suing firearms firms for fueling violence by saturating the urban market with unsafe weapons. Victims are suing, too.

Last week, a Brooklyn jury found 15 gun manufacturers negligent and nine liable in three shooting incidents. It was the first time the industry has lost such a case.

Until then, juries had agreed with the contention of firearms companies that almost any legal product can be made lethal in the wrong hands. Gunmakers, they say, shouldn't be held responsible for the negligence or criminal behavior of individuals—any more than Ford Motor Co. should be held liable for the actions of a drunk driver behind the wheel of a Taurus.

The argument has some legal merit, which is more than one can say for Rep. Albright's radical proposition: Criminally penalize municipalities for doing what every U.S. citizen has a constitutional right to do—be heard in court.

Albright's big-brother bombast is even more hypocritical, given the Republican party's campaign vow to make big government less intrusive in local affairs. Threatening a mayor with arrest is about as intrusive as it gets.

Gov. Jeb Bush opposes the idea of cities suing gun manufacturers, but he'd be making a bonehead blunder to sign his name on a bill as bad as Albright's, which eventually would be shredded in the appellate courts.

Penelas isn't seeking to outlaw guns. He's trying to force the issue of mandatory trigger locks, to protect kids. He also wants dealers limited to selling one gun per month per customer, to eliminate the problem of "straw buyers" who purchase weapons in mass, then sell them illegally (Florida is an infamous bulk supplier of handguns to the Eastern seaboard).

These reforms would cut crime and save lives, without impinging on private firearms owners. But NRA toadies in Tallahassee won't go for anything so sensible.

The same is true elsewhere. That's why so many cities, which bear the terrible social and fiscal cost of gun mayhem, have turned to the courts. In addition to Miami-Dade, New Orleans, Chicago and Atlanta have sued firearms makers. Los Angeles, San Francisco and Philadelphia will soon do the same.

Fearing an anti-tobacco-type onslaught, the panicky gun lobby has turned for rescue to the obedient likes of George Albright. The bill he's sponsoring is merely a knockoff of one recently rammed through the Georgia Legislature, another bastion of deep thinkers.

If such a redneck law passes here, the mayor of every big Florida city immediately ought to sue all the major firearms manufacturers—and then arrange to be arrested on the steps of city hall.

Few juries in this state would convict an elected official for going to court to make their streets safer. They are more likely to give a standing ovation.

June 20, 1999

NRA CLOUT KILLS COMMON SENSE

Thou shalt cower and shirk shamelessly before the National Rifle Association.

That's not from the Book of Exodus—it's from the Book of Wimp, the political bible of the U.S. House of Representatives.

Confronted with an epidemic of youthful gun violence, epitomized by the massacre in Colorado, the House last week acted decisively—not to face the crisis, but to placate the NRA.

Frantically, House members scrambled to derail a Senate measure that would have made it harder for juveniles, convicted felons and known psychopaths to acquire weapons at weekend gun shows.

But don't get the impression that the House was taking the issue lightly. Before killing the gun bill outright, members adopted by a wide majority an amendment that would have allowed states to post the Ten Commandments in public schools.

Yeah, that would have turned the tide.

If only the commandments had been emblazoned on the walls of Columbine High, maybe those two twisted little freaks would have experienced a last-minute revelation. Maybe they'd have thrown down their Tec-9 and their sawed-off shotgun, and dropped to their knees in prayer.

Well, that's what Rep. Robert Aderholt might have you believe. He's the Alabama Republican who proposed The Ten Commandments bill, declaring it would "promote morality and work toward an end of children killing children."

Aderholt is either the most naive goober ever to set foot in Washington, or just another grandstanding zealot.

His bill was a farce, a spit on the grave of every child who's been senselessly gunned down on America's streets.

It reduced a harrowingly complex social phenomenon to something so trite it could be addressed with a simple-minded bumper sticker. Follow the Ten Commandments.

Come on, boys and girls, get with the program! No killing, no stealing, no coveting the neighbor's wife, no taking the Lord's name in vain, no bearing false witness . . .

Sound rules, every one. But home is the place to learn them, and long before Junior reaches high school. By then Moses is competing with Marilyn Manson, and it's not much of a contest.

Because by then your kid is either laughing off the lyrics or trying to live them out. For better or worse, Junior's well on his way—and anyone who believes a religious plaque on the cafeteria wall is going to turn him around is pitiably detached from reality.

Then there's the not-so-minor legal problem with displaying the commandments in schools: The Supreme Court says you can't.

In a Kentucky case, the justices ruled that posting the Ten Commandments in public classrooms breaches the constitutional separation of church and state.

So the House amendment, if it had survived, would have been challenged instantly in court and most likely tossed out. Yet 248 lawmakers, including every Republican from Florida, voted for the Ten Commandments provision, knowing it stood scant chance of enactment.

Then what was the point? To appear concerned, of course, not to mention uprightly devout.

And also to appear as if they were actually doing something about a dire situation, and not just caving in to NRA bullying.

So the whole Ten Commandments idea—even if conceived in earnest— wound up a spurious gesture intended to look righteous. It would have saved not one young life from a bullet.

We got a show and that's all; a decoy. Which is what politicians do when they don't have the guts to do the right thing. Again from the Book of Wimp:

Thou Shalt Cover Thy Ass.

May 31, 2000

THE GUN WAS THE SEED OF THE CRIME

On Tuesday the community of Lake Worth said good-bye to Barry Grunow, the popular middle school teacher who was shot dead by a student on the last day of class.

Grunow was only 35, the father of two small children. He died for no other reason except that a 13-year-old boy had easy access to an unsecured pistol—utter madness that repeats itself all over the country.

Lake Worth is reeling with sorrow and horror, and many people are calling for tougher gun laws. But this is Florida, where the National Rifle Association owns the Republican-controlled Legislature.

The NRA does not want new laws. It says the answer to gun violence is locking up hardened criminals and educating kids about firearms.

Nathaniel Brazill, the boy who killed Grunow, doesn't fit the NRA's pat profile of a fearless gun-toting thug. He was an honor-roll student who got suspended for chucking water balloons. As for a firearms education, he already knew how to aim and fire. There's probably not a teenager in America who doesn't.

The facts of Grunow's murder leave the NRA with no credible stance, just the same old reactionary rant. A kid flipped out, swiped his grandfather's Saturday-night special and shot a teacher. If that .25-caliber Raven hadn't been accessible, Grunow would be at school this week, working on his students' final report cards.

Opportunity is what gave birth to Nathaniel's awful plan—knowing that gun was in the drawer, knowing he could get his hands on it. He wouldn't have plotted to kill anybody with a pocketknife or a rock. The gun was the seed of the crime.

Earlier this year, two Jacksonville Democrats, Rep. Tony Hill and Sen. Betty Holzendorf, introduced a modest proposal that would have required external locks on handguns in homes where children lived or visited. The goal was to help prevent accidental shootings and crimes of impulse.

The law was stridently opposed by the NRA, and it died without debate. In the House, it was "buried" by Rep. Howard Futch, R-Melbourne Beach. In the Senate, it was killed by John Grant, R-Tampa, who chairs the Judiciary Committee. These two fellows are proud lackeys of the NRA. Grant, for example, said he was delighted to hear of a poll showing firearms are present in 37 percent of Florida households with children.

There are many other polls that he and gun lobbyists conveniently choose to ignore, including a recent one by the Associated Press. The result: Mandatory trigger locks were favored by 76 percent of Americans—and 70 percent of gun owners—who were surveyed. This illustrates that the NRA leadership is radically and ridiculously out of touch, even with mainstream firearms owners.

Only a blithering paranoid would claim gun-safety features pose a threat to the Constitution. Both presidential candidates, George W. Bush and Al Gore, say they would sign a compulsory trigger-lock law if Congress passed one. Most manufacturers already offer the safeguards.

Two other states, Maryland and Massachusetts, recently defied the NRA and passed trigger-lock laws. Their legislators, unlike those in Florida, listened to the citizens and not to the money. It's true that you can't legislate against stupidity, but you can thwart it by making a safer product. Automakers fought mandatory seat belts for years, claiming nobody would use them. They were wrong.

Trigger locks won't end Americans' gun lunacy. They are but one small precaution that works only when properly used.

But if Nathaniel's grandfather had locked his pistol, a teacher would still be alive, and a 13-year-old boy wouldn't be facing an eternity behind bars. If such a simple device came with each gun, more parents would use them, and more tragedies would be prevented. One would be enough to justify a law— one life saved.

No such sensible initiative will come from Tallahassee these days—not from the governor, whose cliché-ridden response to Barry Grunow's death never acknowledged the issue that the community is most upset about. And not from politicians such as John Grant, who, as he scuttled the trigger-lock law, cheered the fact that nearly four out of 10 Florida families keep handguns.

Said Grant: "It's good to know their safety is ensured by something other than 911."

Too bad he wasn't there to answer the phone when the 911 call came in from Lake Worth Middle School.

Part

3

13

DEEP POCKETS

February 16, 1990

DIRTY MONEY ISN'T ANYTHING TO BOAST ABOUT

This week's series of articles on dirty money reinforced the axiom that cash gets you anything in South Florida because no one really cares where it comes from.

One of the most embarrassing anecdotes recounted the tale of Mr. Leonel Martinez, a home builder, political supporter and law client of Miami Commissioner Victor De Yurre. The night De Yurre was elected, he was photographed celebrating with Martinez at his side.

The builder also donated to the re-election campaign of Dade Mayor Steve Clark. At the suggestion of the Latin-American Chamber of Commerce, Clark later proclaimed December 10, 1988, as Leonel Martinez Day.

The mayor began: "Whereas: Metropolitan Dade County is proud to recognize the great service rendered on behalf of this community by Leonel Martinez..."

It got thicker as it went. Clark lauded Martinez's "long history of involvement in all facets of this community, supporting many civic, social, patriotic and cultural activities." He commended him for "demonstrating an unwavering commitment to the welfare and progress of Metropolitan Dade County."

The proclamation concluded that "the two million residents of Metropolitan Dade County are immeasurably indebted to Leonel Martinez for his tireless efforts to improve this community's quality of life."

These tireless efforts, according to federal prosecutors, included trafficking in cocaine.

Leonel Martinez was indicted barely six months after his canonization by Mayor Clark, who later blubbered: "I didn't know anything about his background."

So naturally you proclaim him one of our leading citizens. Good move, Stevie.

As if this weren't enough, the county also named a street for Martinez. It's really S.W. 132nd Avenue, but officially it's Leomar Boulevard. If Martinez is convicted, maybe they'll rename it Dirtbag Drive.

Not for a moment do I think that Steve Clark knew what he was doing when he approved Leonel Martinez Day. The mayor spends most of his arduous nongolfing hours handing out plaques, cutting ribbons and making overblown proclamations about people he barely knows. I'm sure it all becomes a blur.

The idea that Martinez might be crooked probably never entered Clark's brain. The guy had some dough, that's all. Other South Florida political figures are getting burned the same way. To avoid future embarrassments, some basic precautions should be taken.

From now on, let's not name a whole street after somebody unless he's dead. Dead people are seldom indicted, and almost never convicted.

If it's absolutely necessary to reward some heavyweight politico with his own "day," the official proclamation should be very carefully worded. A sample boilerplate:

"Whereas: Joe Blow is a resident of Metropolitan Dade County, or at least claims to be, and

"Whereas: Joe Blow has a history of involvement in many facets of this community (even though we have no earthly clue as to what this involvement entails, or whether certain federal agencies have taken an interest), and

"Whereas: Joe Blow would very much like to have something, anything, named for himself, and

"Whereas: Joe Blow has demonstrated an unwavering commitment to the welfare and progress of certain prominent politicians, and

"Whereas: Joe Blow has (as of this morning) not been arrested or convicted of any major felonies in Metropolitan Dade County, and whereas he certainly dresses well and exhibits no visible gunshot wounds, and

"Whereas: Metropolitan Dade County has purchased stacks and stacks of blank proclamations, and we can't just throw the darn things away;

"Now, therefore, be it resolved that we do hereby proclaim Friday, February 16, 1990, as Joe Blow Day, with the understanding that we are taking Joe Blow's word that he's such an upstanding citizen, because he could just as easily be a despicable dope-dealing lowlife scammer and we'd be the last to know."

August 29, 1990

A TELLING LIST: THE DONORS IN GOVERNOR RACE

It's astounding how many Florida politicians are in favor of "growth management." Such a clean, strong-sounding, utterly ambiguous phrase.

And so much easier than coming right out and speaking the unspeakable, which is: We've got too damn many people.

Preliminary census figures show the state's population grew by 31 percent in the last decade, graphic evidence that growth is not being managed at all. People increasingly are disgusted by crime, traffic and urban sprawl, and the candidates know they've got to say something about it.

Consider the positions of the gubernatorial front-runners. Bob Martinez says he's fighting to save the coastlines from overcrowding and rampant development. Bill Nelson says he helped author the first growth management law. Lawton Chiles says the economy has become dangerously dependent on growth-related industries while the quality of life has declined.

Hearing all this, one might believe that our leaders finally have grasped the obvious fact that overdevelopment is ruining Florida. If they'd only pay attention to their own campaign donations, they might figure out how Florida got so loused up.

All the tough promises about preserving our resources and controlling growth haven't scared off the heavy contributors whose livelihoods depend on growth—developers, construction companies, banks, law firms, contractors, real estate brokers.

Millions upon millions have poured into the governor's race from folks who, logically, should be mortified by some of the rhetoric. What's going on here? Perhaps they know something we don't. Perhaps they correctly perceive the "growth-management" kick as political bluster that will conveniently disappear after Election Day.

Thumb through any stack of Gov. Martinez's contribution reports and marvel at the generosity: Lely Development Corp., Naples, $1,000; Hobe Sound Partners, real estate, Boca Raton, $2,000; R. S. Futch, Jr., construction, Ocala, $1,000; Seminole Development Corp., Miami, $3,000; Latin American 8th Street Inc., developer, Miami, $3,000; Marsh Creek Partnership, developer, Jacksonville, $3,000; K. O. Hedin Construction Co., Vero Beach, $1,000; International General Contractors, Hialeah, $2,000; Neil Elsey Associates, developer, St. Petersburg, $1,000; Charles Rebozo, banker, Key Biscayne, $1,000; Florida Rock and Sand Co., Florida City, $3,000; Saxon Properties Inc., developer, Fort Myers, $1,000; and on and on.

Now check a sample of Democrat Bill Nelson's boosters, and witness a similar pattern: BBVK Developers, Fort Myers, $1,000; Plaza Development Group, Miami, $1,000; U.S. Construction Corp., Miami Lakes, $1,000; Firestone Realty Inc., Miami, $1,000; William Hunt, contractor, Pensacola, $1,000; Ceferino Machado, builder, Hialeah, $1,000; Hooker and Dailey Contracting, Fort Myers, $2,000; William Graham, developer, Miami Lakes, $1,000; McCann and Associates, developer, Orlando, $1,000; Bob Moss, developer, Fort Lauderdale, $1,000; Stobs Brothers Construction Co., Miami, $1,000; and on and on.

Nelson's opponent, Lawton Chiles, has limited donations to $100, but hasn't completely squelched the largess of special interests. Chiles recently attended a campaign reception hosted by Arvida, the goliath developer that's trying to bulldoze 1,652 acres of wetlands in western Broward. Although those attending the event gave small contributions, it's safe to assume that Arvida didn't stage the fund-raiser out of the pure shining goodness of its corporate heart.

What happens in election years is that everyone starts throwing money around to cover all the angles; nobody wants to get aced by their competitors. Not all developers and builders are ruthless despoilers of wilderness, but they'd all love to have a governor who returns their phone calls.

Maybe someday we'll have one with the guts to return their money.

April 15, 1991

UNLIKELY VOICE CALLS TO REFORM CAMPAIGNS

Wonders never cease. A feeble cry arises for campaign reform and, lo, the cry belongs to Metro Mayor Steve Clark. Suddenly he wants to ban all political contributions from bankers and bond lawyers doing business with Dade County.

On the surface, it seems a supernatural transformation. "I am anxious," the mayor intoned, "to remove even the appearance of impropriety or favoritism in activities that relate to bond financing."

Stevie, we hardly knew ye. Since when have you lost a moment's sleep over the appearance of impropriety or favoritism? This is a fellow who, during a long political career, has ravenously accepted campaign funds from anybody representing anything. If it was green and had a president's face on it, the Clark campaign would glom onto it.

In his 1984 re-election bid, much of Clark's $500,000 war chest came from builders, real estate developers and land-use lawyers. They adored the mayor because he usually was sympathetic to their projects. He had a soft spot for strip malls.

In 1988, it was the same story—almost half a million dollars, loads of it from firms whose fortunes could be affected by Clark's vote on zoning matters.

Only two weeks ago, as the commission queasily debated new limits on campaign contributions, the mayor fretted that this "honesty kick" might be going too far. Now that was the Steve Clark we all knew.

What happened since then? Was the mayor struck on the noggin by an errant golf ball? Did the spirit of Raul Martinez visit him in his sleep and urge him to mend his ways?

Whatever happened, the change in Clark seemed profound and dramatic. While some of the new commissioners whined and stammered about imposing a cap on donations, there was the mayor—claiming to be a devoted disciple of Lawton Chiles, and pleading for reform.

Perhaps, like the governor, Clark was listening to inner voices. Perhaps one of the voices belonged to Commissioner Joe Gersten. And perhaps that voice was saying: "Stevie, I'm going to take your job in 1992."

Gersten is chairman of the county's finance committee. That means he'll be receiving scads of campaign contributions from out-of-state investment bankers and lawyers specializing in bond issues.

Like most urbanized counties, Dade sells millions of dollars' worth of bonds to pay for public works–type projects. Reviewing the bonds is some of the fastest, easiest money that a law firm can make. It's lucrative, low-risk, boilerplate work—a gravy train. That's why so many firms fight for a piece of the action.

Local politicians are flattered to get political contributions all the way from Wall Street, but it's no tribute to their performance on the County Commission. Bankers and bond lawyers would give money to a chimpanzee if they thought he could steer a deal their way.

Gersten is in a choice position, and that's why Clark is so worried. If Gersten challenges for the mayor's job, it will be the first time in years that Clark has faced an opponent who is bankrolled by special interests as deep-pocketed and influential as his own.

That would explain the mayor's abrupt conversion. What a bold move— banning campaign donations from bond lawyers and bankers! Just what we need to restore the voter's confidence in our integrity . . . with the coincidental side effect of gutting Gersten's campaign coffers.

This is about as close to a brainstorm as the Clark campaign will ever get; subtle it's not. Effective? Sure, if it passes.

But Gersten has another card to play, if he's got the guts. He should agree to the mayor's suggestion—but only if the ban on campaign donations is extended to builders, developers and zoning lawyers who do business with the county.

Just watch what happens then. That blur you'll see at Government Center will be the mayor backpedaling. Reform? Who said anything about reform? Naw, you must be thinking of someone else.

May 29, 1991

COURT ABETS A SHAKEDOWN BY POLITICIANS

Crooked politicians can relax. The U.S. Supreme Court just made it easier to shake down special-interest groups for campaign money.

In a 6–3 vote, the court overturned the extortion conviction of a West Virginia legislator who took several thousand dollars from unlicensed doctors seeking to practice medicine in his state. The legislator then worked to pass a law that would have licensed the doctors without requiring a state examination.

A jury convicted the legislator, Robert L. McCormick, of extortion. The verdict was upheld on appeal. Last week the Supreme Court threw it out. In a ruling that gladdened the hearts of all sleazeballs, the Court said that it's not extortion unless "payments are made in return for an explicit promise or undertaking by the official to perform or not to perform an official act."

As theory, it sounds sensible. In the real world, though, bribery and extortion are rarely arranged by explicit discussion. Only the most witless, ham-handed politician openly solicits money in exchange for favors.

The dirty deed usually is orchestrated by winks, nods, and the most ambiguous of conversations. The risky chore of collecting the payoff generally falls to trusted aides, also known as bagmen. Seldom will you hear a senator holler: "Hey, Frank, where's that bribe you promised?"

Special interests give campaign money to politicians all the time, and usually it's legal. The question of corruption arises when money is tied to a specific favor by mutual agreement—for instance, a payoff in exchange for a vote.

It happens every day, but proving it is hard. The U.S. law against extortion is called the Hobbs Act, and it was designed to prosecute gangsters. Politicians were an afterthought.

In its recent ruling, the Supreme Court applies loan-shark standards to old-fashioned political shakedowns. To make an extortion case, U.S. prosecutors now must show that the payment was either "induced by the use of force, violence or fear," or part of a clear "quid pro quo."

Even the greediest councilman seldom resorts to breaking kneecaps. As for the "quid pro quo," how do you prove a secret deal when both sides deny it? If the extorted party ultimately has got what he wants, he's got no reason to rat on the extortee.

When such allegations do arise, the politician's typical response is righteous indignation. He will heatedly deny any connection between his vote and the wad of money that arrived shortly thereafter. Pure coincidence!

The recent case of Hialeah Mayor Raul Martinez didn't involve campaign funds, but still relied on a broader interpretation of the Hobbs Act. Martinez was charged with extorting almost $1 million in cash and property from developers, in exchange for zoning favors.

Yet some of the government's own witnesses swore—with straight faces—that they'd have steered lucrative real-estate business toward the mayor no matter how he voted. They'd have done it just because he's a swell guy.

Jurors didn't swallow it. The new Supreme Court ruling, however, puts the mayor's conviction in jeopardy. As in the West Virginia case, the Martinez jury was told that proof of threats and explicit extortion wasn't necessary for a guilty verdict; the "wrongful taking" of money and property was enough.

A majority of the high court says no. Consequently, it will be more difficult than ever to make a federal case against a corrupt officeholder.

Hard to believe it's the same "law-and-order" court that's cracked down so hard on the rights of the accused. Recent rulings have given police more power to search without warrants, allowed coerced confessions to stand and lengthened the time that an arrested person can be held with no charges.

The court's anti-crime fervor obviously doesn't extend to politicians. A crook is still safer running for office than he is breaking into one.

March 27, 1994

JEB BUSH SHOULD STOP FLAUNTING HIS FUND-RAISING

Some things you don't brag about.

This week, in only three days, Jeb Bush raised more than $1 million for his gubernatorial campaign. He took his famous mother and father on a statewide tour of cocktail parties and breakfasts, where rich people wrote out checks for $500 each.

The Jebster confidently predicted that his campaign kitty soon will surpass $2.5 million.

Bragging about it is calculated to intimidate other Republican candidates, and even frighten some away from the governor's race. But while the riches of Bush's war chest might daunt his rivals, it will also alienate lots of voters who can't afford yachts and country-club memberships.

Forget all the bunk about campaign reform in Florida. Special interests are once again trying to buy the governor's mansion, and they're off to a spectacular start.

Try this: Walk down the block and ask your neighbors how many have donated to the Jeb Bush campaign. Unless you live in Gables-by-the-Sea or Ocean Reef, you probably won't bump into too many contributors.

That's because regular folks don't send money to political candidates until the campaign actually begins. Meanwhile, the Jebster has been raking in dough for a year. Bankers, corporate lawyers, developers, sugar growers—they're all bankrolling the Bush Family Bandwagon.

It's hardly a partisan vice. Democrats are just as shameless as Republicans about wooing the rich and powerful. Republicans are just better at it.

Sucking up to cash cows is a distasteful chore for many office seekers, and it's possible that first-timer Jeb hates the charade. Anybody with an ounce of self-respect would. Unfortunately, you still can't run a statewide campaign without raising millions.

Every politician faces a moral decision: From whom do I take money, and how much? The answer defines the candidate because it reveals to whom they're willing to be obligated and the depth of that obligation.

Jeb Bush clearly has no qualms about being the darling of land developers. He's one himself. But bragging about it could be political suicide, given the greedy rape of South Florida over the last 30 years.

It's no longer possible to take special-interest money without appearing tainted by it. Voters here are getting wise.

There's also a question of taste. Donors with the most to spend have a fondness for fancy parties, at which their chosen candidate is expected to appear and be charming.

Jeb hauled his parents to 10 fund-raisers at luxurious estates from one end of the state to the other. In between soirees (to prove they hadn't forgotten the travails of the common man), the Bush family dropped by a school and an inner-city community center.

That's the standard drill: Go one place for the money, another place for the votes.

In their defense, GOP leaders say candidates were forced to start scrounging funds early, since state campaign "reforms" cut the maximum individual donation from $1,000 to $500. Poor babies.

Four years ago, Lawton Chiles managed to win election, despite limiting personal contributions to $100. Granted, lots of $100 donations came from corporate heavy hitters, their spouses, kids, second cousins, in-laws and probably family pets.

Capping donations doesn't deprive the wealthy of their right to support a candidate, but it definitely cuts into their clout. Politicians run more honest campaigns when a check from a schoolteacher carries the same weight as a check from the president of Arvida.

Jeb Bush has chosen the unsavory old way of raising money. If he keeps flaunting it, he'll drive off more than just his opponents.

December 1, 1994

METRO PUPPETS HAVE NO SHAME IN BASE DEAL

Christmas has come early for some politically connected land developers. They got a gift-wrapped goody from the Santas on the Metro Commission: Homestead Air Force Base.

The feds will turn over surplus base property to Dade County in 1996. It's a juicy parcel that includes immense runways and about 1,100 undeveloped acres.

Dade commissioners have tied a big red ribbon around it and promised it to a new outfit called Homestead Air Force Base Developers Inc. (HABDI). Its head honcho is Carlos Herrera Jr., president of the Latin Builders Association.

The LBA and its members are heavy campaign contributors to several Metro commissioners. Being the jumpy puppets they are, it's hardly shocking that they would reward the LBA's generosity with a sweetheart land lease. It's the way they did it that's so outrageous.

Commissioners didn't merely embrace HABDI's proposal, they basically voted not to consider any others—including a plan submitted by a wealthy New York entrepreneur, John Grace.

Usually, politicians paying back campaign favors at least go through a charade of competitive bidding. Not this bunch. Metro says public bids aren't necessary with the Homestead project because airport contracts don't require it. How convenient.

Since the arrangement first came to light last July, South Dade home-owner groups have fought to open negotiations to other developers. Many residents supported the Grace plan because they felt it allowed more local input into how the air base would be transformed.

Metro Commissioner Katy Sorenson recently offered an ill-fated resolution calling for a citizen's review panel that would keep watch over the redevelopment of Homestead's base property.

The LBA reacted predictably. Executive Director William J. Delgado said the idea for a citizen's council was a "direct attack to the Latin and African-American communities."

How? The advisory group would have consisted of folks who live near the air base. The LBA claimed that was racist, because those neighborhoods don't have as many Hispanics and blacks as some other areas of the county.

You know the routine. Scream discrimination when the opposite is true.

"A total slap in the face" is what Kevin Broils called the accusation. Broils is black. He also heads the Princeton-Naranja Community Council, which strongly opposes the giveaway to HABDI.

If anyone has been discriminated against, it's John Grace. HABDI's backroom boosters say the air base property shouldn't be leased to some rich guy from New York. They say it belongs in local hands.

Local? HABDI's Herrera is from Hialeah, which is light years from Homestead. Look at the way Hialeah was developed and you understand why residents of South Dade are alarmed.

Herrera has ambitious plans for the air base. He hopes to attract cargo services, a passenger airline, hotels, a farmer's market and even a movie studio. The firm says it initially will put up $10 million cash, with additional funds to be raised from a private stock offering.

Maybe it will turn the old base into a thriving commercial airpark. Maybe somebody else would do it better. We'll never know. The deal was cemented with politics, not merit.

Next week, Dade commissioners will hear HABDI's formal pitch. Expect them to bubble with enthusiasm, as the Latin Builders Association has suggested they should.

Grace stands no chance, nor does anybody else, now that Metro has dispensed with even the pretense of honest competition.

January 14, 1996

WHERE INFLUENCE COMES EASY, NOT CHEAP

One of the most whimsical scenes of any political race is that moment when a candidate gazes earnestly into the TV camera and swears he's not remotely influenced by the truckloads of campaign donations from special interests.

The candidate's pronouncement usually comes with a tinge of indignation at the insinuation that his or her loyalty is available to the highest bidder.

Oh, perish the thought.

Now comes a report by the Center for Public Integrity, a nonpartisan research group, that names the top lifetime contributors to this year's major presidential candidates—and explains what they got for their money.

Plenty, it turns out.

During Bill Clinton's political career, his biggest sugar daddy has been the New York investment banking firm of Goldman Sachs, which has given $107,850.

In addition, the company's former co-chairman, Robert E. Rubin, and his wife donated $275,000 to the New York Host Committee for the 1992 Democratic convention.

After his election, Clinton made Rubin (surprise, surprise) Secretary of the Treasury. The appointment caused no uproar whatsoever, since cabinet posts are traditionally dished out to big campaign contributors.

If Bob Dole gets elected next November, he could stock his administration with California winemakers. According to CPI's report, the Gallo family, its winery and employees have given more money to Dole's campaigns than anybody.

The Kansas senator has received $381,000 from the Gallo winery. An additional $790,000 has been given to the Dole Foundation, a charity for the handicapped.

Dole's actions suggest he's keenly aware of the Gallos' generosity. In 1992, he intervened with authorities so the Gallos could soften the wording required by the government on their wine labels.

And in 1986, as a key member of the Senate Finance Committee, Dole helped pass an amendment to a tax reform law that would spare the Gallo heirs more than $100 million in U.S. inheritance taxes. No wonder he's the toast of the vineyard.

Then there's Sen. Phil Gramm of Texas. His largest benefactor is the National Rifle Association, which has muzzle-loaded his coffers with more than $440,000 since 1979.

No politician in America has collected more money from the gun lobby and, according to the CPI report, "Gramm has not disappointed the NRA." Of 18 major pro-gun bills introduced in Congress in the last decade, Gramm has supported them all, and sponsored many.

Not surprisingly, Gramm and the other presidential contenders aren't eager to discuss CPI's research, which has been published in a new book called *The Buying of the President.*

The money alone is embarrassing for the volume of it. Even worse is what the candidates must do to get it.

While complaining about the vulgarity of fund-raising, they do little to change it. The last meaningful campaign reforms came after Watergate, when Congress couldn't avoid the issue.

Recently a new, bipartisan reform package was introduced. The chance of its passage in an election year, when many officeholders are busy shaking down corporate donors, isn't good.

But even if the reform movement dies again, the candidates should stop insulting our intelligence. Quit pretending the money from Goldman Sachs or the NRA doesn't matter. Quit pretending the pensioner who sends a $5 donation gets the same consideration as the CEO who sends $5,000 to your political action committee.

And quit the self-righteous pretending you can't be bought, when the facts show otherwise. In the immortal words of Ernest and Julio, put a cork in it.

October 31, 1996

BIPARTISANSHIP: THEY JUST CAN'T SAY NO TO DOUGH

The new national poster boy for campaign reform is Jorge Luis Cabrera, the Florida cocaine smuggler who got invited to the White House after donating $20,000 to the Democratic National Committee.

Nobody asked where Cabrera got the money. Nobody ever asks, as long as the check clears.

So Cabrera attended a White House gathering and shook hands with Hillary Rodham Clinton. Another time he got his picture taken with Vice President Al Gore. In the photo, Cabrera is beaming from ear to ear while Gore appears overmedicated.

In any case, the vice president isn't stupid enough to be knowingly photographed with a drug smuggler, particularly in an election year. Gore probably figured Cabrera was just another fat-cat contributor who wanted a memento for his den.

A few months later, Jorge got busted. Now he's doing 19 years, and the Democrats are crimson. Needless to say, they sheepishly refunded the donation.

It should be noted that it wasn't Cabrera's first brush with the law. He'd been busted for drugs twice before, and pleaded guilty to lesser charges. His true occupation was no secret in his hometown of Islamorada, where he masqueraded as a seafood distributor.

The Republicans are having a blast with the Cabrera fiasco, but it just as easily could've happened to them. Neither political party conducts thorough background investigations of its contributors. They don't routinely ask for IDs, aliases or dates of birth so that names can be cross-checked in the crime computers.

That ought to be standard procedure for any large contribution arriving from South Florida. In fact, it wouldn't be a bad idea to put a dope-sniffing dog on the campaign payroll, just to take care of the mail from Miami.

But the problem isn't just the dirty money, it's all of it. Whether given by a coke importer, a tobacco company or the trial lawyers, the aim is to buy clout. The larger the donation, the less likely it springs from the pure golden goodness of somebody's heart.

Under our current sham of election laws, individuals and corporations may give only $1,000 directly to a presidential candidate, but they can donate up to $20,000 each to the Republican and Democratic parties.

And the parties just can't say no. It's amazing they aren't embarrassed more often.

But give Mr. Cabrera some credit as a scammer.

He is the same character who got his picture made with the usually wary Fidel Castro. According to drug agents, several wallet-sized prints of that Kodak moment were found in Cabrera's briefcase when he was arrested.

First, any Cuban American driving around South Florida with personal photos of himself and Fidel either has titanium cojones, or is patently insane.

Second, unless Castro has gone senile, it's doubtful he'd pose for pictures with a hairball doper, even if (as Cabrera claims) he was in cahoots with the guy.

Aide: El Presidente, I'd like to introduce you to a big American cocaine smuggler.
Castro: Excellent! Let's get a snapshot, just you and me!

I don't think so. What's more likely is that Cabrera spread some cash around Havana, and Castro (like most politicians) responded like a shark to a chum slick.

Money doesn't just talk, it shouts. And sometimes you don't need very much to prove that campaign fund raising in our country remains as blindly and corrosively greedy as ever.

As a joke, filmmaker Michael Moore sent Bob Dole's campaign a check made out from the "Satan Worshipers for Dole." Guess what. They cashed it in a heartbeat.

May 14, 1998

NO ALTRUISM IN POLITICAL FUND-RAISING

The governor's race heated up last week when Lt. Gov. Buddy MacKay, the Democratic front-runner, criticized Republican Jeb Bush for accepting a tanker-full of donations from Texas oilmen.

Jeb has raised more than three quarters of a million bucks—$372,000 for his campaign and another $455,000 for Florida's GOP—from supporters of his brother George W., governor of the Lone Star State.

Much of that windfall was oil money, a fact that has prompted MacKay to question the depth of Jeb's oft-stated opposition to offshore drilling.

But here we go again with the politics of cynicism. Suspicions run wild when out-of-state tycoons pour so much loot into a local political race. What are their motives? folks wonder. What do they want here, and from whom?

This, unfortunately, is the skeptical age we live in. Nobody's willing to take a generous civic-minded gesture at face value.

Part of the blame falls on us media jackals for focusing so much on extortionist-style fund-raising and on politicians who auction themselves to deep-pocket donors.

Perhaps it's time to stop painting all "special interests" with the same brush of distrust. Suppose, for example, that the Texas oil guys didn't give all that dough to Jeb and the Republicans in the hope for special favors.

Suppose they shelled out that $827,000 out of a pure love for Florida and an abiding concern for its future.

Let the cynics hoot and snicker. For once we're going to be sunny and positive about the way politics works. For once we're going to give everyone the benefit of the doubt, including Mr. Hushang Ansary of Houston.

He owns a company that makes oil drilling equipment. In February he contributed $50,000 to the Florida Republican party, while his company kicked in another $100,000. (State law bans donors from giving more than $500 to an individual candidate.)

Those worried about oil derricks rising off the Gulf Coast are bound to be alarmed, but there's probably a perfectly innocent, nonsinister explanation of why a big-shot Texan would take such a keen interest in Florida politics.

Ansary told the *Tampa Tribune* there was "absolutely no particular reason" why he contributed so much money, but that sounds like a man who's being modest. Nobody gives away $150,000 for "no particular reason."

Maybe Ansary fell head-over-heels for the Sunshine State on a family vacation to Disney World. Maybe he decided to adopt the place as his second home.

Maybe he sent that wad to the GOP because he loves to canoe the Wekiva River and kayak the Mosquito Lagoon. Maybe he snorkels the Pennekamp reef and drifts for tarpon at Boca Grande. Maybe he goes beachcombing on Sanibel and camping on St. George Island.

Being from Houston, Ansary might sincerely be worried about Florida's poor urban planning and runaway growth. He might be honestly shocked by our overcrowded highways and overcrowded classrooms and diminishing quality of life. He might be losing all kinds of sleep over what's happening to the water in the St. Lucie estuary.

Maybe he even gives money to save the manatee and the panther, and maybe he's absolutely distraught about the decline of the Cape Sable seaside sparrow. Maybe he believes Jeb Bush is the one person who can rescue the cute little peeper from extinction.

Isn't it possible that's why all those Texas fat cats—W. A. Moncrief Jr. of Fort Worth, Cary Maguire of Dallas, Ray Hunt of Hunt Oil—whipped out their checkbooks? It's because they care so darn much about all of us here in Florida. . . .

Naaaah. You're right, that's just plain ridiculous.

November 1, 1998

BUSH APPOINTEES? NOW THAT'S SCARY

Governor Jeb Bush.

The scariest thing about those words isn't Bush himself, by most accounts a decent fellow—devoted husband and father, good neighbor, lover of puppies, etc.

Not a complicated or mysterious guy—just ambitious, as one would expect from the son of an ex-President. He probably wouldn't steal a dime in Tallahassee, but that's not what we should be afraid of.

The scariest thing about having Jeb Bush in the governor's mansion is the folks who will be celebrating the most if he wins.

Oil interests. Big Sugar. Big Tobacco. The megabanks and megadevelopers. And business sharks such as our own beloved Wayne Huizenga.

That's where the Republican party got a big chunk of the $20 million-plus that it has spent running Jeb Bush for governor. And the people who signed those big fat checks are chilling the Dom Perignon for Tuesday night.

That's a spookier scenario than even Stephen King could conjure, because Jeb wasn't given all that money for nothing. It came attached to certain unspoken conditions, and only a fool would believe otherwise.

These heavy hitters, they've got plans for young Mr. Bush. He will be expected to take their phone calls. He will be expected to be their pal. That's why special interests invest so steeply in a political candidate—to buy access.

Jeb says he won't be influenced by their mountainous donations. Bill Clinton said the same thing, yet he interrupted a White House grope session with Monica Lewinsky to take a call from Alfie Fanjul, the Palm Beach sugar baron who donated a heap to the Democrats.

Not me, vows Jeb. The money won't matter. I'll stick to my ideals.

Unfortunately for Florida, he could be co-opted and not even be aware it was happening. As governor he'll be making lots of job appointments to important state regulatory agencies. His choices will directly affect the future of wetlands, coastlines, water quality, highways, schools, parks and more.

Such appointments tend to be partisan, a payback for political support or fund-raising efforts. Bush isn't nearly so scary as the job applications that will be landing on his desk—stooges hand-picked by the same special interests that donated so hugely to the GOP.

That's fine if you don't mind water policy being dictated by cane growers and housing developers, or public transportation decisions being made by highway contractors and rail companies. It has certainly been done that way in the past, and the dreary consequences loom for all Floridians to see.

Just a few scary choices for a few key jobs is all it takes to screw things up even more. And Bush's track record in picking people leaves much to be desired. In 1994, he chose for his running mate an obscure right-winger named Tom Feeney, and surrounded himself with arrogant advisors whose nitwitted strategy cost him the election.

This time around, Bush got off to another embarrassing start by picking Secretary of State Sandra Mortham as his lieutenant governor-to-be. She withdrew after it was revealed she solicited a $60,000 charitable donation from a tobacco firm, then spent some of the dough on picnics and doodads.

At least voters get a say on a candidate's running mate. There is no such check on a governor's personnel picks, which are finalized not at the polls but behind closed doors.

That is what's scary about Jeb Bush—not that he would deviously sell out to the corporate greedheads who bankrolled his election, but that he would do it guilelessly, without knowing any better.

November 10, 1999

A NEW CONCEPT: MERIT OVER MOOLAH

Listen hard, and you can almost hear them squirm.

Miami-Dade Commissioner Jimmy Morales wants to outlaw campaign contributions from people whose firms have county contracts. Such a measure, he says, would be a step toward assuring citizens that their government isn't for sale.

What Morales proposes makes sense. It also makes some of his colleagues jittery, because they—as he does—stand to lose thousands in donations from county vendors seeking favored treatment from the commission.

So there will be plenty of fidgeting at County Hall. The dilemma is familiar: Do you suck it up and do the right thing, or do you grab for the dough?

And how do you grab and not look like you don't care about the integrity of the political process? To which the average Miami-Dade voter might reply: What integrity?

From the airport to the seaport to the commission chamber itself, county government has been steered by cronyism, influence-hawking and outright corruption. Scarcely a month goes by without a new scandal.

In such a dispiriting climate, commissioners become vulnerable at the polls. Even the slimiest of the bunch must strive to appear indignant and reform-minded.

And now comes Jimmy Morales, stirring the pot by offering an actual reform; something with a little substance. Under his proposal, people who own or run companies with county contracts could not give money to candidates running for the Miami-Dade Commission or community councils.

The premise: With tax dollars at stake, vendors ought to be chosen because of their bid qualifications—not because of their generosity to politicians. There's a radical concept, huh? Merit over moolah.

But a loophole in Morales's plan is drawing criticism: People doing business with county agencies still would be allowed to contribute to a commission or council candidate in the district where they live.

Morales says there's no way around it. He says a campaign-reform ordinance would be ruled unconstitutional if it tried to prohibit any voter—county vendors included—from donating to a representative from his or her home area.

Some of Morales's colleagues say the exception would hurt them more than Morales, who represents some of the county's most affluent neighborhoods and the corporate big shots who live there. Theoretically, Morales should be able to raise more campaign bucks than commissioners from poorer districts.

The disparity is undeniable, but Morales has come up with a simple remedy: Commissioners could agree to send back all political contributions from county contractors living in their districts.

"I would be willing to sign a voluntary pledge, along with all my colleagues, to do that. I am willing to give back any checks that I have gotten and not accept any future checks," Morales said.

That's more than a friendly challenge; it's a test of character.

Parting with money isn't easy in the heat of an expensive political race, and the recommendation is making some commissioners queasy. Morales caused similar ripples last year when he pushed for a ban on corporate contributions in county races. Surprisingly, it passed the commission 9–4.

His move to limit donations from county contractors has been praised by Mayor Alex Penelas, who has nothing to lose. The mayor's race wouldn't be affected by the measure. If Penelas runs for re-election, he's still free to take money from anybody.

Of Morales's fellow commissioners, Katy Sorenson has spoken out in favor of the new proposal, while Dennis Moss has voiced misgivings. Said Moss: "I think to some degree we may be trying to over-regulate ourselves."

Some type of "over-regulation" is long overdue. Last year Miriam Alonso raked in an obscene $534,000 to help retain her commission seat; with a $269,000 campaign kitty, Sorenson was no slouch, either.

The heftiest loot doesn't come from the pockets of Joe Voter, but from the bank accounts of those with millions of dollars in county business at stake.

If Morales gets his way, candidates will lose some serious dough from special interests, and the special interests will lose a handy pipeline to the candidates.

That can only be good. Let the squirming begin.

14

POLITICS AS USUAL

December 23, 1988

LET'S TEST LEGISLATORS FOR DRUGS

Gov. Bob Martinez finally came up with something for his new Drug Czar to do: juggle specimen bottles.

This week, the governor proposed a broad urine-testing plan for state employees. The governor said it's just like requiring a driver's exam—and if you've been on a Florida highway lately, you can attest that there are absolutely no lunatics anywhere.

The drug program includes the attempted screening of prospective state workers, and the testing of any current employees if a "reasonable suspicion" of drug use exists.

Interestingly, the governor omitted one key group from his show-us-your-pee program: elected officials.

Apparently Martinez feels that the public welfare is better served by cracking down on clerks and secretaries instead of state senators and representatives and Cabinet members.

In other words, the state will spend truckloads of tax dollars to make sure that the lady who takes your dime at the tollbooth has clean urine—but no such test will be given to those with their paws on the $21 billion state budget.

Heck, all the legislators do is write the laws and spend your money. What possible harm can they cause?

Gov. Martinez's Golden Sprinkler Plan would require urinalysis for all so-called "critical" employees—firefighters, law-enforcement officers, jail guards, even the governor's staff.

Why not the legislators, too? Voting in the state House would seem to be an extremely critical job, and one that demands sobriety. Perhaps the governor would prefer dealing with a Legislature blitzed out of its collective gourd.

But what about his other criterion for urine testing—that is, if an employee causes "reasonable suspicion" that he or she is under the influence of alcohol or other drugs while on the job.

Under these guidelines alone, every legislator could be hauled to the drug czar's specimen booth.

Talk about exhibiting bizarre and erratic behavior—look at last year's ill-fated sales tax on special services. Was that mangled, incoherent document not the product of spaced-out minds?

This is the same bunch of legislators who voted to weaken Florida's handgun laws during an epidemic of armed assaults on police officers. Ask yourselves what kind of politicians would write a law that allowed accused murderers to get permits for concealed weapons.

Nobody is that stupid, so they must have been stoned.

Every spring these geniuses troop off to Tallahassee and behave like they're on a field trip with Timothy Leary. This year they voted momentously on selecting a state pie. They debated bitterly over an official state sand.

They even passed a law ordering police to arrest anyone with an "obscene" bumper sticker—this, at a time when our prisons are overflowing with the most dangerous criminals known to man.

If such acts by the Legislature do not constitute "reasonable suspicion" of drug use, then I don't know what does.

Of course, the governor has a practical political reason for not including elected lawmakers in his drug-testing plan. They wouldn't (literally) stand for it.

They'd feel insulted, humiliated, violated. They'd be offended by the idea of someone confiscating a cup of their urine. They would say it insults personal dignity.

The smart ones would also say that the cost to taxpayers could never justify the minimal results—not to mention the expensive civil lawsuits that are bound to spring up when the labs make a mistake on some innocent person's sample.

And having said all that (mostly to themselves), the Legislature will probably go right ahead and impose the governor's urine plan for everybody on the state payroll but themselves.

How hypocritical that would be. No one has more power than the legislators and Cabinet. No one has more responsibility, or is more directly accountable to the voters. No one makes more decisions that affect more lives in this state.

If we're going to have "clean" government, let's start at the top. Hand out those cups in the halls of the Capitol. Make everybody, not just the little guy, give till it hurts.

MIAMI COMMISSIONER REVEALS A PASSION FOR FRESH VEGETABLES

Two years ago, Miami voters elected Victor De Yurre to replace Joe Carollo. Today they might be wondering what was the point.

While Carollo's paranoid visions generally were limited to Commies and subversives, De Yurre's unusual fantasies apparently focus on fresh vegetables.

Last week, the Downtown Development Authority unveiled a slick new promotional brochure that features the gleaming Miami skyline, a beautiful woman and a seemingly innocent plate of veggies—specifically, carrots, broccoli and sliced peppers.

In critiquing the brochure, some commissioners complained that the picture of the beautiful woman was too suggestive—eyes closed, she's cavorting in the surf, and possibly without benefit of a bathing suit.

Commissioner De Yurre went on to say that he was further offended by the photograph of the vegetables, which reminded him of . . . male genitalia.

If only I were making this up, but I'm not. Study the picture carefully.

Now try to figure out what De Yurre is yammering about. Does the broccoli remind him of pubic hair? And if the carrot is intended to represent the male sexual wand, why are there four of them in the photograph? Does Victor know somebody with four of them?

These are vitally important questions, and we need to get to the roots. We can even envision a brand new field of psychological testing, where vegetable arrangements replace ink blots.

Taking the tourist pamphlet as a whole, there's nothing remotely naughty about it. It is designed as sort of a wraparound postcard. The photography is elegant, the colors are dazzling and the city never looked better.

The best thing about the brochure is that private corporations paid for most of it.

Inside is a fold-out poster that tells all you'd ever want to know about downtown. So what if the prose is tumescent: "Miami has emerged as a pacesetter in film and fashion. Its look is hot and eclectic. Filled with the restless energy of a city in continual transformation."

You said it.

The flap over the model lying on her tummy in the water is inane but not without precedent.

Years ago, the Metro Commission banned a tourism poster that featured a bare-backed woman clad in half a bikini. Instantly the poster became a collector's item, and the slogan ("Miami. See it like a native.") became an indelible subject of lore and parody.

Perhaps with this in mind, city commissioners stopped short of banning outright the new downtown promotional brochure. They did not, however, waste the opportunity to make ninnies of themselves.

By a 3–2 vote, they decreed that no new promotional materials were to be distributed without their prior review and approval. This now gives them an excuse to spend hours looking at color slides of beautiful models cavorting in the water.

In the commission's defense, it's not unreasonable to ask what a picture of carrots (no matter how breathtaking) is doing in a business brochure. Is downtown Miami famous for its carrots? Should it be? Would more Fortune 500 companies relocate here if they knew about our stems and tubers?

Such probing questions were forgotten as soon as De Yurre opened his mouth and said the arrangement of vegetables reminded him of lower male body parts.

What a frightening insight into the commissioner's mind! Obviously this is a fellow who should never be allowed to browse unchaperoned in the produce section of Publix.

If a mere glimpse of naked carrots inflames De Yurre's imagination, what happens when he encounters a particularly sultry yam? Or a patch of young red cabbages, ripe and beckoning . . .

And artichokes! I quote directly from the *Britannica:* "A compact, heavy, globular, plump artichoke, yielding slightly to pressure, with large, tightly clinging, fleshy leaf scales of a good green colour is the most desirable . . ."

Down, Victor, down!!!

July 11, 1990

THE REV. PAT IS GOING TO BAT FOR MARTINEZ

The occult is now a factor in the gubernatorial race.

What else can explain the news that Bob Martinez seeks political salvation in the arms of a TV faith healer?

It's true. Pat Robertson has come to Florida to save the governor from defeat in November.

Yes, Pat Robertson—failed presidential candidate, conspiracy theorist and purveyor of pulpit miracles. A man who has claimed to cure everything from hernias to hemorrhoids in exchange for modest cash contributions; a man who insists that his prayers once scared a hurricane away from Virginia.

Precisely the sort of stable, well-reasoned individual you'd want on the campaign trail. Excellent choice, Governor. Talk about timing. Just when Martinez seemed in danger of slipping back into the political mainstream, he gets adopted as a poster boy of the Far Right.

Robertson and a new group calling itself the Florida Christian Coalition have declared Florida the big prize in a renewed battle for America's moral soul. At the top of the agenda is getting Martinez re-elected.

When the Democrats heard the news, they probably thought they'd died and gone to heaven: "Martinez is getting endorsed by whom? Pat Robertson? *The* Pat Robertson? Oh thank you, God, this is too good to be true."

We're not just talking fringe—this guy is on the fringe of fringe. A sample of Robertson's bizarre ravings: The U.S. government is secretly controlled by the Council on Foreign Relations. God intends to destroy the Soviet Union with volcanoes and the occasional earthquake. The antichrist, age 27, has returned to Earth and awaits Satan's instructions.

Yeah. Probably has a car phone, too.

Republicans must be elated that the same preacher who once predicted a nuclear holocaust for 1982 is now predicting a Martinez victory for 1990.

The governor's advisers say the campaign needs the grassroots enthusiasm of Robertson's followers. The trouble is, Robertson's following is not particularly large. He got stomped in Florida's 1988 presidential primary.

Christian evangelicals, a small segment of the electorate, don't necessarily march to the polls in lockstep. For Robertson to make a serious impact on the governor's race, he'd have to deliver both Protestant and Catholic conservatives—an unlikely coup.

These days his major crusade is against abortion, a subject that Martinez scarcely mentions anymore. Last fall the governor's efforts to toughen abortion laws were crushed by the Legislature and crippled by the state Supreme Court; most Floridians don't want Tallahassee interfering in such private matters.

To resurrect the abortion issue is political suicide, but there's Martinez climbing up on the ledge, with Rev. Pat exhorting him to go ahead and jump. It's so dumb, it's sad.

The governor now finds himself the official standard bearer for a constituency whose priorities include the removal from office of Leander Shaw, the first black chief justice of the Florida Supreme Court.

Shaw is a target because he wrote the court's landmark ruling that restricts the Legislature from interfering with a woman's decision to get an abortion.

It will be interesting to watch the governor try to distance himself from the anti-Shaw witch hunt, assuming he's got enough sense to do so.

Even though Robertson has toned down his act (unlike Martinez, he no longer speaks in tongues), it's still a puzzle why the governor would ally himself with someone considered too extreme for his own party.

Maybe the answer has nothing to do with politics. Maybe the governor sees Robertson as an emissary from that Big Pollster in the Sky.

Consider it a test of holy clout. If Rev. Robertson can whip a full-blown hurricane, he ought to be able to save Bob Martinez's candidacy.

All he needs to do is say a prayer and make Lawton Chiles go away.

June 2, 1994

2 + 12 = 25, SAY MIAMI BEACH MATHEMATICIANS

The Abe Hirschfelds might come and go, but Miami Beach government remains a reliable swamp of deceit and incompetence.

Neither the current city manager nor the Design Review Board can master their basic integers. In particular, they can't tell the difference between the numbers "14" and "25." Or so they'd have you believe.

In its headlong quest to destroy whatever charm South Beach has acquired in recent years, the city approved a high-rise condo at 155 Ocean Drive. The project will be built by German zillionaire Thomas Kramer.

Three pages of the blueprints, submitted by the hotshot architectural firm of Arquitectonica, show a building height of 146 feet, or 14 stories. A memo from city planning director Dean Grandin, Jr., describes the proposal as a "14-story, 42-unit apartment building." Grandin specifies that the tower will be "comprised of two levels of covered parking . . . and 12 floors of residential units."

Hmmm, let's see: 2 plus 12 equals . . . 25!

When the project went before the city's Design Review Board, a planner again gave the height as fourteen stories. The meeting agenda, however, referred to a 25-story structure. Eagle-eyed members of the Design Review Board didn't catch the discrepancy (or so they claim), and approved the condo.

One person who did notice was David Colby, who owns a two-story Art Deco hotel across from 155 Ocean Drive. Colby hired a lawyer and raised a stink, which sent the city into a bumbling paroxysm of butt covering.

Planning director Grandin gave a sworn affidavit saying the Kramer condo was always meant to have 25 floors. The architects concurred, saying whoever put the specs on the blueprints made a boo-boo.

But the most preposterous line came from City Manager Roger Carlton, who assured the commission that the discrepancy was merely a "scrivener's error." Seriously, that's what the man said.

It would take one brain-dead scrivener to mistake the numeral "25" for the numeral "14." Perhaps it's the same one who calculated Carlton's $131,250 salary.

Some city commissions would have canned both Grandin and Carlton after such a fishy debacle. Not in Miami Beach.

Remember the rabid climate in which the stunt unfolded. Last year, under pressure from residents, the city proposed height restrictions for most new buildings. High-rise developers, including Kramer, rushed to beat the deadline.

In only a few months, with Carlton as the main cheerleader, the city approved a half-dozen skyscrapers for the South Pointe area. The project at 155 Ocean Drive squeaked in.

"I can't say I was aware it was 14 stories or 25 stories." That, from Bernard Zyscovich of the Design Review Board. For an architect, he's a bit fuzzy on the details. Naturally he voted for the high-rise anyway.

City attorneys advised board members that a grandfathered project can't be rejected because of its height. That's their laughable alibi for approving a condo that will be a whopping 76 percent taller than they thought.

Are they really that inept, or just selectively attentive?

Monkey business of this sort has gone on for ages in Florida, but usually on a more modest scale. Between approval and construction, a building might mysteriously grow by one or two extra floors, but not 11. That's just plain grabby.

Colby says Miami Beach ought to reconsider the Kramer high-rise because the Design Review Board obviously didn't know what they were voting for. But City Manager Carlton refuses to put the matter back on the agenda and has fixed all official documents to show a height of 25 stories.

A scrivener with a mission.

November 24, 1994

GOP GLUTTONS FEED WEALTHY, STARVE POOR

As details emerge about the ambitious Republican plans to overhaul welfare, public enthusiasm is dissolving into edginess and even alarm.

Thanksgiving brings the surprising news that the new House of Representatives will seek to deny benefits to millions of legal immigrants, many of them elderly, many of them longtime taxpayers.

Another baffling target: the school lunch and breakfast program, which feeds 25 million children daily. The GOP proposal would scrap it, and instead pay each state a lump sum for food assistance.

When we think of government waste, the school-lunch program isn't the first thing that leaps to mind. Americans have always been big-hearted when it comes to the hungry. Given a choice, most of us would rather see our tax dollars spent on needy kids than on Jesse Helms' salary.

The history of child-nutrition laws goes back half a century, and has had strong support from both political parties. In fact, two powerful GOP senators, Bob Dole and Richard Lugar, have fought to strengthen food programs.

At the core of the school-lunch law is the humane premise that no child in a country as rich as ours should go hungry. To toss this responsibility back to the states invites neglect, discrimination and abuse.

Ironically, the debate over food-assistance programs comes in an autumn when U.S. farmers are reaping record bounties of rice, corn and soybeans. Grain elevators are overflowing. In some Midwest towns, hills of corn are piled on the streets.

Good news, right?

Not exactly. The huge harvest is glutting the market, which means farmers are getting lower prices, which means federal subsidies will soon shoot up. The Department of Agriculture predicts that this season's bumper crops will result in direct government payouts of $12 billion to $13 billion to farm interests.

Logic plays no part in the system. Politics rule. The biggest public handouts don't go to old folks or children or immigrants, but to Fortune 500 titans.

Predictably, those who want to slash domestic spending would rather pick on the weak. It's easy to get voters riled up about food-stamp fraud and Medicaid ripoffs, because that's a level of welfare they can understand.

The densely structured tax breaks, subsidies and price-supports contrived for major corporations are more cleverly disguised, but it's "entitlement" just the same. We all pay.

On Tuesday, Labor Secretary Robert Reich suggested that the new Congress should consider terminating as much as $200 billion in "corporate welfare," and use the savings to fund jobs programs.

Such a notion—fair and reasonable, as long as other benefits are being hacked—always causes a nervous puckering in Washington. Goring the welfare ox is a priority, as long as the ox isn't named Exxon or Conagra or U.S. Sugar.

If it comes down to cutting aid to elderly immigrants, or cutting into corporate profit margins, guess whose benefits will be sacrificed?

Nobody argues that the current welfare system is a model of efficiency. It's a mess, bogged by waste, fraud and inertia. Fundamentally, Americans dislike the idea of able-bodied men and women collecting a government check for doing nothing, and too much of that goes on.

But the popular and overdue movement to overhaul "welfare" can't begin until we define it. And we cannot define it without confronting some expensive hypocrisy.

Imagine a country that can't afford $4.5 billion for hungry schoolchildren, but can afford $12 billion for farmers who grew too much food.

Happy Thanksgiving.

December 29, 1994

INTEGRITY IN HIRING SOLD OUT AT METRO-DADE

The only surprising thing about the squalid way in which Dade's new county manager was selected is that some people were genuinely surprised.

They still cling to the quaint fantasy that job applicants are chosen according to ability, that the debate takes place in an open forum, that it isn't steered by conniving special interests, and that Metro commissioners can put aside their egos and ambitions for the sake of the public good.

Since when? Given the current cast of characters, there was absolutely no danger that integrity would influence the process.

Sure, the "search" for a county manager was a charade. Long before the matter came up for a vote, the choice secretly had been narrowed to two main contenders: Cynthia Curry, an assistant manager, and Armando Vidal, the public works director.

Curry is black. Vidal is Hispanic. Both own relatively solid job qualifications, which were pretty much irrelevant. Black leaders wanted Curry as the new manager, while power brokers in the Cuban community lobbied ardently for Vidal.

Blacks versus Latins, us versus them. Same old crap. The only ingredient missing from the mean brew was a token Anglo candidate, to bring out the full complement of racists and xenophobes.

Vidal got the job, but it could easily have been Curry. Vidal's boosters simply did a better job of rounding up votes. It helps, of course, when so many of the commissioners are up for grabs.

Our favorite dictator-in-waiting, Jorge Mas Canosa, made an unsuccessful pitch at Commissioner Maurice Ferre. The proposed deal: If Ferre voted for Vidal, Mas would support Ferre's bid for mayor in 1996.

Ferre didn't bite. He voted for neither Vidal nor Curry.

Commissioner Gwen Margolis didn't play so hard to get. She went for Vidal because Commissioner Alex Penelas (a Vidal supporter) agreed to back Margolis' plan to enlarge the powers of the Metro Commission chairman.

See, Margolis wants to be the next chairman, so she'd like the job to be more powerful than it is now. All in the public interest, of course.

Which brings us to the current commission chairman, Arthur "Bonecrusher" Teele. Poor Art. When the dust finally settles, he'll be remembered mainly for slugging lobbyist Rick Sisser in the schnoz.

Let me suggest that the citizens would be better served if their commissioners spent more time punching lobbyists, and less time kissing their butts.

Nonetheless, Teele's motive for clobbering Sisser was not especially noble. Teele suspected him of planting nasty rumors that Teele (who is black) had bargained away his support for Cynthia Curry's candidacy for the manager's job.

Teele decided that assaulting Sisser was an appropriate way to clarify his position. Being a clever lawyer, he made sure there were witnesses present.

Although the two men have since pretended to reconcile, Teele has run out and bought not one but three guns for protection. Lobbyists don't care. A flamethrower couldn't keep them out of commission offices.

No municipal politics is free of backroom horse-trading, but you'll seldom find a more fetid display than what happened here. The real shame is that the community continues to abet these travesties by encouraging divisive misbehavior.

Hispanic commissioners knew they'd catch hell from many constituents if they supported a qualified black for county manager, just as Teele knew he'd catch hell for supporting a qualified Latin.

As long as voters make ethnicity the issue, politicians are happy to go along. It gives them one more excuse to act dumb, play dirty and sell themselves to the highest bidder.

November 16, 1995

A GIFT OF JOE, JUST IN TIME FOR HOLIDAYS!

Thank you, Lord.

Thanks for finally bringing Joe Carollo back to Miami City Hall. Make that the new "mature" Joe Carollo.

Thanks also to the 14,941 daring souls who chose him over incumbent

Commissioner Victor De Yurre in Tuesday's runoff. Who said voters don't have a sense of humor?

Things had been too dull at City Hall—boringly civil. Not anymore. Now we'll need to start paying attention again.

It was eight years ago when Carollo was booted from office, rejected by a broad multiethnic constituency. Numerous comeback attempts flopped.

But this time, Carollo, now 40, was able to sell himself as older, wiser and more mature. Translation: "I am no longer the vicious, paranoid, race-baiting, back-stabbing maniac I used to be."

It was a good act. Too good, for my own selfish interests. I wanted the old Joe back because the old Joe was dependable—fodder for at least three or four columns a year. A new Joe? Say it ain't so.

Then, between the November 7 election and November 14 runoff, all fears were assuaged. The old Joe surfaced, a familiar hiss in the swamp.

Said he: "Victor De Yurre never met a drug dealer he didn't like."

It's true that De Yurre once took free building materials from a law client named Leonel Martinez, who turned out to be in the cocaine trade. And it's also true that De Yurre got donations from a restaurant owned by another recently convicted drug figure.

But to say De Yurre never met a doper he didn't like implies nasty things beyond the chronically lousy judgment of which De Yurre is guilty.

Then came Carollo's attack commercials on Spanish-language radio. A solemn announcer: "I speak for babies born with birth defects resulting from drug abuse. . . . Say no to drugs. Vote against Victor De Yurre."

In other words: De Yurre was personally responsible for poisoning the unborn. The message was sleazy, unfounded, demagogic—vintage Carollo!

Invoking deformed babies to win cheap votes? So much for "mature." So much for "mellow." Meet the new Joe. Same as the old Joe.

The same one who once announced that Fidel Castro's secret agents had infiltrated the Miami police.

The same one who once likened a black city manager to Ugandan dictator Idi Amin.

The same one who once blocked a Sister Cities convention from meeting in Miami because a few of the delegates came from Eastern bloc nations, meaning they were treacherous commies.

The same one who once kept an Uzi, and professed to equip his car with a dashboard bomb detector.

No, the man was never dull. And it must be said that for all his erratic and reprehensible behavior, the old Joe also managed to get a couple of pretty good laws passed.

For pure entertainment value, De Yurre couldn't fill Carollo's shoes. Victor's best Joe-style escapade happened in 1989, when he objected to a tourist brochure on grounds of lewdness. De Yurre asserted that an artsy photograph of carrots and broccoli looked too much like male genitalia.

It was a nice try, but Carollo wouldn't have stopped there. Joe would've claimed it was Castro's genitalia amidst the veggies.

Give him credit. By winning Tuesday, Carollo overcame a well-financed incumbent, an irredeemably checkered past and the surprise endorsement of this newspaper, which can be the kiss of death.

Thank heaven Joe prevailed. It's a columnist's dream: He's back, he's bad, and he's still loco.

March 28, 1996

TRY MARTINEZ AGAIN? IT'S NOT WORTH IT

Enough already with Raul Martinez. Let the man go.

Not because he's innocent, but because it'll cost a fortune to prosecute him again. It's not worth it.

Those who stand to gain from ditching a corrupt mayor don't seem to care. Most Hialeah voters adore Raul. They'd be perfectly content to let him run the city from a prison cell.

Everybody knows what Martinez did to get himself indicted. Back in the '80s, he made four real estate deals with developers who needed his support for zoning changes. The transactions earned Martinez between $134,000 and $182,000.

The U.S. government called it a shakedown. The mayor said he never promised any favors in exchange for the business.

In 1991, a jury found him guilty of extortion and racketeering. The verdict did not diminish even slightly Martinez's power and popularity.

An appellate court ordered a new trial, which ended Tuesday. This time the outcome was different: a mistrial, with jurors deadlocked 11–1 for acquittal.

Prosecutors say they'll do it again. The mayor says he's being persecuted.

Even if the case against Martinez ended today, it's not a total loss. The trials have been valuable civics lessons, proving beyond any doubt that Hialeah is as relentlessly corrupt as everybody assumed.

There was ex-Councilman Silvio Cardoso, testifying he once gave Martinez $100,000 in consulting fees—even though the mayor had done no consulting.

Cardoso called the money a "gift" meant to win Martinez's support for construction projects. Similar payments to ex-Councilman Andy Mejides were a "bribe," Cardoso explained, because Mejides overtly demanded the money in exchange for his vote.

Such a cagey distinction between gifts and bribes meshed nicely with the mayor's defense. His lawyer said he never extorted extra goodies from developers; rather, they fell serendipitously into his lap.

It's time for the U.S. attorney's office to step back and consider what can be gained from trying Martinez again.

In the years between the mayor's two trials, the courts have narrowed the scope of bribery and extortion. Prosecutors are now challenged to prove a public official isn't just selling influence wholesale, but trading specific votes for specific payoffs.

The message from the Martinez jury this week wasn't encouraging for the feds. If the vote had been 11–1 to convict the mayor, a retrial might make more sense. But an 11–1 vote to acquit signals problems with the indictment.

Even if prosecutors managed to convict Martinez in another trial, it would spark no miraculous outbreak of ethics in Hialeah. Anti-corruption resources would be better spent in places where they are appreciated.

FBI snooping did make a positive difference in other cities with the crooked-mayor form of government. John Lomelo of Sunrise and Alex Daoud of Miami Beach were two gregarious thieves whose esteem among voters declined noticeably when they went to jail.

Hialeah is another world. The air of graft and deception comes from deep in the soil, like radon gas.

The public reacted with scarcely a shrug to the recent suspension of the mayor's old pal, Rafael Sanchez, for allegedly mishandling funds from the Hialeah Housing Authority, and using his position there for financial gain.

Naturally, the mayor replaced Sanchez with another crony.

Some are ashamed by this stuff, and others are numb to it, but most Hialeah voters say they want Raul Martinez as their mayor, no matter what.

I say give the people what they want. They deserve it.

May 30, 1996

CHILES' VETO OF CONSCIENCE DERAILS "TAX TRAIN"

Sometimes it pays to have a governor who isn't worried about re-election.

Lawton Chiles is in his final term of office, and nearing the end of a long public career. Finally he can afford to tell Tallahassee power brokers to buzz off, which is basically what he did on Tuesday.

The governor vetoed an outrageous bill known as the "tax train," which had been passed at the last minute by the Legislature. Most Floridians never heard of it, and there's a reason:

Those who in the wee hours rammed this stinker through the House and the Senate weren't exactly eager to stand up and take credit.

The "tax train" would have provided nearly four dozen substantial tax breaks to a string of corporate and private beneficiaries. They had little in common except well-connected lobbyists and a mutual quest for loopholes.

With time waning in the session, lawmakers hastily pasted together a single bill—a "train," in the benign parlance of the back room—to deliver everybody's goodies all at once.

Among those poor struggling souls seeking tax relief were the folks at IBM, Continental Airlines, Coca-Cola and Time Inc. Others who hopped aboard were chicken farmers, workers' comp insurers and commercial printing firms.

It wasn't modesty that stopped legislators who stoked the "train" from sending out self-congratulatory press releases. They wisely perceived that voters wouldn't be thrilled about the bill because it was a smorgasbord of favors for special interests.

Secretive, 11th-hour giveaways are a bipartisan rite of spring in Tallahassee. Companies and industries who donate money to political campaigns expect more in return than a thank-you note or a basket of fruit. And usually they get it.

This year's tax train was engineered by Rep. Willie Logan of Opa-locka, a Democrat who chairs the House Finance and Taxation Committee. With bracing candor, Logan allowed that the tradition of the tax train is rooted in institutional spinelessness:

"Members don't have the will to vote against most tax exemptions, just like most members don't have the will to vote for more taxes. It's just a nature of the beast."

Which brings us to Gov. Chiles, the creaky old he-coon himself. A more political beast never prowled the corridors of the capitol.

Supporters of the special tax exemptions purposely attached them to legislation the governor liked, a bill that temporarily prohibited imposing a sales tax on Internet providers.

After it steamed through the Legislature, those who stood to benefit from the proposed tax breaks inundated Chiles with beseeching correspondence. They claimed the bill would spur corporate investment in Florida, and create more jobs.

Logan estimated the loopholes would cost the state no more than $15 million the first year, but analysts in the governor's office said the dent in the budget would be closer to $50 million.

So Chiles vetoed it—swiftly.

An aide said it would be indefensible for the Legislature to bestow millions of dollars in corporate welfare while simultaneously slashing services for senior citizens, the disabled, the mentally retarded and the poor.

The governor was angry about those cuts, and his veto of the tax giveaways was an exclamation point. He probably didn't win any Brownie points with IBM, Time Inc. or their hot shot lobbyists, but that's fine.

Chiles no longer needs the campaign donations because he isn't running for anything. These days it's an enviable if unfamiliar position for a politician—to be free to do the right thing for the right reason. What a concept.

October 3, 1996

A CLARION CALL FOR CLEAN LEADERS? NAH.

It would be nice to think Alex Penelas is Metro's first strong mayor because he made integrity the centerpiece of his campaign, and because voters wanted a mandate for reform.

Those who did probably weren't especially comforted by the spectacle of the new mayor dancing at his victory party with the high-rolling lobbyists who helped him win.

The truth is, Penelas was elected more because of his ethnicity than his ethics. That's how Dade votes. The TV ads and turbulent debates didn't change many minds: Cuban Americans went for Penelas, blacks went for Art Teele and the Anglos split almost evenly.

That's not to say Penelas would have coasted, no matter what. His 20-point margin undoubtedly was boosted by the fact he hasn't been caught in any bribery scandals, nor has he been working (as far as we know) undercover for the FBI.

Had Penelas been under indictment, he probably wouldn't have won by more than 10 points. Some voters do draw the line at convicted felons.

The parameters are fuzzier when it comes to garden-variety liars, connivers and deadbeats.

One of Penelas' supporters on the new county commission is Miriam Alonso, a landslide winner even though she was once booted off a ballot for lying about where she lived.

Commissioner Bruce Kaplan was easily re-elected, even though he once tried to weasel a lucrative job out of American Airlines while the company was negotiating with Metro for its $1 billion expansion at Miami International. (Currently, Kaplan is in trouble with a major Customs-fraud case in Peru. He says he's innocent.)

The list goes on, an amazing testament to voter charity. Commissioner James Burke, now a target of Operation Greenpalm, won his seat in 1993 despite being suspended from his law practice for dipping into a client's funds.

Maurice Ferre got elected even though he owed a $56,000 fine for previous campaign misdeeds. He paid it in time for this year's mayoral race, but was vague about where he got the money.

Given the public's history of forgiving and forgetting (not necessarily in that order), only an optimist would interpret Penelas' victory as a clarion call for clean government.

But there is evidence that people are becoming more intolerant of deceit. In Metro's District 7, voters resoundingly snubbed Mavel Cruz, considered the front-runner despite a tendency to lie at the drop of a name.

During the campaign it was revealed that Cruz had illegally claimed two homestead exemptions, fudged her academic credentials and faked an endorsement from Jeb Bush, complete with forged signature.

Aside from all that, she was squeaky clean.

Voters wisely decided Cruz wasn't cut out for office, and instead chose her opponent Jimmy Morales. He was aided by an enthusiastic endorsement from (are you ready?) Miriam Alonso.

Obviously Alex Penelas has an uphill battle. Although he can't control how the other politicians behave, he can definitely set a new tone by keeping his campaign promises, and keeping himself out of trouble.

The real question is whether Dade voters are serious about sanitizing county hall, or whether they're still willing to overlook sleaze.

There's one sure way to find out. His name is Joe Gersten.

If Burke quits the commission, a special election could be held to fill the slot. What better time for Fugitive Joe to return from his South Pacific exile!

You couldn't ask for a better acid test of the new voter "mandate." Come on home, Joey. Give it one more shot.

For old times' sake.

February 26, 1998

TO GET ELECTED IN DADE, FIRST GET INDICTED

It's just not fair. Twelve days isn't enough time to get indicted.

But that's all that remains for James Burke's opponents in the March 10 special election for Miami-Dade Commission, so they'd better think of something fast.

Burke was suspended from the District Two seat after being busted in a slimy bribery scheme. Awaiting trial, he wants his old job back—and clearly the indictment gives him an unfair advantage over the competition.

The same thing worked wonders for Hialeah Mayor Raul Martinez and, more recently, Miami Commissioner Humberto Hernandez. Now it is Burke's turn. He leads all fund-raising with about $24,000—more than both of his opponents put together.

But unlike Burke, neither Dorrin Rolle nor Sherman Henry has been arrested by the FBI. Nor have they been caught on videotape, allegedly discussing a $300,000 payoff for steering county bond business to one of their pals.

Nor have they ever been tracked to Bermuda, picking up $49,750 cash as an alleged down payment on the bribe.

Burke's is a hard act to beat. Maybe if Rolle and Henry had realized sooner what it takes to be a front-runner in Miami-Dade politics, they could have arranged to get themselves indicted, too.

Much of Burke's campaign windfall is from donors who need a compliant vote on the commission and who obviously aren't put off by the corruption charges.

His big supporters include Sergio Pino, ex-president of the Latin Builders Association and a close adviser to Miami Mayor Xavier "I'm Feeling Much Better Now!" Suarez. Pino is trying to hang on to 19 newsstands at Miami International Airport—a lucrative contract now being reviewed by the Miami-Dade Commission.

Another Burke booster is lawyer-lobbyist Tom Carlos, whose developer clients are frequently in need of county zoning variances and other spontaneous acts of kindness.

Also sending a donation was Carlos Herrera, head of the HABDI group struggling to develop Homestead Air Force Base. Burke was an early supporter of leasing the controversial air-base rights to HABDI, without taking a single competing bid.

The feds' investigation of Burke took nearly two years, so his political rivals face a steep challenge. Short of sticking up a bank, there's almost nothing they can do in a mere 12 days to catch the interest of an overworked FBI.

But all is not lost. There are other daring ways to raise campaign funds. Consider the straightforward approach of State Rep. Jim King, who has basically hung a "For Sale" sign around his neck.

Last year, the Jacksonville Republican hosted a secret lunch attended and paid for by lobbyists of the tobacco, beer and health industries. This year King sent letters to 500 lobbyists, thanking them for past donations and seeking more.

"If you've enjoyed the fact that, once committed, you never had to worry about my vote, you should help me," he wrote. "If I've ever helped you 'look good' to your clients by my words or deeds, you should help me."

And this is the guy in line to chair the House Appropriations Committee, overseeing a $44 billion jackpot. Think he'll get some contributions?

Maybe Dorrin Rolle and Sherman Henry should send out a letter like King's. It probably won't get them indicted but it might get them investigated, which in South Florida is the next best thing for a political career.

June 14, 1998

A FEW MINUTES AT CITY HALL

Minutes of the Meeting of the Board of Commissioners, City of Miami.
Meeting called to order at 9 A.M.
New business: Budget Crisis Update.
Mayor and commissioners agree that the budget crisis is still a real big problem.
Old Business: Bi-Monthly Firing of City Manager.
Mayor Joe Carollo announces the regularly scheduled termination of City Manager Jose Garcia-Pedrosa, effective immediately.
Commissioners Arthur E. Teele Jr., J. L. Plummer, Tomas Regalado, Joe Sanchez and Wifredo "Willy" Gort discuss the mayor's decision. Mr. Gort's

motion to override passes 5–0. Former City Manager Garcia-Pedrosa is re-hired and sworn in.

Mayor Carollo announces the refiring of Garcia-Pedrosa, effective "this nanosecond."

Commissioners again discuss the mayor's action. Mr. Plummer moves to override, and the motion passes. The city manager is rehired, and asks the record to show that someone has defaced his nameplate with a purple crayon.

A brief recess is called while the Key to the City is presented to local superstar Jon Secada, who serenades the city manager with a long ballad ending in the line: "Sorry, mi amigo , but you've been canned again."

Commissioner Teele makes a motion to override, but is interrupted by Mr. Regalado, who claims that Mr. Teele is alphabetically out of turn. Mr. Teele argues that first names should count as much as last names, and that "Arthur" comes way ahead of "Tomas."

Commissioner Plummer offers a motion allowing Mr. Teele to move to rehire Mr. Garcia-Pedrosa this time, while Mr. Regalado can do it next time—an opportunity that Mr. Plummer predicts will come "before lunch." Once more the city manager is rehired, and asks the record to show that his microphone, Rolodex and desk blotter have been auctioned off in the parking lot.

Another recess is called while the Key to the City is presented to actor Sylvester Stallone. During the ceremony, Mr. Stallone offers to help City Manager Garcia-Pedrosa clean out his desk, since he has been terminated again by "my old paisano, Crazy Joe, effective like now."

Commissioner Regalado agrees to make a motion to override the mayor, but only if he can do it in iambic pentameter. Other commissioners say they find that meter to be tedious and shopworn, but eventually Mr. Regalado's poem is passed 5–0. Ex–City Manager Garcia-Pedrosa is rehired, and asks the record to reflect that someone has now filled his briefcase with spiders.

Mayor Carollo suggests a long lunch break.

The meeting reconvenes at 1:30 P.M. The city manager reports that, while he was enjoying a salad at Monty's, a "large foul-mouthed macaw" landed on his shoulder and told him he'd again been terminated by Mayor Carollo.

Mayor Carollo asks the record to reflect that the talking bird was in fact a sulfur-crested cockatoo.

Commissioner Sanchez offers a motion in seven different languages to override the mayor. Every version passes unanimously except Urdu, which squeaks by 3–2. Mr. Garcia-Pedrosa is rehired, and asks the record to reflect that someone has now set his favorite humidor afire.

A recess is called while FBI agents upgrade wiretap equipment at City Hall.

Sergeant-at-arms reports Dinner Key is being circled by an airplane towing two banners—one advertising Hawaiian Tropic, and the other announcing another firing of the city manager.

Commissioners discuss who gets to make the next motion. Mr. Teele believes the tallest should go first, while Mr. Plummer believes it should be the oldest.

Meeting adjourns when no one can locate the city manager to hire or fire him.

November 12, 1998

EX-MAYOR LOCO RIDES AGAIN

They don't make straitjackets like they used to.

Mayor Loco is back! The midnight rambler himself, Xavier Suarez, has resurfaced with a daring ploy to regain the office he lost eight months ago because of rampant vote fraud.

His supporters have finished a petition drive that could force another city election next year—and the radical expansion of the mayor's governing powers.

Suarez won't be content merely to recapture his old job—he wants something bigger. He wants to eliminate the post of city manager and assume the day-to-day duties of running Miami.

That's pretty much what he tried last time he took office—hiring and firing frenetically—until somebody pulled him aside and explained the city charter. Mayor Loco prefers no such constraints, next time around.

The petitions submitted Tuesday bear the alleged signatures of about 20,000 Miami voters. All presumably are displeased with Joe Carollo, the mayor and Suarez's arch-enemy.

Carollo (who knows about far-fetched political comebacks) says Suarez's crusade for charter revision is a recall drive in disguise. Carollo also notes that some of the signatures were collected by two of the same Suarez cronies arrested for allegedly corrupting the last election.

Suarez says it's no big deal. He says he used hundreds of signature collectors, the majority of whom have never been arrested for voter fraud.

Now, doesn't that make you feel better?

Think back on what's happened to Miami since Suarez got evicted from city hall. First, hard luck fell upon Humberto Hernandez, Suarez's main ally on the commission and the man who helped him win the controversial—and later discredited—election against Carollo.

Suarez had repaid Hernandez's efforts by appointing him commission chairman, a title that somehow failed to impress prosecutors. Bert now is behind bars for, among other crimes, trying to cover up illegal ballot shenanigans that benefited Suarez.

Meanwhile, the remaining city commissioners grew a spine and adopted modest fee hikes for some municipal services in order to stave off bankruptcy. True, they stalled cravenly until threatened with a state takeover—but at least they finally did something.

As he did throughout last year's mayor's race and four loony months in office, Suarez continues to proclaim—despite unassailable evidence—that Miami's fiscal crisis is a myth propagated by his political foes (who include, apparently, a number of certified accountants).

Let's not forget Mayor Loco's vainglorious trip to Wall Street, where blank stares and bemusement greeted his flaky conspiracy theory, and also his straight-faced plea to upgrade Miami's anemic bond rating.

Removal from office failed to temper Suarez, or improve his math skills. The ex-mayor still derides the special gubernatorial panel appointed to sort out the city's scandalized budget, and scoffs at its conclusion that Miami is basically dead broke.

To drum up support for his election petition, Suarez has campaigned on the grandiose vow to singlehandedly lower fees, improve services and restore the city to solvency. And on the seventh day, he might rest.

As one of the poorest municipalities of its size in the nation, Miami is home to many folks who are barely scraping by, and who'd gladly put their names on any piece of paper that promises a new, better day.

That the promise comes from a self-deluded kook won't be evident until city paychecks start bouncing, and the folks who signed those petitions can't find a firefighter or a cop when they need one.

October 31, 1999

GUTMAN'S A CROOK, BUT HE'S A LUCKY CROOK

To all 32,916 boneheads who voted to re-elect Alberto Gutman: You happy now?

Your baby-faced darling has resigned from the state Senate and is headed to prison, where he richly deserves to be.

Gutman will be remembered as one of the most brazen hustlers ever to troll Tallahassee, which is saying something. The void he leaves in the Republican ranks can be filled just as competently by any pimp off the street.

It's quite a day when the past chairman of the Senate Criminal Justice Committee confesses to being a criminal himself. The fact comes as a surprise only to his myopic constituency and the GOP leadership, all of whom have been living under the same rock.

Gutman had been in and out of hot water for 15 years, and was facing federal indictment at the time of his reelection. It was no petty case, either.

The senator and his wife were up to their grimy elbows in a vast Medicare fraud that, according to prosecutors, cost U.S. taxpayers about $60 million. Gutman's role involved forged patient records, paying cash bribes to crooked doctors and tampering with grand jury witnesses.

Nearly $2 million in phony medical claims were submitted for home-nursing companies in which the Gutmans held a concealed interest. At one point the senator even provided fellow scammers with his voter lists, for names of potential bogus patients.

The crimes dated back to Gutman's days as head of the Senate Health Care Committee—and what salad days they were. Gutman once took $500,000 for brokering the sale of an HMO to a company that had contributed to his political campaign. When news of the arrangement leaked, the senator insisted there was no conflict of interest.

"At no time have I used my office for private gain," he lied.

Gutman was indicted for the Medicare scam in 1997, and he quickly scrambled to cut a deal with the feds. He consented to wear a hidden microphone and help nab other corrupt politicians.

When plea negotiations foundered, Gutman changed his tune. He proclaimed his innocence and announced plans to run for reelection in 1998. In TV commercials he kept a straight face while touting himself as the tough-on-crime candidate. On radio he whined that "liberal Anglos" were out to get him.

He won his District 34 race by a razor-thin margin—but it was still a hoot, considering that details of the 32-count indictment had been well publicized, as had the senator's aborted turn as FBI snitch.

After the votes were counted, Gutman crowed: "This signifies that the charges against me are made up."

Which is the opposite of what he had told authorities in a confession, one year earlier.

It is also the opposite of what he told a federal judge last Tuesday, when he cut short his jury trial to plead guilty to conspiracy.

In exchange, prosecutors will recommend a two-year prison hitch, instead of the 11 years Gutman could have faced. The senator agreed to resign from office and repay $98,000 in tainted payments that had been traced directly to him and his wife.

Gutman is a lucky stiff—lucky to do short time, and lucky he wasn't caught sooner. I feel sorry for all those who had the sense to vote against him, but not for the 32,916 who didn't. Thanks for sending another thief back to Tallahassee.

And how about those lobbyists who gave money to Gutman's legal-defense fund during the 1999 session? Or his bird-brained colleagues, who made him chairman of Miami-Dade's legislative delegation?

Anybody who read the details of the indictment knew it wasn't just smoke, and that Gutman wasn't the target of some mysterious conspiracy. The fact that he'd already tried to plead guilty was a rather large clue.

Another once-popular politician, who got in trouble about the same time, proclaimed: "I look forward to stuffing that case right down the throat of the FBI."

Those smug words came from Jim Burke, who was trying to regain a seat on the Miami-Dade County commission despite pending bribery charges. Voters resoundingly snubbed him, and on October 21 he was convicted by a Miami jury.

Next time Burke should try running for senate in Gutman's neighborhood—unless Al Gutman gets paroled first, and beats him to it.

December 15, 1999

DEAD SERIOUS ABOUT JOKE ON MURDER

An absolutely true news item:

Hialeah Gardens Mayor Gilda Oliveros was suspended December 6 after being arrested for allegedly soliciting the murder of her ex-husband. Investigators say the mayor approached co-workers at City Hall about the plot.

Here are previously undiscovered minutes of a Hialeah Gardens Council meeting, date unknown:

The meeting was called to order at 8 P.M. The clerk presented Council's Agenda.

Item One: The future of Mayor Oliveros's ex-husband.

The floor was given to Mayor Oliveros, who said she wanted to hire a "hit man" to do away with her former spouse. The mayor said this would relieve her of a burdensome distraction and allow her to devote more attention to the job of governing Hialeah Gardens.

Because the city would therefore benefit from the "whacking" of her ex-husband, it was the mayor's view that the murder should be financed all or partly with municipal funds. She recommended using the surplus in the parks and recreation budget.

Several council members said they were willing to second such a motion but only after a ruling from the city attorney.

The city attorney said he could find no provision in the municipal charter that specifically prohibited spending city money on contract homicides.

However, he advised Council that any contract—even a murder contract—must be advertised for competitive bidding.

Mayor Oliveros said she would feel uneasy hiring a killer simply because he was the lowest bidder. Several council members agreed that experience, not just cost, is a crucial consideration in awarding city contracts.

The mayor also complained that widely advertising the proposed murder might alert her ex-husband, prompting him either to flee or notify the authorities.

The discussion was opened to the public. The first speaker, who identified himself only as "Mister X," offered to kill Mayor Oliveros's former husband and discreetly dispose of the remains. In exchange, Mister X asked that his garbage company be awarded the exclusive solid-waste franchise for Hialeah Gardens.

Mayor Oliveros asked Mister X if his services include regular pickup of tree branches and other lawn cuttings. Mister X replied that yard debris would be collected every other Thursday, but it must be neatly bundled, not loose.

The discussion was interrupted by the city attorney, who noted that the city's current garbage contract doesn't expire for three years. Mayor Oliveros said she could not possibly wait that long to be rid of her ex-husband.

A second speaker, wearing dark sunglasses over a red bandanna, volunteered to "off" the mayor's ex-husband for free, if only the mayor would quit acting so stuck-up and agree to go dancing with him.

A brief adjournment was called.

Council reconvened at 8:25 P.M. Mayor Oliveros apologized for the previous speaker. She said he was not a professional killer but actually a floral delivery driver whom she'd met on a cruise to the Caymans.

A third speaker was recognized. He identified himself as "Izzy the Ice Pick" and said he was knowledgeable on the subject of contract murder.

Mayor Oliveros inquired about the average cost of a "hit." The speaker quoted a price of $10,000, half up-front. The mayor then suggested that the speaker be hired to kill her ex-husband under a vendor's permit for "special events," thus avoiding the public bidding process.

While the city attorney went to research the question, the city clerk remarked that "Izzy" looked very much like an undercover policeman she'd once dated.

Another brief adjournment was called.

Council reconvened at 8:57 P.M. The floor was given to Mayor Oliveros, who said she'd been only "joshing" about having her ex-husband killed. Council members agreed they had assumed the mayor was kidding and described her as a "zany practical joker."

The city attorney then offered a hand-written opinion stating that murder was a serious crime, whereas joking about murder was not.

Mayor Oliveros, noting she was now dead serious, called for a motion to table Item One indefinitely.

The motion was made, seconded and passed by a unanimous vote. Council adjourned hastily at 8:58 P.M.

April 12, 2000

ONE HAPPY FIRE SALE IN TALLAHASSEE

Meet the screw-you Legislature.

Sixty-three of 160 members face expiring term limits, so it's one happy fire sale in Tallahassee. Everything goes.

Seldom have so many elected officials so openly pimped for special-interest groups. Seldom have so many greed-sotted bills hurtled so smoothly through committees.

At a time when most Floridians favor stronger growth-management measures, an Ocala lawmaker seeks to gut the state's authority over community planning and give 67 politically slanted "reviewing councils" the power to approve major developments.

It's a perfect recipe for chaos and corruption. Not surprisingly, the idea comes from Rep. George Albright, an attorney for developers. He is also a comedian. He says counties can be trusted to manage their own growth.

The GOP's trust in local authority does not, oddly, extend to farmlands. Sen. George Kirkpatrick of Gainesville is pushing a bill that would prevent counties from passing any laws to regulate agriculture.

Didn't you always want to live next to a pig farm?

Not to be outdone, another Republican, J. D. Alexander of Frostproof, wants taxpayers to reimburse any landowner whose property gets zoned at less than one house per acre.

The bill, hotly contested by counties and cities, would provide another windfall to Big Agriculture. Another surprise—Alexander's granddaddy was citrus tycoon Ben Hill Griffin, Jr.

Penalizing taxpayers for government zoning decisions is an audacious concept that cuts only one way. Conveniently, Anderson's bill wouldn't require big landowners to reimburse the public for new highways, drainage pipes and other goodies that increase the value of their holdings.

The phoniest "property rights" bill skating through this year's Legislature would give away 500,000 acres of state lands to cattle ranchers, timbermen, miners and farmers.

This shameless heist originated with two Republican House members, Paula Dockery of Lakeland and Adam Putnam of Bartow, both of whose families own farmland and would benefit sweetly from the giveaway. (A Senate version of the bill is sponsored by Skip Campbell, a Fort Lauderdale Democrat.)

The lands at issue are submerged at least part of the year as rivers, estuaries, lakes and tidal flats. These always have been open to the public for boating and fishing.

But ranchers and farmers say that they hold title to this wet acreage, pay taxes on it and should be able to use it or sell it back to the state. Opponents say those old legal claims—dating to the 1800s—are flimsy and that property below the high-water line always has been "sovereign."

Judges considering the dispute have ruled in favor of the state. The most famous example is Fisheating Creek in southwest Florida, a slender waterway that had been blocked to public access by the powerful Lyke Brothers company.

After losing that case and others, farm and mining companies devised an end-run around the courts. They went to Tallahassee, where their money always talks loudly.

Today the Dockery-Putnam land grab is rolling through committees of both the House and the Senate. It is opposed by 19 conservation and environmental groups, as well as four of seven members of the Cabinet, sitting as trustees for Florida's public lands.

Such a law would impact every Floridian who loves the outdoors, because there would be a lot less outdoors to love.

Supporters insist that the companies have no intention of fencing off lakes, rivers and shorelines. Of course not! That's why they're going to all this trouble to get their mitts on these unspoiled areas—not to exploit them, but to preserve them for future generations.

What a joke.

Lots of people stand to make millions off the Dockery-Putnam giveaway.

For example, according to the *Palm Beach Post,* the Lost Tree Village Corp. could rake in up to $80 million by developing low-lying islets in the Indian River Lagoon, near fast-growing Vero Beach.

That such an awful bill attracted 63 co-sponsors in the House and 10 in the Senate is all you need to know about what's happening in the capitol this spring.

The short-timers are open for business. It's not really a legislature so much as a flea market.

15

DEALS ON WHEELS

June 2, 1986

NEXT STOP: BUS DEPOT DESPERADOES

A true news item: Missing Florida House candidate Gustavo R. Carbonell surfaced alive and well last week, claiming that he had been mysteriously abducted from a Metrorail men's room and forcibly put on a Greyhound bus to Manhattan. Carbonell announced he was quitting the House race, but asserted that his alleged kidnapping was part of a sinister political conspiracy. In reply, Hialeah Mayor Raul Martinez said that Carbonell should see a psychiatrist.

Federal authorities confirmed this week that they are investigating a small but diabolical terrorist cell that targets politicians and public officeholders.

The avowed mission of the group, known cryptically as the Bus-Stop Brigade, is "to embarrass, disgrace, and degrade certain political figures who might otherwise do anything to get their names in the paper."

According to sources close to the investigation, the gang's preferred tactic is to kidnap its victim, drive him around town until he gets carsick, then buy him a bus ticket to some northern city with exorbitant hotel rates.

Explained one investigator: "Frequently these desperadoes will even arrange for their victim to be seated next to an extremely fat, sweaty person for the entire bus trip. Talk about vicious! These guys make Baader-Meinhof look like the Osmonds."

The Bus-Stop Brigade is now suspected in the strange abduction–bus ride of House candidate Gustavo Carbonell, a Republican who disappeared for several days last week.

"It's the same MO, all right," the investigator confirmed, "only more brutal. Usually the Brigade at least gives their victim a box lunch and a copy of the *National Star,* but this poor fellow was trapped on that Greyhound for 31 hours with nothing, not even a box of Saltines. You've got to ask yourself: 'What next?'"

While political opponents have questioned the veracity of Carbonell's kidnap tale, authorities say it would be unwise to dismiss it as just a dumb hoax.

"Stranger things have happened," recounted one veteran FBI agent. "Last year we had a zoning inspector vanish during a camping trip in Utah. He turned up six weeks later, running a body-waxing salon outside Reno. We've never been able to crack that case, since the victim has terrible amnesia."

In fact, many of those abducted by the Bus-Stop Brigade later complain of chronic memory loss and show great reluctance to answer questions about their ordeal. "This is understandable, considering the emotional pain," the investigator said. "Have you ever seen the Port Authority Bus Terminal?"

The gang apparently selects both Democrats and Republicans as its targets, and claims no political agenda besides "making politicians appear stupendously foolish."

An FBI telex, sent last week to local law enforcement agencies, concluded with this warning: "Judging from the latest abduction, we can only conclude that this radical faction is getting bolder . . . well, if not bolder, certainly sillier."

In Tallahassee, security advisers for Gov. Bob Graham have quietly taken steps to protect the state's chief executive during his current campaign for the U.S. Senate.

"We've ordered the governor to steer clear of all bus stations, and not just Greyhound, either. We're talking Trailways, Red Top, the works," said Ernest "Spud" Delacorte, chief of the Graham security team.

Delacorte acknowledged that Graham initially was "extremely disappointed by this restriction, but now understands the seriousness of the threat."

In Washington, Sen. Paula Hawkins released a statement expressing "shock and dismay that our nation's interstate bus system is being used as a tool of terrorism, particularly against fellow Republicans."

But Hawkins said the Carbonell incident, however tragic, is no reason for panic. The senator added: "I still firmly believe that most people who ride Greyhounds are doing so not under threat of violence, but because they really truly want to."

January 26, 1987

IT WAS A DARK, STORMY NIGHT AS THE MAYOR . . .

An absolutely true news item: Last week the car belonging to Miami Mayor Xavier Suarez was stolen from his house in Coconut Grove. Inside the car was a briefcase containing not only the mayor's gun, but the notes for an upcoming book about "life in the big city."

First Draft

It was the best of times, it was the cruddiest of times . . .

Second Draft

Call me Ishmael.

On second thought, just call me Xavier . . .

Third Draft

"Better hurry," Miss Moneypenny said. "He's in one of those moods."

M stood stood dourly behind his desk. "Nice of you to make an appearance."

"Sorry I'm late," X replied. "Had to jump-start the damn Aston again."

M scowled disapprovingly. "Sit down," he said. "Agent Q has a few items to discuss."

"Let's begin with your gun," Q said. "We think the PPK is a better choice than a Beretta."

"The Beretta works fine," X said coolly. "Just ask the late Mr. Blofeld."

Moneypenny peeked in the door. "A drink, Mr. Mayor?"

"Yes, the usual," X said. "Diet Sprite, stirred not shaken."

Fourth Draft

She came through the door without knocking, but I didn't mind. It was a slow day. Besides, she smelled like Paris and looked like a million bucks.

"I need a man," she said in a low voice, "a man who can help me."

"You came to the right place," I said. "I'm the mayor."

I poured some coffee. She drank it. I poured some more. She drank that, too. "Pour your own," I said finally. She did.

"I don't know who else to turn to," she sighed.

"Enough of the flattery," I said. "What's the problem, babycakes?"

She lowered her eyes. "It's a zoning matter," she said.

My jaw tightened. "What kind of zoning matter?"

"The worst kind," she said. "Think you can handle it?"

I smiled. "Why do you suppose I carry a gun?"

"A gun?" She gave me a smoky look. "I like a mayor who carries a gun. May I see it?"

"Sorry, dumpling, it's in the car."

"Why would you leave it in the car?"

Dames. They're all alike. "Don't you worry your pretty blond head over it," I said.

"But it doesn't sound too bright," she persisted, "leaving your gun in the car. I mean, what if it got stolen? What if some dangerous criminal got hold of it and used it in some hideous crime?"

I leaned forward, stared hard into those baby blues and said, "Just what are you driving at, dollface?"

She got quiet real fast.

"You think I got to be mayor by being stupid! Look up on that wall and tell me what you see."

"A dartboard with Joe Carollo's face on it."

"No, next to that. The sheepskin."

She stood up to take a look. I knew what was coming.

"Oooohh, Harvard," she murmured. "I like Harvard men—even more than they like themselves."

I glanced at my wristwatch. "Any more questions, babe?"

"Just one," the blond lady said. "What are you doing for dinner, Mr. Mayor?"

"Some other time," I said, holding the door. "Sorry, kiddo, but dinner and zoning just don't mix." She blinked away a lonely tear.

Sure, it hurt, but someday she'd thank me. . . .

(PERSONAL NOTE TO THE CROOK WHO STOLE THE MAYOR'S REAL BOOK: If you send the purloined material to Mr. Hiaasen, he would be delighted to return it—along with any helpful criticism you might offer—to Mayor Suarez. The address is One Herald Plaza, Miami, 33132-1693.)

September 12, 1988

IN POLITICS, A HOUSE ISN'T ALWAYS A HOME

Maybe next time, instead of a phony address, candidate Miriam Alonso should try using a Winnebago.

Just drive it around until she finds an election district she likes, park it for six months, then file for a Metro commission seat.

That's better than the musical-homes scheme that just got her booted off the ballot.

Alonso was trying to unseat incumbent Bev Phillips in the District 7 commission race. In last Tuesday's primary, Phillips finished first, followed by Alonso, Charles Dusseau and Armando Bucelo.

The sparks started when Michael Putney of WTVJ reported that neither Alonso nor Bucelo appeared to be living inside District 7, as required by county law.

Before they could run for the commission, both Alonso and Bucelo signed sworn statements claiming to reside in the Southwest Dade district.

But it turned out that Bucelo and family recently purchased a new house in Coral Gables, and had moved out of the other place before election day. Even as neighbors were saying the Bucelos had been gone for two weeks, Bucelo was insisting that he still lived in the vacant house in District 7.

Alonso, meanwhile, claimed she lived at 10835 S.W. 41st Terrace, also inside the district. Strangely, her driver's license and auto registration said she lived on Southwest 12th Street, an out-of-bounds address. Moreover, a man in the house on 41st Terrace swore that Alonso didn't live there and never had.

This is what you call a clue.

Last week Dade Circuit Judge Edward S. Klein rightfully dumped Alonso from the ballot. Judge Klein also ruled that Bucelo could stay in the race, and ordered a new election.

Caught in a lie (and a possible crime), Alonso went whining to the airwaves. With Bucelo at her side, she accused opponent Charles Dusseau of "distorting the process of democracy" by pressing the residency issue.

Some nerve, this guy Dusseau. How dare he demand that all commission candidates obey the law!

Bucelo was particularly outraged that a private investigator watched him leave the wrong house early one morning. Campaign strategist Phil Hamersmith called the surveillance a "scummy" tactic—and few would question Hamersmith's expertise on the subject of scum.

What you've got here are two candidates who tried to sneak around the law and got nailed.

Bucelo stayed on the ballot only because he had a better excuse: He said a lease problem had forced him to move temporarily from the house in District 7.

Alonso wasn't so clever. Barely one month after renewing her homestead exemption on the 12th Street address, she signed the election oath stating that she resided at 41st Terrace—and had for the previous six months.

State officials say it's perjury to lie on election documents, but it will be the turn of the century before Janet Reno's office will ever file charges.

Having violated the residency law, Alonso now has decided to challenge its constitutionality.

Saturday her attorneys marched into the Third District Court of Appeal to try out some desperate arguments. At one point they asserted that a commissioner is required to move to the district only after he or she is elected.

This means you could live in Bismarck, North Dakota, and run for the Dade County commission. (Which, given our pool of local talent, would probably be a big improvement.)

The appellate judges immediately saw Alonso's argument for what it was—a lame stab at creating a loophole. The court upheld Klein's ruling and went one step further by canceling the second primary.

So, pending appeals, it will be Phillips and Dusseau in the runoff. Alonso and Bucelo are out, so they can quit playing house in District 7.

Perhaps they'll pop up in Commissioner Barry Schreiber's neighborhood in time for the 1990 elections. Park their Winnebago down the block and set up legal residence.

Or maybe just a pup tent, a sleeping bag and a can of Sterno.

May 14, 1992

HAS JET-SETTING JOEY SEVERED TIES TO REALITY?

Any moment now, Metro Commissioner Joe Gersten will return from France to confront accusations that he's a dope-smoking sex troller.

As Robin Leach would say, it's all in a day's work for this jet-setting bon vivant, this dapper dynamo, this fast-living fop.

A leisurely spring vacation has given Gersten plenty of time to ponder how his Mercedes-Benz, car keys, driver's license, briefcase, credit cards and gun might have ended up in the hands of drug hustlers.

They say they stole Joey's car while he was having sex with a hooker in a Biscayne Boulevard crack house. Four witnesses, including the hooker, have told this story to police.

From the south of France, Joey exclaimed: Phooey! He said the car was swiped from his driveway in Coral Gables. He said he left the keys and all the goodies inside the Mercedes because he was in an excruciating hurry to get in the house.

While prosecutors try to sort out the two tales, citizens face a wrenching dilemma: Whom do you believe—a county commissioner, or a crack-addict hooker? It's a close call.

Matters are complicated by Gersten's refusal to publicly account for his whereabouts prior to the car theft on April 29. He denies that he visited the crack den, smoked rock cocaine and paid $85 for sex with a streetwalker. Gersten's staff says lowlifes cooked up the wild yarn after they failed to extort money from the commissioner.

Another twist: Phone calls between the prostitute and Gersten's office were recorded by the FBI—with the hooker's consent. These tapes should make for jolly fun at the commissioner's bachelor party.

What little Joey has said about the incident is, admittedly, subject to skepticism. Only a scatterbrain would leave the keys in a Mercedes-Benz. And only a certifiable dolt would leave a handgun sitting there for any passing lunatic to grab.

But let's give Joey the benefit of a doubt. Say he's the innocent victim of a screaming bladder, his own carelessness and cruel circumstance.

Perhaps drug-crazed zombies did wander all the way from Biscayne Boulevard to the Gables in search of wheels. Or perhaps Gersten's enemies concocted the theft as an elaborate smear; through clairvoyance, they knew in advance when he'd be leaving the keys in his ignition!

Still, Gersten's behavior following the allegations is as bizarre as the allegations themselves. A normal fellow, upon hearing himself slimed with accusations of general depravity, would consider his vacation sufficiently ruined. Not Joey.

The man who fancies himself as Dade's next mayor lounged in Nice while his political career crumbled in scandal. Instead of flying home to defend himself against the seamiest of charges—charges that the police are taking seriously—the commissioner luxuriated in a $1,200-a-day hotel and mingled with the beautiful people at Cannes.

Perhaps Gersten has become clinically detached from reality, in which case he needs professional help.

Another possibility is that he isn't as shrewd as his reputation, and simply doesn't comprehend the gravity of the situation. (News Flash: When the FBI is listening in on your phone calls, you've got a little problem.)

A third possibility is that Gersten is scared to come back because he knows the crackheads are telling the truth.

In any event, the commissioner obviously is in no great rush to give a statement to authorities. They haven't heard a peep from him in two weeks.

Gersten's homecoming will be lively and well-attended. Unless he's ready to answer questions, his campaign for mayor is finished—ending not with a whimper, but a bong.

January 28, 1993

MAYOR CLARK VANISHES—JUST LIKE ALWAYS

The man who perfected the invisible-mayor form of government is calling it quits.

Steve Clark has decided not to run for re-election, largely because his job was abolished by a judge. Come March 16, there will be no more mayor of Metro, only 13 commissioners.

In announcing his retirement, Clark said the new mayorless structure will create a "leadership vacuum" in Dade County. Whoever wrote that line for the mayor has a wicked sense of humor. What Clark knows about leadership wouldn't fill the dimple of a Titleist.

In times of crisis, you could depend on him to disappear. He was the David Copperfield of local politics—vanishing during race riots, dematerializing after hurricanes, vaporizing before key commission votes. In 23 years his marshmallow record was intact: He made no courageous stands, took no political risks and contributed not one original, bold idea to government.

He was a blob. An affable, back-slapping, ribbon-snipping blob. But then what did you expect for $6,000 a year? Vision? Courage? In your dreams.

Clark was a developer, and remained loyal to the cause. Builders knew the mayor's vote was a lock, and they dumped a fortune in his re-election campaigns. In gratitude, Clark did exactly what he was told.

Who can forget that memorable moment when the mayor got confused and voted against a $4 million airport expansion? The phone on his commission desk rang instantly, and lobbyist Dusty Melton—who was pushing the project—coldly informed Clark of his blunder. The befuddled mayor interrupted the meeting to call a new vote.

Although the episode was captured on TV, the mayor claimed amnesia when asked about it later. It was vintage Steve.

Then there was his starring role in the Alcee Hastings impeachment hearings. The mayor had claimed that then-Judge Hastings had tipped him to an FBI investigation of alleged zoning crimes involving one of Clark's cronies. Naturally Clark didn't report the leak to the feds. Rather, he was caught whining about it on a secret surveillance tape.

Summoned to Washington, he told his story to Congress. The Senate impeached Hastings on other charges, but rejected the mayor's testimony by a 95–0 vote. So much for credibility.

It's simplistic to credit Clark's political longevity to fat war chests, savvy advisers and weak opponents. He was also a good campaigner, sunny, generous and likable. His presence could light up a Moose Lodge, and there was no place he would rather be, with the exception of the 18th fairway at Biltmore.

The role of Metro mayor was mostly ceremonial—Clark ran the meetings, but his vote carried no extra weight. That's not to say he didn't hold sway. He presided over two decades of runaway development, zoning chaos and sloppy construction. For thousands of innocent people, the price was paid last summer when Hurricane Andrew struck.

To this day, Clark blames only Mother Nature. Forget the grand jury, the wind scientists, the engineers. Sayeth the mayor: "There's nothing we could build today with home construction that would stand."

No wonder it's developers who most deeply lament the mayor's parting. The Latin Builders Association must now find a new stooge on the commission, but that'll be easy.

For the average Dade resident, Mayor Clark's departure won't change a thing. You won't know he's gone because you hardly knew he was there. As for leadership, he was the vacuum within the vacuum. A black hole in deep space.

He ruled by a simple philosophy: When the going gets tough, the tough get a tee time.

July 30, 2000

THE ROVING CANDIDATE

Demetrio Perez is only 23 years old, a youthful University of Miami law student eager to set his course in life.

Tragically, though, Perez has been stricken with Chronic Residential Disorientation, an election-year disorder that evidently runs in his family.

Perez, who is seeking a seat on the Miami-Dade School Board, doesn't seem to know where he lives.

Two weeks ago, when registering to vote, Perez listed his home at 10011 S.W. 80th Ave. He used the same address when he filed to run in the School Board race.

A few days later, though, Perez told elections officials that he lived in an apartment at 13911 S.W. 122nd Ave. "There was some confusion," Perez conceded, when the switcheroo came to light.

The law requires School Board candidates to reside in the district they represent. The original address that Perez gave was in District 6. Unfortunately, he's running for office from District 7.

In the nick of time, Perez's "confusion" evaporated, and he was able to re-call an address conveniently located within the District 7 boundaries. It was a happy ending to a potentially sad but familiar story.

Most normal people are reasonably sure where they live. Every night they return home to the same house or apartment, without the aid of maps, compasses or hand-held navigational devices.

Oddly, local politicians often suffer from bizarre memory gaps when asked to recall their home addresses. The dither that afflicted young Perez is the same type that embarrassed his father, Demetrio Perez, Jr., during the 1996 School Board election.

The elder Perez claimed to be renting a room in District 5, where he was seeking office. But neighbors seldom saw him at the Little Havana house.

Months after prosecutors launched an investigation, the senior Perez said he'd moved to a condo within his district. Investigator Fran Miller, who interviewed him, reported that Perez "did not know his address by memory and had to read it from a piece of paper."

It was pathetic. Luckily for the elder Perez, he's running unopposed this year, so nobody has questioned so much as his Zip code.

Two other School Board members were stricken with similar mental lapses during the last election.

Solomon Stinson stated he lived in District 2, but almost every night his car was parked elsewhere, at a two-story house in Biscayne Gardens. Records showed Stinson received mail there, and even claimed the house for homestead exemption.

All that mysteriously slipped his mind when he filed his election papers. Later his ex-wife surfaced to say Stinson still lived with her in District 2—two decades after their divorce.

A third victim of election-year memory muddle was former board member Renier Diaz de la Portilla, who told officials he was lawfully residing at an address in District 8.

But neighbors rarely laid eyes on him, and a reporter visiting the house discovered it was furnished with only two empty bookcases. Still, Diaz de la Portilla insisted he slept there three nights a week (perhaps by stringing a hammock between the shelving).

Neither he, Stinson nor the elder Perez was charged. Prosecutors closed their investigation, saying the law requiring a candidate to live in his or her voting district gives no clear definition of "residency." A broom closet will suffice, apparently.

In 30 years, only a handful of Miami-Dade politicians have been kicked off the ballot for home-residency discrepancies. They include commission candidate Miriam Alonso (who has since been elected) and Opa-locka Commission hopeful Larry Thompson (who in 1996 couldn't even find a key for the apartment he claimed to call home).

The whole point of district elections is to ensure local representation—a process some say is being contaminated by outside candidates who relocate at the last minute.

Opponents of young Demetrio Perez are suspicious of his 11th-hour change of residence, and it certainly does look fishy. But, given his father's acute attack of fuzziness during the last campaign, it's impossible to rule out some insidious genetic link.

Let's hope that, unlike his old man, young Demetrio won't need to carry his new address around on a piece of paper like a kindergartner.

It would be much better to memorize it, in case he actually decides to move in some day.

August 2, 2000

RAUNCHY JOE GERSTEN CAN STOP RUNNING

Won't you come home, Joe Gersten?

South Florida's funniest fugitive recently got some good news and some bad news.

The bad news: A panel of Australian judges denied Gersten's ludicrous appeal to remain in that country as a "political refugee."

The good news: Miami-Dade prosecutors say they won't charge the ex–county commissioner with any crimes if he returns, because the statute of limitations has run out.

Hard to believe it has been eight years since the raunchy sex-and-drug scandal that sent Gersten—then one of Miami's most arrogant and ambitious politicians—fleeing the country Robert Vesco–style.

It began April 29, 1992, with Gersten reporting his Mercedes had been swiped from the driveway of his gated Coral Gables home. The commissioner claimed that, in a frantic rush to get inside the house and empty his bladder, he'd left the keys in the car's ignition. Cops found the Mercedes tooling around downtown. Inside the car were Gersten's driver's license, gun, briefcase and several photographs of an unidentified nude man.

Things went downhill from there. The drug hustlers who had the car said they took it from a Biscayne Boulevard crack house, where Gersten was consorting with a hooker.

(The hooker said she and the commissioner smoked rock cocaine before he peeled down to his socks—an image so unsavory that even seasoned detectives must have blanched.)

Clueless Joe was vacationing in France when the uproar broke, but he felt no urgency to return and help authorities sort out the mess. In fact, he was a most uncooperative victim.

The hooker and three other witnesses, all with rap sheets, stuck to their story about Gersten's visiting the crack den. Meanwhile, the commissioner's maid and even his fiancée gave statements raising doubts about his claim that he'd been home that fateful night.

Then a cab driver came forward to swear that he drove a man resembling Gersten from a Biscayne Boulevard intersection to Gersten's street in the Gables on the same night.

At long last, Clueless Joe sensed trouble and flew back from Europe, though he refused to give detailed testimony. He blamed his problems on political enemies, prosecutors and reporters. He crowed when hair-sample tests showed he wasn't a regular user of cocaine.

From the sanctum of his defense attorney's office, Gersten launched his re-election campaign. It was a measure of Gersten's clout—and of the moral vacuity of his donors—that he was still able to collect $250,000 and endorsements from some prominent Miami politicos.

The public, however, was unimpressed. The election boiled down to Gersten's word against that of a crack-smoking hooker. Not surprisingly, voters believed the hooker.

Clueless Joe didn't even make the runoff. Afterward, he continued ducking prosecutors until a judge cited him for contempt and tossed him in jail.

There Gersten developed a multitude of phony medical symptoms, and was such a chronic whiner that hardened criminals demanded not to be stuck in the same cell.

Released on bond, Gersten disappeared before a court date in September 1993. Soon he turned up in Australia, grinning like a bloated koala.

Since then, Joey has been laboring to convince Australian authorities of his high moral character in order that he might be allowed to stay forever and practice law.

In seeking refugee status, Gersten insisted he'll be persecuted if he is sent back to the United States, because of vague corruption accusations he has made against then–State Attorney Janet Reno and others.

That Joey wasn't deported the instant he stepped off the plane shows that Australians have a sense of humor. However, Gersten's vacation Down Under could soon be over.

Seven years is a long time to run from anything—especially misdemeanor charges of filing a false police report. And though the statutory clock has run out, Joey still faces a civil contempt citation in circuit court.

Whether he's behind bars or out shopping for a new Mercedes, it would be entertaining to see Gersten back in South Florida, a bawdy distraction in the summer doldrums.

So come home, Joey, to the one place where everybody knows your name. And if you promise never to run for office again, we promise not to ask about the naked guy in those pictures.

16

ELECTIONS, FLORIDA STYLE

November 12, 1985

HOW TO TELL IF AN ELECTION IS OUT OF CONTROL

Any of us who'd begun to think that Dade County had caught up with 20th Century democracy were soberly reminded otherwise last week by the chaotic climax to the primary election. Neil Simon could not have improved on the script.

Here we'd endured the most tedious and hotly contested political race in years—the campaign for Miami mayor—only to have the agony prolonged all night while the ballots were in turmoil, the Ronko Vote-O-Matic computer jammed on overload.

Eventually matters were rectified, but not before elections supervisor David Leahy went on live television and promptly blacked out, something his staff obviously had done much earlier in the evening.

Precisely what went wrong at Election Central remains a mystery, though the official explanation cites human error, computer shortfalls and a phenomenon known as double-counting.

I felt sorry for Mr. Leahy, who is a hard worker, but the more I listened to him try to explain the double-counting, the more confused I got. Evidently it's a lot like compounding the interest on a savings account, except that, unlike bank deposits, votes aren't supposed to grow.

This doesn't appear to be a case of simple fraud. Fraud we could understand; it has a long and colorful tradition in this country's elections. For example, dead people have been voting for years in Chicago. Still, I'm not sure what's worse—people who cheat or people who just can't add. The end result is the same.

Who are last Tuesday's culprits? Nobody's naming names (which makes you wonder what happened to those jokers who came up with Metrorail's ridership projections—could they somehow have gotten new jobs as vote counters?)

Whoever it was, Koko the Talking Gorilla could have done better, or at least explained the foul-up more lucidly.

The bottom line: It took at least eight hours to count, recount and ratify a measly 56,000 votes.

To calculate it another way: Two average human beings, counting every mayoral ballot by hand, could have finished the same job in the same amount of time by spending only 1.02 seconds on each ballot.

Try not to worry about that today when you go back to the polls. Elections officials have promised a smooth performance this time. But, just in case, I've come up with guidelines to help Dade elections officials avoid a repeat of last week's fiasco:

NINE WAYS TO TELL IF YOU'VE LOST CONTROL OF AN ELECTION.

1. You've lost control when precinct workers start fastening ballot cards to the spokes of their bicycles so it makes a real loud noise when they pedal fast.

2. You've lost control if Donkey Kong suddenly shows up on the screen of your elections computer.

3. You've lost control if election headquarters is suddenly surrounded by right-wing guerrillas, whose commander announces that he will personally "supervise" the vote-counting.

4. You've lost control if your precinct captains are caught using knitting needles to punch Happy Faces on the ballot cards.

5. You've lost control when it's discovered that all absentee ballots have been mistakenly forwarded to the Publishers Clearinghouse Sweepstakes.

6. You've lost control if the top vote-getter in the mayor's race is the new music video by David Lee Roth.

7. You've lost control of the election if, at midnight, you find all your precinct workers huddled fervently around a Ouija board and an abacus.

8. You've lost control if the voter registration rolls show more than 4,000 people with the name Bhagwan Rajneesh, all registered Republican and all living in Coconut Grove.

9. You've really lost control if the first TV crew to arrive after the polls close consists of Dick Clark, Ed McMahon and a camera hidden in an ice-cream truck.

January 9, 1994

RENO AIDE LIABLE FOR ACTIONS IN HIALEAH ELECTION

A stunned public reels at the headlines: Authorities investigate possible voter fraud in the Hialeah mayor's race!

Fraud? In Hialeah? There's one for Ripley's.

Opponents of Mayor Raul Martinez allege multiple misdeeds in the gathering of absentee votes. Martinez won the runoff against Nilo Juri by a razor-thin spread of 273 votes, with nearly a 2–1 edge in absentee ballots.

Among the sites energetically canvassed by Martinez supporters was a rest home with mentally ill residents. Twenty-four (including two convicted felons) voted absentee, even though a polling place was located across the street.

It's also been revealed that numerous signatures on absentee ballot applications did not match the voter signatures that were later sent with the completed ballots. Many of the disputed signatures were witnessed by Martinez campaign workers.

In the middle of the mess is Lula Rodriguez, the mayor's sister-in-law. Rodriguez is also a key aide to U.S. Attorney General Janet Reno, which means the Hialeah fiasco is attracting national interest. Rodriguez witnessed 13 of the absentee signatures, and at least one voter—a Raul Martinez supporter—now insists her name was forged.

Documents show that the woman was in the Dominican Republic on the day her ballot was released to a Martinez worker in Hialeah. She was still out of the country when the ballot was returned a few days later—signed.

Lula Rodriguez says she did nothing wrong. She says she flew to Miami for a weekend, and decided to help with her brother-in-law's mayoral campaign. When absentee voters came to get their signatures witnessed, Rodriguez says, she obliged without checking IDs.

No, it isn't so incredible that somebody might have monkeyed with the ballots. It wouldn't be the first time that happened in Dade County.

What is incredible is that Lula Rodriguez would go anywhere near Martinez campaign headquarters. Family loyalty is swell, but what about common sense?

Raul Martinez is a convicted extortionist who ran for office while appealing his case. The people trying to jail him work for the U.S. Justice Department. That would be the same Justice Department headed by Janet Reno, the same Justice Department that now pays Lula Rodriguez's salary.

This is what's known as a "conflict of interest." The risk would have been evident to a ninth-grade civics student.

Federal agents and prosecutors spent many years and probably millions of taxpayer dollars assembling the corruption case against Martinez. He was a major target. It's outrageous that one of the Attorney General's top assistants worked for Martinez's re-election—to the same office he was convicted of betraying.

Perhaps Lula Rodriguez was innocently trying to help family. It's very possible she had no role in the voting shenanigans, and had no clue anything was out of order.

Still, she put herself in the worst place at the worst time. On Thursday, Reno said Rodriguez's conduct will be investigated by the Justice Department's Office of Professional Responsibility. "I will take whatever action is appropriate," she said.

What's appropriate cannot be determined until state and federal agents finish their investigation of the Hialeah election. If Lula Rodriguez signed her name on a single bogus ballot, she's got a serious problem.

It might have been just a foolish mistake, or something worse. The result might be a subpoena, or something worse.

Imagine Reno's surprise. She probably thought her days of worrying about Hialeah were over.

February 19, 1998

IF CROOKS CAN HOLD OFFICE, WHY NOT VOTE?

Convicted felons aren't supposed to vote. It's been that way for a long time, the idea being that criminals aren't morally fit to participate in the political process.

Miami could be the exception.

Considering the recent corruption scandals and unhinged behavior at City Hall, what's the point of barring felons from the ballot box? Could they possibly make worse choices than regular voters have made?

At least 105 convicted criminals cast ballots in the Miami mayoral races last fall. Among those were robbers, car thieves, drug traffickers and killers.

All technically had forfeited their right to vote on the day they were found guilty. By allowing them to register, somebody at the elections bureau slipped up.

But look at it another way. That these felons would take time from their busy days to go to the polls, even illegally, shows they care deeply about city government—certainly more deeply than the thousands of nonfelons who didn't bother to get off their lazy butts and vote.

The truth is, career criminals could bring a valuable insight to the electoral process. In a place like Miami—where for years the government has been run by thieves—the most savvy and knowledgeable voters might very well be those with a rap sheet.

Who better to assess, for example, the unlikely candidacy of suspended Commissioner Humberto Hernandez, indicted on 23 counts of bank fraud and money laundering?

In most law-abiding American cities, Hernandez wouldn't have had the nerve to run for re-election—or, at the very least, he would have been jeered out of the race.

In Miami, naturally, he won by a landslide. He did it by charming lots of elderly Hispanic voters, and snowing others by painting himself as the victim of an Anglo conspiracy.

I submit the outcome would have been much closer, if not different, had more felons been able to take part in the balloting.

In the first place, Hernandez is a lawyer, and most streetwise criminals don't trust lawyers. Secondly, felons have seen and heard just about everything, so they aren't nearly as gullible as ordinary citizens.

Anybody who's been to prison would instantly see through Hernandez's boyish-innocence act. And as for conspiracy theories, Humberto's would sound pretty lame and unimaginative, compared to the ones heard on any medium-security cellblock.

You might assume a shady character such as Hernandez would benefit from a heavy felon turnout, but it's not necessarily so. True, he might draw a few sympathy votes from other indictees, but my guess is the majority of outlaws wouldn't believe a word the guy said, and would be insulted to find his name on the ballot.

Just as normal voters in a normal city would be insulted.

After hearing two weeks of evidence about rampant vote fraud, Miami-Dade Circuit Judge Thomas Wilson Jr. must decide whether or not to call a new mayoral election for Miami.

If he does, he ought to consider suspending the old law and throwing the vote open to all interested criminals. What a bold experiment it would be, with nothing to lose.

City elections can hardly get more tainted than they already are, and the ballot of a well-informed burglar or bank robber would be infinitely preferable to that of a dead person, a nonresident or a forged absentee.

In South Florida, the real menace to democracy isn't from the crooks who vote, but from the ones who run for office.

April 19, 1998

HOW EASY CAN WE MAKE VOTE THEFT?

If Rep. Luis Morse gets his way, it'll be easier than ever to steal an election in Florida.

The Miami Republican has managed to defang a strong voting reform bill by adding a cavernous loophole that would encourage—and legitimize—the seedy pastime of ballot brokering.

If it passes the Legislature, hundreds of political hacks statewide will be empowered to request, witness and collect as many absentee ballots as they can stuff into their grimy pockets.

It's that style of hustling that led to epidemic fraud in last fall's Miami mayoral race. Absentee votes were cast not only by a dead guy, but by candidates' friends and relatives who didn't even live in the city; by people who sold their ballots for $10 on the street; by elderly residents whose votes were altered without their knowledge.

The scandal—and subsequent tossing of election results—made Miami a national laughingstock, the butt of every bad banana republic joke. Embarrassed politicians vowed to crack down.

A bill passed by the Florida Senate would stiffen the penalties for voter fraud, and make it harder for the nonliving and nonresident to participate. It would require two witnesses to all absentee ballots, and would limit to five the number of ballots they could witness in each election. The only exceptions: ballots witnessed by notaries, election supervisors and others who administer oaths.

But the insidious amendment—drafted by Senate sponsor Jack Latvala and accepted by Morse under the watchful eye of Republican staffers—adds political parties to those not subject to the bill's limits. Each party could appoint two "absentee-ballot coordinators" in each House district. These goobers alone could gather and witness an unlimited number of ballots.

So those with the largest motive to swipe an election would be handed the keys to the safe.

Nice work, Luis. Perhaps, for your next trick, you could legalize pickpockets. Call them "wallet-transfer coordinators."

David Leahy, Miami-Dade elections supervisor, says the amendment is a giant step backward because it would license the same runaway solicitations that corrupted the November elections.

Moreover, the Democrat and Republican leadership probably won't use

the inauguration. Those angry retirees who mistakenly punched Buchanan's slot aren't going to shut up and go away. You might not, either, if it were your vote that was lost.

That the future occupant of the White House might be decided by a single county in South Florida is spine-chilling. Given our ripe history of scandal and skulduggery, the rest of the nation is wise to be worried.

November 15, 2000

DO A STATEWIDE RECOUNT

As the whole world awaits the true voting results from Palm Beach County, the Republican party feverishly battles to thwart a hand recount of ballots there.

What's the GOP so afraid of? Losing, of course. Palm Beach is Democratic turf, and a few hundred votes could swing the presidency.

So here comes Katherine Harris, Florida's secretary of state and an unabashed George W. Bush groupie, informing the Palm Beach County canvassing board that it has no legal right to conduct a manual recount.

It's one thing to enforce a statutory deadline for vote certification, as Harris did earlier. It's quite another thing to tell county officials they can't even try to meet that deadline.

Harris's meat-hook interference with a local ballot tabulation is unprecedented, and it illustrates the stark dread with which the Bush camp eyes Palm Beach.

A strategy of obstruction, though, will come back to haunt them. If enough of the country perceives that Republicans deliberately suppressed an accurate vote count in Florida, the legitimacy of a Bush victory will be bitterly disputed long after Inauguration Day.

Meanwhile, the situation continues to degenerate into vaudeville. Lawsuits are flying, judges are ducking for cover and two-bit political hacks from Miami to Tallahassee are slithering toward the limelight.

This serves only to reinforce Florida's image as a backwater Gong Show. If it doesn't end soon, we should change our state song to the banjo duel from *Deliverance.*

There's one solution that neither side can credibly oppose, and it would make most of the lawsuits vanish instantly.

To eliminate the partisan doubts inherent in selective recounts, both parties should agree to a manual recounting in all 67 counties. The logistics would be a pain in the butt, but it might be the fairest way to settle the question of who really won Florida—and the presidency.

Ironically, the Democrats might be less keen on this idea than the Republicans, as a statewide recount easily could end up helping Bush more than Gore.

But a Gore victory resulting from recounts only in Democratic-leaning counties would be just as hollow—and suspect—as a Bush victory achieved by blocking those recounts.

That's why a statewide effort makes sense, even if it takes a couple more weeks. Americans could endure the wait if assured that the outcome would be absolutely irrevocable, and that they finally could turn on a TV without seeing the likes of James Baker or William Daley.

To be sure, a statewide recount poses special challenges. Security obviously is a prime concern, as cheating is possible in any of the 67 counties. One answer is to watch over ballot counters with video surveillance, the way it's done in casinos. If cameras can spot a quick-fingered card shark at a black-jack table, they surely can nab some little old lady stuffing Bush ballots into her bag.

Another question is the precision of the counters themselves. Although widely employed around the country, hand-counting of votes obviously carries a potential for human error. I would suggest using math teachers wherever possible.

No one is more eager than Floridians to end this tawdry tinkling contest; no one is more fed up with the lawyers, the backroom tricks and the hypocritical posturing on all sides.

An all-county recount isn't a perfect solution because it ignores those 19,000-plus nullified ballots in Palm Beach. Unless a judge orders a new election there, which seems unlikely, that controversy is destined to taint a Bush victory.

A published report that the Republicans and Democrats had secretly agreed to a statewide recount proved false, and that's too bad. Polls say most Americans are ready to accept either Bush or Gore, provided the ballot review is seen as thorough and fair.

Yesterday the Palm Beach County canvassing board decided to go ahead and send in its earlier vote totals and proceed today with a manual recount—even if the updated figures won't be accepted.

Add 'em up, what the heck. Katherine Harris might not be interested in the outcome of a one-by-one ballot tally, but many Floridians are eager to know who actually got the most votes here. So is the rest of the world.

Call it morbid curiosity.

November 20, 2000

I, _____, AM OUTTA HERE

The Inevitable Concession Speech [fill in the blanks]:

My fellow Americans,

Our long national nightmare is over. This morning I phoned _____ [Gov. Bush/Vice President Gore] and conceded the presidential election. We had a cordial and very personal conversation that lasted at least 20 _____ [minutes/seconds/milliseconds].

Later, _____ [Gov. Bush/Vice President Gore] called back to make sure I wasn't going to change my mind. I chuckled and told him, "No, Mr. President-Elect, it's over."

And it is, my fellow Americans. At last.

We have an old saying here in _____ [Texas/Tennessee] that goes something like this: _____ [insert appropriate rural maxim].

So when I learned this morning of the court's ruling in _____ [Tallahassee/Atlanta/Washington, D.C.], I knew the time had come to _____ [throw the horned toad into the cactus/turn the rooster loose].

The past few _____ [weeks/months] have tested our democracy as it has never been tested before.

But I'm here today to tell you proudly that America has never been stronger. The presidency itself has seen better times, but the country is holding up fine.

First, I want to thank my wife _____ [Laura/Tipper], my children _____ [insert appropriate kids], and my running mate _____ [Dick/Joe]. All of you helped to make this long journey a most enriching and rewarding experience.

Who could have foreseen that the entire race would come down to the state where _____ [my brother/my opponent's brother] was governor! Go figure. I thought for sure _____ [I had it made/I was having a nightmare].

To all those thousands of loyal friends who worked tirelessly on our behalf, I regret that we ran out of luck, time and _____ [Republican judges/Democratic judges].

I can't help believing that things might have turned out differently if _____ [my old man had more clout/Bill Clinton had never met Monica Lewinsky].

To the voters of Florida and its elections officials, who have endured so much pressure, scrutiny and even scorn, I can only say: _____ [Jeb's really hacked off, so watch your butts/Better get Katherine Harris to save your precious Everglades, 'cause I'm outta here].

And to the people of Palm Beach County, in particular, whose efforts to have their voices heard prolonged this election and brought the eyes of the world upon us, I'd like to say, _____ [Kiss my chad, you old coots/How could anybody accidentally vote for Pat Buchanan! Wait, lemme guess—you left your glasses in the car?].

And, finally, to all the American people, I ask you not to be discouraged by the chaotic events of the last few _____ [weeks/eons]. Democracy isn't perfect; sometimes it can be downright embarrassing.

But I urge you to come together now in support of President-Elect _____ [Gore/Bush], even though he 'won' the election _____ [by a laughably thin margin/by finishing second to yours truly in the popular vote].

Many well-meaning people have begged me not to concede this historic contest just yet. They feel we should continue our court battles as long as necessary, to achieve an outcome reflecting _____ [the true letter of the law/the true will of American voters].

But I believe that the stalemate has gone on long enough and that to drag it out would divide and demoralize the country. In the unforgettable words of _____ [the Dixie Chicks/the Grateful Dead], I _____ [insert appropriate song lyrics].

So today I extend my heartfelt congratulations to our new commander-in-chief and wish him well. And while I know that _____ [48.6 million/48.7 million] of you are disappointed your candidate didn't win, don't feel bad. It's very possible he did.

But that's for history to decide.

As for me, I look forward to returning to _____ [Texas/Tennessee], relaxing with family and friends and _____ [shooting a few quail/writing a 900-page book about the election, to be serialized on my website].

November 22, 2000

FORGIVE ME, FATHER, FOR I HAVE MISPLACED A CHAD OR TWO

A day in the life of a manual vote recounter.

8 A.M.

My first stack of punchcards and here goes: Bush, Gore, Bush, Gore, Bush, Gore . . . Buchanan! Hey, it's a genuine Pat Buchanan vote!

A siren goes off, and I'm swarmed by burley, tight-lipped Democratic and Republican party observers.

The Buchanan punchcard is snatched from my hand and held up to a fluorescent surgical lamp. Then the ballot is photographed, X-rayed, laser-scanned and dusted for fingerprints.

"Good work," says my team leader, a taciturn masseuse named Olga.

10:17 A.M.
My first dangling chad, and I mean dangling.

"Help!" I squeak, and within moments a lawyer for the Democratic National Committee is coming at me with a brass tweezers. I duck out of his reach, only to come face-to-face with some GOP goon wielding an oozing tube of Krazy Glue.

His cologne makes me sneeze—and the dangling chad drops to the floor! In the ensuing scramble, I must've been knocked unconscious, for the next thing I remember is being hoisted by Olga's strong arms.

12:15 P.M.
Lunch break, and tensions are running high.

Republicans have angrily accused one of the manual recounters of eating loose chads—for what purpose, I can't imagine (the same ballot worker, however, has been implicated in the disappearance of Olga's nacho-flavored Doritos).

To play it safe, I retreat to a quiet corner of the auditorium for my usual cup of grape yogurt and a 32-ounce Jolt soda.

Here I'm approached by a shady-looking character who says he'll make it worth my while to "misplace" the next batch of Bush votes in the trunk of a certain gray Volvo, idling by the curb.

I run to fetch a policeman, but when we return the intruder is gone—and so is my yogurt!

1:20 P.M.
My first dimpled chad, and it's a cutie, I must admit.

Again both sides clamorously convene around my counting table, but after a lengthy discussion, it's agreed that the confusing dimple mark favors neither Bush nor Gore.

Microscopic examination reveals that the extraneous indentation on the cardboard was made either by a porcelain denture, or a teething Jack Russell terrier.

"Nice catch," says Olga, giving a smoky wink that leaves me feeling uneasy.

2:35 P.M.
The tedium of recounting is almost unbearable, and I'm afraid some of my fellow workers are starting to crack.

The cops rounded up one poor soul in the parking lot—he was riding in loopy circles on a beach-cruiser bicycle, a handful of Gore ballots pinned in his spokes.

3:10 P.M.

Our work is interrupted by an emergency meeting of the canvassing board, which has received a new legal opinion from Katherine Harris, the secretary of state.

Ms. Harris now says she cannot certify a single vote of the recount unless all ballot boxes are bound with silk ribbons, scented lightly with lilac water and blessed personally by Pope John Paul II.

By a 3–0 margin, the board agrees to "misplace" the secretary's letter for a week or two.

3:45 P.M.

My first pregnant chad has given birth—and it's a bouncing Baby Gore!

Olga is positively aglow, and she gives me a hug that lasts about 17 seconds too long. I fear she has become overly attached to some of us on her team.

5:22 P.M.

Fatigue is taking a hard toll. Several of the counters have been reprimanded for fanning themselves with punchcards, and one lady was caught propping her eyelids open with chads from a discarded Nader ballot.

My own vision is now so blurred that Gore looks like Bush, and Bush looks like Gore. But isn't that how we got into this mess in the first place?

With the U.S. presidency at stake, the pressure to finish is overwhelming. Olga offers to rub my shoulders, and I chase her off with a shot of pepper spray.

7:03 P.M.

My first swinging-door chad, and frankly, I don't give a rip. At this point, they're all confetti.

The Gore people say it's a vote, the Bush people say it's a mistake, and I say, "Bring on the Stoli!"

Olga is group-massaging the entire canvassing board, while the Democrats and Republicans argue about who hid all those punchcards in the toilet-paper dispenser in the men's room.

Me, I'm thinking of taking up origami, with a little help from the good citizens of Precinct 189 . . .

November 29, 2000

RIOTING BY GOP TOURISTS

Last week I got a call from a friend in New York who said, "Turn on the television, I'm sitting here watching your people try to steal the election."

He was talking about the goonfest at the Miami-Dade Elections Department, where rowdy protesters were banging on windows and doors during the presidential recount.

Like many angry viewers around the country, my friend had assumed that he was again witnessing Miami maniacs gone amok. He was wrong.

What he saw was a demonstration imported and paid for by the Republican party and the Bush-Cheney campaign. It's a page right out of the old Richard Nixon playbook, the type of stunt favored by G. Gordon Liddy and the other dirty tricksters.

The difference is, Liddy was smarter about covering his tracks.

Among the screamers who showed up in Miami last week to get their beet-faced mugs on TV were Thomas Pyle, an aide to the House Republican Majority Whip Tom DeLay; Michael Murphy, who works on a DeLay fundraising committee; Elizabeth Ross, who is employed by Senate Majority Leader Trent Lott; and Doug Heye, who works for Rep. Richard Pombo, R-Calif.

These and scores of other zealous young Republicans working on Capitol Hill were given time off, free plane tickets and meal money to come to Florida and raise a little hell at Thanksgiving. According to the *Wall Street Journal,* they even got invitations to a holiday party in Fort Lauderdale, where they were serenaded by Wayne Newton.

Admittedly, we here in the Sunshine State have never been picky about our tourists; basically, we'll take anyone with a pulse and a credit card. But as a point of fairness, we shouldn't be blamed for their bad behavior. The storming of the Miami-Dade elections office wasn't a spontaneous uprising of lawless locals; it was a show staged by visiting yupsters who owe their government jobs to the GOP.

At least Jesse Jackson didn't fly his rallies in from Chicago; most of the folks who showed were actual Floridians.

But having been walloped at the polls in Miami-Dade, Broward and Palm Beach counties, the Bush campaign obviously was worried about a sparse showing in the streets. So they sent reinforcements from Washington, D.C., and elsewhere, and rotated them through all three counties.

According to the *Journal,* one of the chief organizers was Rep. John

Sweeney, R-N.Y. When the demonstration in Miami got ugly, Sweeney was said to have told an aide to "shut it down."

By then things had gone too far. It made for some lively television footage, but it didn't exactly win the hearts and minds of America.

Many people were outraged by the melee, which appeared to frighten the Miami-Dade canvassing board into aborting its manual vote recount.

Never mind that the board had been bumbling around for two weeks and stood little chance of meeting the state Supreme Court's deadline. The Bush camp was determined to manufacture a scene, and it got one.

The confrontation was not only superfluous, it was potentially damaging to the party's own interests. This dumb incident has handed the Democrats new ammunition for their legal challenges and pro-recount campaign.

Judges who view the videotapes of the raucous mini-stampede might well conclude that Miami-Dade elections officials were intimidated into a retreat.

One remedy would be reopening the recount, an inevitably chaotic scenario that not only would prolong the presidential contest but possibly change the outcome.

How ironic if Florida's vote certification gets tossed out and the election results ultimately are recalculated to Gore's benefit—all because of what happened in Miami, where there shouldn't have been a recount to begin with.

By dispatching their aides here to stir things up, these boneheads have risked undoing the election for their candidate, who basically had it won. At the very least, they've given Gore's attorneys a gift-wrapped claw hammer for the upcoming court battles.

Jeb Bush should've warned his brother that sending protesters to Florida was a big mistake.

As everybody knows, we're perfectly capable of making a national spectacle of ourselves with no outside assistance.

17

GOOD SPORT

September 8, 1986

FOOTBALL MUST RID ITSELF OF FOOLISHNESS

The arrival of the college football season annually marks:

  a) a time of tradition and excitement on campus.
  b) the first stirring of autumn.
  c) the signal to buy stock in steroid companies.

In the old days, the only things that football fans ever had to worry about were homefield advantage, the injury report—and of course the point spread.

Now each week is Nerve Time. You cross your fingers and hope that your favorite player's grade-point average doesn't dip into the low fractions, or that he isn't caught with a bag of white powder hidden under the front seat of his 280Z.

There's enough of this going around that you'd think the colleges would catch on. You'd think they'd start teaching athletes a course on Where to Hide Your Stuff, and automatically flunk anyone who answered, "under the front seat of the car," or "in the glove compartment, coach."

A few weeks ago, a University of Miami football player was arrested with some industrial-strength muscle drugs following an alleged altercation with campus police. He says the steroids were left in his truck by a "non-player" with a prescription—which, as alibis go, is a little better than saying the drugs were planted by a Soviet spy.

The season was already off to a rocky start since four UM players were discovered driving fancy cars leased from or provided by a sports agent. When the Hurricanes played the University of Florida in Gainesville this weekend, many of the Gator fans in the stands jangled car keys at the um players—a jeering reference to the so-called Autogate affair.

Being a UF alumnus I can tell you that such displays of wit, however lame, are rare indeed from a football crowd and a welcomed improvement over the usual rock-and-bottle attacks. However, the Gator gesture does seem hypocritical considering that their own athletic department has behaved so crookedly that the football team has been barred from television.

This fetid scandal is best not mentioned in the presence of hardcore UF fans, who week after week stare at blank TV screens and mutter how the cable must be out again in Gainesville.

Meanwhile, in Nebraska, the Florida State Seminoles played against a team that wasn't supposed to be there. Sixty Cornhusker players faced suspensions because of some funny business with their season tickets.

Every player receives a certain number of complimentary game passes, which he is supposed to give only to relatives and student fans. However, some college athletes make a fortune by secretly selling these choice seats for big bucks. In the real world this is against the law; it's known as scalping. The NCAA prefers to call it "assigning complimentary tickets to non-relatives and non-students."

Upon hearing news of the mass suspension, the Nebraska coach angrily declared that none of his players were selling their tickets for money, that the violations were all minor and technical and just plain picky. For a while there was even talk that the Cornhuskers might forfeit the FSU game Saturday night.

Personally I would have tuned in to see a forfeit, just for something different. I was hoping they'd make FSU kick off toward an empty end zone and run downfield with absolutely no one to tackle.

Unfortunately for the Seminoles, the NCAA changed its mind and decided that the whole Nebraska team could play. I'm sure this decision had nothing to do with the fact that ABC was planning to broadcast the game nationally, and that each school stood to lose about $300,000 in TV revenues if there were a forfeit.

Now that the college season has been properly inaugurated, we can anticipate the sounds of sportsmanship old and new—the crack of the helmets, the roar of the crowd and the click of defense lawyers' briefcases snapping open.

September 26, 1986

THINK DOLPHINS ARE IN TROUBLE? JUST YOU WAIT

Even if you detest professional football, you are surely aware that the Miami Dolphins are in dire trouble this season. The crisis has become the talk of all South Florida, edging out the Nick Daniloff affair and the tumult surrounding Don Johnson's new haircut.

In three games the Dolphin defense has given up about a jillion points and is apparently so terrible that this week's opponents, the San Francisco 49ers, have told their punter to go ahead and take Sunday off.

On talk shows the debate heatedly revolves around whether Mr. Chuck Studley, the defensive coach, should be fired, demoted or simply blindfolded and dropped into a vat of boiling Desenex. Distraught Dolphin fans have already figured out that if the team continues at its present rate, it will surrender more points this season than the Denver Nuggets.

The worst part isn't really the losing; the worst part is the excuses. My personal favorites are "lack of concentration" and "failure to execute." These terms are used to explain the phenomenon whereby, when somebody on the other team catches the football, all nearby Dolphins immediately lunge out of the way.

Another distasteful aspect of losing is the excruciating post-game analysis—is the 53-Defense less effective than the 46-Defense? Is man-to-man coverage preferable to zone? Why didn't the weak-side linebacker "stay at home" on the double-reverse? For that matter, why didn't everybody stay at home?

In sportscaster jargon the Dolphins are "struggling," which is the same thing they would have said about General Custer after about the fifth arrow. The football season is young, but already the commentators are running out of excuses for why the Dolphin defense is so miserable. Why not save everybody a lot of creative energy and arrange the post-game alibis in advance:

Game Four (San Francisco 49ers): Dolphins confused because Chuck Studley has suddenly started speaking in tongues. Claims to have lived an earlier life as Visigoth warrior.

Game Five (at New England): Linebackers depressed over poor critical response to Prince's latest album. Insist the CD sounds much better.

Game Six (Buffalo Bills): Pranksters slip chocolate Ex-Lax onto Dolphin lunch trays.

Game Seven (Los Angeles Raiders): Team playbooks stolen, cleverly altered and returned to locker room undetected.

Game Eight (at Indianapolis): Defensive unit mistakenly flies to Baltimore. Apologizes, says they just forgot.

Game Nine (Houston Oilers): Cornerbacks just "can't get up for the game." Claim "life isn't worth living" since *Solid Gold* was moved to a later TV time slot.

Game Ten (at Cleveland): Followers of Bhagwan Rajneesh infiltrate Dolphin team practice, convert defensive back Bud Brown and flee in an unmarked van.

Game Eleven (at Buffalo): Dolphin defense spends the entire first half of the game sitting on the team bus. Studley says Mike Charles dozed off, blocking all exits.

Game Twelve (New York Jets): Morale problems plague secondary after violent pre-game argument over whether Bobby Ewing should be allowed to re-marry Pam on *Dallas*.

Game Thirteen (Atlanta Falcons): Team spirits low after Shula announces "slight mix-up" between urine samples and new Gatorade.

Game Fourteen (at New Orleans): Linemen just "can't get up for the game." Claim to be sorely disappointed by the contrived use of flashbacks in the new Stephen King novel.

Game Fifteen (at Los Angeles Rams): Listless defensive squad termed "seriously distracted" by sliding stock market and poor showing of the dollar against the franc on European money exchange.

Game Sixteen (New England): Dolphins confused after Shula reads a long passage from Kahlil Gibran in the locker room at halftime. Defense promptly gives up a record nine touchdowns in the third quarter, but seems eerily at peace with itself.

April 24, 1987

BASKETBALL TEAM'S NAME NOT HOT ITEM

Now that Miami has finally got an NBA franchise, there are two things we must do immediately:

1) Beg Julius Erving not to retire just yet, and
2) Change the name of our team.

The Heat?

Did Seattle name its team The Drizzle? Is the Minneapolis franchise going to call itself The Slush?

Somewhere along the way somebody held a contest and hordes of well-

- "Cartel Day." Box seats for visiting drug kingpins. Bodyguards get in for half price.
- "John Doe Day." Free corn dogs for anyone in the Witness Protection Program. Just show your fake ID at the concession stand.
- "INS Day." A thousand green cards to be given away during seventh-inning stretch. Check the popcorn box.
- "Meyer Lansky Day." Diamondvision tribute to Miami Beach's most lovable mobster.
- "Money Launderers' Day." First 200 fans with a briefcase get in free.
- "Centrust Day." Beanball contest with wealthy ex-S&L directors taking turns at the plate.
- "DEA Day." Free strip search of everyone in the right-field bleachers.
- "Old Timers' Day." Aging baseball legends struggle three innings in the broiling Florida sun.
- "Paramedics' Day." To be held simultaneously with "Old Timers' Day."

Big-league baseball, Miami-style! Sure, there might be some touchy moments, but nothing a few well-tuned metal detectors couldn't prevent.

It'll take a few seasons to educate new fans. We need to make it clear, for instance, that it's not polite to offer bribes at the ballpark. I don't care what kind of luck you've had with local circuit judges, big-league umpires are off-limits. We've got to draw the line somewhere.

Inevitably, too, the National League will have to come up with a policy regarding animal sacrifices. Certain rituals are said to be effective in hexing an enemy, but who knows how many chickens must die before Miami will ever sweep a four-game series from the Dodgers?

The important thing is, we'll have a baseball team—hot, rain-soaked and sprinkled with poultry feathers, but our team.

Bring on the big boys.

May 22, 1994

UM VS. FSU: A GAME WITH KICK(BACKS)

Here are highlights of the 1995 Payola Bowl, featuring the Florida State Seminoles vs. University of Miami Hurricanes. Because of NCAA sanctions, the game was broadcast only on the Home Shopping Network.

FIRST QUARTER

UM freshman sensation Charles "Speedy Feet" Farquar returns the kickoff into Seminole territory. On the sidelines, former UM players reward Farquar with $50 cash and an assortment of fine cheeses.

After Miami punts, FSU quickly rolls to the Hurricane 15-yard line. But the Noles get a costly delay-of-game penalty when quarterback Claude "Smarty Pants" St. Albin insists that his agent and stockbroker join him in the huddle.

The drive stalls, and FSU settles for a field goal. On the following kickoff, UM's Farquar is knocked down and robbed of the ball by one of his own teammates, the mercurial Benjie "The Deadbeat" Smorker.

Smorker, who admits to having dire credit problems, races 68 yards for a touchdown. Upon returning to the UM sideline, he demands $500, a low-interest home-equity loan and a new pair of Reeboks.

SECOND QUARTER

With emotions rising, Barnett Bank installs an ATM at the Hurricane bench. Coach Dennis Erickson doesn't notice.

With Miami playing the run, FSU's St. Albin tosses a 63-yard scoring bomb. Watching from the sideline (where he's a regular guest), rap star Dr. Drip Doggy Drip offers a $1,000 bounty to any Hurricane who knocks St. Albin out of the game.

Two plays later, the talented Seminole signal-caller is rushed to the locker room on a stretcher. Team doctors gravely describe the injury as a "severe jock-strap wedgie." Four jubilant UM players split the bounty, sweetened by a $75 gift certificate to Pizza Hut.

Still, the half ends with the Seminoles ahead, 10–7.

THIRD QUARTER

On the first play from scrimmage, FSU's gifted tailback, Frank "The Woos" Fleeper, suffers a hip pointer when he lands on a roll of quarters his agent had put in his pants.

Fleeper's loss is offset by the unexpected return of the hobbled St. Albin, who leads the Noles on a 60-yard scoring march. Along the Miami sideline, a furious Dr. Drip Doggy Drip raises the bounty on the pesky FSU quarterback to $2,000, plus a featured role in a new rap video.

UM linebacker Bubba "The Nut Case" Lipschitz rises to the challenge by going after St. Albin with a loaded Colt .38. Lipschitz later explains he needed the bounty money because he was three months behind on his Jet Ski payments.

The attempted shooting draws an automatic 15-yard penalty, but on the very next play Lipschitz recovers an FSU fumble and rambles unmolested for a Hurricane score.

American Express opens a full-service counter on the Seminole sideline, but Coach Bobby Bowden doesn't notice.

FOURTH QUARTER

A bomb concealed in a cash register explodes in the FSU huddle, and again St. Albin departs on a stretcher. Twenty-three Miami players scramble to claim the bounty.

On the next play, Seminole backup Phil "Noodle Arm" Grossberg is intercepted by UM's hard-hitting safety, Vlad "Ape Fingers" Agnew, who is immediately presented with a brand new Miata and a set of steak knives.

With seconds remaining, Dr. Drip Doggy Drip climbs a pile of Wells Fargo bags to give an emotional pep talk. The Canes score on the next play, edging FSU 21–17.

The victory hoopla is marred when confused UM players steal the Gatorade and dump the ATM on Coach Erickson's head.

August 14, 1994

THE SORRY LOT OF A STRIKING BASEBALL PLAYER

Bums! Brats! Ingrates!

For Zeke "Cheese Fingers" Farqua, the scrappy but unheralded utility infielder-outfielder for the Florida Marlins, the insults raining from the bleachers stung hard.

"These fans," says Zeke, "they don't understand. Not all of us are zillionaires. I got mortgages, lawyers, agents. That forty-unit time-share I'm building over on Marco. Not to mention a major frigging IRS problem."

Zeke Farqua is at the last place he expected to be in August: home. Baseball is on strike.

The turquoise Marlins duffel lies discarded in the sauna of Zeke's modest Key Biscayne penthouse. Inside that clay-scuffed bag is the Louisville Slugger that had carried Farqua to a .194 batting average this season, a personal best after four vagabond years in the majors.

"You think I wanted to go on strike? I had a chance of breaking .200 this year. A damn good chance." He looks away, biting his lower lip. "Man, to come so close . . ."

Zeke is tired of hearing the dispute between ball players and team owners characterized as millionaires vs. millionaires. "OK, so the average big-league salary is $1.2 million. But not everybody makes that kind of dough. Me, I only get $750,000, nondeferred."

I tell Zeke it still sounds like good money. His eyes flash.

"Hey, it took me four hard years to get where I am. Besides, how many good seasons do I have left? Most of my buddies quit by 33 or 34. I'm already 29. What'm I supposed to do when I'm out of baseball—learn a skill? Go to school? Get a job?"

He laughs bitterly. "I'm looking at, like, 40 years of retirement. That's expensive, man. It's not like I got jockstraps full of Krugerrands stashed in the backyard." He shakes his head. "I took a bad hit last fall. Mutual funds."

On the walls of Zeke's apartment are photos and newspaper highlights of a dogged, albeit forgettable, career:

"Farqua's Bunt Lifts Reds over Phils"

"Braves Edge Padres on Farqua Sacrifice"

"Gooden Hits Batter, Mets Drop Third Straight"

When I ask Zeke about the Gooden incident, he beams.

"Bottom of ninth, bases loaded, we're tied 1–1. Doc's throwing real good, but I'm patient. I take five straight fastballs, run the count to 3-and-2. The last pitch is a screamer on the inside corner—so what do I do?"

Zeke coils with an imaginary bat, re-creating the moment. "What do I do? I let it hit me! Stick out my elbow and bingo. Doc hollers bloody murder, but the ump points to first base and off I go. In comes the winning run!"

He sighs and sits down. I say, "You're really going to miss it, aren't you?"

"Tell you what I'm gonna miss," he snaps. "I'm gonna miss my September IRS payment if I don't get some serious liquidity. That means selling off stock, my friend, and that means capital gains."

After Zeke calms down, he talks about pride. No career should end like this. His brief stint with the Marlins was frustrating—a stubborn bout with gingivitis kept him on the disabled list for nine weeks. Days after rejoining the team, he was sidelined again with a painful plantar wart.

"When I was younger, I could play hurt," Zeke says ruefully. "Not anymore."

He opens a suitcase and starts packing. There's a big trading-card convention in Dallas. "Barrel of laughs. I sit there like a robot, autographing baseballs at five bucks a pop. Ha, and they call it a game!"

"Five dollars for one autograph?"

Zeke looks up. "What—you think I should ask for six? Seriously?"

April 2, 1995

RADICAL RULES MAY BRING FANS BACK TO GAME

Major-league baseball, due to begin tonight at Joe Robbie Stadium, has been postponed so that the real Florida Marlins and the real New York Mets can hit the StairMaster.

Fan apathy is so thick you can cut it with a knife. When the season finally starts, only the most loyal or morbidly curious will go to the games. Many fans will stay home, defiantly tuned to hockey or bass-fishing infomercials.

Even before its labor crisis, baseball was in no shape to alienate ticket holders. It's not the most fast-paced or physically taxing of sports, and many folks would rather watch Dan Marino or Michael Jordan on their worst days than endure nine scoreless innings on a sweltering summer afternoon.

If baseball is to recover its popularity, radical rule changes are needed—at least until the bleachers start filling again:

- No MORE RELIEF PITCHERS.

    So what if a guy's having a tough night. For $3 million a year, he can damn well stay out on the mound and keep throwing sliders until he gets somebody out.

    In the meantime, fans will get to see some hitting—doubles, triples, maybe even home runs. For a few franchises this will be an exciting new experience.

- No MORE MANAGERS.

    Once you get rid of relief pitchers, there's no need for somebody whose main job is chatting with them. The speed of the game cannot be accelerated as long as paunchy middle-aged men are allowed to interrupt play by strolling back and forth between the mound and dugout.

    If an umpire needs abusing, let the team owners descend from their skyboxes and do it themselves.

- No MORE DROPPING THE BAT AT HOME PLATE.

    Base running is baseball's most thrilling aspect, but imagine the extra thrills (and higher scores) if runners not only carried their bats, but were allowed to use them offensively on the base paths.

    It should, for example, be legal for a bat-wielding runner to swat a pick-off throw back at the pitcher. Likewise, a grounder dribbled to the shortstop could be batted safely into the outfield by a runner dashing between second and third.

Ty Cobb was infamous for breaking up double plays with his wicked slide. Think of what he could've done with a 34-ounce Louisville Slugger.

• No MORE EXTRA INNINGS.

Eliminate those sadistically tedious 16-inning marathons. If a baseball game is tied at the end of nine, it ought to be settled in a strictly limited overtime, like football.

Then, if the score remains knotted after overtime, a player selected from each side would meet at home plate for a chaw-spitting contest to break the deadlock. Games "decided by expectoration" would be denoted in the box scores with EX.

Teams would be permitted to keep two "designated spitters" (DS) on the regular-season roster, with a third available for the playoffs.

• No MORE FOUL BALLS.

Currently a batter is allowed to slice an infinite number of fouls without being called out. That rule often results in lengthy at-bats, during which fans have enough time to visit the restroom, buy a hot dog, and finish the annotated *War and Peace*.

Baseball games would be more action-packed (and blessedly shorter) if infielders and outfielders were made to chase foul balls through the crowd, while hitters ran the bases.

Nothing would draw strike-weary fans back to the ballpark as fast as the prospect of seeing Jose Canseco or Barry Bonds vault into the thirteenth row and try to pry a pop fly out of a little kid's fingers.

Talk about excitement. Talk about your "suicide squeeze."

April 27, 1995

UM DRUG POLICY: IF YOU FAIL, TRY AND TRY AGAIN

After days of controversy and rumor, an attempt to clarify the University of Miami's drug policy for football players:

• Urinalysis will be conducted several times during the season. It will be random, except in cases where the athlete accidentally finds out in advance by means of fax, e-mail, Day-Glo messages spray-painted on his locker, or airplanes circling the practice field with large banners that say:
"DRUG TEST MONDAY! DRUG TEST MONDAY!"

- The results of all urinalysis shall remain confidential. Access shall be restricted to the player himself, his defense attorney, the coach, the athletic director and the weekend crew of ESPN.
- If an NFL team inquires about a player's drug test, the university shall respond according to its long-standing policy of "Don't ask, please don't ask."

Penalties for drug use are:

First offense: The first time a player tests positive, it will be explained in no uncertain terms that marijuana stays in urine FOR WEEKS AND WEEKS, while cocaine flushes out in a couple days.

Second offense: A player who tests positive twice will be required to take off the headphones of his Walkman during future drug counseling.

Third offense: A player who tests positive three times will receive an automatic one-year suspension, unless he's a first-string All-American and Top Five draft choice, in which case he will be lectured very sternly indeed, and warned for the umpteenth time that marijuana stays in your urine FOR WEEKS AND WEEKS — GOT IT, CHOWDERHEAD?

Fourth offense: A player who tests positive four times will be banned from both dancing and singing in all team videos.

Fifth offense: A player with five positive urine tests will receive a double-secret suspension from the team, and will automatically be enrolled in a 12-step rehabilitation program at the university's School of Business.

There, counselors using the "Tough Love" approach will explain—with bar graphs, pie charts and actuarial tables—the massive monetary losses facing the player if his NFL draft status should slip because of a college drug scandal.

Sixth offense: A player who tests positive six times will automatically be banned from the team, unless he's a first-string All-American and potential Top Five draft choice, in which case he'll be benched for a whole entire game.

It shall be purely a coincidence if the suspension is imposed during a game against Temple, East Carolina State or even a more hapless opponent. The suspension can be rescinded only in the unlikely event that the Hurricanes are in danger of losing said game (and thus a lucrative bowl bid), in which case the suspended athlete will be permitted to play.

However, he will be strictly forbidden from participating in traditional sideline activities such as butting helmets with his teammates, or shouting "Hi Mom!" at the TV cameras.

Seventh offense: A player with seven drug violations shall be removed from the team, expelled from the university and made to repay his scholarship money.

The only exception shall be made if the seventh failed drug test occurs before a nationally televised bowl game in which the University of Miami has been invited to participate.

In that case, the player's urine shall automatically be sampled again, and shall be sent in a Gatorade bottle by fourth-class mail to a small mountain laboratory in Gstaad, Switzerland, for review.

It shall be purely a coincidence if the results of the urinalysis aren't available before the aforementioned Orange/Rose/Sugar Bowl game, or even before the NFL draft.

November 17, 1996

AN ETIQUETTE GUIDE FOR UM FOOTBALL FANS

An absolutely true news item: University of Miami Athletic Director Paul Dee has published a code-of-conduct guide for distribution to fans at home football games.
Rough Draft 7 might've looked like this:

1. USE OF ALCOHOL

Alcohol shall be used only in moderation at the Orange Bowl. "Moderation" is hereby defined as the upright consumption of beer and/or hard liquor from cans, bottles, flasks, jugs, coolers, carafes, decanters, pitchers, crocks, urns, bowls, tureens, canteens, wineskins and 55-gallon drums.

However, the sale of alcohol via intravenous drip will be discontinued by vendors after the third quarter of every game.

2. USE OF OBSCENITIES

Profanity, ethnic slurs and graphic sexual terminology shall not be directed at opposing players or coaches unless such language is purposely elicited by goading, taunting or provocation.

Actions by the visiting team that shall justify the use of multisyllabic obscenities by UM fans include but are not limited to (a) making a first down; (b) completing a forward pass; (c) recovering a fumble; (d) blocking a field goal; (e) wantonly entering the end zone without permission; (f) scoring more points than the Hurricanes during the allotted 60 minutes of play.

3. USE OF VIOLENCE

It shall be the policy of the Orange Bowl and of the university to discourage violence at all home football games. "Violence" is hereby defined as a flagrant assault with fists, truncheons, bottles, dental probes, PVC pipes (Schedule 40 and higher), baseball bats, cutlery, golf equipment or hickory limbs (see Appendix IV, "Possession of Hardwoods [native]").

4. USE OF EXPLOSIVES

Fans at the Orange Bowl shall be strictly forbidden from possessing, constructing or igniting explosives, except in instances when such devices may be necessary to neutralize boat horns or other obnoxious distractions in the stands.

5. PROJECTILES, UNAUTHORIZED

Fans shall not hurl the following objects onto the field of play: coconuts, bowling balls, cinder blocks, artificial limbs, car batteries, large reptile eggs, deep-sea outriggers, dead chickens, live chickens, urinal cakes, toaster ovens, napalm canisters or pieces of the Orange Bowl itself (i.e., chairs, rails, awnings, plumbing fixtures).

6. PROJECTILES, AUTHORIZED

To sustain a festive game-day spirit, Hurricane fans shall be permitted to toss the following relatively harmless objects onto the field: Seedless grapes, cold cuts, Junior Mints, handfuls of dog food (dry only), articles of personal clothing and soft-tissue body organs.

7. RESTROOM ETIQUETTE

It shall be the strict policy of the Orange Bowl and the university that stadium restrooms shall be utilized only for their designated purpose, and only by ticketholders whose gender and species are indicated by the symbol on the door.

Fans waiting to use the restrooms should form an orderly line, and should resist the urge to use nonauthorized receptacles such as sinks, ashtrays, trash cans or tote bags of unsuspecting ticketholders.

8. VOMITING ETIQUETTE.

As a matter of courtesy, drunken fans should always make a good-faith effort to reach a restroom before vomiting.

In such instances where a restroom is too far away, closed for repairs or obstructed by other drunken fans, then it is always preferable to vomit on one's self (i.e., feet, lap, knees) or at least in the general vicinity of one's self.

Under no circumstances is it considered permissible or prudent to vomit on another UM ticketholder, particularly in the upper deck (see Appendix IX, "Discharge of Firearms [unregistered]").

Part

4

This precipitated such a holiday fest of political back-slapping and celebration that a key fact of the ruling seems to have been overlooked: It does not exonerate Sergio Pereira of anything. It does not proclaim his innocence. It does not even suggest that the Hot Suit Case be abandoned.

All the order says is that Pereira shouldn't have been charged with three counts of grand theft, but one. While the county manager is alleged to have possessed seven stolen suits from the infamous Marino Duplex, the special prosecutors cannot prove that he didn't buy these suits all at once, instead of in three separate visits.

If this seems kind of picky, it is. Lawyers are paid to be picky.

To buttress Sergio's plea for dismissal, his attorneys dug up a 1951 decision called *Hearn* v. *State of Florida*. Fittingly, this was a case about cattle rustling—a standard of conduct against which all public officials should be tested.

In this instance, a fellow named James E. Hearn and some pals stole nine cows and two calves from a range in North Florida and tried to sell them up in Alabama. The rustlers were arrested and charged with two larcenies, since one cow belonged to one rancher and the others belonged to another.

Justice moved swiftly in those days. Hearn was convicted of the first charge in the morning and went on trial for the second charge that very afternoon, with similar results.

However, on appeal the Florida Supreme Court ruled 4–3 that, because all the cattle were stolen at the same time, Hearn should have been prosecuted for only a single act of larceny.

"This principle also governs receiving stolen property," Sergio Pereira's attorneys argued this week. "In our case, the State cannot prove that Pereira purchased the seven suits at different times, therefore it cannot exclude the possibility that the purchase of the seven suits, or any combination thereof, occurred at the same time. Accordingly, the State cannot charge Pereira with three separate offenses."

Fine. The Hot Suit prosecutors can abide by the judge's order and still follow the will of the grand jury by simply refiling the indictment as one count of grand theft.

This means the case would go to court. Finally, Pereira would get an opportunity to take the witness stand and fully explain how he came to buy rustled, cut-rate suits from an old "friend" whose business had been previously shut down for the same shenanigans.

Obviously, the special prosecutors are under enormous pressure to forget the whole case. Defense attorneys say that they've come up with all kinds of juicy tidbits about one of the state witnesses, and that five of the seven suits might not be stolen after all. Presumably the leak of such information is designed to spare prosecutors the toil and expense of trying to prove their case.

Anytime a powerful public figure is arrested, the establishment loses its stomach for letting the justice system work. It's a big, sticky mess, having one of the old gang up on a felony rap. Regardless of the outcome, nobody wins any political brownie points.

Judge Gersten probably wants to go to trial about as much as he wants a live grenade tossed in his lap. Meanwhile, the county commissioners are so eager to bury the case that they convened on Thanksgiving Day to reinstate Pereira, heedless of the possibility that they might just have to suspend him all over again.

Defense attorneys George Yoss and Hank Adorno, once so eager for a quick trial, now say the charges against their client should stay dropped. Interesting, since the most important material fact of this case hasn't changed.

The county manager bought stolen suits, period. Whether it was two or 200 doesn't matter. Whether he bought them on one visit or a dozen doesn't matter. Did he know, or should he have known, that the suits were hot? This is the accusation, and only a trial can settle it.

Dumping the indictment now, on an easily corrected technicality, would mean that Dade County justice isn't just blind, it's double-jointed.

July 10, 1989

LAWYER ADS ALWAYS LEAVE YOU LAUGHING

The most hilarious commercials on television might be banned from the airwaves if the Florida Bar gets its way.

The Bar wants to clamp down on lawyers who advertise. Some of those lawyers are fighting back and have formed a new group that loftily calls itself Citizens Against Censorship. The CAC has just launched a TV campaign to convince Floridians that consumers benefit from lawyer advertising.

In one way, we do. Television is entertainment, and nothing is more entertaining than watching a David Singer commercial at 2 in the morning.

My favorite is the one with a squirmy little brat in the barber chair. The barber tells the kid to sit still or he'll cut his ear off, and the kid whirls around and says something like: "If you do, I'll hire attorney David Singer to sue you."

Then Mr. Singer himself appears, amused and avuncular, to say that "no case is too small" for his considerable talents. This is wonderfully crude and empty-headed advertising, and it works like a charm on its target audience—potential clients whose intelligence quotient barely exceeds that of wet concrete.

Some people who watch these commercials actually believe that nice young David Singer or sharp-dressing Jeffrey Orseck will personally accompany them to court, when in fact both men are usually much too busy.

The leadership of the Florida Bar feels that some TV ads demean the profession and damage the already battered image of lawyers. Consumers might argue that the commercials are actually enlightening and informative, because they confirm what we've always suspected is the root of many lawsuits: naked greed.

It's interesting that TV commercials are used almost exclusively by personal-injury lawyers in search of fresh accident claims. Why don't downtown zoning lawyers ever do television? Or divorce lawyers ("Married to Scum? Let us take him to the cleaners!")?

Likewise, probate lawyers could have a ball on prime time: "Gonna croak soon? Call the firm of Grab, Swipe and Scrounge for your Last Will and Testament. We're not only cheap, we're fast! Inquire today for special deathbed rates!!!"

And think of the excitement if local criminal defense lawyers started doing TV commercials: "No Bust is Too Small! From grams to kilos, from mail fraud to murder, from robbery to RICO—we'll help you beat the rap . . . and, best of all, you won't have to sell your Ferrari to pay our fee!!"

The possibilities are boundless, and perhaps this is one reason why the Florida Bar is so worried. Having witnessed the unabashed tackiness of some personal-injury advertising, many lawyers dread what might happen if the TV fad spreads to other legal specialties.

Under the plan proposed by the Bar leadership, dramatizations would be forbidden in lawyer advertising. No screeching car crashes, no tearful testimonials—just the lawyer's name, phone number and credentials. There's even talk of requiring a disclaimer advising TV viewers that it's unwise to choose an attorney the same way you do an underarm deodorant.

From the audience's standpoint, the dignified approach is no fun at all. We'd miss those side-splitting late-night lawyer ads, with their hokey prop law books and their unctuous solicitations to help any poor wretch who's ever torn a hangnail in a fender bender.

Fortunately, that stalwart guardian of the U.S. Constitution—the advertising industry—has rallied forth to defend the cause. Ad agencies have joined TV lawyers in warning that a crackdown on legal-services commercials is really an assault on the First Amendment.

"It's just the beginning," predicts Susan Gilbert, a prominent South Miami ad executive. Today they're going after lawyers, she says; tomorrow it might be car dealers.

No, Susan, not here. Not in America! In this country we cherish the right to have our intelligence insulted. It's something that we will always fight for, just like David Singer, long into the dark of night.

July 23, 1990

OLD SPARKY SHOULD GET DEATH SENTENCE

Amazing but true.

Exactly 112 years after Thomas Edison invented the incandescent lamp, the great State of Florida still grapples with the theory of electricity.

Old Sparky is on the fritz.

Today in Starke, so-called electrocution experts will gather to perform a battery of tests on the electric chair, the Gothic death seat reserved for the most heinous of criminals.

I can't imagine what qualifies a person for the title of "electrocution expert," and I'm not sure I want to know. One could make an argument that the only true experts on the subject are, without exception, deceased.

Nonetheless, today's panel will try to determine if Old Sparky is operating properly. The last time the chair was used, on May 4, a serious glitch developed: When the switch was pulled, cop-killer Jesse Tafero's head caught fire. Tafero didn't expire until the executioner sent three separate charges through his smoldering body.

Prison authorities explained this ghastly malfunction as a freak incident. They blamed it—I swear—on a faulty sponge attached to Old Sparky's headpiece.

The sponge had been purchased from a store (obviously not a specialty shop) in downtown Starke. It replaced a natural sponge that had been used on the heads of prisoners in previous executions.

According to the Department of Corrections, the store-bought sponge proved unsuitable (to say the least) for conducting heavy jolts of electricity, and the fibers ignited during the Tafero execution.

This is not a demented Monty Python routine. It is the official explanation.

Sometimes it's scary to watch state government in action. You can forget about solving our mess of a highway system. Forget about cleaning up the Everglades. Forget about saving the children in HRS.

We can't even get an electric chair to work.

The concept of electricity, as applied to executions, is not complicated. A switch is pulled and thousands of volts are sent through electrodes into the prisoner, who dies from the shock.

It is a terrible thing to see; we are assured it's swift and painless, but this is pure speculation. Those who witnessed the Tafero execution probably will carry the memory to their graves.

The debacle was grisly enough to prompt the appellate courts to postpone three subsequent executions. Florida now finds itself forced to prove that our electric chair is not, in fact, a device of human torture.

Testing Old Sparky requires a certain amount of guesswork. It's easy to measure how much current is passing through the electrodes; calculating its effect on brain and flesh is something else.

Consider the problem scientifically: How do you test an electric chair? It's not like a portable hair-drier or a VCR; *Consumer Reports* doesn't rate these things.

The lethal nature of the machine limits the scope of experimentation. A public outcry would occur if they ever tried to test it on a gerbil or a monkey.

As for the new sponge, I suppose they could strap the headpiece on a ripe grapefruit and see if it catches fire. Still, it wouldn't be quite the same as using a human being.

Some would say that the more agony associated with executions, the better. There are those who would probably cheer if we dropped Death Row inmates in a tank of ravenous piranhas.

But the law proscribes us to be slightly more civilized than the violent killers we punish. While I agree that there are some crimes for which death is the only just penalty, it shouldn't be performed with a Rube Goldberg contraption.

Recognizing the gruesomeness of electrocution, many states have switched to giving lethal injections. What happened to Tafero suggests that Florida should do likewise, and junk Old Sparky for good.

The final result of injections is the same, without the sparks or the smoke or the Frankenstein ceremony. A society that practices capital punishment ought to keep up with the technology.

May 9, 1993

THE HOUSE HONCHO THAT COKE BUILT

Move over, Horatio Alger. Meet Pablo Valdes, a success story for modern times.

Valdes came to Florida on the Mariel boatlift. In a few years, he became a big-time developer of Hialeah Gardens and a very wealthy man. He was even featured in a cover story in the *Latin Builders Association* magazine.

Valdes was living the American dream, or so it appeared. But while thousands of other immigrants were making their fortunes the old-fashioned way—sweat, sacrifice and hard work—Pablo had found a shortcut. Here's how: Smugglers brought him huge amounts of cash to invest in housing developments in Hialeah Gardens. Over the years, he built almost 800 homes, many of them with laundered drug profits. He could have honestly called his subdivisions Kilo Lakes or Cocaine Meadows, but he chose more conventional names, such as Biltmore Estates.

Pablo prospered until early 1989, when he was visited by federal agents. They were on the trail of a coke dealer, and that trail led to Valdes. Quickly he did what all desperate dirt balls try to do—cut himself a deal.

And what a deal, too. Reporters Jeff Leen and Alina Matas dug up the details: In October 1990, Valdes agreed to forfeit $4 million in drug-stained property and admitted to laundering $100,000. The true sum was closer to $7 million, but who was counting?

Valdes vowed to help agents nail high-level coke traffickers and corrupt public officials. To some prosecutors, the information looked promising. Pablo got to stay out of jail and run his business as if nothing was awry.

Although the plea agreement was opposed vigorously by the Drug Enforcement Administration and FBI, then-U.S. Attorney Dexter Lehtinen approved it. The terms remained secret.

Pablo continued to prosper. He developed three new subdivisions. He cruised around town in a Jaguar or a Lincoln, depending on his mood. He donated money to political candidates. Mister Model Citizen, that was Pablo.

Those who'd bought his houses had no idea that cocaine had built them. They had no idea they were dealing with a criminal. When some of their yards began to flood, residents laid tiles to push the water back. When the city of Hialeah Gardens cited them for illegal construction, the residents said it wasn't fair.

"What they should be doing," one homeowner declared, "is going after the developer." If only they had known.

While his customers' lawns filled with stinky water and worms, under-cover ace Pablo Valdes was providing intriguing leads but no major drug figures to the government. Eventually, the only people he snared were a teller and a bank vice president whom he'd allegedly recruited to help deposit drug cash.

The feds dutifully indicted the pair, resigned to chase minnows while the shark himself swam free. For two years, prosecutors assembled cases against the teller and the bank officer, while Valdes went on building homes and living the good life.

On Thursday, prosecutors glumly decided to drop charges against the bank officer because their star witness, Pablo Valdes, had turned out to be a liar. U.S. District Judge Stanley Marcus, a former prosecutor, was exasperated. He called the case a "disgrace."

Not for Valdes. He came to this country with nothing, and became rich by breaking the law. When he got caught, the government generously adopted him and protected his good name. Not only was Pablo allowed to stay out of jail, he was allowed to stay wealthy and respectable, too.

Talk about a land of opportunity. Talk about dreams coming true. The story of Pablo Valdes is enough to bring a lump to your throat.

Straight from the stomach.

March 3, 1994

CASTRATION BILL SOUNDS TOUGH, BUT IT'S IMPOTENT

The war on violent crime has a new buzzword: castration.

In Tallahassee, the Senate Criminal Justice Committee has approved a bill that would allow the "chemical castration" of repeat rapists.

In Okeechobee, a county judge named Ed Miller is a hero for writing that a local sex offender should have been "castrated and hung by the neck."

Regardless of which was to come first, a lynching would make castration superfluous. Still, Judge Miller made his point. The hometown folks cheered, even if the Judicial Qualifications Commission didn't.

The idea of emasculating rapists isn't original, but U.S. courts have consistently prohibited the practice as unconstitutionally cruel. In 1992, a child molester in Houston volunteered himself for a castration, but not a single doctor could be found to perform the operation. The defendant eventually reconsidered.

Seldom has the subject of involuntary genital adjustment been so widely discussed as it is today. Perhaps lawmakers are emboldened by the public's fascination with the fate of John Wayne Bobbitt's penis.

After weeks of excruciatingly explicit testimony and talk-show jokes, it's difficult to imagine anyone being too shocked by a debate over castration legislation.

Whether it would deter rapists is highly questionable. In these crime-conscious days, sounding tough is every politician's aim—and there's no tougher word than *castration*.

Florida's so-called "Bobbitt bill" caused an outcry when it was introduced by Sen. Robert Wexler of Boca Raton. In its current form, the law would allow a judge to order chemical castration for a rapist convicted of a second offense. (If we can't cut 'em off, let's nuke 'em!)

The term *chemical castration* is politically catchy, but clinically misleading. Castration typically is the permanent removal of testicles. Chemical castration is the injection of a drug that reduces the sex drive.

Rapists would receive injections of Depo-Provera, along with counseling and prison time. The effects of the substance are reversible.

Wexler says other countries have successfully used chemical castration to reduce rapes by repeat offenders. Rape victims have testified in favor of the law, but others—including women's groups—oppose it. A similar bill died 10 years ago.

The theory of chemical castration presumes rape is a crime of hormonal urges. Many experts say it's more often an act of rage. Rendering a rapist impotent won't remove his anger or his ability to carry out a sexual assault. Many brutal rapes are committed with something other than an erect penis.

Wexler says the threat of chemical therapy will deter serial rapists, but that presumes they think rationally and are able to exercise self-control. If that were true, the prospect of state prison would be a sufficient deterrent. It's certainly nastier than a temporary loss of sex drive.

The Bobbitt bill has been denounced as inhumane and even likened to the Nazi drug experiments of World War II. That's quite a reach, but it makes for colorful rhetoric.

Putting moral arguments aside, a basic problem with legalizing chemical castration is that it can't work. Prosecutors would be tied up for years by rapists fighting Depo-Provera as unconstitutional. It's possible they'd win, too. These days, ironically, the only court-approved injections are lethal ones.

Wexler's new solution to rape is as judicially impractical as the old-fashioned one suggested by Judge Miller. Both sound tough. Both touch a public nerve. Both grab headlines.

But neither stands a ghost of a chance of coming to pass.

July 13, 1997

DEATH PENALTY DEBATE MIRED IN GRISLY DETAILS

Does the human brain literally cook when zapped with 2,300 volts?

That's one of the grislier questions being asked in a Jacksonville courtroom—a needless diversion of time, legal talent and taxpayer money.

Once again the issue is Old Sparky, Florida's temperamental electric chair. The last man to sit in it, Pedro Medina, briefly caught fire when the skullcap malfunctioned because of "unintentional human error."

Attorneys for the next inmate in line on Death Row, convicted cop killer Leo Jones, promptly stalled his execution by assailing the electric chair as a form of cruel and unusual punishment.

Now both sides have gathered to debate the finer points of electrocution—how long the prisoner remains conscious, how much agony (if any) is suffered, how many minutes until clinical death occurs.

The state contends that the chair usually works fine, rendering the inmate instantly unconscious and free of pain. Some pathologists have said Old Sparky's three massive surges dissolve brain matter to pudding.

However, a neurophysiologist who examined Medina's brain testified Thursday that it showed "normal cell anatomy" and was "not cooked in any way."

This would be a fascinating discussion if you had a TV show called "The Intra-cranial Gourmet," but it's pointless in the broad emotional battle over capital punishment.

That the electric chair is a gothic anachronism goes without saying. Whether it induces an unconstitutional amount of pain can never be determined, because the only guys who could tell us are dead. All other accounts are speculation.

In any case, the strongest argument against the chair isn't humanitarian, but pragmatic. It drags out the process of capital punishment.

Based on the delays and litigation generated by Old Sparky, no one should be more opposed to it than proponents of the death penalty. As long as Florida employs an electric chair, murderers will get another potentially long road of appeal.

All other executions have been on hold since the Medina fiasco March 25. Texas, meanwhile, continues to thin its Death Row population at the record-setting pace of one per month. Like most states, it has discarded the chair and switched to lethal injection.

Florida's lawmakers aren't that bright. Some have said they believe electrocution is a bigger deterrent to murder than a toxic needle is—a theory without a speck of factual support or insight into the psychology of heinous homicide.

The other popular argument for the electric chair is easier to understand: Capital punishment ought to be excruciating, to repay the killer for all the pain he caused his victim.

Problem is, the courts prohibit eye-for-an-eye treatment of convicted criminals. Whether you agree or not doesn't matter; the law won't change.

The more controversial a method of capital punishment is, the more legal challenges it faces from Death Row. That means elongating the already-grinding and costly appeals process.

Texas wised up to the electric-chair dilemma. While lethal injection has its occasional glitches, at least no one's scalp ignites during the procedure.

There are ghouls on Death Row for whom an agonizing demise might seem just, especially to the victims' families. The Supreme Court, however, allows no such accommodation.

Politicians know it, yet they continue to talk tough about the electric chair. Ironically, as long as they cling to fitful Old Sparky, capital punishment in Florida has no chance of being either swift or certain.

We will, however, learn more than we care to know about the precise boiling temperature of the brain.

September 11, 1997

LUNETTA'S ODDS FOR A PLEA DEAL SEEM ROSY

Every time Ted Klein picks up a newspaper, he's probably holding his breath—or calculating how much to raise his fee.

Klein is the attorney for king wharf rat Carmen Lunetta, ex-director of the Port of Miami. Klein is a fine lawyer, but he's no magician. And only a feat of magic can save his client now: the wave of a wand, to make all those FBI agents disappear.

Scarcely a week goes by without fresh headlines exposing more deceit and chicanery by Lunetta while he mismanaged Dade's huge, bustling harbor into unfathomable debt.

The latest revelation: A California construction firm got $10 million in public funds for dredging it didn't do. Lunetta personally arranged the payout, supported by phony paperwork, and then tried to cover it up. The dredging company is now mired in bankruptcy.

A few days earlier, another bombshell: Lunetta used a legitimate Miami shipping agency as a funnel for thousands of dollars to friends and associates for questionable, vaguely documented services.

One Lunetta golfing chum, Janison Foreman, collected $108,800 for "promotional" work, although nobody has been able to explain what he did to earn the money.

Apparently a man of multiple talents, Foreman was also dispatched by Lunetta to monitor the port's fiscal health—a task already assigned to professional accountants and auditors. Collectively they did such a bang-up job that the port was $22 million in the hole by the time Lunetta resigned this summer.

He hasn't yet been charged with any crimes, but it seems probable. If the feds keep dredging, they'll have so much evidence they'll need a barge to haul it upriver.

That there was looting and misuse of public money on a massive scale is obvious. The big unanswered questions are: How much of the booty was kicked back to Lunetta, and which of his cronies will be the first to give him up to prosecutors.

Ted Klein is no dummy. He knows that more ugly front-page revelations are bound to come.

But from recent events he should also know there's reason for hope. It springs from, of all things, a squalid little scandal called Operation Greenpalm.

The lesson: In Miami, being busted for corruption isn't the end of the world. Far from it.

Look what happened to former City Manager Cesar Odio, caught on tape counting out a big fat bribe. He copped a plea and was sentenced to a whopping one year in prison, plus a $100 fine.

Only one year for selling his office, selling out the citizens he was sworn to serve. Incredible but true.

As a matter of fact, all the major Greenpalm crooks have been allowed to plea-bargain for country-club time. It's unlikely any of them will spend much more than two years behind bars, barely long enough to polish their tennis games.

Those headlines, though infuriating to many in South Florida, could only have buoyed the optimism of Klein and attorneys for other potential Port of Miami indictees.

A trial would be time-consuming, expensive, risky—and harrowing for lots of important people, people who knew about or benefited from the casual plundering of the port. From those nervous quarters, at least, a Lunetta plea deal would be cheered.

And if a guy like Odio, whose crimes were recorded by electronic surveillance, can skate away with one measly year in prison, Lunetta's prospects for a similar slap on the wrist seem rosy indeed.

He and Klein ought to curl up outside the U.S. attorney's office, and wait for the Plea Bargain Fairy to come out.

May 31, 1998

POLITICIAN'S LAWYER NEEDS A LOT OF PITY

There's Miami Commissioner Humberto Hernandez, smirking like the class clown as he surrenders (yet again) on serious criminal charges.

And I feel a peculiar pang of sympathy, not for the feckless Humberto but for his attorney, of all people. Defense lawyers don't get much pity—or expect it—but I can't imagine a more dispiriting job than trying to defend a slug like Bert.

The task falls to Jose Quinon, of whom we'll be seeing plenty. When the suspended commissioner goes to trial for alleged bank fraud and money laundering, Quinon will be at his side. He'll be there again when Hernandez is tried on these new charges of covering up ballot fraud in November's election.

Quinon is one of Florida's top defense aces, but he's best known for representing big-time drug dealers, not small-time politicians. I don't envy him for taking on Hernandez as a client.

Say what you will about cocaine smugglers, they usually know how to behave once they're busted. They don't grin idiotically at TV cameras while being hauled away in handcuffs. Rather, they often make efforts to hide their faces, or at least bow their heads until they reach the lockup.

Because even in the grubby world of drugs, embarrassment is an appropriate reaction to being arrested on television in front of one's family and friends (not to mention strangers who might someday be sitting on the jury). Laughing on the way to the paddy wagon is not advisable conduct.

Another advantage to representing dope smugglers over politicians: Most dope smugglers know when to shut up.

They don't spout off before they're arrested, and they don't spout off after they're arrested. They don't make self-serving (or self-incriminating) speeches. They don't ride in parades. They don't stage pep rallies on court-house steps.

And they don't go on talk radio to promote nutball conspiracy theories, or claim to be an innocent victim of ethnic persecution (especially when the prosecutor shares the same ethnicity).

Smart defendants understand the importance of keeping a low profile. Apparently that's impossible for an egomaniac like Hernandez.

One can imagine Quinon's dismay when the already-indicted Humberto chose last fall to run again for the City Commission. And one can imagine Quinon's deepening gloom as the vote-fraud scandal unfolded, and evidence increasingly pointed toward his client.

To rig a public election while out of jail on a $500,000 bond—nobody possibly could be that stupid. Or so Quinon must hope.

Those holding low opinions of lawyers will assume Quinon must be secretly pleased by Hernandez's latest arrest. More work, more money—right?

Not necessarily. Another drawback to defending a politician over a dope smuggler: Smugglers pay whatever it takes, because they can afford to.

Politicians, by contrast, rarely have such deep pockets. Those in trouble usually got there by hustling somebody for dough.

Even those with real jobs aren't always at the apex of their profession. As a lawyer Hernandez has been fired from the city attorney's office, rebuked by the Florida Bar for chasing ValuJet mourners, and busted by the feds. None of that's good for business.

A smuggler who runs short on legal fees always has a way to raise more cash. But a suspended city commissioner? Once out of office, he can't even shake down a guava tree.

So Jose Quinon probably won't get rich off the Hernandez case. Maybe he's doing it because he's got a soft heart, or because he likes a stiff challenge.

Wait until he hears the surveillance tapes. At least dopers know enough to speak in code.

August 20, 1998

JURY DUTY HAS ITS REWARDS

Thanks to the case of Miguel D. Moya, some folks might think twice before trying to squirm out of jury duty. It's no longer just a civic duty, it's a potential jackpot.

Moya, a ramp worker at Miami International Airport, took four months out of his life to serve as jury foreman in one of South Florida's biggest drug trials.

And what did he get in return? The deep personal satisfaction of serving a vital role in the process of justice—plus about $500,000 in cash, according to prosecutors.

Citizen Moya was arrested this week and charged with bribery, obstruction of justice and witness tampering. The feds say that in exchange for a payoff, he engineered the 1996 acquittals of powerboat racers Willie Falcon and Sal Magluta on 17 cocaine smuggling charges.

Nobody doubts that Willie and Sal are capable of bribery, but seeking out the jury foreman would show not only audacity, but an ironically abiding faith in the system.

The foreman is supposed to be the jury's leader; supposed to be articulate and persuasive. Theoretically, if you're going to pay off anybody, that's the one.

But not all jury foremen are too swift, as evidenced by the number of dumb and jumbled verdicts in high-profile cases. If the charges against Moya are true, Willie and Sal lucked out. They bought somebody who actually understood the facts of the case, and knew how to dismantle it verbally.

The feds made a priority of prosecuting the high-flying Magluta and Falcon, accused of importing 75 tons of cocaine. Some witnesses were murdered before trial, and others vanished. A detective said Falcon and Magluta offered him a 1,000-kilo bribe.

Their acquittal was shocking, and had bizarre political fallout (U.S. Attorney Kendall Coffey decamped to a local strip joint, where he not only licked his wounds but allegedly chomped a dancer. He denied the bite, but resigned from office).

Jurors recalled that foreman Moya had argued emphatically for acquittals, and that ultimately six holdouts caved in. Afterward Moya told the *Herald:* "The testimony of the 27 witnesses didn't coincide with the physical evidence. No one wanted to believe these . . . people."

But he also acknowledged that deliberations got so tense that other jurors "wanted to fight me." They believed Magluta and Falcon were guilty.

Today, Willie and Sal are doing time on other charges. Moya himself has pleaded innocent to tainting the jury, though he will have to explain a few eyebrow-raising purchases: new cars, a $31,000 Mako outboard, a jaunt to Hawaii, a $198,500 house in Tavernier and the inevitable Rolex (not the typical timepiece of airport ramp workers).

People usually think of jury duty as an inconvenience, not a golden opportunity to get rich. It'll be interesting to see if more start volunteering to serve, now that Moya's alleged windfall is in the headlines.

Recently I sat on a jury in a cocaine case. The defendant wasn't as flashy or rich as Willie and Sal. He was just some young guy—one of more than 100 picked up many months after allegedly selling $40 worth of crack to a police informant.

We acquitted him as fast as possible. It was a terrible case—not one cop or drug agent witnessed the "crime," and the surveillance video was so murky that prosecutors didn't want us to see it. That's because the face of the man on trial was nowhere to be found on the tape.

I didn't get bribed to vote for acquittal, and I'd bet the other jurors didn't either.

Not long ago I ran into our foreman in a restaurant, and he certainly wasn't sporting a Hawaii-grade tan. Call me naive, but I didn't bother to check his wrist to see if he was wearing a new Rolex.

September 3, 2000

NO CORRUPTION'S TOO LARGE FOR RUNDLE TO MISS

How surprising to learn that 443 public employees and officials have been prosecuted during the tenure of Miami-Dade State Attorney Katherine Fernandez Rundle.

The statistic, provided by Rundle's office, is meant to refute the widespread conception that she's soft on corruption. Running for reelection, Rundle wisely has deduced that voters are fed up with bribery and graft.

"Aggressive," is how she describes her prosecutorial record. *Illusory* is another word for it.

Of the 443 prosecutions, 283 ended in convictions. In a third of those cases, adjudication was withheld, leaving the defendants with spotless records.

And who were the defendants? Police officers, jail guards, teachers, garbage collectors and other public employees. These were not unimportant cases, because many involved bribery, fraud or misconduct on the job.

But among the accused were few of the big fish—the politicians who have sold out and given Miami-Dade its reputation as a putrescent pit of corruption.

Rundle prosecuted only 10 elected officials between 1994 and 1999. Most of the cases were penny-ante, netting plead-outs and small fines.

One of those glowingly cited: State Rep. Carlos Valdes, convicted of defacing an apartment hallway with graffiti. (Given that the numbskull's crime was caught on videotape, a pre-law student could have nailed him.)

Rundle's only marquee prosecution was that of Miami Commissioner Humberto Hernandez, convicted in 1998 of covering up voter fraud in the municipal elections. Hernandez was booted from office and sent to jail—undeniably good news for taxpayers.

It would be nice to report that his election shenanigans were uncovered by the state attorney and her intrepid team of investigators, but that's not what happened.

The case was cracked by this newspaper in elaborate, embarrassing detail. Whenever evidence of a blatant crime is presented on a silver platter, a state attorney is left with few options but to press charges. That's not aggressive prosecution; it's reactive.

In Florida, state attorneys must run for office, which makes them politicians. Generally, they don't seem keen on investigating other politicians.

As in many cities where graft is entrenched, virtually every major corruption case in Miami has been tried by federal prosecutors, not the state.

Rundle and others say that's because the Justice Department has more resources, and federal trial rules make prosecutions easier.

That's true, but it is no excuse for local law enforcement to shy away. Florida has tough laws against officeholders taking bribes, fixing bids or stealing votes—and prison time awaits those who get caught.

Rundle's track record is better than that of her predecessor, Janet Reno, but that's not saying much. Reno had no appetite for snooping into the mysterious sudden wealth of certain prominent politicians.

On the other hand, nobody in Reno's office was having explicit phone conversations with a convicted multiple murderer.

Three secretaries employed by Rundle spent hundreds of hours chatting intimately with a jailed hit man who had turned witness against a notoriously vicious smuggler.

As a result, the prosecution dissolved in chaos, and the cocaine case was moved to Orange County, where the infamous Griselda Blanco was allowed to plea-bargain.

Later one of the secretaries sued Rundle's office and won a $235,000 verdict for sexual harrassment by a male prosecutor.

It was one of those only-in-Miami fiascos, and it didn't inspire confidence in the state attorney. The issue wasn't lack of talent—Rundle has many dedicated, talented lawyers—but strength of leadership.

In a community where cynicism is epidemic, Rundle can't skate by on dubious statistics. With corruption, as with any type of crime, the number of prosecutions is meaningless if the crime doesn't abate.

And no one in his or her right mind would contend Miami-Dade politics has been cleaned up, that the crooks have been routed and integrity rules the day. The bums still are in office, and they're still lining their pockets. Citizens deserve a state attorney who considers corruption a full-time priority, not an election-year fad.

"Aggressive" prosecutors don't wait for a scandal to break. They break the scandal before it makes headlines.

19

SCHOOL DAYS

May 14, 1986

SCHOOL BOARD DOESN'T PRACTICE WHAT IT PREACHES

After the Dade School Board's stellar performance last week, you should be grateful that these characters aren't out in the classrooms, teaching your kids—particularly if the subject is ethics.

Led by Robert Renick and Holmes Braddock, the board rejected a strong conflict-of-interest policy proposed by member Janet McAliley. Braddock argued that a new ethics code was unnecessary because board members are immutably wholesome and honest, and their activities are thoroughly covered by state law.

That's funny. Only a few days earlier, board member Kathleen Magrath admitted failing to report a $1,000 cash campaign contribution from Albert San Pedro. Look up the law on that one.

What was so revolutionary about McAliley's proposal? Among other things, it would have:

- Prohibited school board members from taking gifts from lobbyists.
- Prohibited board members from going on travel junkets paid for by companies doing business with the school system.
- Forbidden board members from holding a private interest in those companies.
- Barred members from voting on any matters in which they stood to make outside financial gain.

To ordinary folks, this sounds like a big improvement over the fuzzy state ethics law. After all, the school board controls a mammoth budget of $1 billion—the kind of sum occasionally known to invite favoritism, kickbacks and graft.

To some board members, though, McAliley's proposal was unfair and elitist.

That's what Braddock said. He's got a state Ethics Commission opinion saying it's not a "prohibited" conflict for him to sell insurance to a major school contractor. And when time has come to renew the contractor's arrangement with the school system, Braddock has voted yea.

No conflict, you understand, just coincidence.

Ironically, teachers, principals and other school employees are governed by a stronger ethics policy. They are forbidden from accepting expensive gifts from school vendors, from taking free junkets, and from begging personal discounts from firms doing business with the schools.

Guess who prescribed these tough guidelines: the school board members. And guess who exempted themselves?

McAliley says it doesn't make sense. "I think if it's good enough for the staff, it's good enough for those of us who impose it on the staff."

The high moment in last week's debate came when Renick actually said: "If we want to talk about ethics, if we want to talk about tightening things up, where do we stop?"

Yeah, Bob, better watch out. This darn honesty kick could really get out of hand.

The spark of last week's action was simple. Some board members were mortified by the suggestion that they no longer be allowed to shake down school employees for campaign contributions.

Putting the arm on teachers and principals is a dirty little election year ritual that guarantees incumbent board members a fat war chest. McAliley's proposal wouldn't have stopped school workers from voluntarily contributing to board members' campaigns, but it would have muffled the crass solicitations.

Not long ago Dade school administrators received special invitations in the mail. They included $50 tickets to "testimonial" dinners for Braddock and fellow board member Bill Turner.

Say you were an assistant principal hoping for a promotion—would you attend the fund-raiser, or send the tickets back with regrets?

It's this kind of institutionalized extortion that has to stop, and sooner or later it will.

The board members who killed McAliley's conflict-of-interest proposal are Turner, Braddock and Renick. All three are up for re-election this year, and what a splendid opportunity for the voters of Dade County to teach these guys a lesson in elementary civics.

January 22, 1988

COURT DECISION FORCES STUDENTS TO AVOID ISSUES

The U.S. Supreme Court's stamp of approval on high-school censorship carries an impact far beyond constitutional encroachment.

Writing for the 5–3 majority, Justice Byron White said that a Missouri high-school principal was within his rights to delete from the student paper two full pages of articles about birth control, divorce and teen pregnancy.

"A school need not tolerate student speech that is inconsistent with its 'basic educational mission,'" Justice White wrote—as if social relevance has no place in the classroom.

The case involved Hazelwood East High School, where in 1983 principal Robert E. Reynolds objected to an article about teen pregnancy because he felt it didn't adequately conceal the identity of students interviewed. It was a privacy question—but one the high court scarcely addressed.

Instead, the majority said that because the student newspaper was published as part of a journalism class—true for most high-school papers—Principal Reynolds was simply exercising his power to control the curriculum.

Here the court tied itself in a knot trying to justify its decision. A newspaper produced by students is no more "curriculum" than a banner at a football pep rally.

Still, the court's ruling won't have its most chilling effect on good high-school papers; they are good because of administrators smart enough to allow them to be good. Almost always they have a sharp faculty adviser who acts not as a censor, but more in the role of consultant.

A good example is teacher Brenda Feldman at Coral Gables Senior High; she doesn't tell her students what to print, but she tells them what the fallout might be. "Ultimately, the decision is up to them, but at least it's an informed decision."

Schools such as Gables in Dade County and South Plantation in Broward have award-winning newspapers because they have advisers and principals committed to letting the kids do what journalists do.

That means printing stories about issues that are not only timely but sometimes sensitive. It means student reporters going out and asking hard questions that some administrators won't want to hear, and printing answers they won't want to read.

Where the Supreme Court has done the most damage is in high schools with mediocre papers supervised by weak or frightened administrators.

Thanks to Justice White, nothing will get better here because nothing of substance will ever get printed.

We all suffer for this, in both the short- and long-term. As thorough and skillful as real newspaper folks like to think of themselves, one thing we don't do very well is write about teenagers and their problems—until there's a crisis.

A horrifying example is the recent story about two Dade teens who died playing Russian roulette in the same house, eight days apart. As astounding as it seems to parents, police say this kind of macho gun play was a party pastime among the group.

To sort out this tragedy, we as reporters can go out and try to interview friends of the victims, but I don't think anybody could do a better job than a journalist their own age. And I don't think any story is more important, or of greater interest to students in this community today.

And there is no better place to publish it than in a high school newspaper.

Some principals reading this would never allow an article about teen suicide to get in the way of prom news. It is a shame to think the Supreme Court played into their hands.

The First Amendment issue aside, the Hazelwood decision is troubling for what it suggests about the court's view of public education.

If schools are indeed meant to prepare our kids for the grown-up world, what lesson is imparted by teaching them to avoid the issues, to duck controversy, to close their eyes to what's going on around them? What do we possibly gain by rewarding them for not asking the tough questions?

July 12, 1989

SCHOOL BOARD FLUNKS MATH ON BOND ISSUE

Exactly 16 months ago, the voters of Dade County agreed to spend $980 million to help build 49 new schools and renovate 161 old ones.

When it comes to kids, taxpayers can be generous. Approval of the construction bond issue was hailed as a bright victory for education, an enthusiastic public declaration that children are the top priority.

Today there are no new schools, only new taxes. The voters who dug so deeply into their pockets last year are now being told that it wasn't deep enough. Much of the money spent so far has gone to consultants, who are proven experts in the field of spending other people's money.

No one doubts that the new schools will be built, but the question is when, and for how much. On Monday the school superintendent asked for a tax increase of 21 percent—the latest and largest of disconcerting fiscal surprises.

Just last week we learned that renovations have been delayed at 10 schools, and budget problems are forcing future elementaries to shrink by 10,000 square feet on the drawing board.

We also learned that school administrators were urgently seeking a way to avoid a projected $171 million shortfall in the building fund—big trouble, before the first new school goes up.

The shortage is caused by heavy dipping into the building budget to pay for certain operating expenses of the school system. Though allowed by law, this switcheroo raises questions about how all the money is being managed—or whether *managed* is even the right word. *Juggled* is more like it.

Remember back in March 1988 when the bond issue received strong support from many political leaders, educators and community activists? In the end, most voters recognized the need to upgrade existing schools and build more of them—even at a tax boost of $75 or more per house.

Combined with other tax sources, the sale of school bonds would create a huge $1.5 billion kitty to finance the ambitious building program. But the bulldozers and cement mixers didn't crank up right away. First the School Board wanted to hire professional consultants to help plans go smoothly.

Selecting the firms took time. Big-shot lobbyists were hired. Behind-the-scenes politicking took place. Stakes were high, because consultants generally charge 1 to 2 percent of a total project cost.

Finally, in December, the School Board selected CRSS Constructors and William-Russell and Johnson. The contract was to run through June 1990 at a fee of $11.5 million, including $480,000 for executive travel, supplies and equipment.

This is a whole heap of money, but school officials promised that hiring experts would save them millions more, in the long run.

The first thing noticed by the razor-sharp consultants was how far behind schedule the building program had lagged (due partly to the fact that it had taken so long to pick the consultants). Also, it was announced that more money was needed than what the voters originally had been told (due partly to the fact the building fund was being depleted by consultant fees).

At this point, you're thinking to yourself: Boy, am I in the wrong line of work! How do I get in on this consultant gig?

Only part of the proposed 21 percent tax increase is meant to cover the shortfall in the school building program. Still, parents have to wonder what's going on. Last year's celebration over the bond issue has turned into this year's ulcer.

Voters thought they'd be building new schools for the kids. They didn't know it would take so long to lay the first brick, and they didn't know they'd be paying private consultants to snarf up part of the jackpot. Over the five-year course of the project, the fee could go higher than $35 million.

Maybe the money is well spent. It's hard to argue with the fact that the school system desperately needs help balancing its own checkbook.

Yet it is curious that there's one piece of advice you never hear from these high-priced consulting firms: Stop spending so much money on consultants.

March 21, 1990

DON'T BET ON LOTTERY CASH FOR SCHOOLS

Last month, state Education Commissioner Betty Castor complained about a lottery commercial being aired on television.

The ad featured Lottery Secretary Rebecca Paul walking through a bustling classroom, and speaking in upbeat terms about the tonnage of money raised for schools by lottery sales.

Castor said the commercial left the wrong impression that the education system relies substantially on the lotteries. The implied message was that Floridians should keep playing the numbers if they want their schools to prosper.

After a review, lottery officials decided that the commercial was not misleading, and left it on the air. In a way not intended, they might have performed a public service.

The latest figures show that lottery funds are increasingly being used for education needs that formerly came out of general revenues. To put it another way: Since 1987, the lottery money has ballooned from 2 percent to 12 percent of what the state spends on schools.

Despite assurances to the contrary, the future of Florida's students is becoming more dependent on how many lottery tickets are sold at the corner convenience store. This is a dangerous trend, and one that lottery opponents had warned against four years ago.

The good news is that the lottery is bringing in much more than even its most ardent boosters had predicted; last year ticket sales hit an astonishing $2 billion. By law, 35 percent of the gross is plowed into an "Education Enhancement Trust Fund" that benefits public schools, community colleges and state universities.

As conceived, the lottery money was to be used for improvements and special programs in education. It was specifically not to be used as a substitute for existing budget resources.

In fact, millions of dollars in lottery income have been spent in innovative ways that its organizers had always hoped for—on a new preschool program for underprivileged kids, for instance, and on new computers for the classroom.

But more and more lottery money is being grabbed to pay for basic necessities such as school buses and teacher training. Last fall, the Legislature helped itself to $161 million in lottery dough to prevent cuts in education spending.

You might say, so what? The money's just sitting there, why not use it?

It's risky, for one thing. To budget for education based on projected Lotto sales leaves our school systems vulnerable to the public's gambling habits. If lottery games go into a slump, which has happened in some other states, education could suffer.

This possibility was on the mind of lottery supporters when the measure was passed back in 1986. Sen. Jack Gordon of Miami Beach wanted a guarantee that, no matter what happened with the lottery, the level of spending for education would remain a steady percentage of the state budget.

That hasn't happened. Each year the Legislature is spending a smaller share of the budget on schools, and reaching deeper into the lottery stash. Says Gordon: "There's no law preventing the use of lottery money to substitute for general revenue. So the temptation is always there."

The trend is worrisome to Gordon and many others. The Florida Chamber of Commerce and the teachers' associations have criticized lawmakers for ignoring the intent of the law, and for weakening the integrity of the education budget. A report by the chamber asserted that, without the lottery, Florida would be forced to spend almost $1 billion more annually on schools to keep up with inflation and the increase in students.

So what was once envisioned as a bonus to schools is getting to be a crutch. We probably won't even notice, as long as the lotteries continue to thrive. But if hard times come, and people stop lining up to play, the impact could be serious.

Once we start relying on gambling revenues to buy our children's school buses, the stakes of this game get very high indeed.

November 20, 1994

PRAY LEADERS TURN PREACHING TO REAL ISSUES

Leaders of the new Republican-led Congress are promising swift action on the country's most pressing issues.

And what's more urgent than a constitutional amendment allowing voluntary prayer in public schools? Just about anything.

Try passing a health-care plan, salvaging the welfare mess, reforming campaign laws, or containing the deficit. That's hard work, and it will require time and deep thought.

The school prayer amendment is pure show business, an easy slam dunk for Newt Gingrich, the new House Speaker. He promises it will be at the top of the agenda when the new Congress convenes in January. President Clinton hints that he might support the measure.

Politicians of both parties have an occasional fondness for hollow acts of symbolism. Appearance is what matters. In this case, it's the appearance of endorsing wholesome family values.

Ever since 1962, when the U.S. Supreme Court banned organized prayer in public schools, members of Congress regularly have attempted to overturn the rulings with constitutional amendments. In the meantime, children who wanted to pray had to do so silently on their own time.

There's no evidence that deprivation of an official prayer period causes students to grow up to be serial killers, dope dealers, porn stars or even crooked TV preachers. Yet many politicians (from Jesse Helms to Marion Barry) claim that taking prayer out of schools has contributed to the unraveling of sturdy old-fashioned virtues.

On the other side are civil libertarians who say that school prayer violates the separation of church and state, and is unfair to those whose religious views are in the minority. The point is sound, in the case of organized readings from a specific Scripture.

But it's hard to see how a student would be permanently harmed by a neutral minute of silence before classes begin. These days the trauma starts after the opening bell.

In all the debate, few are addressing the question of what a school prayer amendment would actually do. The answer: not much. It's nice to think that a few moments of quiet worship will help fix the country's serious social ills, but it won't. The most you can say is that it probably couldn't hurt.

I don't care one way or another about an amendment allowing silent prayer, but I do worry about the high cost of getting it adopted. Passage in the

Congress requires a two-thirds vote in both houses. Then it moves to the states, where three-quarters of the legislatures must approve it.

For lawmakers seeking to avoid tough work on complex issues, the school prayer controversy is like paid vacation. It's a swell opportunity for headline-grabbing speeches about the moral rot in America, or the dangerous erosion of the Bill of Rights.

From Washington, D.C., to every statehouse, days and days will be spent grandstanding on the prayer question—precious time that could otherwise be used to tackle substantive laws, laws that might even have an impact on education, jobs and crime.

Students who want to can already pray, privately and whenever they choose. The prayer amendment isn't meant for them, it's meant to win over the parents. That's where the votes are.

It will take several years for politicians to put prayer back in the public schools. By then, even more kids will have good reasons to pray.

Pray they don't get mugged for their lunch money. Pray the crackheads on the corner don't hassle them on the way home. Pray Dad's sobered up, and won't clobber them when they walk in the door.

Pray that somebody in Washington wakes up.

March 29, 1998

COKE DAY LESSON LEAVES A BAD TASTE

If some schools in Miami staged a "Coke Day," the cops would storm in with field lab kits and specially trained dogs.

But at Greenbrier High in Evans, Georgia, "Coke Day" was dedicated to a soft drink, and the whole thing was the administration's idea.

Greenbrier was competing with other schools in a national contest sponsored by the Coca-Cola Bottling Co. The big prize: $10,000. Students were to spend the day being educated by Coke officials about the wonders of Coke.

You've probably heard what happened. Senior Mike Cameron was suspended for wearing a Pepsi shirt to school. Principal Gloria Hamilton said Cameron was punished because the Pepsi apparel showed disrespect for the visiting Coca-Cola team.

What splendid values to be teaching today's kids! Forget individuality. Dismiss from your mischievous young minds any thoughts of freely expressing yourself. And God forbid you should have a sense of humor, or let it show in front of your classmates.

Because it's all about money, boys and girls. For 10 grand you can darn well dress right and button those lips . . . until someone passes you a cold, refreshing Coke.

Cameron was unaware that sporting a Pepsi T-shirt posed a seditious threat. "That's my personality," he told reporters. "I don't like to follow the trend of everyone else."

Well, this'll teach the little whippersnapper—a one-day suspension and a blot on his permanent record. Next time an idiotic trend comes along, young Mr. Cameron will know enough to follow it, and dutifully too.

Because it's all about money, son.

Just as Nike and Reebok have bought their way into collegiate sports, soft-drink firms have become a high-profile presence on public-school campuses. In exchange for exclusive vending rights, Coke and other companies donate money and even underwrite capital projects such as athletic stadiums.

Dr Pepper, for example, has pledged $3.4 million to a Texas school district, while Pepsi is spending $2.1 million on Jefferson County, Colorado, public schools.

Such a problematic trade-off wouldn't come up if local lawmakers adequately funded education. But that doesn't happen in Georgia, Texas, Colorado or anywhere else. The more strapped for cash a school is, the easier it is to say yes to a corporate benefactor.

Nor can one blame the soft-drink companies for aggressively reaching out to the youth market—it sure works for Big Tobacco. Research shows customer loyalty begins at a young age, and the sooner you can reach them, the more loyal they tend to be.

So what's the harm in letting high schools compete for Coke or Pepsi or Dr Pepper dollars? For one thing, carbonated sugar drinks aren't good for kids. But let's accept the theory that a few rotten molars or a few extra pounds of flab are a small price to pay for a new gym or $10,000 worth of textbooks.

That still leaves the values conflict, epitomized by the boneheaded decision to suspend Mike Cameron for his Pepsi prank. The actions of the Greenbrier principal mortified even Coca-Cola honchos, who recognized the fiasco as a public-relations bonanza for the competition. (Pepsi, of course, wasted no time sending the school a $500 check.)

For Cameron and all the students at Greenbrier High, Coke Day turned out to be very educational indeed. It taught them that money is more important than freedom of choice. It taught them that silence is more desirable than dissent, that conformity is better than being different.

And it taught them there's no shame in selling out, if the price is right. Being true to your school is as easy as being true to your school's officially licensed cola.

June 7, 1998

IT'S A VICTORY FOR FREE SPEECH

I never heard of a school being burned down by its graduating class, but that's what William Clarke III must've been worried about.

He's the Northwestern High principal who recently decided his top students wouldn't be allowed to give speeches at the upcoming commencement.

The brusque break in tradition stemmed from last year's event, in which the valedictorian chided administrators for not being supportive enough—hardly a wild-eyed call to anarchy, but enough to rattle Clarke. He slapped a gag on this year's potential rabble-rousers.

One was valedictorian Vivechkanand Chunoo, a science whiz known as "V" to classmates. He has amassed a stratospheric grade-point average of 5.326, basically an A++. Not far behind was salutatorian Jessica Figueroa.

Many educators would be proud of kids like these, happy to let them share their feelings with teachers, classmates and parents. Many would say kids like these have earned, after four hard years, a moment in the spotlight.

What was Principal Clarke afraid of? Publicly he didn't say, but his actions made it plain. Words are what he feared.

One thing about bright kids: Often they know how to use words. Since the first day they toddled into pre-K they've been drilled on the importance of reading and writing. They've also been taught—if teachers are doing a good job—the value of keen inquiry and independent thinking.

And when the best teaching sticks, you don't end up with meek, unquestioning drones. You end up with some very sharp young people who have things to ask and things to say, and who know how to express themselves. They might not always be right, but it's hypocritical not to listen.

These days there's plenty to worry about, even dread, in public schools. Guns, gangs, drugs, nut-case violence. But speech? Clarke seemed to think that's dangerous, too.

But we can't tell a kid to use words instead of fists, and then stuff a sock in his mouth.

The Miami-Dade School Board forbids principals from censoring the text of graduation speeches. Clarke tried to skirt that rule by canceling the speeches altogether.

Before they were even written.

See, Clarke had no idea what Chunoo or Figueroa planned to say at the commencement. They might've sermonized on the nuclear threat from Pakistan, for all Clarke knew.

But free speech is risky—that's one thing you learn in history class. Apparently the principal couldn't risk hearing his administration tweaked, even by the best and brightest students.

It would have been quite a dispiriting send-off for the class of '98: Here's your diploma. Now sit down and shut up.

When Chunoo learned the speeches had been axed, he objected in a polite and thoughtful letter to the School Board. Officials summoned Principal Clarke, and after a meeting Friday he wisely changed his mind.

Chunoo and Figueroa will speak, freely, at Northwestern's graduation June 18. It should be a good day for the students, and for their principal as well.

This month, in thousands of high schools all over the country, valedictorians and salutatorians with boggling academic records and luminous futures will give speeches.

Some will be fiery, some will be dull. Some will be clever, some will be sophomoric. Some will be stirring, some will be trite. But all will be heard because that's the custom, and also because it's the smart thing to do, listening to these folks who'll be running the planet in a few years.

Even if listening means getting our egos bruised occasionally.

June 28, 1998

MIAMI HIGH: THE FRANCHISE

Not everybody loves a winner.

The Florida High School Activities Association could force Miami High to forfeit as many as 84 victories compiled by its boys' baseball, basketball and soccer teams. The FHSAA says the school broke rules regarding the recruitment and transfer of athletes.

Recruiting? Gone are the days when only big-name colleges scoured the hinterlands for potential superstars. Now big-name high schools do it, too.

One reason for Miami High's phenomenal success is that some of its top athletes come from other districts, other counties, even other countries. For example, only three of the 15 players on its state championship basketball team have been verified as living within the school's attendance boundaries.

Picky, picky, picky, reply Stingaree boosters. They blame the FHSAA probe on jealous sniping from rival schools. But in March a *New Times* article exposed how Miami High's sports program systematically imports fresh talent from elsewhere.

Its top basketball player, Udonis Haslem, was from Broward. Any coach there would have been thrilled to have the 6-foot-8 Haslem on the roster, but he wanted to play at powerhouse Miami High.

The problem was, Haslem had to move here to qualify. He says he did, but the FHSAA is skeptical, with reason. Haslem claimed he moved with his father to an efficiency apartment they shared with a man described as an assistant coach of the Miami High basketball team. (Coaches aren't supposed to provide housing to players, but that's another issue.)

When questioned, Haslem couldn't recall the location of the apartment. Another small problem: School records listed his phone number as a Broward exchange. (That didn't stop this newspaper from naming Haslem its Class 6A-5A player of the year for Dade. Next time we'll broaden the category to "Commuter Player of the Year.")

The FHSAA alleges wrongdoing in other Miami High sports. Deputy Commissioner Ron Allen found that an assistant baseball coach had signed up two players from Mexico and helped them with their enrollment papers.

According to Allen, one of the ballplayers didn't qualify as a transfer and was unable to document his previous education. (However, at Miami High he maintained the necessary grade-point average, aided immensely by the A's he received in every class taught by—and here's a coincidence!—baseball coaches.)

The school's highly ranked soccer team is also in trouble because one player was too old to compete. Consequently, the squad could be made to forfeit all 21 victories. The player in question was Jose Amaya, a 20-year-old sophomore. Rules say high-school athletes can't be older than 19 years and nine months.

Miami High administrators have said clerical errors caused some of the problems in the athletic program. This week, the school filed its response to the FHSAA, and the organization is expected to impose sanctions soon.

On campus, the fear is that the Stingarees will be forced to surrender their basketball championship. Indignant alumni are raising money for lawyers to defend the trophy. Lesson: Be true to your school, even when your school isn't too truthful.

It doesn't seem to matter that so many Miami High players are hired guns brought in from other parts. Some fans want a winner, period, and they couldn't care less whether their star players live on Flagler Street or in Finland.

Forget the old-fashioned notion of a school as a neighborhood institution, with neighborhood kids and neighborhood pride. Think of Miami High as much more than that. Think of it as a franchise.

July 8, 1999

LOOK, SEE JACK MAKE THE GRADE

Jack runs fast.

Jack is a star football player at a big Miami high school.

Run, Jack, run!

Jack likes school. The coaches are very nice, and some of the teachers are, too.

Jack's favorite class is Physical Education! His second favorite class is the History of Physical Education. His third favorite class is the Science of Physical Education. His fourth favorite class is wood shop.

All Jack's favorite classes are taught by his coaches. They give Jack mostly A's and B's.

But not all his schoolwork is fun. Sometimes there are books! Books can be hard.

See Jack try to read. Jack reads slowly. Some words are too big.

See Jack try to spell. Jack spells poorly. Jack appears unsure of the relationship between vowels and consonants.

Now see Jack try to punctuate a sentence. On second thought, never mind.

Sometimes there are also numerals in Jack's schoolbooks. This is called math. Math can be hard, too.

Jack's favorite numeral is 6. That's how many points you get for a touchdown. Jack is good at scoring touchdowns, but he is not so good at math.

Jack is pretty sure that 6 times 6 equals 47.

Jack could be taught to read much faster, and to multiply and divide perfectly, but that would take too much time away from football practice.

Run, Jack, run!

Not all of Jack's teachers are as nice as the coaches. Some teachers get disappointed when Jack doesn't come to class for three or four weeks, or turns in blank paper for his homework.

Sometimes the teachers get so upset they give Jack a D or an F on his report card.

This is bad. If Jack gets too many D's and F's, he won't be allowed to play football for the school! Then the team won't win as many games, and the coaches will look like big fat losers.

So, sometimes, when Jack gets a really bad grade, the coaches quietly ask someone in the school office to switch Jack's bad grade to a C or even a B.

Now Jack looks smarter than he really is! Now he can keep playing football!

See Jack run. See Jack score. See the people cheer. Someday Jack wants to play for the Miami Dolphins. Statistically, this is about as likely as Britney Spears calling up Jack out of the blue and inviting him over for a private skinny-dipping party.

Jack is a good high school athlete, but there are many thousands of good high school athletes in America. Very few of them will make it to professional sports.

Jack's coaches don't talk much about that. They just tell Jack to try real hard and do real good on their team. They want to win every game. They want to be state champs!

Not long ago, Florida gave out letter grades to all public elementary, middle and high schools. The grades were based on how well the students scored on academic tests.

Jack's school got a D. This was very bad. (Jack wondered why somebody didn't just sneak into the computer and change the D to a better grade.)

In all, 600 Florida schools got D's for achievement. Seventy-eight others got F's, which is even worse.

If Jack's school falls to an F more than once, the students can ask for special money to switch to a private school instead. This money is called a voucher.

Some of Jack's senior classmates are disappointed because it's too late for them to get vouchers. They had hoped for an actual education in high school.

But Jack isn't disappointed. He likes school. He's learning a lot about P.E. If it were up to Jack, his school would get an A+++, for axcellence!

Go, Jack, go.

February 20, 2000

ENTER HENRY FRAIND—EXIT OPRAH

Here's a multiple-choice problem for the next FCAT achievement test:

Oprah Winfrey wants to feature a local high school as a success story on her top-rated television show. Do you:

(a) eagerly make all the necessary arrangements.
(b) proudly notify the students, parents, staff and faculty.
(c) tell Oprah to take a hike.

If you answered (c), you're qualified to be Miami-Dade's deputy superintendent of schools, the second most powerful administrator. That job is now held by a certifiable chowderhead named Henry Fraind.

You've all seen His Rudeness on television. He is the school district's one and only spokesman, through whom all media queries must go. In another era, he would have made a splendid Minister of Information for the KGB.

One thing about Fraind: He's consistent. He treats everyone with equal disdain. Not long ago, parents at one Miami-Dade school requested that a popular stand-in teacher not be transferred. Fraind publicly told them to butt out. Said they ought to pay more attention to parenting and leave school hiring to the experts.

When you're as important as Henry, it's easy to forget who's paying your salary.

Last month, producers of the *Oprah Winfrey* show asked to include North Dade's William H. Turner Technical Arts High in a program about successful, trend-setting schools. Folks at Turner Technical were thrilled, understandably. Here was an opportunity to show the nation what could be accomplished with new ideas in urban education.

Enter Henry Fraind. Exit Oprah.

He told the producers to go elsewhere. He said the TV crew couldn't tape at Turner Tech because privacy releases hadn't been obtained from parents of the students.

Later, attempting to justify his obstructiveness, Fraind blamed Oprah's staff for submitting its request on short notice. He also said Turner's principal forgot to pass out the permission slips before school was dismissed.

Said haughty Henry: "Rules are rules."

A normal person in Fraind's position—chief of media relations—would have done whatever was necessary to get those kids and teachers on Oprah's show. A normal person would have recognized it as a once-in-a-lifetime chance and personally would have phoned every single parent for approval, if that's what it took.

But Fraind isn't normal. He's arrogant and petty and power-hungry.

By his edict, those who know most about what's happening in the schools aren't supposed to talk to the media. Teachers aren't allowed to give interviews. Same goes for school principals and their staffs.

Henry Fraind speaks for everyone—even the superintendent. Seldom will you see or hear from Roger "The Dodger" Cuevas, except at school-board meetings. In times of crisis, Fraind does all the yakking, and Cuevas wants it that way.

When it was recently revealed that several close relatives of Fraind and Cuevas had gotten jobs with the school system, it was Fraind who came forward to insist that no special treatment had been given to family members.

And when news leaked out that the failing grades of numerous star high-school athletes had been mysteriously changed to passing grades, it was Fraind who announced the launch of an investigation.

Given such embarrassing headlines, you'd think a deputy superintendent might rejoice at some upbeat news about the public schools. You'd think he would have done backflips at the prospect of showcasing Turner Tech to the whole country.

Not Henry. If he doesn't get to be on TV, nobody gets to be on TV.

The Oprah fiasco wasn't the first time he sabotaged positive publicity. He also nixed an HBO special on a 10-year-old student filmmaker, a Court TV documentary and an ABC news story about an inner-city teacher buying her own school supplies.

Now Fraind singlehandedly has managed to demoralize a first-rate high school. Twenty-three teachers and staff members at Turner Tech have written an angry letter to Cuevas, with copies to the School Board.

Fraind will try to tap-dance his way out of trouble, but lately he has been on thin ice. Some board members are grumbling about the need for a new media liaison. The sooner the better, because Henry's a disaster.

Surely, another job can be found for him somewhere in the vast bloated bureaucracy of the school system, a job that won't require contact with parents, principals or the press.

If Fraind is allowed to stay where he is, don't expect any more calls from Oprah. Next time it's more likely to be Mike Wallace.

March 19, 2000

DUMB AND DUMBER

With each new headline, more Miami-Dade parents must be asking themselves: How dumb is our school board?

Plenty dumb, to be sure. But dumbness alone can't explain the odd behavior of certain board members, and the administrators who work for them.

Obviously, other deficiencies plague the nation's fourth-largest school district: incompetence, cronyism and good old-fashioned political fixing. Example: The board's decision last summer to pay $2 million more than one of its own appraisals for a future West Kendall high school site.

On the surface, the deal looks like simple bungling by arithmetically challenged politicians. Wrong. It was a deftly choreographed screwing of taxpayers that brought grins to the speculators who unloaded the property, and to the lobbyist who engineered it.

The School Board wound up paying $116,500 an acre for land that appraisers had valued at $94,333 and $110,000 per acre, respectively.

Worse: Board members weren't even told about a third appraisal that pegged the property's worth at only $75,000 an acre. That's because the district's land acquisition director, Tabitha Fazzino, decided the low appraisal was "garbage."

Later, Fazzino said she couldn't recall making the remark. She said she didn't submit the lowest estimate to the school board because "I was getting married and going on my honeymoon at the time. Honestly, I didn't remember the third appraisal."

Just slipped her mind, huh?

How fortunate for the landholders and their lobbyist, Dusty Melton. Coincidentally, he and Fazzino had lunch during the negotiations. She insists—and this time we're asked to trust her memory—that no lobbying took place.

When it came time to vote on the school-land purchase, board member Solomon Stinson led the charge, followed by Michael Krop, Robert Ingram, G. Holmes Braddock, Betsy Kaplan and Perla Tavares Hantman.

Despite the lower appraisals, Melton's clients were paid $116,500 an acre for 60 acres. The price didn't faze those six School Board members one bit.

If only they were so generous when it came to maintaining the schools after construction.

Last week, fire officials revealed that scores of Miami-Dade schools are plagued by potentially perilous code violations.

Moreover, the problems were made known to school officials some time ago, and little has been done to fix them. A peculiar state law lets fire inspectors screen public schools, but not act on code violations.

One would think that fire safety would be a top priority in any school system—after all, what's more important than a child's life?

Plenty, judging by the nonchalance of Miami-Dade school administrators. They'd rather spend money buying land for new classrooms than repairing the old ones.

Miami Beach Senior High, for example, is so badly deteriorated that parents, faculty and students fear it's a fire hazard. Elected officials in several communities have voiced similar concerns about the schools, and are calling for legislation that would force the school district to bring its buildings up to code.

Inspectors discovered all sorts of dangers, including broken or painted-over alarms and, in at least one school, no alarms at all. It's enough to terrify any parent with kids in the public schools.

On Monday, fire officials confronted the School Board with their findings. Under a glare of media focus, several board members finally managed to manifest concern.

Shame would have been the appropriate response, but none was evident. Superintendent Roger Cuevas, the invisible man himself, agreed to meet with fire authorities to discuss the situation—a virtual guarantee that nothing will get done for years.

In the meantime, there's a better-than-average chance that your child is attending school at a firetrap. Funds that could be used to make the place safe are instead being spent on other pet projects, including extravagant, politically greased land deals.

This goes beyond stupidity, and into criminal neglect. One spark is all it would take. One spark, one fire, one dead child.

The board has no excuse for letting schools crumble. With a $3.7 billion budget, even nine first-graders could find the money for new fire alarms.

Not so, however, for the alleged grown-ups running the school district.

August 20, 2000

SMOKING OUT FIRE HAZARDS IN OUR SCHOOLS

Rough draft of an open letter from Miami-Dade Schools Superintendent Roger Cuevas:

Dear Frantic Parents,

As you are keenly aware, questions have been raised about alleged fire hazards in our public schools, and about the district's somewhat unhurried response.

We feel this situation has been grossly exaggerated by the media. With opening day of classes only one week away, it's time to clear the air—and to put your minds at ease.

Yes, it's true that of 212 Miami-Dade schools inspected by July 20, only 36 met the state fire code. And we'll concede that fire alarms in at least 80 schools either needed repairs, or didn't function at all.

And what mother or father wouldn't be disturbed to hear three experienced fire marshals describe conditions in the schools as "life-threatening"?

But such rhetoric is, if you'll pardon the expression, inflammatory. All along we've said our schools are basically safe, and we'll keep saying it as long as none of them burn down.

In the meantime, your School Board has taken steps to address these issues in a more prudent, responsible way. It wasn't easy finding money for alarms, sprinklers and emergency exits in our lean, no-frills $3.7 billion budget, but I'm pleased to report we were able to scrounge up about $30 million.

Remember, that's $30 million we normally would have blown on inflated real estate, obsolete office buildings or bogus construction overruns. But we decided to bite the bullet this one time, and put the kids first.

Unfortunately, it's too late to finish many of the fire-safety improvements before the school year starts. That's why we recently unveiled our innovative "fire watchers" program. You might have read about it in the papers and thought, "This is a joke, right?"

It's not. We here at the School Board take the threat of fires (and fire-related litigation) very seriously.

Several trained "fire watchers" are being hired to patrol the halls of seven Miami-Dade schools where the alarms don't work. Their mission is to report anything suspicious, such as raging flames, toxic fumes or billowing smoke. Once a blaze is detected, a fire watcher first will notify the fire department, and then begin dashing from classroom to classroom hollering "Fire! Fire!" or "Good God, we're all going to fry!" or something along those lines.

At this point, students will assemble alphabetically in single file and evacuate in a calm, orderly fashion. Some of you have expressed doubts that a few foot sentries can cover a large campus such as that of Carol City High, which has 2,700 students. It's a legitimate concern. Therefore, we're asking each parent to assist our new fire-safety campaign by purchasing a smoke alarm and sending it to school with your child on opening day.

These simple devices can be found at any hardware store for $10 to $20, and they fit easily into most student backpacks. (Don't forget the batteries, please!)

Teachers will collect the smoke alarms after the Pledge of Allegiance on the first day of classes. By the end of the week we hope to have all of them mounted on wall locations throughout your child's school.

The results promise to be dramatic. Carol City High, for instance, would have 2,700 operative fire-detection devices where now it has junk. Code, schmode, I call that progress!

Maybe if all schools were equipped with just one smoke alarm per student, those finicky fire marshals would get off my case for a while.

To all you parents who have written and phoned my office, I want you to know how much your input on fire-safety matters is appreciated. We've already adopted some of your suggestions.

As of today, for example, the ban on students bringing live ammunition, barbecue grills, propane tanks, dynamite, Semtex, gasoline and marine flares has been expanded to include twigs, dry leaf matter and old newspapers.

In addition, we will continue to strongly discourage cigarette smoking, particularly in the elementary-level grades.

Finally, many of you have been inquiring about school uniforms. Unfortunately, the manufacturer has informed us they are not currently available in asbestos or any other fireproof fabric.

If you have more questions, don't hesitate to call. With the help of our intrepid fire watchers, we look forward to a safe, smoke-free school year!

20

HOLIER THAN YOU

May 9, 1986

DEAR DR. CARL, TELL US ABOUT SEX PLEASE...

Students at Barry University picked up their newspaper this week and saw a big white hole where a story was supposed to be. The story was about birth control, and Barry's administrators decided it shouldn't be published at a Catholic school.

So the article was yanked before the newspaper went to press, leaving the aforementioned abyss on the front page.

The university is operating on the interesting premise that birth control information is unnecessary, since sex is the farthest thing from the minds of most healthy college students. Being raised a Catholic, I can appreciate this kind of logic.

Still, you've got to wonder: What happens on the outside chance that one or two Barry students actually need to know something about you-know-what? We certainly don't want them prowling around off campus, asking touchy questions.

So this is for them. If they can't read it in the *Barry Buccaneer,* at least they can read it here. (Incidentally, the editors were nervous about this column, so I took out the item about the trapeze and the vat of warm caramel.)

Dear Dr. Carl, (Note: The author is not a doctor. He just likes the way it looks in front of his name.)
What is the difference between "making love" and "fooling around"?
"Making love" is a term invented in 1962 by a TV soap opera writer who couldn't get the phrase "fooling around" into her script. In the mod-

ern lexicon, people over 25 are considered to be "making love," while anyone younger is just "fooling around."

Dear Dr. Carl,

How reliable are birth control pills?

The prevention rate of the pill is about 99 percent. By contrast, the "rhythm method" of contraception carries roughly the same odds of success as you winning the New Jersey state lottery.

Dear Dr. Carl,

How do most young people first learn about sex?

Unfortunately, national surveys tell us that most teenagers learn about sex by studying the lyrics of the first Ozzy Osbourne album, particularly side one. The next most common source of sexual information is the National Geographic documentary *Intrepid Mud-People of the Rain Forest.*

Dear Dr. Carl,

Is it true what they say about malt liquor?

Yes, I'm afraid so.

Dear Dr. Carl,

What is meant by the phrase "going all the way"?

The term "going all the way" was invented in 1957 by columnist Ann Landers, who had it copyrighted as one of several amusing euphemisms for sexual intercourse.

Dear Dr. Carl,

What's a euphemism? Can I buy one at the drugstore? Do I need parental consent?

No, no. A euphemism is simply a polite expression often substituted for a graphic one.

Dear Dr. Carl,

You mean like "heavy petting"?

Exactly. Except that nobody knows precisely what "heavy petting" means. The prevailing scientific definition is "rolling around with your clothes on."

Dear Dr. Carl,

Is it possible to get pregnant that way?

Oh yes. Being the creative little mammals we are, humans can get pregnant just about anywhere—at home, in the car, at the beach, even while weatherstripping a grain silo. That's why access to sound birth control information is so important.

Dear Dr. Carl,

So exactly what did Barry University censor from its newspaper?

It was a national poll showing that many college students are misinformed about contraception. Can't imagine why.

Dear Dr. Carl,

If sex education is so important, why are adults so uptight about it?

Simple. They're terrified that you might be doing what they were doing when they were your age.

May 16, 1986

CABLE-PORN BILL IS JUST FUZZY IN ITS INTENTIONS

As if to prove they've got too much time on their hands, our fearless leaders in Tallahassee have now tackled the subject of pornography on cable television.

So far they haven't actually managed to define porn, but they assure us that they've got a pretty good handle on what it might be.

Armed with this private moral certitude, the House is mulling a new law that would make it illegal for cable companies to broadcast "indecent" material into your home. (The assumption being that you are somehow strapped into your La-Z-Boy recliner, and unable to get up and change the channel.)

Under this measure, if HBO, MTV or any cable network broadcast a scene deemed naughty by some enterprising state attorney, the local cable firm could be prosecuted and fined up to $2,000.

Someone who buys the Playboy Channel isn't really expecting to see Julie Andrews singing in an Alpine meadow, but forget common sense. The backers of this bill say they only want to protect our kids. As House Speaker James Harold Thompson reportedly proclaimed, "Censorship in the name of good wholesome living isn't so bad."

The proposed law says:

"Matter is indecent when, under contemporary community standards for cable television, it is patently offensive and is a representation or verbal description of (a) ultimate sex acts, normal or perverted, actual or simulated; (b) masturbation; (c) human sexual or excretory organs or functions; (d) a display, description or representation in lurid detail of violent physical torture or dismemberment of a person."

Some of this deft legal terminology deserves scrutiny.

Contemporary community standards. All of you contemporary types probably are wondering: Exactly what are these "community standards"? Are they tacked up somewhere at the local post office? And who made up the list? Can we write to Rockville, Maryland, for a free copy?

Representation in lurid detail of violent physical torture. This would automatically ban all professional wrestling from pay TV.

Human sexual or excretory organs. Excretory organs! Does this mean no noses and armpits?

Ultimate sex acts. Presumably every cable-movie sex act will have to be closely reviewed and classified as either preliminary, penultimate or ultimate. Finding someone to conduct this screening shouldn't be difficult—we all know people who've spent their whole lives searching for the ultimate sex act.

Normal or perverted. You know the old saying: One man's sheep is another man's prom date.

Patently offensive. The word *patently* is derived from the well-known sexual term "patent leather shoes."

The original version of the "clean-cable law" even included a few choice words about the hazards of televised nudity. This section was quietly deleted when it was pointed out that, by dint of a nipple or two, movies such as *Kramer vs. Kramer* could be ruled obscene under this law.

The force behind the cable-porn bill is not some seething, leisure-suited fanatic. Rather, it's moderate Herb Morgan, the Democratic chairman of the Rules Committee and one of the most highly regarded members of the House.

Morgan is a Sunday school teacher and deacon at his Tallahassee church. He's retiring from the legislature after this session, and the cable-porn bill—in which he fervently believes—is a going-away present from his colleagues.

The bad news is, the measure is arbitrary, unenforceable and hopelessly vague. The good news is, it faces powerful opposition in the state Senate, where it will likely die.

Have a happy retirement anyway, Herb. And if you don't want to see sex on television, steer clear of *Dynasty,* tune out *Donahue* and for God's sake don't buy Hugh Hefner's channel.

Please let the rest of us alone. We want our MTV.

June 13, 1986

IRATE PREACHERS ASK LORD FOR A MIGHTY SMITE

. . . and God bless my mom and dad, and my little dog, Biff. And, while You're at it, could You please drop a cinder block on Mr. Justice Brennan?

As you've probably heard, some fundamentalist preachers are so disgusted with their Spiritual Enemies that they have formally appealed to God to forthwith smite them dead.

Explaineth the Rev. Greg Dixon of Indianapolis: "We've been doing this for some time. It just hasn't been made public."

No wonder. The Lord probably takes His smitings quite seriously, and doesn't wish to be swamped by cheap and frivolous requests. A few years ago some zealot publicly prayed for God to "quickly and utterly" put the Heavenly Snuff on Alexander Haig—and look at all the good it did. The guy's practically a regular on *Nightline.*

Even so, God's phone is ringing off the hook. Some Texans have assembled in solemn prayer to ask Him to please extinguish the state attorney general, while a Baptist congregation in Los Angeles has nominated U.S. Supreme Court Justice William J. Brennan Jr. to be fatally smote. (The Brennan request is explained thusly: The judge believes a woman has a right to have an abortion, therefore he is a murderer, therefore he must be murdered.)

Who knows what God or His secretary does with such strident prayers, but I suspect that His threshold of wrath is considerably higher than that of the average preacher. A full-bore intergalactic smiting is a serious thing, and it's doubtful that God would waste one on someone as lowly the Texas state attorney general.

But what exactly is a Heavenly Smote? Good question. I'm not sure I've ever seen one, but these are the smitings most frequently cited, in descending order of degree:

- Getting struck by a lightning bolt. This certainly looks like an act of God, though history seems to contradict. Hardly any infamous blasphemers, scoundrels, killers, tyrants or sleazeballs have been smote dead by lightning. In fact, the only celebrity I know to get hit by lightning was Lee Trevino, a golfer who not only survived, but got a swell job afterwards as a network sports commentator.
- Being swallowed into the core of the earth without a trace. This doesn't happen very often, except to drug informants, punk-rock stars and people

with messy IRS problems. Most likely God has nothing to do with these disappearances.

- Having a ball-peen hammer dropped on your head from the 37th floor of a downtown construction site. This is a tough one to call. When is such an episode a true Heavenly Smite, and when is it just plain rotten luck?
- Having a flaming meteorite crash through the roof of your townhouse. OK, OK, this isn't just rotten luck. Your number is definitely up.
- Getting crushed to death by Rosemary Clooney in a crowded movie theater. It's hard to believe that even a vengeful Lord would pick such a fate for a sinner.
- Eating a plate of bad clams. No question about it, this is the ultimate message from God.

As the pray-for-death movement gains steam, some observers have questioned if death is necessarily the punishment God prefers.

For instance, wouldn't it be possible to pray for a half-smite? You know—where the Target Heathen isn't actually killed, just humiliated or badly inconvenienced. Arrange for him to step on some chewing gum, for example, or have all his clean laundry stolen out of the dryer. That's the kind of smiting some of us could go for.

Yet a few fundamentalists insist that the Bible gives God free rein to do all the killing He wants, and we should feel free to solicit Him, if only as a last resort. This is big news to millions of churchgoers who've been wasting their breath praying for prosperity, good health, peace and world harmony.

Heck, I think of the hours spent as a kid saying those monotonous rosaries—Hail Mary, over and over and over—when all the time I could have been praying for Nikita Khrushchev to get hit by a truck.

July 21, 1986

THANK HEAVEN 7-ELEVEN'S LIBRARY IS SAFE FOR ALL

What a pleasure to report that it's safe again for all God-fearing citizens to venture into 7-Eleven for their boysenberry Slurpees.

The parent company of 7-Eleven, Southland Corp. of Dallas, has responded to the Meese Commission by hastily removing from its stores the twin evil influences of *Playboy* and *Penthouse* magazines.

This is a relief for all us parents who harbored a dread that our sons might someday, in a frenzy, vault the counter to sneak a peek at Miss July. Now Mr. Jere W. Thompson, president of Southland, has banished such publications because of "a possible connection between adult magazines and crime, violence and child abuse."

I was so relieved by Mr. Thompson's display of civic concern that I dropped by two of his convenience stores last week to sample some of the approved newspapers and magazines. Guess what—scarcely a breast, bosom or buttock to be found! Well done, Thompson, you old smut-buster.

Thanks to your vigilance, the shelves of 7-Eleven are once more a rich trove of wholesome family reading. Take a look:

- "Glamour Boys of Carnage!"—A psychological ode to sex killers Ted Bundy and Christopher Wilder, featured in the August issue of *Front Page Detective*. On page 26, you'll also see a police photograph of a nude murdered man in a bathtub full of blood—but don't worry, Mom and Dad, there's not a naked female breast in the whole magazine.
- "White Slavers Kidnap U.S. Girls in Europe"—Valuable travel tips from the July 15 issue of the *Sun* tabloid, including an account of "perverted intrigue" and an actual photograph of a "raped and drugged" female tourist.
- "Have Fun with Guns!"—From *The Basic Guide to Guns and Shooting*, an impassioned firearms instructor reveals: "The modern repeating handgun . . . is the answer to social predation."
  Brings a lump to your throat, doesn't it?
- "Maniac Made the Brunette Die 3 Times!"—From the July issue of *Inside Detective*, a quaint torture tale to share around the family hearth. Don't miss the tasteful photo on page 32: a young stabbing victim strung up to a tree.
- "Q & A with Sgt. Slaughter"—From the September issue of *The Wrestler* magazine, an interview with one of wrestling's leading intellectuals ("I love a knock-down, drag-out brawl as much as the next man!"), plus a photograph of our hero gouging an opponent's bloody face with a two-pronged ice pick.
  And who says there are no role models for kids today!
- "Lovely Mexican Girls—"A recurrent ad in the staples of 7-Eleven's magazine rack: "Hundreds of attractive young Mexican girls offer friendship, love and marriage to men of all ages. Personal service!" What a nice idea, sort of like the Campfire Girls, I guess.
- "Crimson Footprints Beside the Battered Nude!"—Whoa, parents, don't be scared off by the caption. This issue of *Inside Detective* contains no offensive photos of nudes, just one measly decomposed corpse on page 32.

- "Mom & Boyfriend Kill Baby by Pouring Pepper Down Its Throat"—More unusual home recipes, courtesy of the *Sun.*
- "The Gay Hustlers Thought Murder Was a Laughing Matter!"—A little something to amuse the kids on that long bus ride to summer camp. This tale is bannered in the August issue of *True Detective.* As a bonus for science buffs, the same issue shows a dead body crawling with—how shall we put this—fly larvae.
- "Fitness Recipes for Better Breasts"—Wait a second, how did this rubbish slip by? From the July issue of *New Woman* magazine, an illustrated article about special exercises for you-know-what. Oh geez, what's that—a picture of a topless woman! Aaaggh! And bare buttocks on both pages 38 and 39!

Get Dallas on the phone, pronto. Thompson! Quick, send the Magazine Purification Squad—yeah, there's still trouble in the 7-Elevens. I know, I know. Today a nipple, tomorrow a sex massacre.

Read all about it.

March 25, 1987

GOD FINALLY SPEAKS TO ORAL ROBERTS

God was reading the newspaper the other day when he came across an item that really aggravated Him.

He called the Heavenly Operator and asked him to dial a number in Tulsa. The phone rang several times before a familiar, sonorous voice answered: "Oral Roberts speaking."

"We've got to talk," God said.

"Who is this?" Oral Roberts demanded.

"You know who this is. This is God."

"Get outta here," Oral Roberts said. "Who is this, really?"

"It's Me," God said. "I'm not kidding."

"Prove it."

God sighed and hurled down a couple of major lightning bolts.

"OK, OK," Oral Roberts said, tremulously. "Take it easy."

"Who told you to go fast in a belfry?" God asked.

"You did," Oral Roberts replied. "And it's not a belfry, it's an imperial prayer tower."

"Whatever it is, get down from there," God said. "You're making a dern fool out of yourself. While we're on the subject, who gave you permission to go around begging money in My name?"

"You did."

"I did not," God said.

"Then it was someone who sounded just like You," Oral Roberts said. "Maybe Rich Little."

"Never mind," God said. "It says here in the paper I was supposed to kill you off if you didn't raise $8 million by March 31."

"That's what You told me," Oral Roberts insisted. "You said You would call me home."

"No, no, I said I would call you at home. That's because I can't ever get through on that stupid 800 number for the ministry."

"I guess I misunderstood," Oral Roberts said, sheepishly.

God said, "Brother Roberts, let me clue you in. If I got vengeful—I mean, seriously ticked off—I wouldn't just 'call you home.' I might have a flaming meteor drop on your head, or a blinding monsoon wreck your condo, or maybe arrange for you to get hit by a bus. This is known as serious smiting."

There was a pause on the Tulsa end. "You'd do that?" Oral Roberts asked.

"Remember that awful movie with John Denver and George Burns?"

"*Blasphemy!*" Oral Roberts boomed.

"Forget blasphemy, it was the dumbest script I ever saw. For that I smote L.A. with an earthquake."

"Geez," said Oral Roberts.

"We all get in moods," God said. "The point is, you've got no business saying that stuff about Me on TV. You're hurting My credibility. Like the time you claimed you saw a 900-foot Jesus."

"But I did!"

"Right. And I suppose the Virgin Mary looked like Fay Wray." God drummed His fingers, and the heavens over Oklahoma thundered. "Brother Roberts, what about this guy in Florida who gave you the $1.3 million?"

"A miracle, Lord! The bank says he's good for it."

"Excellent," said God. "So you'll just endorse the check and send it on up to Me."

"Pardon?"

"You heard me, Brother Roberts. I know some folks who could really use the dough, needy types. You might have heard of them—the poor."

"Hold on now, God. What're you bugging me for? Did you catch Falwell on *Nightline* this week—that was a $600 suit! Or why don't you call up Jim and Tammy—they're really loaded. Have you checked out their place in Palm Springs? We're talking seven figures, Lord."

"Brother Roberts, shall we discuss your Learjet?"

"Come on, you expect me to fly coach? Satan flies coach."

Sternly, God said, "Oral, I want that check on My desk by the close of business hours, tomorrow."

"Or what? I suppose You'll really call me home."

"Better than that," God said. "I'll send a 900-foot bill collector named Meathook. Think about it, Brother Roberts . . . and don't call me, I'll call you."

February 22, 1988

AND LO, THEY SWAGGERED TO ALL-TELL MOTEL

Today's sermon, from the Book of Ramada, Chapter 2, Verse 1: "Jimmy Swaggart Gets a Motel Room."

And yea, as the sun went down, he felt a deep need to lay prone. And along the way he met a harlot, and she said unto him: "There's a place up the road by the pancake house. Whaddya say?"

And though weariness lay heavy upon his eyes, a strong urge took hold of his better judgment, and he checked his wallet.

And the woman mocked him, saying, "I haven't got all night, pal."

And as he put his wallet away, he thought of many things, none of them pure. And he said unto the pushy harlot: "This place you speak of, woman, does it take Diner's Club?"

And, lo, they traveled together to this place, which in its time was known as a motel. And together they entered the vestibule, which in its time was known as a lobby.

And there he met a man who made him question his very faith; a simple and plain-spoken man, who in his time was known as a desk clerk.

And the desk clerk said unto to him: "Nice hair, Elvis."

And in anger he replied to the desk clerk: "Speak to me as a Christian, boy!"

And the desk clerk said, "Hey, I seen you on TV, right?"

And, being a man of supreme vanity, he replied unto the desk clerk: "I am on cable every Sunday morning. Eight million viewers."

And the desk clerk rejoiced, saying: "I can't believe it, Jim Bakker in my motel!"

And in anger he smote the desk clerk repeatedly, and in a thunderous voice proclaimed that nay, he was not the nefarious Jim Bakker. And the desk clerk was full of sorrow, saying, "I always get you guys mixed up."

And the harlot spoke up in a shrill voice, saying unto the chastened clerk: "How about a room, buddy? While we're still young."

And the desk clerk said: "How many nights, Mr. Swaggart?"

And at that instant the devil took hold of his tongue and he said to the desk clerk: "You mean I gotta pay for the whole night?"

And the desk clerk meekly said unto him: "We don't rent by the hour, Reverend. State law."

And so he agreed to take the room, and the desk clerk handed unto him a slip of paper, which was in its time known as a registration card. And this he completed with a fountain pen.

And when the desk clerk read what he had written on the registration card, his eyes filled with amusement. And the clerk said unto him: "That's some daughter you got there, Mr. Swaggart."

And the harlot rolled her eyes and made a remark of profound crudeness. And he said in a low voice unto the desk clerk, "She is a good girl, but she has lost her way."

And the clerk replied, "Whatever you say, Mr. Swaggart."

And it came to pass that the woman herself became restless, tapping a scarlet fingernail on the face of her wristwatch and saying unto him, "The meter's running, Slick."

And so he implored the desk clerk to move with haste, and secure for them a room for the night; and he decreed that this room should have a king-sized bed, and also a Magic Fingers machine that might soothe his troubled flesh.

And the desk clerk gave unto him a roll of quarters for this machine, and also some extra towels with light starch. For this he was thankful, and he pressed unto the desk clerk's hand a piece of money, which in its time was known as a tip.

And further he beseeched the desk clerk not to remark upon his visit to anyone, especially rival TV evangelists who might use it against him before the next Arbitrons were out.

But, lo, even as he spoke, a man hidden from view was taking his photograph. And though the quality of the photograph was poor, it was plain to all that the woman was definitely not his daughter.

And when this became known, the heavens trembled, his enemies rejoiced, and a great voice spoke sternly unto him late one night.

And the voice admonished him for succumbing to the sinful ways of Satan, and yet it pressed him for more details. And in its time this voice was known as Ted Koppel.

March 4, 1988

WHEN IT'S ROBERTSON, YOU HAVE TO HAVE FAITH

The polls say that TV evangelist Pat Robertson is not expected to do well in Florida on Super Tuesday.

This is a shame. We've never had a faith healer in the White House before, and President Robertson would be very exciting to watch.

Back in 1981, he was a smash at the Full Gospel Business Men's Fellowship in Philadelphia. There is a videotape of this performance that gives you an idea of what an entertaining president Robertson could be.

Right off, he tried to heal a man with a fractured skull, but the man couldn't be located in the crowd (probably too shy), so the Rev. Robertson closed his eyes and went on:

"God's healing people all over this place," he intoned. "A hernia has been healed. If you're wearing a truss, you can take it off. It's gone!" He really said this. A detailed account was published in the *Washington Post.*

From hernias the Rev. Robertson moved along to tougher prey.

"Several people are being healed of hemorrhoids and varicose veins," he proclaimed. "Thank you, Lord."

Then he tackled somebody's ulcer. After that, tooth decay and gum disease. Even a sinner with crooked toes.

"The Lord is straightening out these toes on somebody right now," he declared to the multitudes.

What a great show! If this guy were elected president, we could look forward to the most exciting inaugural in the history of the republic—the chief executive, healing people from the steps of the Capitol! As an act of charity, he could start with the Democrats.

When he was the star of the 700 Club, the Rev. Robertson offered personal prayers for certain viewers who phoned in with arthritis, bladder problems, even cancer. Those who got good results were mentioned prominently by the preacher on his TV show.

I can't imagine why Robertson hasn't tried this system on the campaign trail, as it seems like a sure way to get votes, not to mention donations.

Admittedly, some people are disturbed by the prospect of this fellow getting anywhere near the Oval Office. They just don't understand. The Rev. Robertson has a special "insight."

For instance, he said he predicted that Iran would fall a few years ago because "the prophet Ezekiel knew it."

In 1979, the Rev. Robertson announced that the U.S. government had been taken over by the Trilateral Commission and the Council on Foreign Relations. Ask yourself: Has anyone actually proved him wrong?

In 1980, the Rev. Robertson declared that the anti-Christ was among us, a man "approximately twenty-seven years of age who is now being groomed to be the Satanic Messiah." I firmly believe this, and I also believe that today this man is a car salesman, somewhere in North Miami.

In 1981, the Rev. Robertson announced that the Bible specifically says that God will destroy the Soviet Union with earthquakes and volcanoes. Now, I can't find this anywhere in the Bible, but then I've got a very old edition.

Likewise, I also believe the Rev. Robertson when he says that he personally prayed a hurricane away from Virginia. This is a useful talent for a president—we would never have to worry about any World Series games getting rained out.

And I also believe the Rev. Robertson when he says his Christian Broadcasting Network knew where the hostages in Lebanon were being held and didn't tell the White House. Just like I believe him when he says George Bush secretly orchestrated the exposure of his preacher pal, Jimmy Swaggart, as a sexual basket case.

And, most of all, I believe the Rev. Robertson's warning that the Soviets have intermediate missiles in Cuba—missiles that about two dozen different U.S. spy satellites haven't been able to see.

I believe this so fervently that I won't have time to vote for the Rev. Robertson myself on Tuesday, as I will be frantically digging my new bomb shelter in the backyard and afterward trying on trusses.

April 20, 1990

WATCHDOGS HELP PROMOTE 2 LIVE CREW

A bunch of Florida television stations sent crews to Gainesville the other night. They hoisted their satellite dishes outside a nightclub in anticipation that the rap group 2 Live Crew would be arrested while performing on stage.

An Alachua County prosecutor had threatened to do just that if the Crew sang the dirty versions of its songs. No doubt the entire citizenry of Florida would have slept better, knowing that a bunch of musicians had been tracked down and captured in the act.

The most interesting part of the TV coverage was the long line of young people who had shown up with $12.50 to see 2 Live Crew in person. Many had never heard of the group until Gov. Bob Martinez launched his obscenity campaign against the album *As Nasty As They Wanna Be*. Some of the fans had come to the concert as a protest; others just wanted to see what all the fuss was about.

Thanks to the governor, 2 Live Crew is packing them in wherever it plays. Thanks to the governor, the album has reached more young people than the promoters had ever dreamed possible. The band is now a household name, and a rallying point for civil libertarians.

Nothing like being the target of a moral crusade to sell a few million records. As more grand juries across the state find the Crew's lyrics obscene, more kids clamor for the music.

It backfires like this every time, yet Martinez and other self-appointed guardians of morality never seem to learn. Either they're not very bright, or they're getting a cut of the album royalties.

Years ago, Terry Southern and Mason Hoffenberg wrote a novel called *Candy*. The book caused an uproar because of its raunchy sexual content; some newspapers refused to advertise the book, and it was banned from stores in Tampa and other cities.

Immediately it became the secret mission of every red-blooded American male teenager to obtain a copy of *Candy* and sneak it to high school, where its compelling narrative passages (including, I recall, a brief romance on a pool table) could be shared with all who would listen.

The more controversy *Candy* generated, the more copies were sold. This is an equation as old as censorship itself. Tell people they can't have something, and they'll crawl naked over broken glass to get it. The quality of the work is secondary to the principle of free will.

A few years back, Marlon Brando made a tedious movie called *Last Tango in Paris,* which was denounced as pornography on the basis of a single scene that involved a man, a woman and a stick of butter (or possibly margarine).

As a result of all the protests, millions who would not have otherwise bothered with this film went to stand in line. Soon it became the hip thing to see. It became . . . art!

This is what's happening with 2 Live Crew.

As one not easily shocked, I'll admit to being completely grossed out by some of the words to Crew rap songs. Whether they are obscene or not isn't for me to say. Certainly everyone lining up at that Gainesville nightclub knew exactly what they were paying to see.

Richard Pryor is hilarious in concert; he's also profane. So is Eddie Murphy. So is Andrew Dice Clay. So is Sam Kinison. Without the F word, these guys don't have an act. But arresting them would make no sense at all, except to their press agents.

What's got the governor so upset about 2 Live Crew is the way that the group sings about sex. Without getting specific, let's just say true love is not a recurring theme. Then again, what do you suppose the Beatles were talking about when they wrote "Why Don't We Do It in the Road?"

And if you've heard Jimmy Buffett in concert, you know that one of his all-time great sing-along numbers is "Why Don't We Get Drunk and Screw?" This is not an ode to carpentry.

Yet during every show, thousands of fans (sometimes with their kids) happily belt out the bawdy lyrics. No one gets corrupted by it. No one gets arrested for it. The moral fiber of the free world remains intact.

February 11, 1991

STATE SMART TO JETTISON *PLAYBOY* CASE

Prosecutors in Broward saved themselves a huge embarrassment by dropping obscenity charges against the Miramar grandmother who sold a *Playboy* magazine to two teenagers.

A trial only would have meant more headaches for the Broward state attorney's office, which is still smarting after the 2 Live Crew acquittals. The *Playboy* case was an even larger turkey, but this time the sheriff isn't to blame. This time it's the Miramar police.

Elaine Ott, 52, was working as a cashier at a Mr. Grocer on the night of February 1. She was new to the job. Unknown to her, a couple of Miramar plainclothes officers, Jill Schroeder and Mario Bonis, were hanging around the store on a robbery stakeout.

Soon, however, the eagle-eyed cops witnessed what they believed was another serious crime: As $3.95 cash changed hands, Mrs. Ott handed the March issue of *Playboy* to two 16-year-old boys from Carol City.

The officers perked up. Apparently they'd received a tip that *Playboy* sometimes contains pictures of bare breasts, including nipples. Sure enough, the March issue displays numerous naked body parts of women in Cuba, a famous swimsuit model, and the very grown-up daughter of an FBI language specialist!

State law prohibits the sale of material "harmful to minors." The Miramar officers decided that *Playboy* fit the bill. Undoubtedly they meant well—perhaps fearing that impressionable 11th-graders might, upon viewing Havana's nubile splendors, rush to North Perry Airport and hijack a plane.

Mrs. Ott might not have realized that her customers were only 16 (since one of them stood 5-foot-11), but the cops moved swiftly. She was busted, photographed, fingerprinted, strip-searched, jailed and charged with a third-degree felony.

When prosecutors heard about the arrest, they surely groaned in despair: not again. Not after the 2 Live Crew debacle. Compared to Luther Campbell's lubricious lyrics, *Playboy* is an oracle of Puritan restraint; the March issue even has a column about the recklessness of promiscuity.

No jury this side of the Bible Belt would've convicted Elaine Ott of anything. Big-time defense lawyers already were volunteering their services, while the magazine was enjoying a public-relations bonanza.

It took prosecutors exactly one day to dump the case. They must've asked themselves (as did thousands of other bewildered taxpayers), didn't these cops have anything better to do?

True, Miramar is a sleepy suburb compared to other Broward cities. According to the Florida Department of Law Enforcement, only tiny Sea Ranch Lakes has a lower per-capita crime rate.

But folks in Miramar do occasionally get robbed. As a matter of fact, it happened to Mrs. Ott's husband on the night after she was arrested. Richard Ott was behind the counter of the same convenience store when a man walked in, pulled a gun and swiped $40.

This time, the police stakeout team wasn't there to witness the crime. The robber got away.

After Mrs. Ott's arrest, Miramar Police Chief Ben Galante said about the only thing he could say: "My officers have followed the state statutes and took action."

The word *action* is a slight embellishment of what happened at the Mr. Grocer, and *Playboy* in no way fits the statutory definition of obscenity. But Galante can be forgiven for overstating the case. It was not a good week.

If he sincerely wants to protect the youth of America from the evils of convenience stores, his officers' time would be better spent busting clerks for peddling junk food, beer and cigarettes—all demonstrably more "harmful to minors" than *Playboy*. Nobody ever got lung cancer from ogling nipples.

Even though the crime beat in Miramar is sometimes slow, Chief Galante would be wise to leave the sex stuff to the big boys. One Nick Navarro on the streets is plenty.

March 3, 1996

HYPOCRISY DID IN MEMBER OF "GOD SQUAD"

Don't look now, but there's one less Christian soldier on the "God Squad."

That's what a group of religiously conservative state lawmakers humbly call themselves. No longer shining among their moral beacons is one Marvin Couch, a Republican representative from Oveido.

On February 22, he was arrested in the parking lot of an Orange County shopping center. Sharing the front seat of his truck was a young woman who was not, by any stretch of the imagination, humming a Bible hymn.

Couch was charged with soliciting prostitution, committing lascivious acts and exposing himself in public. He admirably has admitted to the deed, remorsefully confessed to others, and on Friday announced his resignation from the Legislature.

Said Couch: "I have sinned against my God, my wife, my children and the citizens I represent."

Ironically, the citizens whom Couch represents would probably have been the first to forgive him—if it weren't for the "God Squad" nonsense.

The public can show compassion for an honest person with weaknesses, but it has no tolerance for a self-righteous phony who preaches family values by day and trolls for hookers by night. The sex isn't nearly as offensive as the hypocrisy.

Couch has been a steady yeoman for the "religious" right, which remains preoccupied with butting into other people's bedrooms. Last fall, he was one of 15 lawmakers who signed a huffy letter chastising the Walt Disney Co. for making health insurance available to partners of homosexual employees.

The legislators hinted at consumer retaliation if the company didn't rescind the policy, which they said mocked "the sanctity of marriage." Disney refused to buckle, recognizing the letter as a flimsy stunt contrived to please extreme fundamentalists.

You saw the same posturing last week in South Carolina, where the GOP presidential hopefuls groveled disgracefully for the anti-gay, anti-choice, pro-prayer vote. To firmly hold these beliefs is one thing, but to embrace them purely for political opportunism is another.

Couch was hardly one to lecture on the sanctity of marriage. I don't really care if he liked to play find-the-periscope with prostitutes, but I do care that he passed himself off to voters as a paradigm of Christian rectitude.

God Squad? Try the Hugh Grant Fan Club.

What happened to Couch happens with poetic frequency to holier-than-thou crusaders. Those who rail loudest against the imagined sins of others seem to harbor the dirtiest secrets.

Televangelist Jim Bakker turned out to be a world-class embezzler as well as a fornicator. The lachrymose Jimmy Swaggart blamed "demons" after California cops stopped him with a streetwalker and a stack of skin magazines.

Closer to home was born-again Doug Danziger, who as vice mayor of Fort Lauderdale campaigned to rid the city of nude dance clubs and adult book stores, asserting they fostered prostitution.

Danziger, it turned out, was intimately knowledgeable on the subject. One of his sweaty trysts with call girl Kathy Willets was immortalized on videotape, leading to his hasty resignation.

All these guys have moved on with their lives, and Marvin Couch will, too. Since the charges against him are misdemeanors, he likely won't do any jail time.

The humiliation might be punishment enough. Vice agents spared few details in their report of the incident. Even the prostitute arrested with Couch had a beef: She complained that he offered her $30 for sex—but had only $23 in his wallet.

That's when she should've figured out he was a politician.

March 6, 1997

LESS MARRIAGE, LESS DIVORCE: START PRAYING

The new leadership of the state House of Representatives wants to reinstate prayer in schools, restrict abortions, outlaw same-sex marriages and make it harder for opposite-sex couples to get divorced.

Sure, go ahead and laugh. You and your snarky heathen friends.

But it's a glorious new day in Tallahassee, and the new Speaker of the House, Republican Dan Webster, is a darling of the fire-breathing Florida Christian Coalition.

And, by God, those folks intend to legislate some serious morality around here.

Forget school overcrowding, crime, growth management and campaign reform. Florida's got bigger problems, such as gay couples wanting to get married.

True, they aren't exactly stampeding the courthouse, but we all know how these dangerous fads get started. First, one guy on your block marries another guy. Then some woman on the corner marries another woman. Soon everybody wants to try it and, before you can say "Roy Cohn," the whole darn state's gone fruity!

This cannot be tolerated. If legislators do nothing else noteworthy this year (and it wouldn't be the first time), the session can be a triumph as long as they act to fortify the institution of heterosexual marriage.

To that end, another proposed reform is the toughening of Florida's no-fault divorce laws.

What a cunning strategy: Discourage couples from splitting up by making the experience even more grueling and heart-wrenching than it already is. One sure deterrent is to put some "fault" back into divorce.

The Christian Coalition–backed proposal is opposed by degenerate sinners (mostly Democrats), who believe that ending a marriage ought not to be always time-consuming, bankrupting and acrimonious.

But does the Bible not state: "A man and woman who desire to break their union shall do so only with mighty difficulty; they shall both be commanded to go forth and hire attorneys and private investigators, and to put forth lengthy depositions and tedious financial affidavits. Such a journey to dissolution shall be long and humiliating and absurdly expensive, and rife with such recrimination that all parties hence shall raise their eyes to the Heavens and implore, 'O, what hast Thou wrought, with yet another subpoena?'"

All right, maybe the Bible doesn't phrase it exactly in those words, but it's all right there, between the lines.

Since divorce apparently is one of the dire menaces facing Florida, it's up to our lawmakers—moral beacons, every one—to step in. Why shouldn't husbands and wives who no longer can stand the sight of each other be forced to stay together in seething, spiteful misery?

The important thing is to preserve the institution, at all costs. Let's bring that divorce rate down, even if it causes the homicide rate to shoot up.

And forget all those worrywart "experts" who claim that unhappy marriages create a terrible environment for kids. There probably are deep spiritual lessons to be learned from watching two parents holler, spit, curse and hurl small household appliances at one another.

As long as they're opposite sexes, of course.

And not only should loveless couples remain married, they should have more children, too—even if they don't want them and can't take care of them.

Sure, youngsters from turbulent homes are bound to have tough times, but Rep. Webster and the Christian Coalition aren't unsympathetic. Why do you think they're so keen to put prayers back in public schools?

That way, kids can take a moment before morning assembly to pray that Mom and Dad won't slit each other's throats over dinner.

In Tallahassee, you see, the family comes first.

June 19, 1997

OLD-FASHIONED DISCRIMINATION BACK IN VOGUE

On behalf of God-fearing heterosexuals everywhere, I'd like to thank the Metro-Dade Commission for snuffing out another dangerous gay-rights ordinance.

It was a close call, too. This week's vote was 7–5.

It might have been even closer, if several hundred members of the local Christian Coalition hadn't shown up to pray, sing hymns and wave their Bibles.

Some of the protesters actually began speaking in tongues, which made them only slightly less articulate than the commissioners themselves.

Then again, the commissioners didn't need to say much on the issue of gay rights. That's because they took the sly and unusual step of killing the ordinance on first reading.

That meant there'd be no public discussion, which saved everybody the inconvenience of having to listen to both sides.

What a breath of fresh air, in this age of tedious "political correctness." Finally we've got some politicians who aren't afraid to offend the sensibilities of thousands of tax-paying citizens; politicians who aren't afraid to stand up for a little intolerance.

If passed, the ordinance would have outlawed discrimination based on a person's sexual orientation. That would have meant you couldn't lawfully refuse to sell a house or rent an apartment to someone solely because they were a homosexual.

Nor could you invoke that reason to deny them a credit card, or a bank loan—or even a job. Can you imagine such a world, where a person's private lifestyle can't be used against them?

Thankfully, Dade County is blessed with at least seven public servants who believe in old-fashioned values, who remember a time when *discrimination* wasn't such a naughty word.

Most inspiring about the vote was the way black and Hispanic commissioners put aside their differences and joined together in a common goal of keeping gays in their place.

It was a veritable rainbow coalition of prejudice—Miriam Alonso, James Burke, Miguel Diaz de la Portilla, Natacha Millan, Dennis Moss, Pedro Reboredo and Javier Souto. And, in the audience: throngs of cheering Christians.

For many, the uplifting scene brought back memories of 1977, when a similar gay-rights law was overturned here in a hotly debated referendum. Then, opponents were led by born-again songbird Anita Bryant.

Twenty years later, Anita's gone but the tune remains the same. Commissioners who killed the ordinance said they did so because they were morally opposed to homosexuality.

James Burke expressed "spiritual concerns." Pedro Reboredo said the law would have sent "the wrong message." Javier Souto offered up a resolution in praise of "traditional family values."

Only Commissioner Bruce Kaplan, who sponsored the gay-rights ordinance, branded the defeat an act of "cowardice." Ha! I think it took courage.

Courage, in a place like South Florida that depends so heavily on tourism, to rise up and declare to millions of potential visitors: We don't like your kind.

Just because commissioners did it without the customary debate or public hearing doesn't mean they were gutless or ashamed. They were just in a big hurry to do the right thing.

It would've been so much easier to cave in to crybaby economic concerns and pass the law. Oh noooo, we can't afford to offend the gays and lesbians. They spend a fortune down here!

What hypocrisy. No, our commissioners took the honest road. They chose to make a statement and damn the consequences.

Heck, money isn't everything. Surely there'll be other tourists to fill the hotel rooms left empty by the ones we're running off; also, builders and investors and business tycoons.

You know, the good kind. Heterosexuals.

March 1, 1998

IT'S NEVER YOUR FAULT IF THE DEVIL MADE YOU DO IT

Another prominent preacher is in trouble, and you know what that means: Satan strikes again.

The Rev. Henry Lyons, president of the National Baptist Convention USA, has been indicted in St. Petersburg on charges of racketeering and grand theft.

He has admitted making "serious errors in judgment" and caving in to "human weaknesses and frailties." He said the devil led him astray.

The same devil who lined up that hooker for the Rev. Jimmy Swaggart, I'll bet. The same devil who coaxed the Rev. Jim Bakker to embezzle all those millions.

Why, it's the gospel according to Flip Wilson and Dana Carvey! Watch out for that sneaky Satan.

Rev. Lyons stands accused of trying to swindle $330,000 from various companies and groups. Among his alleged targets was the Anti-Defamation League, which had donated nearly $250,000 to help rebuild black churches that had been burned down by arsonists. Most of the money never got there.

Meanwhile, Lyons was keeping secret bank accounts, buying fancy cars, jewelry and a time-share in Nevada. There's the $700,000 house he sometimes shared with a female former employee, who also happened to be a convicted embezzler.

When Lyons' wife found out about the fancy love nest, she tried to torch the place. That's when the preacher's secret life came to light.

Turns out the devil was all over this fellow's case. For example, he somehow talked Lyons into lying about the size of his organization—and not a little lie, but a whopper.

Lyons liked to brag that the National Baptist Convention USA had 8.5 million members—about 7.5 million more than it really had, according to the *St. Petersburg Times.*

The result was to mislead business partners, churchgoers and others. Lyons and pals would sell membership lists to companies while pocketing most of the fees as a "commission."

Darn that Satan. He even persuaded the preacher to become an unregistered lobbyist for the military regime of Nigeria, best known for its political assassinations, corruption and human-rights abuses.

But Lyons put in a good word with U.S. congressmen, and was rewarded by the Nigerians with $350,000. In these matters the IRS and other authorities have taken a keen interest.

The revelations brought this from a remorseful-sounding Lyons: "God has placed on my heart the burden of transforming my errors and misfortunes into a personal testimony that Satan knows no bounds, that he can reach up to the highest levels—even the church—and lay temptation at your footstep."

Footstep, doorstep, you get the picture. It's definitely not a speech you'll hear from most accused racketeers. Mafia guys, for instance, would never stoop to blaming the devil for their legal problems. They don't rat on anybody.

The truth is, your average thief wouldn't dream of trying the "Satan defense," for fear of being laughed out of the courthouse. Indicted preachers, however, have no such qualms.

So far, the Baptists are standing behind Lyons. It remains to be seen whether a jury buys the theory of Satan as an unindicted co-conspirator, but the preacher isn't taking any chances. To share the pulpit he has hired F. Lee Bailey.

Praise the Lord, and pass the alibis.

September 3, 1998

OWN WORDS BITE BITING POLITICIANS

Dubious history was made last spring when an influential member of Congress openly referred to the President of the United States as a "scumbag."

The name-caller was Rep. Dan Burton, the Indiana Republican who chairs the House Government Reform and Oversight Committee. Burton, who portrays himself as morally upright, offered his coarse description of Bill Clinton in a newspaper interview.

In this country, anyone is free to call the commander-in-chief a scumbag (or other unsavory receptacle) without fear of reprisal. But politicians who hurl such insults run a serious risk, as the overly pious Mr. Burton is finding out.

This week he's been dashing around Washington, warning people that he's not perfect, either. He says a snoopy journalist from *Vanity Fair* is doing an article that delves unflatteringly into his personal life.

Burton even volunteered the fact that his long marriage has undergone "rocky" periods, which is almost exactly what so-called scumbag Bill Clinton said in 1992 after Gennifer Flowers surfaced.

The *Vanity Fair* article won't be published for a while, which makes Burton's pre-emptive attack all the more awkward. Defending one's self against racy allegations that haven't yet been printed is a sure way to ignite—not squelch—public curiosity.

Burton himself raised the subject of his marital problems, then refused to get specific. "It's nobody's business," he declared.

Which is almost the same line used the other night by our so-called scumbag president, when confessing to White House intimacies with Monica Lewinsky.

It's debatable whether America deserves to know—or even gives a hoot—

which elected officeholders cheat on their wives. It does become important, though, if it reveals one of Clinton's most rabid critics as a hypocrite and a phony.

What's happening to Burton is the nightmare of every partisan hatchet man. He's in danger of getting sliced and diced with his own self-righteous Veg-O-Matic.

Notice how the smart ones have been relatively reserved in their comments on the Lewinsky affair. Neither House Speaker Newt Gingrich nor Senate Majority Leader Trent Lott has been foolish enough to do the fire-and-brimstone act, or to call Clinton names.

It's not because they're more dignified or respectful than Burton. They're just smarter. They know what's out there: lots of other potential Monicas and Gennifers who've been cozy with prominent—and prominently married—politicians.

All it takes is one woman to tune in the nightly news and see her ex-lover sanctimoniously bashing Clinton's lack of integrity. All it takes is one of them to get ticked off, pick up a phone and call a reporter.

Notice also how many of the President's critics are careful to say the issue in the Lewinsky case is the lying, not the sex. Most Americans agree, according to polls.

The sex issue makes lots of folks edgy, but nowhere is the discomfort more acute than Capitol Hill, former stalking ground of Bob Packwood, Gary Hart and others.

It's unlikely that Dan Burton's name will be added to Washington's priapic pantheon. But his defensive statements this week—offered without context or detail—suggest that the upcoming *Vanity Fair* story won't be a profile of perfect rectitude.

And whose would? But Burton asked for this trouble by fervidly using his congressional pulpit to assault Clinton's morality. When you do that, you'd better be morally bulletproof yourself.

Plenty of Americans might agree with Burton's crude knock of the president, but they don't need to hear it from a congressman with tawdry secrets of his own. That's the pot calling the kettle scum.

21

HIT THE ROAD

November 18, 1987

HERE'S A ROUTE WORTH 4 STARS FOR METROMOVER

In a burst of wild optimism, the County Commission recently voted to spend $240 million of public funds to extend the Metromover tracks south to Brickell Avenue and north to the Omni shopping mall.

Don't pinch yourself, it's no dream.

Already dozens of excited commuters are surging toward their respective Metrorail stations in anticipation of the moment when they can ride the train all the way from the Dadeland Thom McAn to the Omni Thom McAn!!! And then afterward maybe eat lunch at that little place that serves microwave lasagna!!!

Yes, these are giddy times, but let's not get carried away.

For those of you who don't know about the Metromover, it's that cute little empty car that goes around and around on a rail through downtown Miami. Metromover hooks up to the Metrorail, which is a shiny elevated train that serves as the vital link between the Hialeah racetrack and Vizcaya.

Metrorail is currently operating at about 160,000 daily riders below projections, while the transit system loses about $87 million annually. Last year county commissioners promised not to make Metrorail any bigger until they found a way to pay for it.

In the meantime, the U.S. Urban Mass Transportation Administration reported that extending the Metromover would add fewer than 2,000 riders a day and cost taxpayers $15.20 per passenger. The report (disputed by the county) basically concluded that it would be cheaper for Uncle Sam to give everyone cab fare to get around downtown.

As the debate dragged on, the county's Dogpatch excuse for a bus system was getting worse. UMTA said putting more buses on the road should be a priority over Metromover—since buses serve more people, and needier ones.

The county promptly decided to raise bus fares from 75 cents to $1 to help pay for the Metrorail deficit. In addition, social programs for the underprivileged were cut back.

When it came to Metromover, the commission was brave enough to ignore not only its own promise of fiscal responsibility, but the U.S. transit report as well. The system will be extended, even if there's no way to pay for it, even if it means that bus service will get worse.

Only three commissioners—Barbara Carey, Barry Schreiber and Jim Redford—made the argument that it's dumb to keep stuffing a $1 billion turkey.

Still, the visionaries prevailed. The downtown boys showed up with buttons and bows, and cheered the Metromover vote. Anything to bring a few warm bodies into the lobby of Venetia.

The publicized reason for adding the new Metromover legs is to draw more riders. But some experts remain skeptical that the general public will stampede the turnstiles just for a bird's-eye view of the Sears Tower.

Maybe they're right. If Metromover is ever to become a smash success, it's got to run some place where everybody wants to go.

Some place like Joe's Stone Crab.

Now we're talking crowds. Build the Metromover on pilings along Government Cut, straight out to South Beach. Have it stop right at Joe's doorstep—hop off the train, give your name to the maître d' and get in line. This is a route that nobody could fault, except maybe the parking valets.

Sure, it would be expensive, but money obviously is no object where mass transit is concerned. And sure, a Joe's Metromover would benefit the affluent instead of the poor, the elderly and the blue-collar work force—but you can say the same for the other Metromover plan.

The added advantages of a Joe's Express Route are obvious:

a) It would triple the Metromover ridership overnight.
b) It would bring thousands more tourists to and from Miami Beach.
c) It would make the world of fresh shellfish accessible to many who would never otherwise get a chance to experience it.

An extravagance? You bet. Unaffordable? So what. We're talking stone crabs, folks. You want a world-class community, or not?

July 20, 1988

ALL ABOARD! LET DADE TAKE YOU FOR A RIDE

To save money, Dade County Manager Joaquin Avino wants to cut back on Metrorail service. This is like putting a dead person on a low-cal diet.

Avino suggests reducing the number of cars per train and scheduling rush-hour departures every 7½ minutes instead of six. He also wants to discontinue late-night train service unless it's paid for by sponsors of special downtown events, such as concerts and basketball games.

As long as we're plucking a billion-dollar turkey, let's go all the way. Why not run just one train with one car, one time every day? Cancel stops at all underused Metrorail stations: Just have the engineer slow down to, say, 15 miles an hour, then open the doors briefly in case anybody wants to dive aboard.

This is not so far-fetched. It's hard to cut service when there's not much service to cut.

The other night I got inspired to take the train to the Robert Plant concert at the new Miami Arena . . .

To avoid arena traffic, I park as far away as possible, the Dadeland South station. I see two trains, and ask which one is leaving next. Obediently I board with other concert-goers. We wait. We wait some more. I check my watch. Since Cheap Trick is the opening act, I'm not exactly heartsick about being a little late.

Then a voice on the intercom instructs all of us to get off this train immediately and board the other one. We do. The train pulls out.

All goes well. The arena is great, Robert Plant is terrific.

Midway through the show I realize that I'm not sure how late the Metrorail will be running—there are conflicting reports—and I get this distressing mental image of hitchhiking back to Kendall.

So I cleverly slip out before the encore and head for the train. At the Metrorail turnstiles I encounter uniformed cops stuffing cash into Hefty bags. Even in Dade County, this seems unusual.

Affording them the benefit of the doubt, I hand the cops a buck and they let me on the platform. Many minutes pass, but the train doesn't move. Other passengers start to grumble. More time passes.

Then the truth becomes obvious: This isn't the last Metrorail train, it's the only bloody train!

So we steam for 25 minutes, missing Plant's encore (which, naturally, includes a Zeppelin medley). On the Metrorail there's idle talk of hijacking a northbound train and getting a bunch of really big guys to pick it up and turn it around on the tracks. This plan is not consummated.

Eventually the concert ends, the train fills up and we head south.

But the fun isn't over. Back at the Dadeland station's parking garage, the elevators have been automatically shut down by computer. The result: No Metrorail passengers can get up to their cars without ropes and pitons.

Eventually I locate a sympathetic security guard who reprograms an elevator to take me to the fifth (and only the fifth) level of the garage. God knows what happened to the other riders; they might still be trapped.

When I finally get to the parking attendant, she announces with a perfectly straight face: "Five dollars."

"It's supposed to be a dollar," I point out.

"You need a receipt from one of the machines," she says.

Apparently the Metrorail parking-receipt machines (don't even ask) take only a dollar in coins, which I didn't have. I explain this to the parking lady, and swear that I really am an actual train rider. When I try to tell her about the Plant concert, she stares at me, dazed and confused.

"Let me get this straight," I say. "First you turn off the elevators so I can't get my car out of the garage. Now you want to charge me five bucks?"

"Without a receipt," she says stoically.

"And you wonder why no one rides this damn thing."

From her expression, though, it was clear she didn't wonder why. She knew. On the bright side, at least she wasn't stuffing the money in a garbage bag.

March 20, 1989

DOT'S WAY: TEAR IT UP, THEN WAIT

Advice to South Florida drivers: Buy stock in Bob's Barricades.

The DOT is D.O.A.

Somehow the state road department is nearly broke. Many highway improvement projects have been stalled, as have $20 million worth of badly needed tollbooth renovations from the Golden Glades to Lantana.

Much of the tortuous obstacle course that commuters face each day is now cemented in place until autumn, possibly longer.

How did this mess happen? Where was the eagle eye of Gov. Bob "Give-Me-a-Whack-at-That-Budget" Martinez? Not on the Department of Transportation, obviously.

We are led to believe that the road crisis caught the governor by surprise. Only seven months ago, his transportation people were unveiling grand plans to rebuild the Golden Glades interchange. Then, one day, somebody glanced at the DOT ledger and happened to notice a cash shortfall of $700 million.

The official explanation was a beauty: In its haste to complete these projects in record time, the road department spent more money than it had in the bank. Recent audits have revealed the DOT as a sinkhole of mismanagement where everybody wrote checks but nobody bothered to balance the checkbook.

Incompetence is always a prime suspect in Tallahassee follies, but $700 million worth of incompetence is hard to imagine. Somebody up there is either incredibly stupid, or incredibly crooked.

One way to find the truth is with a statewide grand jury. Certainly the waste-hating Martinez would support such an important investigation and would instruct his DOT appointees to cooperate fully.

In the meantime, exasperation rules the highways.

It's bad enough that the state recently jacked up turnpike tolls, but the agency also laid off 115 part-time tolltakers and reduced the hours for the rest. This has caused crazier-than-usual traffic jams at the busiest urban toll plazas.

Not only do we get to drive on torn-up, detoured, dangerously congested highways, we also get to sit in long, hot lines to wait for the privilege—and then pay more tolls than anyone else in the state.

Here's the best part: DOT's finances are so hopelessly mangled that some legislators say there's only one recourse: Raise the gasoline tax by a nickel or dime a gallon.

Martinez has gallantly vowed to veto any such measure. However, he has yet to announce his scheme for rescuing the DOT from its own blundering.

Typical of the state's shrewd judgment was the decision to take over the anemic Sawgrass Expressway, which is losing about $15 million a year. The Sawgrass now draws an estimated 30,000 drivers daily; just to break even, ridership would have to triple overnight.

The highway is such an asphalt tundra that an estimated 80 percent of motorists don't even bother to put coins in the unattended toll baskets. Still, the developers and land speculators for whom the Sawgrass was built are now so desperate for traffic that they want to lower the tolls.

Broward officials were delighted to dump this turkey on the DOT, but now the dodge has come full circle. Several key Broward road improvements—actual intersections, with real cars and everything—have been cut from the construction schedule under the state's emergency austerity plan.

The reason: the cost of bailing out the Sawgrass. Turnpike travelers all over the state will be glad to know that part of their higher tolls are subsidizing a greedy 23-mile mistake in West Broward.

In a magnificent twist of logic, transportation officials predict a positive result from the upcoming highway quagmire: It will encourage more drivers to use mass transit.

Maybe this was the DOT's secret plan all along—boost support for car pools and buses by creating the worst imaginable nightmare for the solo commuter.

Rip up at least one section of each major highway in South Florida, raise the tolls, then fire the tolltakers—all during the heart of the tourist season!

Somebody should have thought of this a long time ago.

November 20, 1989

HEY, NEAT IDEA: TIE UP ROADS, SCARE FOLKS OUT

Gridlock for everybody!

Bob Martinez strikes again, only this time he's right.

Gridlock is just what Floridians need to dramatize what's happening to this state. Nothing like two hours in oozing traffic on a potholed, truck-choked highway to demonstrate the results of mad growth and lousy planning.

People need a frightening jolt of reality to see the disaster ahead, and the governor has come through with flying colors.

His threatened veto of a new gas tax killed a $650 million-a-year highway plan that was proposed last week in the Legislature. The money would have been used to repave old roads, to build new ones and to subsidize mass transit.

Think about the scenario if lawmakers had gotten their way. Just suppose (and you'll have to use your imagination) that the Department of Transportation was actually able to complete a few decent roads before the end of the century—roads that weren't already obsolete by the time they were finished.

A zany fantasy? Perhaps. Under Martinez, the DOT has bungled its finances so badly that it had to jack up the tolls while laying off toll-takers. Highway construction projects are taking so long that teams of skilled archaeologists couldn't locate the original blueprints.

Yet just imagine—as the Legislature dared to do—a Florida ribboned with spacious, safe, smoothly paved highways. This is the worst thing that could ever happen.

Such breezy thoroughfares would only attract more industry, more tourists, more land speculators, more people migrating permanently to Florida. In other words, more growth—the one thing we don't need.

Before long, the new highways would be just as congested and crumbling and dangerous as the old ones. Commuters would be just as short-tempered and miserable; the only difference is, there'd be millions more of them.

Meanwhile, some new governor would be fighting over gas taxes with some new bunch of legislators.

Luckily, today we have a governor who is shrewd enough to see the future for what it is, a governor who is not afraid to shift the gears of this great state firmly into neutral.

I admit that I've underestimated his cunning. I fell for all that macho blather about his being a pro-growth, pro-development, pave-to-the-grave kind of guy. Now it appears that this was all a clever, politically expedient charade.

The Bob Martinez who said no to the gas tax is one radical dude. He wants people out of this state, and he wants them out now.

What better way to thin the ranks than to impose the specter of total gridlock! Is there a more wretched place on the planet than the Palmetto Expressway at 5 in the afternoon? Or the Golden Glades in the morning? Dante himself would despair at the vision.

Here in South Florida, we commuters have adjusted to such coagulated travel by disconnecting our horns and arming ourselves with the latest in semiautomatics. This will be a new and exciting experience for residents of fast-growing Orlando and Jacksonville and Tampa.

The brilliance of the Martinez strategy was its smoke screen. He said he opposed hiking the gas tax because he's against new taxes, period—a Republican mantra that has served the party well.

In this case, though, the true result is a concrete defeat for traditional GOP power groups—developers and bankers. By state law, communities can ban new construction if adequate roads aren't completed first. Without a gas tax, you won't see many new roads. Without the roads, you won't see many new high-density condo villages.

Don't think our wily governor didn't realize this. Slowly his secret plan for a sane and less populous Florida is taking shape: To make this place livable again, it must first be seen as unlivable. What with the high crime, vanishing coasts and dwindling water supplies, we're well on the way.

Maintaining the highway crisis is crucial to the plan. People will quit moving to Florida only when it becomes dreadfully clear that, once they get here, they can't move at all.

August 22, 1990

TRUST—DON'T COUNT ON IT FROM TURNPIKE DRIVERS

When the turnpike scrapped the fare-card system in exchange for coin drops, the goal was to make commuting in South Florida a smoother, more carefree experience.

Perhaps this works in other parts of the civilized world, but here it's different. Here hundreds of motorists remain stymied by the concept of placing a quarter in a toll taker's hand; paralyzed behind the steering wheel, they refuse to budge from the lane as they await . . . who knows? Perhaps a divine signal to accelerate.

Unfortunately, the long-term plan for modernizing the turnpike relies on three crucial premises:

- People know how to count.
- People know which direction they're traveling.
- People are honest enough to pay.

None of these suppositions should be taken for granted in South Florida.

Some of our immigrants are still learning the difference between dimes, nickels and quarters. So are many locals. It's the same with directions. The terms *north* and *south* remain distant abstractions to many of us. (As a shining example of native intelligence, in Monday's column I mistakenly located the Holiday Isles resort on Plantation Key instead of Windley Key, where it most definitely is.) But the major obstacle to the jillion-dollar turnpike project is its dependence on the inherent honesty of motorists—a faith epitomized by a device known as a coin basket. The driver drops his money in the basket, a light turns green and away he goes. Theoretically.

The current plan calls for installing coin baskets at all plazas in three years (which, in DOT years, is approximately the length of the Bronze Age). You're asking, why will this take so long? How complicated can a basket really be?

The delay is the result of a protracted bidding dispute over the $37 million contract. Until the toll baskets are in place, human beings will staff all the lanes.

My contention is that human beings will always be needed to staff the toll lanes because unmanned baskets don't work. On the more remote legs of Broward's Sawgrass Expressway, running the tollbooths is so popular that anyone naive enough to stop deserves a receipt that says: "SUCKER!" On parts of the busier Turnpike Extension, the basket lanes are blocked late at night because so many drivers were zooming through without depositing any coins.

At blame is a seed of old-fashioned dishonesty, but also frustration. The baskets are currently designed in such a clever way that the coins frequently get stuck in various secret crevices. Rather than waiting for a toll guard with a Roto-Rooter, lots of drivers just say to hell with it and stomp on the gas.

Turnpike spokeswoman Susan Daniels says the new baskets will be "high tech," and will spin the coins in such a way that they shouldn't clog. It sounds like a great way to get your fingernails yanked out, but maybe it'll work.

Unfortunately, no technology has been invented that solves the problem of scofflaws—or, in the jargon of the DOT, "lack of compliance."

A few gentle souls still believe that, if they run a toll basket, a massive steel barricade will automatically pop out of the pavement and stop their car. Most drivers know better. Unless a cop happens to be watching, toll cheaters get away.

This is why we'll always need humans at the toll plazas. Drivers are less likely to cheat when somebody's watching, even if that somebody can't do a darn thing to stop them.

There's one other chronic problem with coin baskets, something I hesitate to mention. It's the problem of pranksters depositing extraneous items in lieu of coins. In South Florida these goodies could be anything from bubble gum to hand grenades to human body parts. I don't care how fast the coin basket is spinning, this sort of stuff will clog it up.

Maybe in the next three years they'll invent a toll collection machine that really works down here—one with a giant mechanical arm that reaches out, seizes the driver by the throat and says: "Pay it, Bozo!"

October 6, 1996

REASONS TO WIDEN U.S. 1 ARE A STRETCH

How'd you like Florida's Turnpike to empty out on your street?

That's the neighborhood disaster awaiting the Upper Keys if the state moves ahead with its plan to four-lane the 18-Mile Stretch between Florida City and Key Largo.

Essentially it will be an extension of the turnpike extension, delivering at high speed thousands more vehicles into what is already one of the most log-jammed, accident-plagued parts of Monroe County.

Folks who live there are livid, with good reason. All aspects of their lives will be affected by the southbound deluge, because everything fronts U.S. 1: the schools their children attend, the stores where they shop, their churches.

At a recent hearing, angry residents displayed a petition with 6,001 names against the Stretch project. Even the Key Largo and Islamorada Chambers of Commerce have come out against it.

But the Department of Transportation remains gung-ho, and the permits are controlled by the South Florida Water Management District, which has never met a backhoe or a bulldozer it didn't like.

Proponents of the road widening say it's long overdue. The project is necessary to make the trip to the Keys safer, they say, and to expedite hurricane evacuation.

Those of us who drive the Stretch frequently don't need to be convinced it's a perilous, nerve-racking experience. But adding more cars seems a bizarre solution, and one some experts believe will backfire.

Today, some of the bloodiest wrecks on the Stretch occur on the four-lane segments. More significantly, a substantial increase in traffic volume into the Upper Keys means more congestion—and more accidents—down the road.

The hurricane argument for widening the Stretch is even more suspect. Keys residents evacuate more quickly and efficiently than anyone in Florida, and they've now got two safe routes out: U.S. 1 and County Road 905 across Card Sound.

It's possible to make the 18-Mile Stretch safer without turning it into an autobahn, but the Chiles administration isn't interested.

The latest "compromise" is a proposed three-lane mutation, two going north and one going south—with an extra southbound lane prepared but not paved. Just for practice, I guess.

Nobody's been fooled. The DOT wants four lanes, period.

Interestingly, support comes mainly from those who don't live near Key Largo or drive the Stretch as often as commuters who do. It's easy to cheer for offloading the turnpike on U.S. 1 when it's not your third-grader crossing the road every morning.

The driving forces behind the Stretch expansion are politically connected developers, road contractors and pro-growth forces, including some of the same greedheads involved in the Port Bougainville fiasco years ago, on North Key Largo.

To understand one reason why people are worried, look at Florida City. Peddling itself as the gateway to the Keys, the place is deliberately morphing into a mega–rest stop, a charmless gauntlet of mini-marts, fast-food franchises and gas stations.

Key Largo is no stranger to tacky self-exploitation—if it weren't for John

Pennekamp State Park, many tourists would keep driving—but business leaders there finally have wised up to the fact that more isn't necessarily better.

What's always made the Keys so special, and so alluring to visitors, was how different it was from Miami, Fort Lauderdale and the rest of urban Florida.

That won't be so true if the Stretch is four-laned. No matter how fast you can drive, everything you're trying to escape will be waiting when you get there.

February 28, 1999

TERRIBLE TOLL ON COMMUTERS

Tolls will soon double from 25 to 50 cents on four major Miami-Dade expressways, and many disgruntled commuters are wondering: What are they doing with my money?

One thing they're doing with your money is using it to collect more money. The toll increase will finance new and better tollbooths.

It's a teeth-grinding irony of commuting, because there's no worse cause of gridlock, accidents and general mayhem than an urban toll plaza. In the short term, nothing would do more to relieve congestion and improve highway safety than bulldozing every last one of them.

But siphoning money from motorists is such a lucrative component of urban transportation systems that the placement and design of tollbooths get as much engineering attention as the highway itself.

With the toll hike approved last week, the Miami-Dade Expressway Authority hopes to raise $20 million to finance bonds for road widening, express lanes, a truck tunnel to the Port of Miami-Dade—and, of course, tollbooths.

For instance, a fancy new plaza is in the works for State Road 836. Currently 10 ordinary-looking toll lanes greet eastbound motorists heading toward downtown Miami. These facilities will be replaced by a modernistic overhang, with a special pass-through lane for drivers holding annual passes.

It sounds very sensible and efficient. In fact, everything the Miami-Dade Expressway Authority (and the Turnpike Authority and all the other road-building authorities) promise to do always sounds sensible and efficient.

But things often don't turn out that way. Take those high-tech electronic "smart signs" that display up-to-the-minute traffic alerts. They were supposed to have been installed eons ago on Interstate 95. Fortunes have been wasted, and still the goofy things don't work.

Similarly advanced technology is planned for the toll roads. If they manage to get the "smart" signs functioning in our lifetime, the first news flash to drivers should be: "HEY, CHUMPS, LOOK WHAT YOU PAID FOR!"

Another slick idea was automatic coin baskets. Remember how these simple machines were supposed to save jillions by replacing human toll collectors?

Not quite. At most toll stops, drivers with exact change get a two-for-one treat: Every coin basket comes with its own human being, whose job is to clear the loose change out of the contraption whenever it jams, or to pick up the quarters tossed on the ground by myopic motorists.

(Here's how to save some serious dough: Rip out the stupid coin baskets and put all those people back inside tollbooths, where at least they can sit down.)

No one would dispute that it's expensive to build and maintain good highways. Most commuters don't mind paying, as long as they see positive results.

Until 1984, both 836 and State Road 112 (the Airport Expressway) had westbound toll plazas. They were, like their eastbound counterparts, nightmares of coagulated chaos, especially during afternoon rush.

Then somebody decided to raise the eastbound fare from 10 to 25 cents and rip down the westbound plazas altogether. Revenues soared. Traffic hummed. Commuters cheered.

Expressway Authority members say they'll consider removing all tollbooths if the Miami-Dade Commission dedicates a source of revenue for mass transportation. That might require boosting taxes, so don't hold your breath.

Meanwhile, plans call for new, speedier "premium lanes" for drivers who can afford a higher toll. Soon you can be mired on the Dolphin at 9 A.M., while Lexuses, Beemers and Cadillacs go flying by in their own exclusive lane.

Talk about road rage.

June 24, 1999

A "TRAIN TO NOWHERE"

"By the year 2000, people will be saying, 'By gosh, how did we live without it?'"

That was Metro commissioner Bev Phillips back in 1985, speaking in defense of Metrorail. It is now nearly 2000 and people are saying:

"By gosh, were we insane?"

Metrorail was, and remains, one of America's most infamous mass-transit failures. Now, in a hastily scheduled late-July election, Miami-Dade voters will be asked again to invest prodigiously in the "train to nowhere."

Metrorail is the chief beneficiary of Mayor Alex Penelas's proposed one-penny sales tax hike. The plan is to expand the current 21-mile rail system by adding new lines to South Beach, the airport, the seaport and the Broward line.

To do all that, the county needs to raise billions or lose out in matching U.S. funds. (State, federal, local—it hardly matters. Every dime is from taxpayers.)

Three times Miami-Dade voters have rebuffed a transportation tax. This year Penelas has sweetened the package by vowing to remove tollbooths from four busy expressways, which should draw weary commuters to his cause.

Penelas also asked—and the commission agreed—to hold the vote July 29, a Thursday. The mayor insists he's only trying to meet an August deadline to apply for federal money, but the practical effect of staging an off-day midsummer election is to minimize voter turnout.

The fewer voters who show up, Penelas knows, the better the chance of a tax hike passing.

Until a few months ago, he opposed raising the sales tax from 6.5 to 7.5 cents on the dollar. Now he says it's the only way to get Miami-Dade moving again.

Experts agree that the solution to easing gridlock isn't more highways, which are obsolete and overcrowded by the time they're finished. Experts also agree that something must be done urgently to get a dedicated source of funding for a long-range transit plan.

A one-cent tax hike isn't unreasonable if the money is intelligently spent. The question is why the county wants to invest 10 to 15 times more in Metrorail (a proven flop) than in the bus system (which large numbers of people actually use).

It would be grand if commuters had fallen in love with the train, but for many reasons they didn't. Built with a projected daily ridership of 200,000, it's now lucky to sell 50,000 tickets a day—a number that's been essentially flat since 1994.

Ridership not only hasn't grown, it hasn't even kept pace with the population. Any way you cut it, 25,000 daily round-trips in a county of 2 million is pathetic.

Meanwhile, nearly a third of Miami-Dade's 600-odd buses have racked up more than 500,000 miles. They belong in a junkyard or maybe a museum, but not on the road.

Penelas wants to spend $170 million to double the bus fleet over time. How about tripling or quadrupling it instead? The benefits to many neighborhoods would be instant and demonstrable—already five times more people use buses than ride the train.

Building each new rail line is predicted to take five or 10 years. The cost? Anybody's guess.

To paraphrase Ronald Reagan, it would be cheaper to buy everyone on the train their own bus.

But be certain that lots of well-connected folks—-property owners, engineers, contractors—stand to make big bucks from such a drawn-out public-works extravaganza. Metrorail II will be a gravy train, just like Metrorail I.

And once done, it'll continue to gush red ink.

So while it might be nice not to hassle with tolls on the Dolphin Expressway, remember: The half-dollar you're saving, and plenty more, will be snatched by other fingers from your pocket.

That, and politics, is all that keeps Metrorail rolling.

October 29, 2000

VOTERS SHOULD DERAIL THIS BOONDOGGLE

The biggest I.Q. test for Florida voters this year is the proposed bullet-train amendment to the state constitution.

This knuckleheaded scheme would require construction of a high-speed rail connecting Florida's five largest metropolitan areas. Sillier yet, the amendment commands that the train itself must go at least 120 mph.

Significantly, the ballot language says nothing about how much this gobbler would cost, exactly where it would go or who'd pay for it. The answer to the latter can be found by looking in the mirror.

This is more than just another wacko idea. If Amendment One passes, it means Florida's constitution will codify an unlimited expenditure of taxpayer funds on a project with no blueprints, no budget and no precedent.

Historically, such wild boondoggles have been initiated in the Legislature, where there's at least the pretense of accountability.

Backers of the bullet train initially tried that tactic and, in fact, wheedled the state out of millions, ostensibly for feasibility studies and surveys. Backed by the ever-ambitious Department of Transportation, a deal was cut with a private consortium to build high-speed rail lines linking Miami, Orlando and Tampa.

The plan stood no chance of turning a profit and, worse, would have